Promoting Prosperity in

Mississippi

EDITORS:

Brandon N. Cline
Mississippi State University

Russell S. Sobel
The Citadel

Claudia R. Williamson
Mississippi State University

Published by the
Institute for Market Studies at Mississippi State University

 **MISSISSIPPI STATE UNIVERSITY**™
INSTITUTE FOR MARKET STUDIES

admin@ims.edu
www.ims.msstate.edu

Published by the
Institute for Market Studies at Mississippi State University

MISSISSIPPI STATE UNIVERSITY™
INSTITUTE FOR MARKET STUDIES

The Institute for Market Studies at Mississippi State University was created in 2015
to support the study of markets in order to provide a deeper understanding
regarding the role of markets in creating widely shared prosperity.

Institute for Market Studies, Mississippi State, MS
admin@ims.edu • www.ims.msstate.edu

Nothing in this publication should be construed as an
attempt to aid or hinder passage of any legislation.

Book design by Finney Creative, Inc. © 2018

Printed in the United States of America

ISBN 978-1-7320353-0-0

Promoting Prosperity in Mississippi

Edited by Brandon N. Cline,
Russell S. Sobel, and
Claudia R. Williamson

TABLE OF CONTENTS

Preface

What creates prosperity? Why are some states rich and others poor? Why does Mississippi consistently rank as one of the poorest states in the nation? Can anything be done to move Mississippi 'out of last place'? These questions are often raised by our students and fellow Mississippians. This book addresses each of these questions by identifying areas in which Mississippi can improve its economic conditions.

In this book, we identify key areas for Mississippi economic policy reform. Twenty-one scholars, ten of which are from or work in Mississippi, have contributed original policy research. All twenty chapters were written specifically for Mississippi with a shared goal to promote prosperity in the state. While some of the chapters contain complex policy reforms, we have made every effort to present the concepts and ideas in a way that is understandable to the average citizen, the person who can benefit the most from this information.

The first three chapters of the text summarize the basic economic principles necessary to achieve economic prosperity. These three chapters present the principles behind the reforms proposed in the subsequent seventeen chapters. Each chapter was written independently and offers unique insight into different areas of state policy reform. While the topics covered range from tax reform, education reform, healthcare, corporate welfare, occupational licensing and business regulatory reform to criminal justice reform, and natural disaster recovery efforts, there is a clear unifying framework underlying the conclusions reached in each chapter. The theme throughout is that economic growth is best achieved through free market policies, policies which are based on limited government, lower regulations, lower taxes, minimal infringement on contracting and labor markets, secure private property rights, low subsidies, and privatization. Policy based on these principles allows Mississippians to have more rights and more choices in their lives.

We hope that readers come away with a better understanding of capitalism's true potential to generate the long-run economic growth necessary to make Mississippi more prosperous, as well as ideas for policy reforms that could accomplish it in our lifetimes. This book illustrates that if Mississippi embraces economic freedom, the state will experience more entrepreneurship, increased business and capital formation, higher labor productivity and wages, and overall economic growth. Our main goal is to provide the scholarly, academic research that can inform state policy decisions and open a much needed dialogue on growth-oriented policy reform in Mississippi.

We focus on long-run policy improvements. Thus, the analysis is not an assessment of any particular administration or political party. Instead, this book can be thought of as a blueprint of possible economic reform proposals that use scientific evidence as a guiding principle. We emphasize that our unifying framework, which shapes the conclusions drawn in each chapter, is based on economic science, not politics. All authors address their respective topics by relying on academic research. Topics and policy conclusions were not based on any particular political agenda, political party, or political expediency. Instead, the authors relied on cold, hard facts and data with references to published academic literature to develop policy reform suggestions specific for Mississippi. In fact, many reforms suggested may not be politically possible.

The inspiration for this book came from *Unleashing Capitalism*, a series of books using economic logic to improve state policy in West Virginia, South Carolina, and Tennessee. We owe thanks to more people than we could possibly list. We are indebted to our colleagues and the Finance and Economics advisory board at Mississippi State University who helped review chapters and provide invaluable feedback. We thank Ken and Randy Kendrick, Earnest W. and Mary Ann Deavenport, and the Pure Water Foundation for the funding necessary to embark on a project of this magnitude. We also thank our friends and family for their support, and for putting up with the long working hours that went into conducting this research. Most importantly, we would like to thank the staff and supporters of the Institute for Market Studies at Mississippi State University for publishing this book. Without their support, this book would not have been possible.

Let's start promoting prosperity in Mississippi!

Brandon N. Cline, Ph.D.
Associate Professor of Finance
Mississippi State University

Russell S. Sobel, Ph.D.
Professor of Economics and Entrepreneurship
The Citadel

Claudia R. Williamson, Ph.D.
Associate Professor of Economics
Mississippi State University

PART 1

Introduction: The Role of Government and Economic Growth

1

The Case for Growth

Russell S. Sobel and J. Brandon Bolen

The Case for Growth

Russell S. Sobel and J. Brandon Bolen

Mississippi needs policy founded in a vision of a better future for its children and grandchildren. If done correctly, policy reform has the potential to drastically increase the well-being of Mississippians within a generation. Within a few generations the state could be at the top of the national income rankings, rather than the bottom. This progress requires policy reform undertaken with the explicit objective of increasing the rate of economic growth and sustaining it over the long term. This reform must be based on science, not politics. That is, Mississippi needs to adopt policies that have been proven to increase growth in other states, and to abandon policies that have decreased economic growth in Mississippi and in other states.

To begin our quest to understand which policies promote, and which hinder, economic growth this introductory chapter outlines the main arguments for why economic growth should be considered as one of the most important policy priorities in the Magnolia State.[1]

The Have's and the Have Not's

How wide are the differences in standards of living across states? How does average income in Mississippi compare with that of other states? Figure 1.1 (on the following page) shows the most recent data available on per capita personal income for all fifty U.S. states.

With a 2016 per capita personal income of only $35,936, Mississippi ranked 50th, making it the poorest U.S. state. Average income in Mississippi is about 72.5 percent of the U.S. average of $49,571. What this implies is that the average person in the United States as a whole has roughly 38 percent higher income than the average Mississippian. This disparity isn't just with states in the North or West. Two of Mississippi's neighboring states (Arkansas and Alabama) have 10 percent higher per capita personal incomes, and the others (Louisiana and Tennessee) have 20 percent higher per capita personal incomes.

---

1   This chapter is based on Sobel and Daniels (2007), Sobel and Leguizamon (2009), and Sobel, Clark, and Leguizamon (2012).

Figure 1.1: Average Income by State, 2016

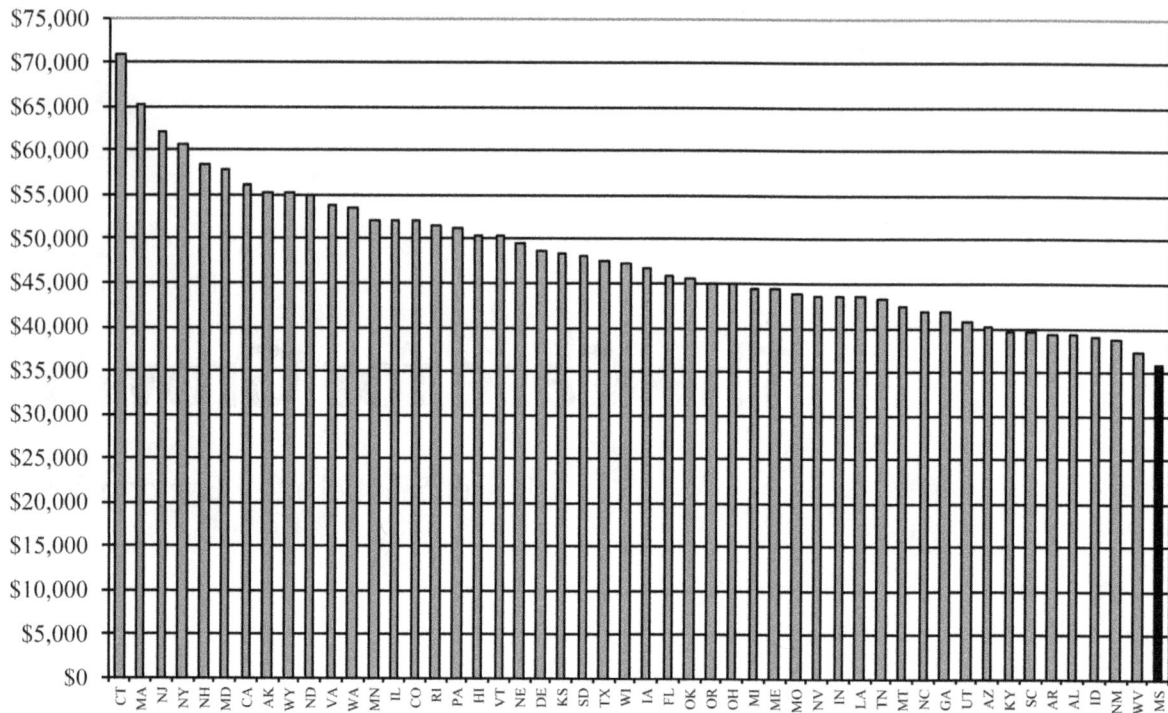

Source: Bureau of Economic Analysis (2017). Per capita income data is in 2016 dollars.

Prosperity does indeed cease at the Mississippi border. The border counties in each of Mississippi's neighbors have higher per capita personal incomes than their Mississippi counterparts. The differential at the Tennessee border is perhaps the most striking. At the county level per capita income is, on average, $6,184 higher in the five Tennessee counties that border Mississippi than in the six Mississippi counties that border Tennessee. A similar income disparity of $5,261 exists when examining the border county differential with Louisiana. There are many other measures of personal, family, and household income and in some, like median household income, the differentials are even greater (the border county median household income differential with Tennessee is $6,934). A similar, but smaller, disparity exists along the Arkansas and Alabama borders.

Figure 1.2 (next page) shows per capita personal income by county in Mississippi. Per capita personal income ranges from $18,598 in Issaquena County (the 3rd poorest county in the United States in 2015), to $57,964 in Madison County (the only county in Mississippi with a per capita income higher than the national average). There is a noticeable clustering of low income counties in the northwestern region of the state bordering the Mississippi River commonly referred to by Mississippians as "the Delta." As a region historically dependent on agriculture, the Delta has experienced high poverty rates, dwindling populations, and a loss of employment opportunities in recent decades.

Do the low per capita income levels of the Delta explain why Mississippi has experienced the lowest average per capita income in the country each year since 1930? In short, the answer is no. The average per capita income in the Mississippi Delta is $32,800, which is significantly lower than the average of $35,200 elsewhere in the state. While a difference of $2,400 is worth noting, Mississippi would still rank last in the country in per capita personal income if the counties of the Delta were excluded.

Mississippi has a hard-working labor force, a bounty of natural resources, wonderful recreation opportunities, major transportation rivers, and other significant advantages. From a purely economic perspective, there is no reason Mississippi should be so low in the national income rankings. So why does the average Mississippian earn significantly less than the average citizen in other states? One fundamental problem is that despite its many advantages, Mississippi has been unable to get its economic policies right. Getting these policies right is the key to increasing prosperity.

Figure 1.2: Mississippi Per Capita Income by County, 2015

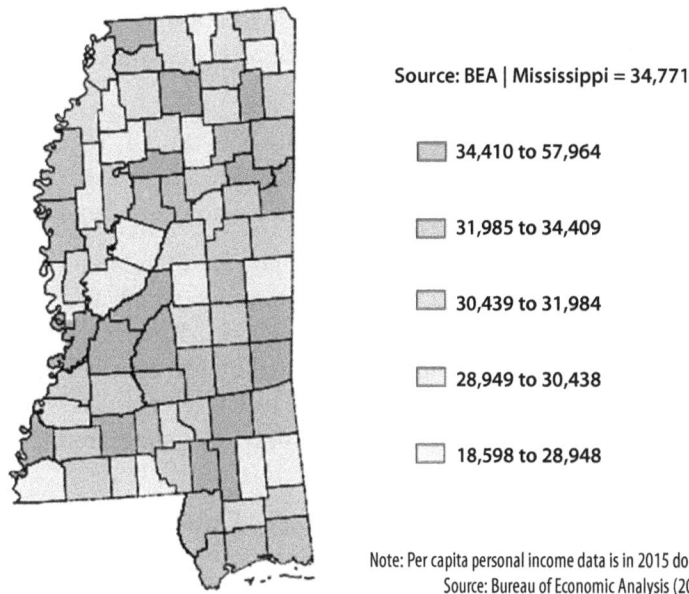

Source: BEA | Mississippi = 34,771

☐ 34,410 to 57,964

☐ 31,985 to 34,409

☐ 30,439 to 31,984

☐ 28,949 to 30,438

☐ 18,598 to 28,948

Note: Per capita personal income data is in 2015 dollars.
Source: Bureau of Economic Analysis (2017).

Just One Percentage Point: Will Our Children Be Better Off?

Large changes in wealth and prosperity cannot be generated overnight. Places that are prosperous today went through stages of development. What prosperous areas have in common is that they were able to sustain higher rates of economic growth over longer periods of time.

Figure 1.3 shows Mississippi's average growth rate of per capita personal income for three periods of time: 1971 to 1985, 1986 to 2000, and 2001 to 2015. This is the 'real' growth rate, or the growth rate after adjusting for inflation.

During the 1986 to 2000 period, Mississippi's average real rate of economic growth was 2.1 percent, which was the 14th highest rate of growth among U.S. states at that time. During that period, Mississippi experienced 9 years of rapid growth above two percent and 5 years above three percent. This was a slightly higher growth rate than the 1.9 percent Mississippi had achieved earlier in the 1971 to 1985 period.

Had Mississippi been able to sustain this rate of growth, faster than the average of other states, Mississippi would have soon climbed up the national income rankings. Unfortunately, economic growth in Mississippi slowed after the mid-1990s, falling to 1.1 percent between 2001 and 2015. While growth slowed in many states due to the economic down-

Figure 1.3: Mississippi's Declining Rate of Growth

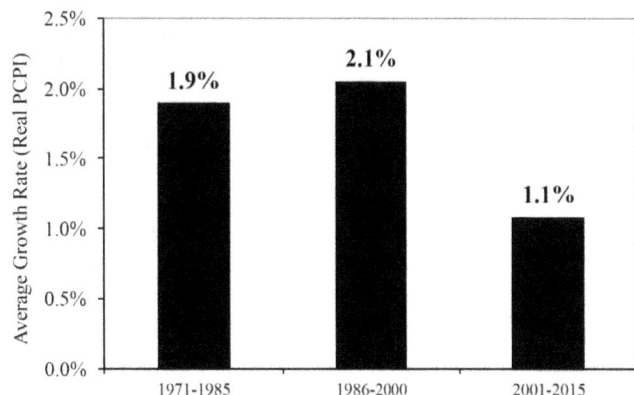

1971-1985: 1.9%
1986-2000: 2.1%
2001-2015: 1.1%

(Average Growth Rate (Real PCPI))

Source: Bureau of Economic Analysis (2017), Bureau of Labor Statistics (2017). Note: All per capita personal income data in Chapters 1 and 2 are adjusted for inflation to constant 2010 dollars using the Consumer Price Index unless otherwise noted.

turn during the period, Mississippi's growth rate decreased even relative to other states falling from the 14th highest growth rate among U.S. states to the 23rd highest growth rate. Even excluding the recent recession years, average growth from 1996 to 2008 was only 1.7 percent, a significant decrease from the growth of the previous period. Thus, the recession is not the reason for the slowdown in Mississippi's growth.

While some might think the difference between 1.1, 1.9, and 2.1 percent seems small, nothing could be further from the truth. Even small differences in growth, over long periods of time, add up to significant differences. This is the topic to which we now turn our attention.

Figure 1.4 shows the history of income growth in Mississippi, adjusted for inflation, along with several alternative future projections. One projection simply takes Mississippi's recent rate of real per capita economic growth over the 2001 to 2015 period, 1.1 percent, and forecasts it into the future. The other two projections show what the future would hold if Mississippi's growth were increased back to the 1971-85 rate of 1.9 percent or the 1986-2000 rate of 2.1 percent. These real growth rates are not unrealistic. Both were actual growth rates experienced in other U.S. states from 2001-2015, and previously experienced in Mississippi itself.

The last year of historical data shown in the figure is 2016, a year in which the average income in Mississippi was $32,649. Let us consider the simple question of what the average income will be in one generation, or twenty years into the future, in 2036. At the historical growth rate of 1.1 percent, average income in Mississippi would be $40,635 in 2036.[2] What if instead growth could be increased to 1.9 or even 2.1 percent? Under these alternative scenarios, average income in 2036 would instead be $47,573 and $49,475 respectively. Thus, going from a 1.1 percent to a 2.1 percent rate of economic growth results in a difference

Figure 1.4: Which Future for Mississippi?

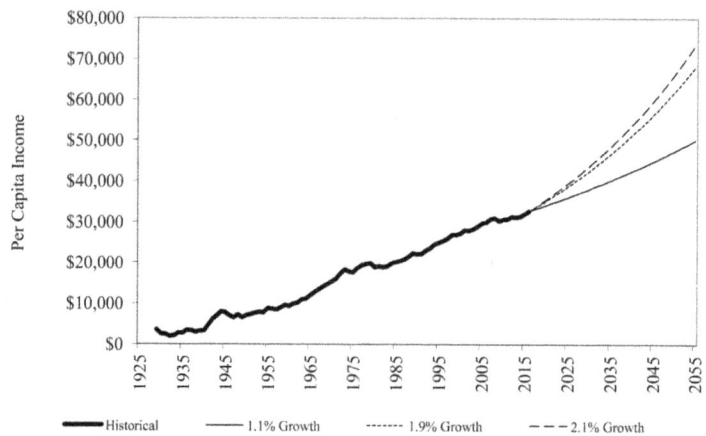

Note: Per capita income is adjusted for inflation to constant 2010 dollars. Sources: Bureau of Economic Analysis (2017), Bureau of Labor Statistics (2017)

of almost $8,841 in average income one generation out into the future. Also, remember that we are considering average income *per person*. The average family size in Mississippi is 2.58 persons (from 2010 Census data), so the impact of this difference on the average family is roughly 2.5 times this amount—or a substantial $22,810 difference in family income under the two alternative scenarios 20 years into the future.

What if we look even farther into the future? What about two generations? By 2056, just one year beyond the forecast period shown in Figure 1.4, the differences grow even larger. Instead of average income being $50,573 in 2056 at a growth rate of 1.1 percent, it would be $69,317 at 1.9 percent, or a whopping $74,973 at 2.1 percent. Make no mistake about it, over two generations a one percentage point increase in Mississippi's rate of growth means a difference of almost $25,000 in per capita income.

Perhaps a better way of looking at the data is to ask, at what date in the future will average income in Mississippi hit $50,000? To put this figure in perspective, it is approximately the current average income

---

2   All dollar values for future years are given in today's dollars—or 'real dollars'—that have already been adjusted to take out the impact of inflation on the purchasing power of money in the future because we are using a real, inflation adjusted, growth rate.

Promoting Prosperity in Mississippi

level in Alaska, North Dakota, and Wyoming. At Mississippi's historical 1.1 percent rate of growth it will hit $50,000 in the year 2055. At a 1.9 percent rate of economic growth, this date would instead be 2039—or sixteen years earlier. At a 2.1 percent rate of growth it becomes 2037—or eighteen years earlier. Increasing economic growth by just one percentage point moves the date at which the average Mississippian will have an income level of $50,000 forward by almost an entire generation.

Rather than relying entirely on future projections, it is also useful to consider a few specific historical income comparisons. Consider the cases of Mississippi and two states that twenty years ago, in 1996, were very similar to it in terms of income, Montana and Oklahoma. Figure 1.5 presents this data. In 1996, the average income in Mississippi was $25,433, while Montana and Oklahoma had average incomes of $27,142 and $27,936 respectively. Montana ranked two spots ahead of Mississippi (48th) and Oklahoma five spots ahead (45th).

Over the next twenty-year period, Mississippi was able to sustain a 1.3 percent rate of growth, Montana 1.9 percent and Oklahoma 2.1 percent. After twenty years, less than one generation, Mississippi's 2016 average income of $32,649 is about $5,860 less than the average income in Montana and $9,033 less than average income in Oklahoma. The result is that while Mississippi has remained 50th in the national income rankings, Montana has risen to 38th and Oklahoma has risen to 28th.

Figure 1.5: State Growth Comparisons

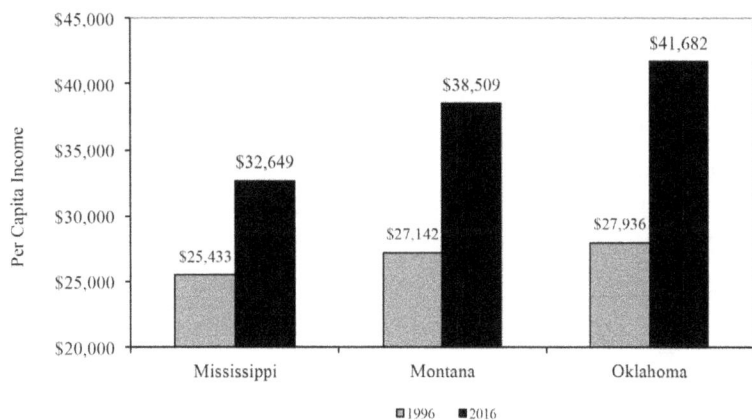

Note: Per capita income is adjusted for inflation to 2010 constant dollars. Source: Bureau of Economic Analysis (2017)

It almost seems unbelievable that such small differences in growth can produce such large differences through time, but they can. A well-known financial formula called 'The Rule of 70' helps us to understand the importance of time and economic growth rates in generating prosperity.[3] According to this rule, an area's standard of living will double every X years, where X equals 70 divided by the rate of economic growth:

The Rule of 70: *Years it takes for income to double* $= \dfrac{70}{\textit{Annual rate of economic growth}}$

So, a state that sustains a 1.3 percent growth rate, as Mississippi did over the last two decades, doubles its living standards roughly every 54 years (70 ÷ 1.3). A state that sustains a growth rate of 1.9 percent sees its living standards double approximately every 37 years, and a state that sustains a growth rate of 2.1 percent doubles its income in only 33 years.

As these numbers clearly illustrate, small differences in the rate of economic growth produce big differences in standards of living when they are sustained over long periods of time. The principle at work here is the same one responsible for the 'miracle' of compound interest. Mississippi currently ranks 50th

---

3   Alternatively, this is sometimes referred to as the 'Rule of 72' which produces similar results, but is divisible by more whole numbers making it easier to use in simple calculations.

in average income. If all states continue their current (2001-2015) real per capita growth rates, 20 years into the future Mississippi will have climbed two spots to rank 48th. If instead Mississippi could increase growth back to just 1.9 percent, its ranking in twenty years would be 32nd. If Mississippi could manage to grow again at 2.1 percent, it would rank 29th in the nation within one generation. If that 2.1 percent could be sustained for forty years, Mississippi would rank as the 20th richest state in the nation in 2056.

As the experiences of other states illustrate, these large leaps in the income rankings are possible. Within a fifteen-year period, North Dakota moved up 32 places from 42nd to 10th, Wyoming jumped 23 places from 31st to 8th, South Dakota rose 18 places from 37th to 19th, Vermont improved 10 places from 30th to 20th, and Montana moved up 11 places from 47th to 36th. All of them did this the same way—by sustaining high rates of economic growth over the 15-year 1995 to 2010 period.

From Rags to Riches: It Can Be Done

Because economic growth rates vary considerably more across countries than across U.S. states, some international comparisons of long-run growth are even more impressive. An often cited example is the comparison between Hong Kong and Argentina. Approximately fifty years ago, Argentina was almost as rich as many European nations, while Hong Kong was relatively poor. Due to their differing policy climates, today Hong Kong is one of the richest countries in the world while Argentina has fallen behind. This example is often pointed to as proof of how little a country's natural resources matter for growth. Hong Kong, after all, is essentially a rock island in the ocean. Argentina, in contrast, has a wealth of natural resources. Like Argentina, Mississippi's abundance of natural resources by itself cannot guarantee a fast rate of economic growth.

Figure 1.6 shows the levels of per capita income in 1960 and 2014 for five countries: the United States, Venezuela, Argentina, Japan, and Hong Kong. In 1960, while the United States was the richest of the group with a per capita income of almost $15,000, Venezuela was not far behind at $10,600. Japan and Hong Kong, on the other hand, were relatively poor. Their average citizens had only 25 percent as much income as the average citizen in the United States (per capita incomes of roughly $5,000 and $3,750 respectively).

These countries followed very different paths over the next forty-two years. Growth rates were most rapid in Hong Kong (4.5%) and Japan (4.5%), while growth was virtually non-existent in Argentina (0.8%) and Venezuela (0.7%). Over the same period U.S. per capita income growth averaged somewhere in the middle of these other countries (2.5%).

Fast forward two generations. By 2014, Hong Kong was wealthier than

Figure 1.6: International Growth Comparisons

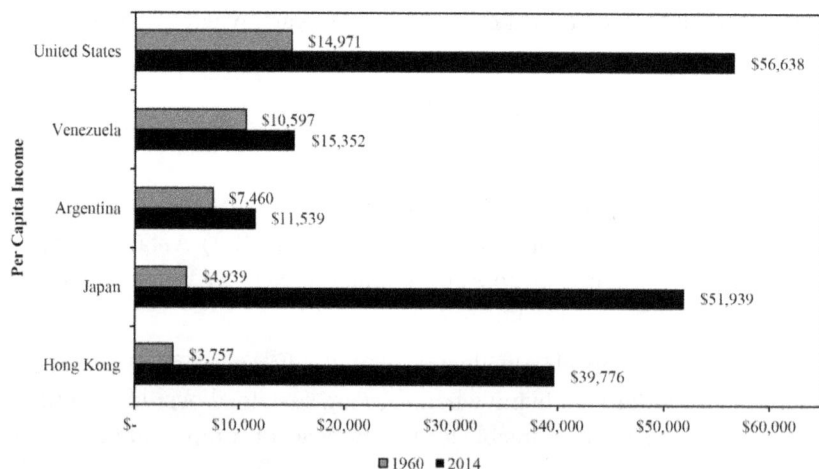

Note: Per capita income is adjusted for inflation to 2005 constant U.S. dollars. Sources: Summers and Heston (1994) and World Bank (2017).

most European countries, and Japan was not far behind the United States. Both are true 'rags to riches' stories. In contrast, the average citizen in Argentina is only $4,000 richer than his or her grandparents and the average citizen in Venezuela is only $5,000 richer. Today the average citizen in Argentina or Venezuela has only a fraction of the income that citizens in the other three countries have.

Meridian versus Charlotte: A Tale of Two Cities

Returning closer to home, let's take a more detailed look at the long run trends in Mississippi relative to other states. Because of their similar histories, Mississippi and North Carolina are interesting to compare. In the late 1800s, the cities of Meridian, Mississippi and Jackson, Mississippi were almost identical in terms of average income, educational levels, and populations to the city of Charlotte, North Carolina. Jackson, actually had about an 80 percent higher population than Charlotte prior to the Civil War, but even by 1870 the populations were roughly identical (4,234 versus 4,473). Similarly, in 1890 the population of Meridian, Mississippi was roughly equal to the population of Charlotte, North Carolina (10,624 versus 11,557). Like Meridian and Jackson, Charlotte was in a state with a significant rural population, and also relied heavily on industries which dwindled through time (for Charlotte this was textiles and tobacco). Even as recently as the 1950s Jackson's population remained about three-fourths the size of Charlotte, with similar demographic factors (134,042 versus 98,271). Over the subsequent decades, however, Charlotte has grown into a crowning jewel of the South, with a population more than 4 times larger than Jackson and 17 times larger than Meridian (731,424 versus 173,514 and 41,148 in 2010).

Virtually all of Charlotte's new jobs and businesses were in industries that could have located anywhere. Charlotte's numerous new bank headquarters are an example. Nine Fortune 500 companies now have their corporate headquarters located in the Charlotte metro area. There was no special geographic reason, such as a specific natural resource or even a sea port, giving Charlotte an advantage over Meridian or Jackson in its ability to attract and nurture these businesses. The question of interest is why these seemingly similar cities diverged so drastically. As we have seen, over such a long period of time, even small differences in growth rates can produce large differences in income. What made it possible for Charlotte to sustain a higher rate of growth over such a long period of time? The answer is simply that North Carolina had a set of policies in place that were more conducive to economic growth than did Mississippi.

Economic Growth and Human Well-being

At this point, some readers might be questioning whether income is really a good measure of personal well-being. While increasing income certainly helps everyone afford more of the things they want, there is more to life than material possessions. We also care about our families, our health, and our overall safety. While growth may increase our income and standard of living, how does it affect these other measures of personal well-being? By focusing on growth, can we also achieve other goals as well? Let us look at the evidence.

People want to lead long healthy lives, and this requires access to quality healthcare. Figure 1.7 (on the following page) shows how two important measures of health and longevity differ between groups of the highest income and lowest income states. Without exception, citizens in high income states live longer, healthier lives. The average high income state ranks 6th out of 50 in terms of the life expectancy of its citizens. The average low income state ranks only 40th. In terms of health care quality, the picture is the same. Richer states do better, while poorer states like Mississippi do worse. The average high-income state ranks 8th in terms of health care quality. The average low-income state ranks 41st. Because Mississippi is a lower income state, it is also one of the less healthy placing 49th in the U.S. health rankings, and 50th in life expectancy.

This difference is not limited only to physical health; it also appears in measures of mental health. People in lower income states suffer from the highest rates of mental illness (almost 20.2 percent in the lower income states compared with only 17.2 percent in the richer states)[4]. This difference is likely due to the lower levels of stress at home and in the workplace that higher income brings.

In addition to our own health, we also care about the well-being of our families and children. All parents want their kids to have stable families,

Figure 1.7: Health Indicators by Income Level

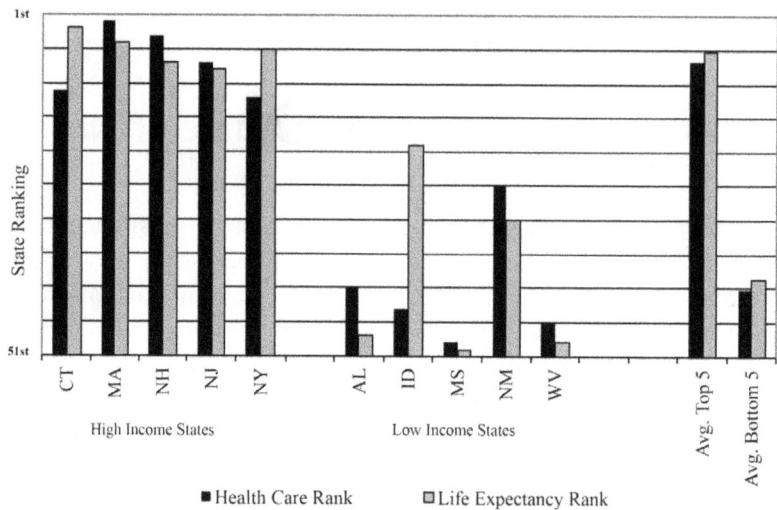

Sources: U.S. News and World Report (2017), Measure of America (2017).

live in safe neighborhoods, and receive a good education. Does having higher income levels lead to these as well? Figure 1.8 presents the evidence. Families living in the five states with the highest incomes experience lower divorce rates than families in the five lowest income states (7.4 versus 10.6 on average). Richer families have fewer money problems destroying their marriages and more money to spend on family vacations and leisure activities. Furthermore, higher income leads to safer neighborhoods. For instance, states with higher incomes have lower rates of violent crime (3.1 versus 3.6 on average).

Our children benefit from economic growth not only in terms of safety and stability but also in the area of education. Children growing up in high income states are far more likely to graduate from high school. The five highest income states have higher percentages of the population graduating from high school

on average than the five lowest income states. Higher income states have more children graduating from college as well (35.1 percent versus 23 percent college educated population, not shown in figure). Not only does more education increase a child's future earning potential, enhancing the state's prospects for growth in the future, but people with higher levels of education report higher levels of job satisfaction and overall happiness in their lives.

Figure 1.8: Divorce, Crime, and Education

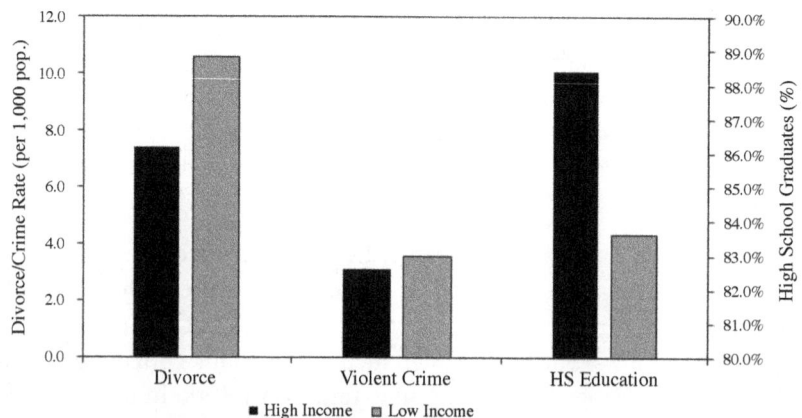

Sources: Measures of America (2017) and Center for Disease Control and Prevention (2017).

---

4   Substance Abuse and Mental Health Services Administration (2012)

The evidence is overwhelming. Economic growth not only makes us materially richer; it helps to accomplish our other goals as well. The objective of growth is really about creating a future for Mississippi where families are not only wealthier, but also happier, healthier, safer, and better educated.

Conclusion

This introductory chapter has explained how even small differences in economic growth rates can produce substantial differences in the quality of life within a generation or two. If Mississippi refuses to undertake policy reform, and continues its current trend, Mississippians will remain at the bottom of the national economic ladder.

In contrast, a better and richer Mississippi is possible to achieve within our lifetimes. An increase in Mississippi's rate of real per capita economic growth, back to the 1.9 percent level sustained from 1971 to 1985, would result in a ranking of 32nd twenty years into the future. An increase back to the 2.1 percent level sustained from 1986 to 2000 would result in Mississippi becoming the 29th richest state in the nation within one generation, and the 20th richest state in the nation within two generations.

More importantly, this growth does not have to come at the expense of other things people value—to the contrary, these other areas are also enhanced by economic growth. Reducing crime, improving health outcomes, and increasing education are frequently discussed policy agenda items, but improvements in these areas are a symptom of growth, not a cause. Policy reform that increases economic growth and prosperity in Mississippi will *automatically* result in reductions in crime and health problems, and increases in educational attainment. These social ills are a result of poverty, not a cause of it, and focusing on policies targeted in those areas to produce economic growth is simply putting the cart in front of the horse.

But can policy reform actually increase growth by a meaningful amount? Evidence from both the experience of U.S. states and countries around the globe suggests the answer is yes. In the next chapter we turn to the next important question: Which policies are most conducive to creating and sustaining long-term economic growth in a state?

References

Bureau of Economic Analysis, U.S. Department of Commerce. 2017. *Annual State Personal Income* [electronic file]. Washington, DC: U.S. Department of Commerce. Online: http://www.bea.gov/regional/index.htm (cited: June 21, 2017).

Bureau of Labor Statistics, U.S. Department of Labor. 2017. Consumer Price Index [electronic file]. Washington, DC: U.S. Department of Labor. Online: http://bls.gov/cpi/ (cited: June 21, 2017).

Measure of America, Social Science Research Council. 2017. *Human Development Index: 2013-2014* [electronic file]. Brooklyn, NY. Online: http://www.measureofamerica.org/download-agreement/ (cited: June 21, 2017)

Sobel, Russell S., and Susane J. Daniels. 2007. The Case for Growth, Chapter 1 in Russell S. Sobel (ed.), *Unleashing Capitalism: Why Prosperity Stops at the West Virginia Border and How to Fix It.* Morgantown, WV: Center for Economic Growth, The Public Policy Foundation of West Virginia: 1-12.

Sobel, Russell S., and Susane J. Leguizamon. 2009. The Case for Growth, Chapter 1 in Peter T. Calcagno (ed.), *Unleashing Capitalism: A Prescription for Economic Prosperity in South Carolina.* Columbia, SC: South Carolina Policy Council: 7-20.

Sobel, Russell S., J.R. Clark, and Susane J. Leguizamon. 2012. The Case for Growth, Chapter 1 in J.R. Clark (ed.), *Freedom and Prosperity in Tennessee.* Chattanooga, TN: The Scott L. Probasco Jr. Chair of Free Enterprise: 1-16.

Substance Abuse and Mental Health Services Administration. 2012. *National Survey on Drug Use and Health Report: 2011-2012.* [electronic file]. Washington, DC: U.S. Department of Health and Human Services. Online: http://archive.samhsa.gov/data/2k14/NSDUH170/sr170-mental-illness-state-estimates-2014.htm (cited June 22, 2017)

Summers, Robert, and Alan Heston. 1994. *The Penn World Tables (Mark 5.6)* [electronic file]. Cambridge, MA: National Bureau of Economic Research.

U.S. Census Bureau. 2010. *Families and Households: 2010* [electronic file]. Washington, DC: U.S. Census Bureau. Online: https://www.census.gov/prod/cen2010/briefs/c2010br-14.pdf (cited: June 21, 2017).

U.S. Centers for Disease Control and Prevention. 2017. *Marriage and Divorce.* 2017. [electronic file]. Washington, DC: U.S. Department of Health and Human Services. Online: http://divorce-laws.insidegov.com/saved_search/States-With-Highest-Divorce-Rates (cited: June 21, 2017).

U.S. News and World Report. 2017. *Best States for Healthcare* [electronic file]. Washington, DC. 2017. Online: https://www.usnews.com/info/features/about-usnews (cited: June 21, 2017).

World Bank. 2017. *World Development Indicators* [electronic file]. http://data.worldbank.org/data-catalog/world-development-indicators (cited: June 21, 2017).

2

The Sources of Economic Growth

Russell S. Sobel and J. Brandon Bolen

2

The Sources of Economic Growth

Russell S. Sobel and J. Brandon Bolen

The previous chapter made the case for why increasing the rate of economic growth in Mississippi should be considered one of the top policy priorities. However, policy reform to promote growth should be based on evidence of what has worked, and what has not worked in Mississippi and other areas. Evidence was presented in the previous chapter that economic growth is faster in states like Vermont, Oklahoma, North Dakota, South Dakota, and Montana; and in countries like Hong Kong and Japan. How can this be replicated in Mississippi? Can we uncover which policies tend to promote prosperity? These are the questions we address in this chapter.[1]

As we will soon see, there is one thing that high-income and fast-growth places generally have in common: they have adopted sound economic policies and backed them up with sound political and legal systems that firmly protect property rights and prohibit fraud, theft, and coercion. By doing so, they have created a level playing field for prosperity to take root. As economist Dwight Lee writes:

> No matter how fertile the seeds of entrepreneurship, they wither without the proper economic soil. In order for entrepreneurship to germinate, take root, and yield the fruit of economic progress it has to be nourished by the right mixture of freedom and accountability, a mixture that can only be provided by a free market economy. (1991, 20)

The Process of Economic Growth

To understand economic growth and the best way for government policy to promote it, we must first delve deeper into the relationship between economic inputs, institutions, and outcomes.

An economy is a *process* by which economic inputs and resources, such as skilled labor, capital, and funding for new businesses, are converted into economic outcomes (e.g., wage growth, job creation, or

---

1 This chapter is based on Sobel and Hall (2007a), Sobel and Hall (2009), and Sobel, Clark, and Hall (2012).

new businesses). This concept is illustrated in Figure 2.1. As the large arrow in the middle of the figure shows, the economic outcomes generated from any specific set of economic inputs depend on the 'institutions'—the political and economic 'rules of the game'—under which an economy operates. The important point is that some rules of the game are better than others at producing prosperity.

Several analogies will help to clarify. First, let us consider a basketball game. The players, the court, and the basketballs are all inputs into the process. The 'institutions' in this context are the rules under which the game is played. Some examples of these rules are the time length of the game, the length given on the shot clock, the rules on fouling, and the three-point line rule. Examples of the measurable outcomes are the score, the winning team, the number of fouls, etc. The important point is that the outcomes will be influenced by which rules of the game are chosen. The reason for this is that the rules of the game affect the choices and behavior of the people playing the game. If, for example, the rule that shots made from behind the three point line were changed so that these were now worth only one and a half points, we would expect players to respond to this rule change in a predictable manner. As the point value of those longer shots decreased, fewer players would attempt them.[2]

While a basketball example might sound hypothetical, Clemson University economists Robert

Figure 2.1: Inputs, Institutions and Outcomes

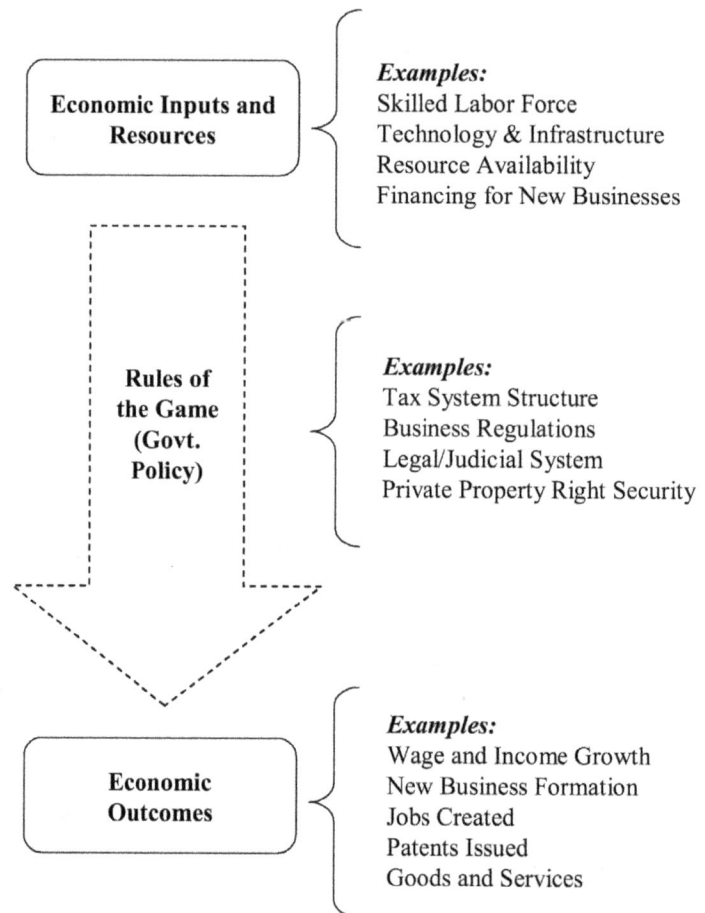

Examples:
Skilled Labor Force
Technology & Infrastructure
Resource Availability
Financing for New Businesses

Examples:
Tax System Structure
Business Regulations
Legal/Judicial System
Private Property Right Security

Examples:
Wage and Income Growth
New Business Formation
Jobs Created
Patents Issued
Goods and Services

Source: Hall and Sobel (2006).

McCormick and Robert Tollison (1984) found that while adding an additional referee to a basketball game was expected to result in more fouls being called, a slower-paced game, and less scoring, the addition of these rule changes to ACC basketball had precisely the opposite effect. The result was fewer fouls, a faster pace, and more scoring. The explanation? Knowing that fouls were more likely to be called by referees, players changed their behavior and committed fewer of them.

To take another example, consider for a moment the board game "Monopoly." The 'institutions' in this analogy are again the rules under which the game is played. Imagine if a new rule were created making it legitimate to steal the property cards of other players if they were not looking. The play and

---

2   This change in the rules would also alter the incentives in the selection of players, or investments in resources for an economy. Coaches would now have a much weaker preference for players who could make longer shots.

outcomes from a game of "Monopoly" would be significantly different under these different institutional rules, as players would alter their behavior in response to them. Not only would this rule change increase the rate of theft among players, it would also result in fewer properties being purchased, less investment (houses or hotels) on the properties, and more resources being devoted to trying to protect their property cards from being stolen (and more effort into trying to steal the property of other players).

As a final analogy, consider the process of baking cakes. In this context, the ingredients are the inputs, the 'institutions' are the oven, and the outcomes are the delicious cakes that result at the end. The main point is obvious—if the oven is not working, simply putting more ingredients (inputs) into the oven does not result in more cakes coming out the other end. Too many government policies at every level of government fail to realize this, and keep pouring money into programs that attempt to increase the inputs into the economy when the real problem is that the oven is broken due to failed economic policies. An economy cannot spend its way out of problems that are caused by weak institutions. Rather institutions must be improved, and this, and only this, will result in investments in inputs paying dividends at the other end of the process.

This model makes it clear that by improving institutions, or the rules of the game under which the Mississippi economy operates, it can change economic outcomes for the better. When institutions are weak, even places with abundant natural resources or other inputs have difficulty becoming prosperous. Mississippi, and the countries of Argentina and Venezuela, fit into this category of resource-rich areas that have not been able to sustain economic growth (as was noted in the previous chapter).

The important point is that our daily economic lives are played out under a set of rules that are to a large extent determined by government-enacted laws and policies. These political and legal 'institutions' as economists call them, are what create the incentive structures within the state economy. Prosperity requires that Mississippi get the rules right.

Adam Smith's Question:
Why Are Some Places Rich and Others Poor?

Adam Smith, the 'father of economics,' published the first book addressing the set of topics we now consider 'economics' in 1776. In his book, titled *An Inquiry into the Nature and Causes of the Wealth of Nations*, Adam Smith (1998 [1776]) attempted to answer a single question: Why are some nations rich and others poor? Economic science has come a long way in 230 years, and volumes of published research now clearly provide the answer to the question Adam Smith posed long ago. The answer is fundamentally the same one arrived at by Adam Smith.

In a nutshell, he found that countries become prosperous when they have good institutions that create favorable rules of the game—rules that encourage the creation of wealth. Smith further concluded that the institutional structure that best promotes prosperity is an economic system of capitalism backed up by sound political and legal institutions. According to Smith, an economy becomes prosperous when they use unregulated private markets to the greatest extent possible, with the government playing the important but limited role of protecting liberty, property, and enforcing contracts. Over 230 years of published scientific evidence now supports Smith's conclusion.

Capitalism is not a political position or platform, it is an economic system—a set of institutions or rules that define the 'economic game.' Capitalism's institutions produce prosperity better than the alternative of government control, not only in terms of financial wealth, but in terms of other measures of quality of life. Adopting institutions ('rules of the game') consistent with the economic system of capitalism has the potential to generate outcomes that better accomplish the common goals of all political parties: prosperity, wealth, health, family, security, etc.

The Rise and Decline of Economic Freedom in Mississippi

While most people tend to think of capitalism and socialism as alternative and discrete forms of economic organization, in reality government policies tend to lie somewhere on a continuum between these two extremes. What differs on this continuum is the degree to which the government uses its power to enact direct command and control policies that intervene into the private sector. Some countries, like North Korea, have governments that use a command and control approach to organizing nearly the entire economy. These countries lie at the extreme socialist end of the capitalist-socialist spectrum. Other countries, such as China, are nominally socialist but rely considerably more on the private sector in organizing their economies. Some countries have moved from one end of the continuum to the other, like the former Soviet Republics of Estonia, Latvia, and Slovenia (formerly part of socialist Yugoslavia), who all adopted radical reforms that moved them toward capitalism.

On the other hand, most market-based economies have a much larger degree of government intervention and control than is envisioned under pure capitalism. Within the last two decades, a significant advance in our understanding of this continuum was the publication of the *Economic Freedom of the World* index created by economists James Gwartney (a former Chief Economist of the Joint Economic Committee of Congress) and Robert Lawson.[3] They derive an index measure for each country placing it on a scale of zero to ten, where ten represents the greatest degree of 'economic freedom', i.e., reliance on capitalism, and zero represents the greatest degree of 'economic repression', i.e., reliance on government control of the economy. In the most recent index, the United States scores 7.75 out of 10, ranking it the sixteenth most capitalist, or free-market, economy in the world. However, the United States has fallen eight spots since 2008, and now ranks below Canada. The countries ranking as the most capitalist in the world are Hong Kong, Singapore, New Zealand, and Switzerland.

Because state and local policies vary within the United States, Dean Stansel, José Torra, and Fred McMahon create an index of the *Economic Freedom of North America*, ranking U.S. states and Canadian provinces by the degree of free-market orientation within each state or province.[4] Among U.S. states, Mississippi ranked 40th in the most recent index, for year 2014 data. In 1995, however, Mississippi was ranked 25th in this index. Figure 2.2 shows how Mississippi's economic freedom rank has changed.

From 1989 to 1995, Mississippi's economic freedom ranking improved nine places, from 34th to 25th among U.S. states. Since that time, particularly in the late 1990s, economic freedom has been on the decline in Mississippi, falling in recent years to its lowest rank recorded (42nd).

Does the 'market-friendliness' of Mississippi's policies help to explain its recent economic performance? Recall that Figure 1.3 from Chapter 1 showed Mississippi's per capita income growth over the last few decades, and that there was a slight improvement in Mississippi's growth from 1986-2000, followed by a subsequent large decline in economic growth. Figure 2.3 shows the remarkable correlation between Mississippi's economic freedom and 3-year moving average per capita income growth. Here, Mississippi's 3-year moving average per capita income growth is measured on the left y-axis, while its economic freedom ranking is on the right y-axis.

---

3   Online at: http://www.freetheworld.com. The most recent edition is the 2016 report (Gwartney, Lawson, and Hall 2016).

4   Online at https://www.fraserinstitute.org/studies/economic-freedom. The most recent edition is the 2016 report (Stansel, Torra, and McMahon 2016) which includes annual rankings through 2014. Rankings reported in this chapter have been recalculated among only U.S. states (i.e., excluding Canadian provinces and Mexican states).

Figure 2.2: Mississippi's Economic Freedom Rank

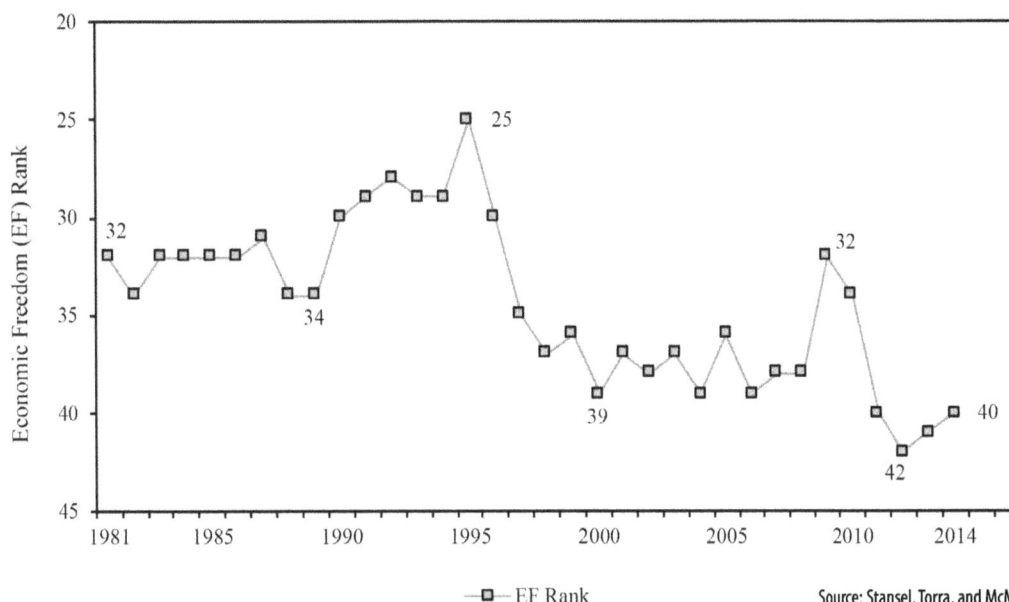

Source: Stansel, Torra, and McMahon (2016).

Figure 2.3: Economic Freedom vs. Prosperity in Mississippi

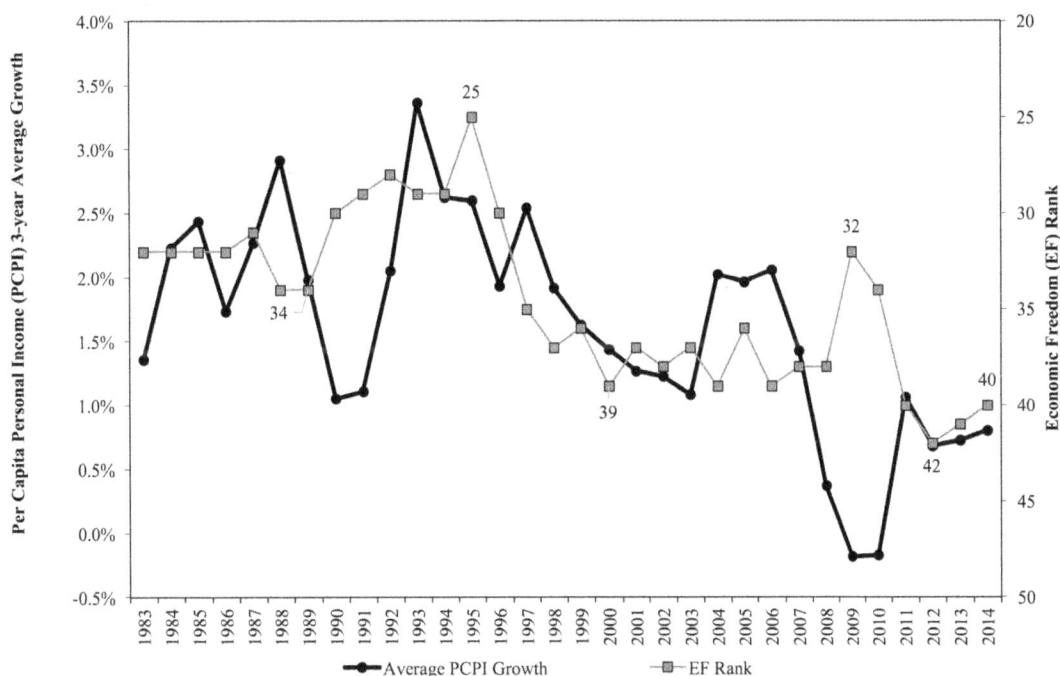

Source: Stansel, Torra, McMahon (2016) and Bureau of Economic Analysis (2017).

First, it is worth noting that the graph includes two recessionary periods that impacted growth in Mississippi (and all states) independent of state economic policies. These two downturns are visible in the figure, the first in 1990-91 and the second in 2007-09. Abstracting from these two national events, one can clearly see the close relation between economic freedom and economic growth, especially in the period between the two recessions, and since the recent recession. Perhaps the most important correlation occurs from the mid-1990s to the mid-2000s when as Mississippi's economic freedom declined from 25th in 1995 to 39th by 2000, growth in Mississippi fell by almost two percentage points.

The point should be obvious, for Mississippi to improve economic growth it must again move toward policies that embrace capitalism and free markets. If Mississippi continues its downward trend that began in the early to mid-1990s, the state's economic ranking is likely to suffer, and Mississippi will remain at the very bottom of the national economic rankings.

To help illustrate how Mississippi relies on capitalism less than some of the other U.S. states, it is worthwhile to examine one of the major components of the economic freedom index, government spending as a share of the state economy, shown in Figure 2.4.

Figure 2.4: Government Control of the Economy

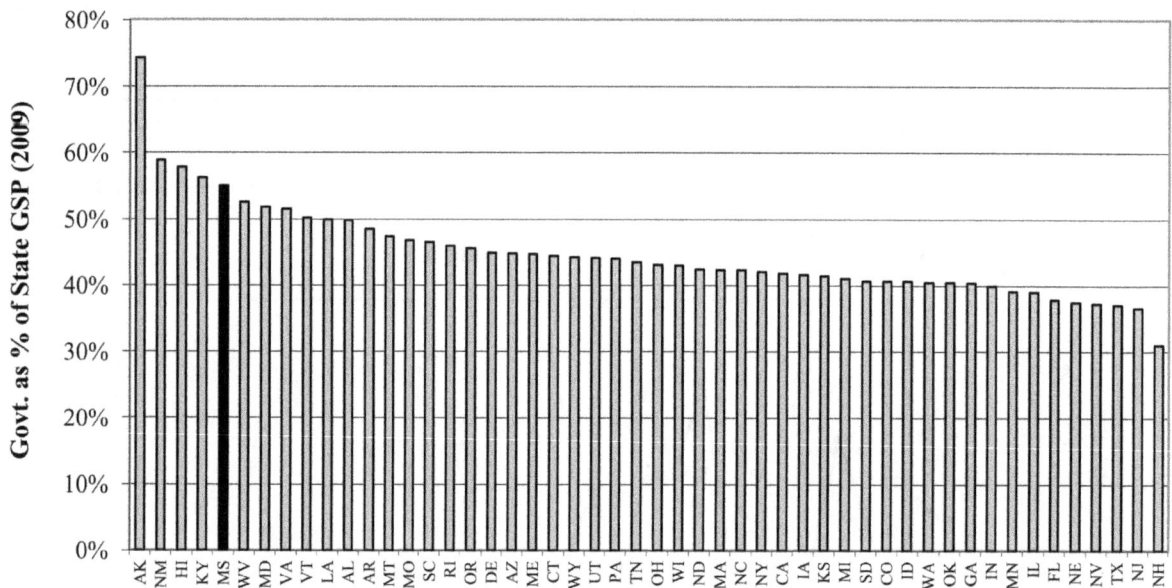

Source: Stansel, Torra, McMahon (2016).

How much government spends relative to the total size of a state's economy is a good measure of the extent to which government controls the allocation of economic resources in a state. Government spending is, of course, only one component of the overall economic freedom index, which also includes measures of government regulations, relative tax rates, and threats to private property.

Looking at spending alone, relative to the other U.S. states, Mississippi has the 5th largest government share of state economic activity. Combined, all federal, state, and local government spending in Mississippi amounts to 55 percent of the state economy leaving less than half of the state's economic resources available to the private sector. For comparison, in the most free market state, New Hampshire, government controls only 31 percent of the economy, leaving roughly 69 percent to the private sector.

While the above data include federal spending, if one computes the ranking based on state and local spending alone, Mississippi fares even worse—moving up to 4th highest share of government across states. In other words, the issue of too much government control and spending relative to other states is a state and local spending issue, not a federal one.

Changes in Mississippi's government size as a share of its economy is one of the key factors that led to the trends in economic freedom shown earlier. Figure 2.5 shows Mississippi's ranking in the size of government component of the economic freedom index. Here lower numbered rankings (implying smaller government control) are better, and higher numbered rankings (implying more government control) are worse, as the size of government enters negatively into the computation of the overall economic freedom index. The axes in the figure have been reversed accordingly so that a decline in the size of government (and thus an improvement in economic freedom) is represented by the data lines moving upward.

Figure 2.5: Mississippi's Government Size Rankings

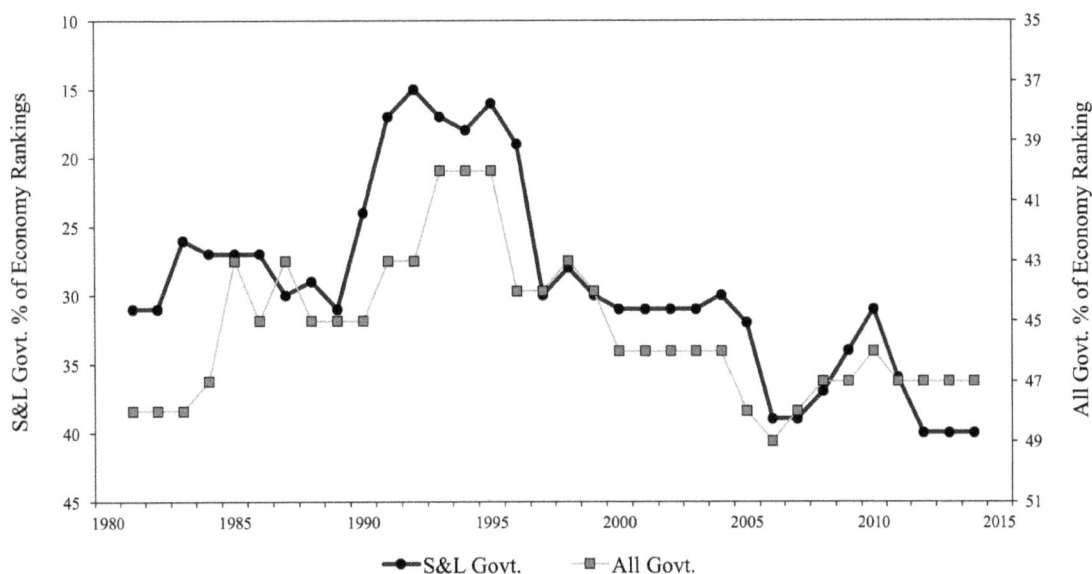

Source: Stansel, Torra, McMahon (2016).

Up until around 1995, by either measure Mississippi was moving in the right direction, with government spending and control of the economy falling, and Mississippi's rank relative to other states improving. As we saw in the prior graphics, this reduction in government size as a share of the economy during that period resulted in improved economic freedom and faster economic growth in the state. Since the mid-1990s, however, government spending has risen significantly as a share of the Mississippi economy, from around 45 percent to an average of 54 percent from 2000 to 2014. The expansion in the size of government peaked in 2006 at 71 percent following Hurricane Katrina and the infusion of federal funds following the disaster. Even when 2006 is omitted from the calculation, total government spending still averaged 53 percent, a significant increase from previous decades.

Excluding federal spending, Mississippi's state and local (S&L) spending as a percentage of the total economy has also risen from an average of 17 percent in the early-1980s to an average of 24 percent from 2009 to 2014. Mississippi, which once had the 15th *best* ranking in its state and local size of government indicator now has the 10th *worst* ranking.

The pattern shown by the data is obvious. During the period prior to 1995, Mississippi's government was shrinking as a share of the economy, and economic growth was rapid. Since that time Mississippi's government sector has grown substantially and as a result Mississippi's rate of economic growth has fallen dramatically. International studies across OECD countries suggest that a nation's economic growth rate falls by 1 percentage point for every 10 percentage point increase in government spending as a share of the economy.[5] This interestingly, is roughly the amount by which Mississippi's economic growth rate has fallen as its government sector expanded by 9 percent of the state economy since the mid-1990s.

Mississippi's Other Economic Policy Rankings

Not only does Mississippi's economic freedom ranking show the need for policy reform, but nearly every other national index of business climate agrees. Mississippi's most recent rankings in the major national indices of state business climates are presented below.

Mississippi's Business Climate Rankings:[6]

40th   Fraser Institute's *Economic Freedom of North America* (2016)

47th   CNBC's *America's Top States for Business* (2016)

50th   Beacon Hill Institute's *State Competitiveness Report* (2015)

46th   Milken Institute's *National State Technology & Science Index* (2016)

43rd   Institute for Legal Reform (ILR) / Harris *State Liability Systems Ranking Study* (2015)

48th   Forbes *Best States for Business* (2016)

50th   Information Technology & Innovation Foundation's *State New Economy Index* (2014)

28th   Tax Foundation's *State Business Tax Climate Index* (2017)

Mississippi generally ranks below average, and mostly near the bottom in the national business climate rankings. The poor ranking is not just in the economic freedom index. These indices are to one extent or another measuring the same thing; Mississippi's lack of reliance on capitalism.

Because business firms and citizens alike can easily locate across a state border to avoid policies, but still take advantage of similar regional, geographic, transportation, or weather advantages, having worse policies than your neighboring states can be a big disadvantage in economic development. Unfortunately, Mississippi is in this situation. Of the eight business climate rankings presented, Tennessee beats Mississippi in all eight. Alabama and Arkansas outrank Mississippi in six of the eight rankings each, and Louisiana is higher ranked in five of the eight. Of Mississippi's neighbors, Tennessee is definitely the 'one to beat' in that it ranks in the top 20 in five of the eight business climate rankings presented.

The one area of Mississippi's business climate that has shown some improvement in recent years is the legal system ranking, although much more is needed in this area. Since the inception of the ranking in 2002, Mississippi has risen from 50th to 43rd. Most of the improvement has occurred during the 2012 to 2015 period when Mississippi jumped from 48th to 43rd. This is in jeopardy however if the proposal to move to partisan election of judges in Mississippi becomes law.[7] Studies clearly show that states with elected judges, especially if they are elected in partisan elections, have worse legal systems than those states with an appointment mechanism for selecting judges.[8] Nonetheless, there is a substantial need of liability and tort reform in Mississippi. The Institute for Legal Reform estimates such reforms, alone, could boost employment in the state by 1.07 to 2.89 percent.[9]

---

5   See Gwartney, Stroup, Sobel, and Macpherson (2018), page 588.

6   These rankings can be found on line at the following websites, http://www.freetheworld.com, http://www.cnbc.com, http://www.beaconhill.org, http://www.milkeninstitute.org, http://www.instituteforlegalreform.com, http://www.forbes.com, http://www.taxfoundation.org, and http://www.itif.org/.

7   See Gates (2017) regarding House Bill 496.

8   See Sobel and Hall (2007b), Hall and Sobel (2008), and Hall and Sobel (2009).

9   See http://www.instituteforlegalreform.com/states/mississippi.

The taxes most in need of reform in Mississippi to increase economic growth are the taxes that fall on capital investment (such as property taxes on machinery, equipment, intangibles, and inventories). As we will discuss in the next chapter, capital investment–expenditures on things like machinery and equipment that increase the productivity of labor–is a key driver of economic growth. Unfortunately, Mississippi levies some of the highest taxes in the nation on capital investment, a big factor limiting the economic growth prospects of the Magnolia State.

As an example, Mississippi's effective property tax rate on industrial property is among the highest in the nation. A study by the Minnesota Center for Public Finance Research that appears in the *2009 Competitiveness Redbook* published by the National Association of Manufacturers provides a ranking of the tax burden on a representative manufacturing business with $25 million of property consisting of $12.5 million in machinery and equipment, $10 million in inventories, and $2.5 million in fixtures. Mississippi has the fourth highest tax burden in the country with an annual property tax bill of $1,291,050, which amounts to a 2.582 percent effective tax rate. For comparison, in the lowest tax state, Delaware, this same business's property tax bill would be $238,840 (an effective rate of 0.478 percent). Thus, the annual property tax bill for an identical manufacturing business in Delaware is less than one-fifth of the tax bill they face in Mississippi.

In 2016, Mississippi adopted a reform that will help as long as it is upheld, a graduate phase-out of its capital stock tax that begins in 2018 and will be fully implemented by 2028. Along with the reductions in corporate and individual income taxes that are scheduled to begin phasing in at that time, this should improve some of Mississippi's poor tax climate rankings and improve growth.

Like a three legged stool, a state's tax system, legal system, and regulatory code must all be well designed to support economic growth. While we have briefly discussed Mississippi's legal and tax codes, reforms to the state's regulatory structure also warrant discussion. The true burdens of regulation on a state's business climate are often very hard to quantify and measure. Most of the cost is reflected in the expenditures of the business rather than as a category of government spending, and in addition many of the regulations have hidden costs through the higher prices to consumers that result. Lastly, many regulations are local, so there is variance even within a state. However, while the true burden of regulations are often hard to quantify, relative measures of regulatory are available. For example, Mississippi ranks 30th in the Forbes index subcomponent on regulatory climate.

One significant problem with regulations–in all states–is that there is no natural "profit and loss" mechanism that serves to indicate which regulations, once in place, are performing well and which are not. Identifying which current regulations are ineffective or fail to create benefits that exceed economic costs is difficult, and getting these regulations repealed through the political process is often even more of a challenge. One obvious area for improvement in Mississippi has to do with its lack of a sunset provision. While sunset provisions–those that force regulations to be reconsidered and fight to stay in place–have been shown to result in significantly improved state regulatory climates, Mississippi's sunset provisions were terminated over three decades ago.[10]

The most comprehensive study of state rulemaking, "52 Experiments with Regulatory Review: The Political and Economic Inputs into State Rulemakings," was conducted in 2010 by Jason Schwartz from the New York University School of Law's Institute for Policy Integrity. Schwartz gives Mississippi a "D" in its regulatory review system. Schwartz (2010, pp. 371) noting that "Mississippi offers no centralized, substantive review of agency regulation... and its periodic review is both standard-less and unrealized..."

---

10 See note (i) in table 3.27, Summary of Sunset Legislation, in Council of State Governments (2010), and also Baugus and Bose (2015).

Promising bills have, however, been proposed in the Mississippi Legislature that could improve Mississippi's regulatory process by requiring agency review and sunsetting of rules that aren't reviewed within five years.[11] Clearly there is room for improvement in Mississippi's system of regulatory review. What is needed is a meaningful requirement for an independent, non-governmental, body to undertake a serious and transparent review of state rules, and a process that would require all regulations to sunset if they cannot justify renewal after a certain period of time in place.

What is Capitalism? The Concept of Economic Freedom

While everyone has a general idea of what economists mean by the term 'capitalism' it is important that we now define it more precisely. Fundamentally, capitalism is an economic system founded on the private ownership of the productive assets within an economy. These include land, labor (including your person), and all other tangible property (e.g., cars, houses, factories, etc.) as well as intangible property (e.g., radio waves, intellectual property, etc.). Individuals are free to make decisions regarding the use of their property, with the sole constraint that they do not infringe upon the property rights of others.

The freedom of action given to private owners under a system of capitalism is why the index that ranks states and countries is called the 'economic freedom' index. Economic freedom is synonymous with capitalism. More specifically, the key ingredients of economic freedom and capitalism are:

- personal choice and accountability for damages to others,

- voluntary exchange, with unregulated prices negotiated by buyers and sellers,

- freedom to become an entrepreneur and compete with existing businesses, and

- protection of persons and property from physical aggression, theft, lawsuits, or confiscation by others, including the government.

The concept of capitalism is deeply rooted in the notions of individual liberty and freedom that underlie our country's founding and are reflected in the Declaration of Independence and U.S. Constitution. Economic freedoms are based in the same philosophies that support political and civil liberties (like the freedom of speech and the freedom to elect representatives). Individuals have a right to decide how they will use their assets and talents. On the other hand, they do not have a right to the time, talents, and resources of others.

Because private property rights, and their protection, are critical to economic progress, it is worthwhile to be more specific about private property rights.[12] Private property rights entail three economic aspects: (1) control rights – the right to do with your property as you wish, even to exclude others from using it, so long as you do not use your property to infringe on the property rights of someone else; (2) cash flow rights – the right to the income earned from the property or its use (i.e. being the 'residual claimant,' which is also critical for enabling the property to be used as collateral for loans); and, (3) transferability rights – the right to sell or divest of your property under the terms and conditions you see fit.

---

11 See Wilson (2017) and Sanders (2017). In particular, under H.B. 1265, state rules that aren't reviewed in five years by the state agencies that made them would sunset; while H.B. 1112 would require a thorough and regular review of state agencies.

12 Note that the appropriate definition of property rights are those of protective rights—that is, rights that provide individuals with a shield against others who would invade or take what does not belong to them. Because these are nonaggression or 'negative' rights, all citizens can simultaneously possess them. In the popular media some people argue that individuals have invasive rights or what some call 'positive rights' to things like food, housing, medical services, or a minimal income level. The existence of positive rights require the forceful redistribution of wealth, which implies that some individuals have the right to use force to invade and seize the labor and possessions of others, and such invasive rights are in conflict with economic freedom. If you can ask "at whose expense" at the end of a statement about a claim of someone's right, it is not—and can not be—a real right. Real rights, such as the right to your life or free speech, do not impose further obligations on others (other than to avoid from violating your right). The right to property does not mean you have a right to take the property of others, nor is it a guarantee you will own property—rather it is a right that protects legitimately acquired property against the aggression from others who would take it.

A government policy that weakens any one of these components of property rights weakens property rights in general. Taxes, for example, restrict the cash flow rights associated with property and so weaken private property rights on that dimension.[13] Regulations, on the other hand, restrict how owners may use their property, infringing on control rights, and weakening private property rights on that dimension. Outright takings, or other forms of outright expropriation, by removing the property from an owner's possession (such as eminent domain, especially when allowing the state to remove the property from an owner's possession and transfer it to another private owner) actually weaken property rights on all of the dimensions considered above, making property a 'contingent right' (contingent on the state's arbitrary will) rather than an 'absolute right' guaranteed and protected by law.

In order to nurture capitalism, government must do some things but refrain from doing others. Governments promote capitalism by establishing a legal structure that provides for the even-handed enforcement of contracts and the protection of individuals and their property from aggressors seeking to use violence, coercion, and fraud to seize things that do not belong to them. However, governments must refrain from actions that weaken private property rights or interfere with personal choice, voluntary exchange, and the freedom of individuals and businesses to compete. When these government actions are substituted for personal choice, economic freedom is reduced. When government protects people and their property, enforces contracts in an unbiased manner, and provides a limited set of 'public goods' like roads, flood control, and other major public works projects, but leaves the rest to the private market, they support the institutions of capitalism and the resultant prosperity it creates.

Capitalism, Democracy, and Constitutional Constraints

It is also important to distinguish between economic freedom and democracy. Unless both parties to a private exchange agree, the transaction will not occur. On the other hand, majority-rule voting is the basis for democracy. When private mutual agreement forms the basis for economic activity, there will be a strong tendency for resources to be used in ways that increase their value, creating income and wealth. The agreement of buyer and seller to an exchange provides strong evidence that the transaction increases the well-being of both. In contrast, there is no such tendency under majority rule. The political process generates both winners and losers and there is no assurance that the gains of the winners will exceed the cost imposed on the losers. In fact, there are good reasons to believe that in many cases policies will be adopted for the purpose of generating benefits for smaller and more politically powerful interest groups— even when those policies impose much greater costs on the general public. Elected officials must cater to the special interest groups who provide votes and support for their political candidacy—they have to if they want to keep getting reelected.

The reason why the political allocation of resources is problematic is that when the government is heavily involved in activities that provide favors to some at the expense of others, people will be encouraged to divert resources away from productive private-sector activities and toward lobbying, campaign contributions, and other forms of political favor-seeking. We end up with more lobbyists and lawyers, and fewer engineers and architects. Predictably, the shift of resources away from production and toward plunder will generate economic inefficiency. We will return to this idea in more detail in Chapter 3.

Unconstrained majority-rule democracy is not the political system that is most complementary with capitalism—limited and constitutionally constrained government is. Constitutional restraints, structural procedures designed to promote agreement and reduce the ability of interest groups to exploit consumers

---

13 In addition, because the value of a property asset is determined by the present discounted value of the net income from the property's ownership, taxes often directly impact the current market value of property to the owners. Insecure cash flows due to taxes also inhibit long-term contracting and lending.

and taxpayers, and competition among governmental units (federalism and decentralization) can help restrain the impulses of the majority and promote economic freedom.

As Supreme Court Justice Robert Jackson emphasized in *West Virginia State of Education vs. Barnette* (1943, 638), "one's right to life, liberty, and property, to free speech, a free press, freedom of worship and assembly, and other fundamental rights may not be submitted to vote; they depend on the outcome of no elections." The fundamental principle is that there needs to be safeguards preventing democratic governments from enacting policies that infringe on the property rights of citizens, just like the rules preventing it from infringing on the rights to free speech and worship. When property rights are secure so that owners can use their property in the ways they see fit without the fear of the property being seized, overly regulated, or taxed, the foundation for economic freedom, prosperity, and growth is created.

What Capitalism Is Not:
Being Business Friendly Does Not Mean Giving Away Favors

Before moving on, one additional point needs clarifying. There is a difference between what economists call capitalism and what some might consider 'business-friendly policies.' When government gives subsidies or tax breaks to specific firms or industries that lobby but not to others, this is at odds with the institutions, or rules of the game, consistent with capitalism.

When it becomes more profitable for companies and industries to invest time and resources into lobbying the political process for favors, or into initiating lawsuits against others, we end up with more of these types of destructive activities, and less productive activity. Firms begin competing over obtaining government tax breaks rather than with each other in the marketplace. They spend time lobbying rather than producing.

In addition, by arbitrarily making some industries more (or less) profitable than others, private sector economic activity is distorted in those sectors relative to other sectors. For growth, market-determined returns (profit rates) and market prices should guide these investments, not government taxes and subsidies. Capitalism is about a fair and level playing field for everyone. This does mean lower overall levels of taxes and regulations—ones that are applied equally to everyone.

Business subsidies may visibly create jobs, but the unseen cost is that the tax revenue or other resources necessary to fund these subsidies generally destroy more jobs than are created. They result in a *net* reduction in economic activity. The problem, politically, is that these losses are not as visible. When every taxpayer in Mississippi has to pay, say, $1 more in taxes to fund some multi-million dollar subsidy, this reduced spending spread out all over the state ends up causing job losses at businesses all over the state. Government subsidy programs can, thus, transfer jobs around the state, but on net the overall impact is negative.

When business interests capture government's power things can go just as bad for capitalism as when government power is held in the hands of less business-friendly groups. For example, when companies can get government to use the power of eminent domain to take property from others, or use lobbying or connections to get special tax favors, subsidies, or exemptions for their business, this policy climate is not conducive to capitalism either.

Economic progress, growth, and development are not about having business take over government policy making. Unconstrained democracy is a threat to capitalism regardless of who is in power. Progress is not about turning policy over to a specific industry; instead it is about being competitive across the board to attract many new types of businesses in different locations. It is about an environment in which small rural entrepreneurs can compete and thrive in the global marketplace that is now becoming more connected to them through the Internet. It is about creating more high-paying jobs across the board.

Mississippi has a bad record when it comes to granting these special favors, including millions of dollars in incentives given to Hattiesburg's Stion Corporation , Canton's Nissan plant, West Point's Yokohama Tire plant, Senatobia's Twin Creeks solar panel company, Hinds County's Continental Tire plant, and Columbus' KiOR facility. These incentives are not only extremely costly, often costing up to $200,000 per job created, and sometimes ineffective as these firms close or relocate prior to fulfilling their job creation promises, but more importantly, they simply create the wrong policy climate—one that encourages all firms to try to invest in seeking favors from Mississippi's state government.

As a case in point, in 2010, Mississippi spent $27.7 million in a loan to build a facility in Senatobia, Mississippi for Twin Creeks, a solar panel company who pledged to create 500 jobs but never employed more than 25 employees before going out of business. In an effort to recover taxpayers' money, the state settled with the company for the rights to possible royalties worth up to $10 million and the rights to Twin Creeks' future shares of lawsuits and antitrust claims. Additionally, as of June 2017, Mississippi is suing the KiOR plant in Columbus, another failed business, for $77 million accusing the company of fraud. However, it is not only these failed and fraudulent cases of misallocated taxpayer dollars that create poor incentives for businesses, but any case where political favors choose economic winners rather than the private market.[14]

Government officials often cite the necessity to offer these credits to entice firms to locate in the state. However, the only reason the incentives are necessary is due to the high taxes and policy burdens on these types of firms in Mississippi to begin with, such as the property taxes discussed earlier. The problem is the underlying policies, and the solution is to reform the policies that keep Mississippi from being competitive in the first place. These incentives would not be necessary if Mississippi had a more competitive economic policy structure.

When governments give favors to some businesses but not others, it is unfair to the competitive market process as unsubsidized Mississippi firms must now compete with the politically-favored, subsidized firms for employees, resources, land, and consumers. All firms in Mississippi should have a good business climate, without having to devote time, effort, and resources toward political lobbying and favor seeking to get it. Many of Mississippi's businesses—including small entrepreneurs—simply do not have the political power to even begin to negotiate a better business climate like these large companies. The resources devoted toward offering these special favors to big businesses would be better spent doing across the board, broad-based tax reductions that apply to all of Mississippi's entrepreneurs and businesses.

Institutions and Growth: A Closer Look at the Evidence

Nobel Prize winning economists F.A. Hayek, Douglass North, and Milton Friedman won their Nobel awards for contributions to our understanding of why (and how) capitalism creates such remarkable prosperity. The reason why so many economists are in agreement on this issue is because the evidence is so clear. Let us take a closer look at the evidence on the relationship between capitalism and prosperity.

First, let us compare states' reliance on capitalism, the *Economic Freedom of North America* index, and state per capita income. This is shown in Figure 2.6 on the following page. The trend line shown in the figure clearly has a positive slope. Thus, the states whose citizens have the highest average incomes are the states that rely most heavily on capitalism. The poorest states are those that rely most on government.

How does the economic freedom index correlate with other measures of economic activity? Figure 2.7 shows, for the top 5 and bottom 5 ranking states in the economic freedom index, seven measures of economic prosperity and entrepreneurial activity. To provide a picture uncomplicated by the recent national

---

14 See Wright (2013) and Amy (2017).

recession, this data is from prior to the recession. The table shows the averages for these two groups of states on these important indicators of prosperity, as well as the difference between the averages for these two groupings of states.

The states listed in the top of the table, those with the best institutions, are uniformly more prosperous than the states with the worst economic institutions. The differences in economic outcomes are striking. Looking at the averages given near the bottom of the table, average per capita personal income is $5,618 higher, and the poverty rate is 3.1 percentage points lower, on

Figure 2.6: Reliance on Capitalism and Prosperity

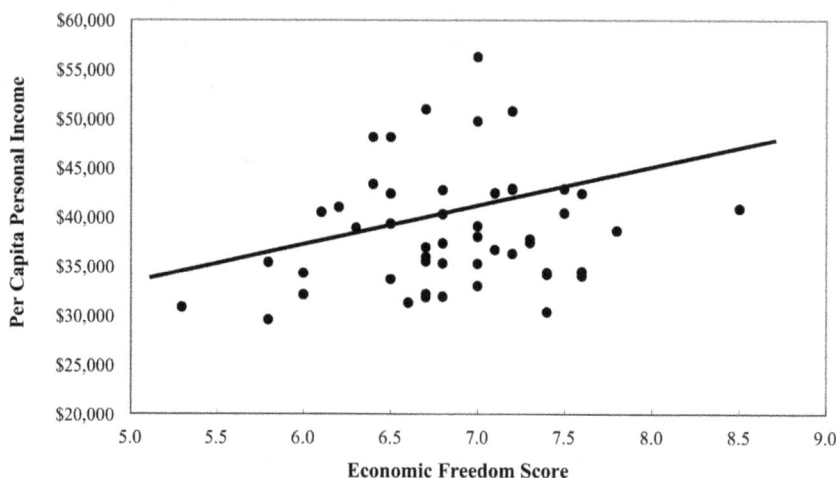

Sources: Sobel and Hall (2009).

Figure 2.7: Capitalism's Economic Record

State	Economic Freedom Index (2005)		Economic Performance Measures		Measures of Entrepreneurial Activity (annual averages)				
	Score	Rank (among U.S. states)	Per Capita Personal Income (2008)	Poverty Rate (2007)	Venture Capital Investment Per Capita	Patents Per Capita (per 100,000 pop.)	Sole Proprietorship Growth Rate	Establishment Birth Rate (all firms)	Establishment Birth Rate (large firms only)
Top 5 States									
Delaware	8.5	1	$40,852	10.3%	$60.97	52.6	5.5%	13.1%	14.2%
Texas	7.8	2	$38,575	16.3%	$113.29	25.9	3.3%	12.8%	12.0%
Colorado	7.6	3 (tie)	$42,377	11.5%	$333.22	37.1	4.6%	14.2%	13.0%
Georgia	7.6	3 (tie)	$33,975	14.3%	$103.63	14.6	4.0%	13.5%	11.7%
North Carolina	7.6	3 (tie)	$34,439	14.3%	$82.57	19.5	3.5%	11.7%	10.3%
Bottom 5 States									
Montana	6.0	46 (tie)	$34,256	14.1%	$14.30	12.6	1.9%	12.0%	10.7%
New Mexico	6.0	46 (tie)	$32,091	17.9%	$10.08	16.3	2.7%	12.1%	10.8%
Maine	5.8	48 (tie)	$35,381	12.2%	$34.96	9.3	3.0%	11.2%	9.5%
Mississippi	5.8	48 (tie)	$29,569	20.7%	$18.53	5.6	3.4%	11.1%	9.7%
West Virginia	5.3	50	$30,831	17.1%	$0.00	0.0	2.8%	9.5%	8.6%
Average - Top 5 States			$38,044	13.3%	$138.74	29.9	4.2%	13.1%	12.2%
Average - Bottom 5 States			$32,426	16.4%	$15.57	8.8	2.8%	11.2%	9.9%
Difference (Top minus Bottom)			$5,618	-3.1%	$123.16	21.2	1.4%	1.9%	2.4%

Source: Sobel and Hall (2009).

average, in those states with the best economic institutions. Examining the measures of entrepreneurial activity, a similar pattern emerges—states with the most economic freedom have higher rates of entrepreneurial activity. Relative to the states with the least economic freedom, those with the most have venture capital investment $123.16 higher per capita, a rate of patents 21.2 higher per 100,000 residents, a growth rate of sole proprietorships 1.4 percentage points higher, an establishment birth rate almost 2 percent higher, and a birth rate of large establishments 2.4 percentage points higher. This strong relationship between economic freedom and rates of entrepreneurship has been well documented at both the state and national levels.[15]

Because Mississippi ranks in the bottom of the pack on economic freedom and business climate measures, the measures of entrepreneurship and prosperity for Mississippi also suffer like in other states near the bottom. Relative to other states, Mississippi's level of venture capital investment, patents, and large firm births fall well below average.

Evidence from Across the World

While state comparisons are probably the most valuable for Mississippi policy reform, it is worthwhile to spend a moment looking at some additional evidence on the relationship between reliance on capitalism, or economic freedom, and prosperity from around the world. This is meaningful because as mentioned earlier, there are much larger differences between countries than between U.S. states. The majority of countries in the world indeed rely less heavily on capitalism than does Mississippi, but their fate can help us understand what is in store for the state if policy keeps moving in the wrong direction.

Figure 2.8 shows the average income level within four different groupings of countries in the *Economic Freedom of the World* index. Countries are divided into these groups based on their scores, and again higher numbers mean a heavier reliance on capitalism, rather than political planning, to organize their economies. The pattern in Figure 2.8 is clear and is the same pattern we saw across the U.S. states above. A heavier reliance on capitalism makes countries more prosperous.

Figure 2.9 shows a similar graph for the relationship between reliance on capitalism and income growth rates over the 1990-2014 period for countries of the world. Those relying least on capitalism are not only poorer to begin with (looking at average income levels), but they are also becoming worse off through time. As their negative growth rates show, average income is actually falling through time in these countries.

Figure 2.8: Capitalism and Income (International Data)

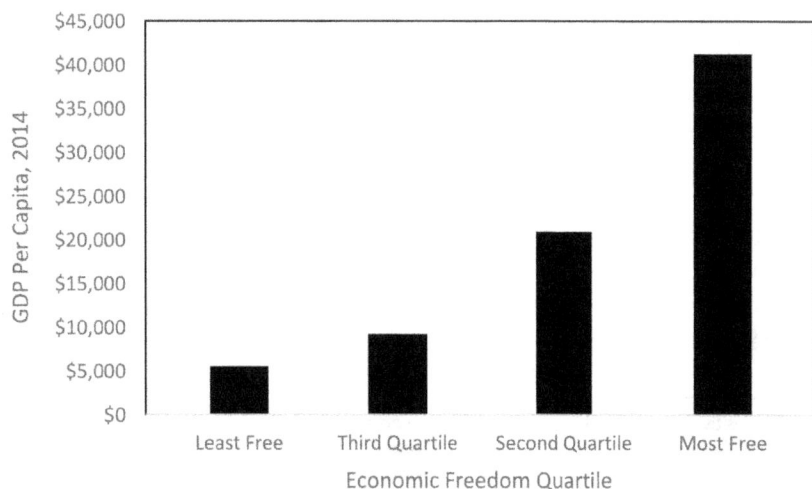

Source: Gwartney, Lawson, Hall (2016).

---

15 See Kreft and Sobel (2005) and Sobel, Clark and Lee (2007).

At the opposite end of the spectrum are countries that rely heavily on capitalism and have both high incomes and high growth rates as a result.

In summary, the international evidence bears out the same conclusions as the evidence from U.S. states. Those areas embracing capitalism are richer and grow faster, and those areas that do not are poorer and grow slower.

Figure 2.9: Capitalism and Growth (International Data)

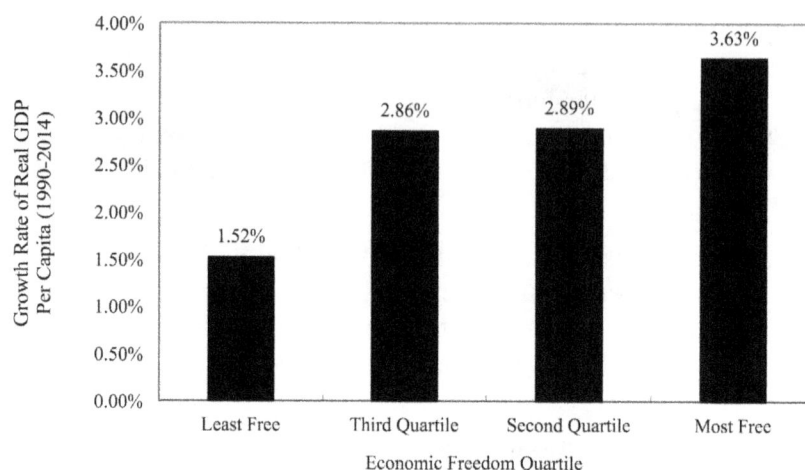

Source: Gwartney, Lawson, Hall (2016).

Could Other Things Account for These Differences in Prosperity?

Up to this point we have relied on presentations of simple correlations to establish the linkage between good institutions and prosperity. Some readers might wonder if these relationships hold up to closer inquiry after controlling for other factors that might account for observed differences. This is the realm of academic journal publications, and for our intended audience, the details behind this analysis would be uninteresting.

Rather than attempting to present these more detailed results here, we instead point the reader to the following published articles on this subject contained in the accompanying footnote to this sentence.[16] All of these articles are published in academic journals, in which authors submit papers that are reviewed anonymously by other scholars from across the globe in a scientific manner. Papers generally go through revisions and must pass a high level of scrutiny. These studies confirm the conclusions we have shown in this chapter, namely that economic freedom promotes prosperity.

It is worth noting that this literature does provide evidence rejecting some popularly held notions of what other factors might explain these differences in prosperity. Areas rich in natural resources, for example, do not necessarily grow faster than those areas with none. The previously mentioned case of Hong Kong (a rock island in the ocean) and how it has grown rapidly versus resource-rich countries with slow or negative growth, such as Venezuela and Argentina, are good examples. Geographic climate variation, or just plain luck, does not explain the differences observed across countries or regions or states either. When we see the borders between countries—like the two sides of the former Berlin Wall separating wealthy, capitalist West Germany from relatively poor, socialist East Germany—it is clear that institutional differences, differences in the rules of the economic game, are the true source of differences in prosperity.

---

16 The positive relationship between economic freedom and growth has been shown to be robust in a large number of studies. Gerald Scully (1988), for example, finds that politically open countries that respect private property rights, subscribe to the rule of law, and use markets instead of government to allocate resources, grow three times faster than countries that do not. Harvard economist Robert Barro (1996) finds a positive relationship between economic freedom and growth. Gwartney, Lawson, and Holcombe (1999) take into account demographics, changes in education and physical capital and find that economic freedom is still a significant determinant of economic growth. John Dawson (1998) finds that economic freedom positively affects growth and it does so by directly affecting the productivity of capital and labor and indirectly through its influence on the environment for investment. This is consistent with Hall and Jones's (1999) finding that policies consistent with economic freedom improve labor productivity. A very nice overview of the findings of this literature can be found in Berggren (2003) and, more recently, Hall and Lawson (2014).

Conclusion

This chapter has presented evidence that areas relying on capitalism—the protection of private property through constitutionally limited political institutions and sound legal institutions—are more prosperous. We began with a review of the economic evidence on the sources of prosperity and growth. Beginning with Adam Smith, over 230 years of evidence suggests that reliance on capitalism is the best route to achieve increases in living standards. States and countries relying more heavily on capitalism not only have higher income levels and faster average income growth, but also faster and more even growth across the income distribution.

One key component in reforming policy in a manner conducive to growth is to ensure the security of private ownership rights. This implies protection of persons and property from unreasonable aggression, theft, lawsuits, or confiscation by others, including the government. This is why having a weak legal system is devastating to the underpinnings of a free-market economy. Too often these violations of private property sneak in under the guise of regulations that require costly actions on the part of property owners, or restrict their ability to use their property as they see fit.

In addition to the legal foundations necessary for capitalism, governments must also refrain from attempting to control the state's economy by spending citizens' incomes for them through high taxes and government expenditures. Large rates of government employment, ownership of land and of productive assets, and high government spending, beyond some basic functions, reflect the government attempting to drive the economy rather than leaving this to the private sector. There is no getting around the fact that the private and government sector shares in the state economy add up to 100 percent. The goal should be to increase the share controlled through the private sector and diminish the share controlled through the public sector. The evidence clearly shows that prosperity follows as a result.

References

Amy, Jeff. 2017. KiOR Lawsuits Story. *StarTribune*, June 13. http://www.startribune.com/investors-get-4-5m-in-biofuel-case-under-federal-settlement/427650193/.

Barro, Robert J. 1996. Democracy and Growth. *Journal of Economic Growth* 1(1): 1-27.

Baugus, Brian, and Feler Bose. 2015. Sunset Legislation in the States: Balancing the Legislature and the Executive. Mercatus Research, Mercatus Center at George Mason University, Arlington, VA. https://www.mercatus.org/system/files/Baugus-Sunset-Legislation.pdf.

Berggren, Niclas. 2003. The Benefits of Economic Freedom: A Survey. *Independent Review* 8(2): 193-211.

Bureau of Economic Analysis, U.S. Department of Commerce. 2017. *Annual State Personal Income* [electronic file]. Washington, DC: U.S. Department of Commerce. Online: http://www.bea.gov/regional/index.htm (cited: June 21, 2017).

Council of State Governments. 2010. Summary of Sunset Legislation, table 3.27 in *Book of the States*. http://knowledgecenter.csg.org/kc/system/files/Table_3.27.pdf

Dawson, John. 1998. Institutions, Investment, and Growth: New Cross-Country and Panel Data Evidence. *Economic Inquiry* 36(4): 603-619.

Gates, Jimmie E. 2017. Bill Would Make Judicial Elections Partisan. *The Clarion-Ledger*, January 16. http://www.clarionledger.com/story/news/politics/2017/01/16/bill-to-make-judicial-elections-partisan/96633558/.

Gwartney, James D., Robert A. Lawson, and Randall G. Holcombe. 1999. Economic Freedom and the Environment for Economic Growth. *Journal of Institutional and Theoretical Economics* 155(4): 1-21.

Gwartney, James D., Robert A. Lawson, and Joshua C. Hall. *Economic Freedom of the World: 2016 Annual Report*. Vancouver, Canada: Fraser Institute, 2016.

Gwartney, James D., Richard L. Stroup, Russell S. Sobel, and David A. Macpherson. 2018. *Economics: Private and Public Choice*, 16th Edition. Boston, MA: Cengage Learning.

Hall, Joshua C., and Robert A. Lawson. 2014. Economic Freedom of the World: An Accounting of the Literature. *Contemporary Economic Policy* 32(1): 1-19.

Hall, Joshua C., and Russell S. Sobel. 2006. Public Policy and Entrepreneurship. *Center for Applied Economics Technical Report* 06-0717. Kansas City: Center for Applied Economics.

Hall, Joshua C., and Russell S. Sobel. 2008. Is the 'Missouri Plan' Good for Missouri? The Economics of Judicial Selection. St. Louis: Show Me Institute, Policy Study #15.

Hall, Joshua C., and Russell S. Sobel. 2009. Judicial Selection Methods and Legal System Quality, Chapter 4 in Russell S. Sobel (ed.), *The Rule of Law: Perspectives on Legal and Judicial Reform in West Virginia*. Morgantown, WV: Center for Economic Growth, The Public Policy Foundation of West Virginia: 25-49.

Hall, Robert E., and Charles I. Jones. 1999. Why Do Some Countries Produce So Much More Output Per Worker than Others? *Quarterly Journal of Economics* 114(1): 83-116.

Kreft, Steven F. and Russell S. Sobel. 2005. Public Policy, Entrepreneurship, and Economic Freedom. *Cato Journal* 25(3): 595-616.

Lee, Dwight R. 1991. The Seeds of Entrepreneurship. *Journal of Private Enterprise* 7(1): 20-35.

McCormick, Robert E., and Robert D. Tollison. 1984. Crime on the Court. *Journal of Political Economy* 92 (2): 223-235.

National Association of Manufacturers. 2009. *2009 Competitiveness Redbook*. Washington DC: National Association of Manufacturers, Association of Washington Business, and Washington Research Council.

Sanders, Jon. 2017. Rulemaking Reform Clears Out Clutter, Grows Economy. *USA Today*, February 7. https://www.usatoday.com/story/opinion/columnists/2017/02/07/ rulemaking-reform-clears-out-clutter-grows-economy/97590072/.

Schwartz, Jason A. 2010. *52 Experiments with Regulatory Review: The Political and Economic Inputs into State Rulemakings*. New York, NY: New York University School of Law, Institute for Policy Integrity, Report No. 6.

Scully, Gerald. 1988. The Institutional Framework and Economic Development. *Journal of Political Economy* 96(3): 652-662.

Smith, Adam. 1998 [1776]. *An Inquiry into the Nature and Causes of the Wealth of Nations*. Washington: Regnery Publishing.

Sobel, Russell S. 2008. Testing Baumol: Institutional Quality and the Productivity of Entrepreneurship. *Journal of Business Venturing* 23(6): 641-655.

Sobel, Russell S., and Joshua C. Hall. 2007a. The Sources of Economic Growth, Chapter 2 in Russell S. Sobel (ed.), *Unleashing Capitalism: Why Prosperity Stops at the West Virginia Border and How to Fix It*. Morgantown, WV: Center for Economic Growth, The Public Policy Foundation of West Virginia: 13-36.

Sobel, Russell S., and Joshua C. Hall. 2007b. The Effect of Judicial Selection Processes on Judicial Quality: The Role of Partisan Politics. *Cato Journal* 27(1): 69-82.

Sobel, Russell S., and Joshua C. Hall. 2009. The Sources of Economic Growth, Chapter 2 in Peter T. Calcagno (ed.), *Unleashing Capitalism: A Prescription for Economic Prosperity in South Carolina*. Columbia, SC: South Carolina Policy Council: 21-48.

Sobel, Russell S., J.R. Clark, and Joshua C. Hall. 2012. The Sources of Economic Growth, Chapter 2 in J.R. Clark (ed.), *Freedom and Prosperity in Tennessee*. Chattanooga, TN: The Scott L. Probasco Jr. Chair of Free Enterprise: 17-46.

Sobel, Russell S., J.R. Clark, and Dwight R. Lee. 2007. Freedom, Barriers to Entry, Entrepreneurship, and Economic Progress. *Review of Austrian Economics* 20(4): 221-236.

Stansel, Dean, José Torra, and Fred McMahon. 2016. *Economic Freedom of North America: 2016 Annual Report*. Vancouver, Canada: Fraser Institute.

Wilson, Steve. 2017. Mississippi Legislature Could Reduce Regulatory Burden with New Laws. *MississippiWatchdog.org*, February 9. http://watchdog.org/288002/regulatory-burden-mississippi/

Wright, Megan. 2013. State Reaches Settlement with Failed Twin Creeks. *Mississippi Business Journal*, January 16. http://msbusiness.com/2013/01/state-reaches-settlement-with-failed-twin-creeks/.

Cases Cited

West Virginia State of Education vs. Barnette, 319 U.S. 624 (1943).

3

Why Capitalism Works

Russell S. Sobel and J. Brandon Bolen

3

Why Capitalism Works

Russell S. Sobel and J. Brandon Bolen

The previous chapter showed that increased reliance on capitalism has allowed other states and countries to become more prosperous. To promote capitalism in Mississippi, its political and legal institutions must do two things: (1) strongly protect private property rights and enforce contracts; and (2) refrain from adopting policies or undertaking actions that infringe on voluntary actions and contracting in the private sector.

Unfortunately, governments often enact policies that interfere with capitalism without fully understanding the economic consequences. While policy makers in Mississippi and other states are indeed smart and reasonable people, most do not have formal training in advanced economics. To ensure that the true economic consequences of policies are better understood, elected officials and citizens must become more knowledgeable about a few basic principles of economics. We hope this chapter will help to accomplish that goal. For readers wanting to learn more, we suggest the easy-to-read book, *Common Sense Economics: What Everyone Should Know about Wealth and Prosperity*, by James D. Gwartney and his coauthors listed in the reference to this chapter.[1] With better knowledge of fundamental economics and the basic structures that operate within an economy–the reasons why and how capitalism works–policy makers can make better state policy decisions.

In this chapter we discuss these basic economic principles, including the concepts of wealth creation and entrepreneurship.[2] In addition, we examine the concept of 'unintended consequences'–or secondary effects–the reason why, for policy making, good intentions simply are not enough to guarantee good outcomes.

Voluntary Exchange, Wealth Creation, and Value Added

While we tend to think of our wealth in dollars, true wealth has nothing to do with paper money itself. Total wealth in a society is not a fixed pie waiting to be divided among us. Wealth, instead, is con-

---

1   We also suggest the equally easy-to-read classic, *Free to Choose* by Nobel Laureate Milton Friedman and his wife, Rose Friedman.

2   This chapter is based on Sobel and Leeson (2007), Sobel and Leeson (2009), Sobel, Clark, and Leeson (2012).

stantly being created by each of us; the 'economic pie' grows each day. Wealth is created through both production and exchange. An example will help to illustrate.

Suppose that two neighbors trade a bushel of hay for a load of wood. Both are now better off; after all, they were only willing to trade with each other because each wanted what the other person had more than what they traded away. Both have become wealthier in every sense of the word even though no new money has been printed, nor existing money passed around.

On an everyday basis, money only represents wealth to people because it measures the quantity of these trades—or purchases—we can undertake when we exchange money that we earn from producing at our jobs for the goods and services produced by others. A man on a deserted island with $1 million is very poor indeed without anything to purchase with the money. On the other hand, a man deserted on an island with no money, but a group of other people, will be much wealthier because of his ability to produce and exchange with others—even in the absence of paper money on the island.

Taking the example further, suppose a group of island castaways decided that half of them should dig holes and the other half should fill them in. After a full-day's work, they would have nothing to show for this effort; nothing was produced. Holes were dug and filled again. No wealth was created, even though people worked very hard.

Wealth would be created if instead half the tribe collected coconuts and the other half fished. Now they would have dinner. Suppose one castaway invents a new tool that increases the number of fish she can catch. This invention would further increase wealth; there is more food at the dinner table. In fact, the new tool might increase productivity so much that only half as many castaways are needed fishing, and the extra castaways are free to labor at a new task such as building a shelter, further increasing wealth. As these examples illustrate, there is a close link between prosperity, or 'wealth,' and the quantity, quality, and value (or usefulness) of the output produced. Prosperous places—those with high levels of income and wealth—become that way by producing large quantities of valuable goods and services.

One difference between this castaway analogy and our daily economic lives, however, is that we might anticipate the castaways sharing the fruits of their labor, for example, splitting the fish caught that day. In a large and advanced economy it no longer works this way. Instead, each of us gets paid in dollars, or money income, for what we produce at our jobs. We then go to stores and exchange that money for the goods and services produced by others at their jobs.

The amount of income we earn is determined by both the prices people are willing to pay us for what we are producing and how many units of it we can produce. For individuals, states, and nations, income is determined by the value of output. A worker with a backhoe will be more productive than a worker with a shovel and will earn more as a result. An entrepreneur producing apple pies will be more prosperous than one producing mud pies because people place a higher value on apple pies (and thus are willing to pay more for them).

This logic leads to one obvious, and simple, litmus test that can be used to decide if a suggested new policy or law is good, or bad, for the Mississippi economy—does it increase, or decrease, the net amount or value of output (of goods and services) produced in the state. Regulations, such as those adopted in some European nations for example, which restrict the workweek to 35 hours clearly result in reduced output, and reduced standards of living as a result. For a tax-funded government program, this principle must be applied by looking at the *net* change in output—that is, one must properly account for the reduced output caused by the taxes or other resources necessary to fund the policy.

One of Adam Smith's insights in his previously mentioned 1776 book, *An Inquiry into the Nature and Causes of the Wealth of Nations*, is that labor productivity, the main determinant of wage rates, is increased through specialization and the division of labor. When labor is divided into specific tasks, like workers in an assembly-line, they can produce more as a group than could have been produced individually. The same holds true when individuals specialize across different occupations and industries.

However, according to Smith, our ability to specialize, thereby increasing our productivity and enhancing our wages, depends on the size or 'extent' of the market to which we sell. When consumer markets are larger in size, smaller specialized stores can survive that could not have survived in a smaller marketplace. Oxford's population, for example, is able to support two general purpose pet stores, each carrying a broad line of products. In a place like Jackson, however, a dozen or more such stores can flourish, with a greater extent of specialization, some focusing on saltwater fish, while others may focus on birds and other reptiles. Increasing the size of the markets to which Mississippi's goods and services sell could increase wealth by allowing Mississippians to specialize more specifically in areas where they do best.

Population growth in metropolitan areas would be one way of increasing market size. But another way to increase market size is to enact policy reform that better enables the businesses in Mississippi to sell and compete in larger national and global marketplaces and expand their customer base. To compete in these markets Mississippi businesses need to be on a level playing field with their competitors. Mississippi's taxes and regulations are a competitive disadvantage to firms located in the state. The higher prices Mississippi businesses must charge for their products greatly limits the markets in which they can compete. If these tax and regulatory costs could be reduced through policy reform, firms could offer more competitive pricing, increasing their market shares and the extent of their markets. This would allow both the businesses themselves, and their workers, to become more specialized and earn higher incomes as a result.

In addition to specialization and the division of labor, capital investment also increases labor productivity. Higher levels of education (more 'human capital') and better machinery, buildings, and tools to work with (more 'physical capital') can help our citizens produce more output and generate more income. Recent capital investments in the auto industry provide a good example of this. Modern robotics and automation allow workers to position, spin, and move the parts they are assembling much more easily and quickly. With this new capital equipment workers are more productive and earn higher wages as a result.

But new factories, better machinery, and equipment are expensive. They require large investments in assets and property. In Mississippi, taxes (such as property taxes on capital equipment), regulations, and lawsuits decrease the return from capital investment and thereby lower the inflow of capital into the state. As we discussed in Chapter 2, Mississippi has among the highest property taxes in the nation on a representative manufacturing facility's equipment and machinery. This results in Mississippi's workers being less productive—and earning less as a result.

The income a state produces from its output depends not only on *how much* is produced (which can be expanded through specialization, division of labor, and capital investment), but also on the price per unit, or *value*, of the goods and services produced. A company trying to sell mud pies will generate less income than one producing apple pies. Income can be increased not only by increasing labor productivity, but also by raising the value per unit—or 'value added'—of Mississippi labor.

However, the answer to the question of which specific uses of Mississippi's resources create the most value, and thus income, is not obvious. In fact, the answer is so complex that it is not something any one person or group of people knows, not even a group of expert economic planners. It is an answer that must be *discovered* by individuals in the private sector through the decentralized process of entrepreneurship, a process of private trial and error. This is the topic of our next section.

Before moving on, however, let us complete our discussion of the process of wealth creation started above. As we pointed out, in a real-world economy things work a bit differently than in the castaway example because we must first earn income by producing goods and services. Only then do we use that income to acquire the goods and services produced by others. The ability to turn our income into prosperity and wealth through exchange is the second important part of this process.

As consumers, we turn income into wealth through the acquisition of goods and services like food, clothing, shelter, and recreation. In our shopping, we search out and negotiate with potential sellers from around the globe. We spend time and effort on this search because maximizing the value we get from our limited budgets makes us wealthier. Finding a product we want to buy at a lower price increases our wealth because we now have more money to spend on other things.

This is the reason why restrictions on the ability of citizens to freely engage in trade with people from other geographic areas through tariffs, quotas, taxes, and other restrictions, destroy wealth. Individuals cannot generate as much value and happiness from their limited incomes. Not only are there fewer options to select among, but also the taxes and regulations make things more costly for us to purchase, reducing our ability to stretch our budgets and turn our income into wealth.[3] This is one reason to avoid adopting policies that interfere with, tax, or restrict Internet purchases.

As this section has discussed, our well-being is the result of both production and exchange. Becoming more prosperous can be accomplished by increasing the amount of wealth created in the state through: (1) increasing in the quantity, quality, and value of goods and services the state's citizens produce, and (2) increasing the number and value of the voluntary exchanges the state's citizens make, both with other Mississippians and with people from around the world.

Policy reform that lowers taxes and regulations can help achieve these goals because it results in: (1) increased specialization of labor and increased capital investment–increasing labor productivity and wages; (2) increased ability of residents and businesses to buy and sell with individuals from across the state, nation, and globe; and (3) more private sector entrepreneurship that allows the decentralized decisions of workers and business owners–rather than government planning–to help search out and identify the ever-changing bundle of goods and services that creates the most value and income for Mississippi.

Entrepreneurship and Discovery

Of the many potential things Mississippi could produce with its resources, it should set its sights on those having the highest value in the marketplace. However, this target is an ever shifting one, with new opportunities arising and others dwindling every day. One important reason the economic system of capitalism is especially good at generating prosperity is because it does a good job at chasing this ever-moving target through the continuous process of entrepreneurship and discovery.

Sifting through these many combinations is a difficult task because the number of possible combinations of society's resources is almost limitless. Two quick illustrations will help to clarify the vastness of these opportunities. First, think for a moment about the typical automobile license plate. Many have three letters, a space, and three numbers. There is a formula for calculating the total number of 'combinations'– the total number of possible different license plates–that could be created using these three letters and three numbers. The answer is more than you might think: 17,576,000. Second, let us consider the number

---

3   If the benefits from the spending undertaken with the tax revenue, or from the regulation, are things we value highly enough, the tradeoff might be worth it. Of course, if this were the case, we would expect citizens to voluntarily contribute to the cause, or privately regulate the activity, being considered. But when the value created by government policy is lower than our losses from the resulting higher prices and more limited availability of goods and services, society's well-being is reduced.

of possible ways to arrange a deck of cards. Even with only 52 cards, there is a mind-blowing number of possible ways to arrange them—the answer is a 68 digit number:

80,658,175,170,943,878,571,660,636,856,403,766,975,289,505,440,883,277,824,000,000,000,000

With this many ways to rearrange a deck of 52 cards, the astonishing implication is that each and every time you shuffle a deck of cards you are most likely making a new ordering of cards that has never been seen before, and is likely never to be seen again. In fact, even if every human that has ever lived on the Earth did nothing but shuffle cards 24 hours a day their entire life, and even unrealistically assuming they could shuffle the deck 1,000 times per second, we would have not even come close to making it through a fraction of the number of total possible arrangements of the deck throughout all of human history.[4]

Now, returning to the economy, we clearly have more than just three letters and numbers, or 52 cards, with which to work. Instead, we have thousands of different resources that could be combined into final products. With this many inputs to work with, the number of possible different final product combinations that could be produced is almost infinite.

Entrepreneurship is important because it is the competitive behavior of entrepreneurs that drives this search for new possible combinations of resources that create more value. A vibrant entrepreneurial climate is one that maximizes the number of new combinations attempted. Some of these new combinations will be more valuable than existing combinations and some will not. In a market economy, it is the profit and loss system that is used to sort through these new resource combinations discovered by entrepreneurs, discarding bad ideas through losses and rewarding good ones through profits. A growing, vibrant economy depends not only on entrepreneurs discovering, evaluating, and exploiting opportunities to create new goods and services, but also on the speed at which ideas are labeled as successes or failures by the profit and loss system.

From an economic standpoint then, business failure has a positive side; it gets rid of bad ideas, freeing up resources to be used in other endeavors. In our example, where half of the castaways were digging holes and the other half filling them in, business failure would be equivalent to the half that were filling in the holes going out of business and losing their jobs. A capitalist economic system causes this failure and then replaces it with a profitable business that installs underground piping in the holes to provide running water.

A vibrant economy will have both a large number of new business start-ups *and* a large number of business failures. Minimizing business failures should not be a goal of public policy. Instead the goal should be to maximize the number of new combinations attempted, which also implies having a lot of failures. In an economy where all entrepreneurs—even those with crazy and marginal ideas—can try them out in the marketplace, there will be a lot of business failures. The benefit is that it increases the odds that we will stumble on that one-in-a-million new major innovation, or the next Fortune 500 company. Business failures are a natural result of the uncertainty involved in knowing whether a new idea will meet the 'market test.' From an economic perspective, it is better to try 100 new ideas and have 60 fail, than to only try 50 and have 30 fail. By doing so, we end up with 20 additional new businesses.

Noted economist Joseph Schumpeter (1934 [1911]) stressed the role of the entrepreneur as an innovator who carries out new combinations of resources to create products that did not previously exist. The result of these new combinations is entirely new industries that open considerable opportunities for economic advancement. In Schumpeter's view, the entrepreneur is a disruptive force in an economy

---

4   For an insightful and more through demonstration of the process of computing combinations for a deck of cards see
    http://www.worsleyschool.net/science/files/deck/ofcards.html.

because the introduction of these new combinations leads to the obsolescence of others, a process he termed 'creative destruction'.

The introduction of the compact disc, and the corresponding disappearance of the vinyl record, is just one of many examples of this process. Cars, electricity, aircraft, and personal computers are others. Each significantly advanced our way of life; but in the process of doing so, other industries died or shrunk considerably. Economists today accept Schumpeter's insight that this process of creative destruction is an essential part of economic progress and prosperity and that capitalism is uniquely suited to foster it.

A point worth clarifying is that it is much better to have a decentralized profit and loss system sorting through these new combinations, than a government approval board or decision-making process. The reason is that the incentives facing public officials can be very different than the incentives facing venture capitalists and entrepreneurs. While each venture capitalist and entrepreneur brings different motivations to the table, ultimately their success or failure is determined by whether their idea generates wealth.[5] This is the 'market test' we alluded to earlier. The same is not true for public officials in charge of handing out tax incentives or low-interest loans. They may have other concerns beyond creating wealth. For example, officials may be concerned about *where* a new business is located in order to maximize political support among voters. But there is no reason to think that this decision corresponds with the most economically advantageous one.

In addition, there is no individual, or group of individuals, that could be in charge of this discovery process. There is nobody, not even those seemingly in the best position to know, who can predict which business opportunities are the most viable in advance. For example, Ken Olson, president, chairman and founder of Digital Equipment Corporation, who was at the forefront of computer technology in 1977, stated: "There is no reason anyone would want a computer in their home." Today his remark sounds funny because we all have computers in our homes, but at the time even those in the infant computer industry did not see this coming. An even better example might be the story of Fred Smith, the founder of Federal Express Corporation. He actually wrote the business plan for FedEx as his senior project for his strategic management class at Yale. While we all know in retrospect that FedEx was a successful business idea, Smith's professor at Yale, one of the leading experts on business strategy, wrote on his paper in red ink: "The concept is interesting and well-formed, but in order to earn better than a C the idea must be feasible."

The point? Even smart professors, business leaders, and government officials cannot possibly pre-evaluate business ideas and identify those that will be most successful and those that will fail. A thriving economy is created when individual entrepreneurs have the freedom to try new ideas, risking their own assets, or the assets of their private investors, and the profit and loss system is used to decide their fate. While some policy makers may think solar power is the future of the state economy, the truth is that Mississippi's future is yet to be discovered, and when it is, it will likely be in something that is not yet invented or known at the present time. In the end, it is Mississippi's *citizens* that must discover the future for the state, not the state political process.

---

5   It is important to recognize that from society's perspective the profits earned by entrepreneurs represent gains to society as a whole. Because entrepreneurs must bid resources away from alternative uses, production costs reflect the value of those resources to society in their alternative uses. Thus, profit is only earned when an entrepreneur takes a set of resources and produces something worth more to consumers than the other goods that could have been produced with those resources. A loss happens when an entrepreneur produces something that consumers do not value as highly as the other goods that could have been produced with those same resources. For example, an entrepreneur who takes the resources necessary to produce a fleece blanket sold for $50 and instead turns them into a pullover that sells for $60 has earned a $10 profit. Since the price of the resources used by entrepreneurs reflect the opportunity cost of their employment in other uses, the $10 profit generated by the entrepreneur reflects the amount by which they have increased the value of those resources. By increasing the value created by our limited resources, entrepreneurs increase overall wealth in a society.

In addition, many good ideas die because entrepreneurs simply can not put together the initial level of resources necessary to comply with the many rules, regulations, and permissions necessary to open a business in Mississippi. We will never know if one of these could have been another FedEx. If we want a thriving economy, Mississippi must find ways to make it easier and less costly for entrepreneurs to try to test their ideas in the marketplace.

To promote entrepreneurship, government often attempts to enact new programs, such as state-run venture capital funds, government-funded or subsidized business incubators, economic development authorities, or even to create new positions within the education system aimed at expanding entrepreneurship education within schools and colleges. Unfortunately, these policies grow the government sector, and *shrink* the private sector. The simple fact is that the public and private sectors sum to 100 percent of the economy, and expansion of government spending means reductions in private spending, and of the resources available within the private sector. One wonders, for example, whether the hundreds of millions of tax dollars spent on incentives for Continental Tire, Nissan, Stion Corporation, Toyota, KiOR, and Yokohama Tire would have created more jobs and opportunities had this money simply been left in the private sector's hands.

Entrepreneurship is the means by which we discover ways to increase the value created by the state's labor, physical, and natural resources (or economic inputs, in the framework of Figure 2.1 in Chapter 2). Successful entrepreneurship expands the overall economic pie and allows us to generate more wealth and prosperity. To encourage growth, policy reform must reduce the burdens on entrepreneurial start-ups and learn to tolerate business failures.

Adam Smith (again): The Invisible Hand Principle

Under capitalism there is no captain of the ship, no central economic planning authority making the decisions for the economy as a whole. How, in the absence of this central economic planning, can an economy thrive? Adam Smith's most important insight was the concept of 'the invisible hand' of the marketplace which provides the answer to this fundamental question.

Smith's insight was that the incentives under capitalism are arranged in such a way that even though we all pursue different goals and objectives to advance our *own* economic interests, we are in turn faced with strong incentives to pursue those actions that also create the most wealth for society as a whole. An example will help to illustrate Adam Smith's invisible hand principle in action.

Suppose the price of maple lumber increases because of higher consumer demand for maple furniture. This single price change will change the incentives faced by decision makers throughout the economy, likely resulting in changes in which properties are harvested, the percent of maple sent to sawmills versus other uses, the incentive of non-furniture makers to substitute away from maple, etc. The 'signals' sent by these market prices are what enable our workers and businesses to identify changes in which goods and services create the most value. Price signals not only tell us when new opportunities are arising; they also help us to find out when what we are doing is no longer as highly valued, or when the resources we are using have found an alternative use in which they create even more value.

Nobel Laureate F.A. Hayek (1945) stressed that unregulated prices are a necessary ingredient for a functioning capitalism-based economy. The information contained in prices about buyer preferences, relative scarcity, and the cost of production is essential to good business decision making. However, these all-important prices are often missing in the government sector.

For policy, taxes should be viewed as prices people pay for the goods and services they receive from government. If a private firm provided roads, water, and sewers, it would extend service to any new development willing to pay a price high enough to cover the firm's costs of reaching and servicing the area. When government runs these services, however, the prices it charges are often out of line with true costs. This can result in development not being undertaken when and where it should be; or being undertaken when and where it should not. Policies should be designed to avoid interfering with market prices; and when possible, we should also attempt to set taxes and user fees for government provided goods and services at levels more analogous to market prices. Additionally, consumer choice mechanisms can often be introduced into government provided goods and services, such as with school voucher (i.e., parental choice) programs—as long as the money follows their choice—to help infuse more of a profit and loss system into government provision.

Spontaneous Order:
A Thriving Economy is a Result of Human Action, not Human Design

Nobel Laureate F.A. Hayek (1967) contributed to our understanding of economic progress by realizing that much of the economy is the 'result of human action but not human design.' What Hayek had in mind with this distinction was that many institutions are not consciously designed. Rather, they are the result of the efforts of many individuals, each pursuing their own ends, whose activities create order through time. The English language is one example, as is the common law and a successful economic system. No one person or group of people can sit down and create these things by human design.

Hayek called these outcomes 'spontaneous orders.' Another example of spontaneous order is the marketplace itself—the nexus of interpersonal relationships based on producing, buying, and selling goods and services. When there are large gains to be had, Hayek pointed out, these relationships spontaneously arise without any central economic planning.

Hayek's concept can be illustrated with an example. Suppose a college in Mississippi added a new dormitory on campus that was separated from the classroom buildings by several acres of undeveloped land. The college could hire someone to plan and pave the sidewalks in advance so that students could walk to campus. Alternatively, students could be allowed to have one semester in which they tracked through the woods on their own, creating their own pathways. The college could then retrospectively pave these pathways. The deeper and wider a pathway is, the wider the sidewalk is made. Many of the road systems in the United States are the result of this process in which trailblazer's paths were then used by wagons, and eventually the larger ones paved to become major highways.[6]

The important difference is that when a system is allowed to arise naturally it will be much more likely to satisfy the true desires of those involved and create the most value. One university in Ohio that pre-planned its sidewalks has subsequently had to install benches and holly shrubs to discourage people walking 'in the wrong places' and making trails in the grass. Students simply were not using the 'planned' sidewalks. Spontaneous orders work better with human nature and help to accomplish our specific goals in the most efficient manner. The 'unplanned' sidewalks simply go where people need them the most.

While we have explored Smith and Hayek's reasons why an economy organized as a 'ship without a captain' is best, let us now turn to the reasons why having a strong captain in control can prevent prosperity.

---

6   A more in-depth illustration of this idea for interested readers is given in the famous "I, Pencil" essay by Leonard Read, available at the Foundation for Economic Education's website http://www.fee.org/pdf/books/I,%20Pencil%202006.pdf.

Good Intentions Are Not Enough:
The Prevalence of Unintended Consequences

As we mentioned in the introduction to this chapter, what often happens is that new policies restricting capitalism are enacted because they 'sound like good ideas.' Unfortunately, these policies frequently have unintended consequences that work against the very goals they were intended to achieve.

The minimum wage is a good case in point. While many people are in favor of the minimum wage law, they support it because they think it helps low income families. The published scientific evidence, however, rejects this view and instead concludes that the minimum wage actually makes the intended beneficiaries worse off.[7] So, for the same reason—the goal of helping those in need—economists are generally opposed to minimum wage legislation. This position can only be reached by examining all of the other indirect changes that happen as a result of a minimum wage, such as less worker training, fewer employee benefits, and most importantly fewer jobs and higher unemployment for low-skilled workers.

Again, it is important to remember that economics is a science, not a political position. We care little about the publicly *stated* intent or goal of the policy, and rather evaluate policy based on published research that examines real-world evidence. Good intentions are not enough to guarantee good outcomes. A few more examples will help to illustrate this important point.

The employment provisions of the Americans with Disabilities Act (ADA) were passed with the intention of lowering barriers to employment for disabled persons. The legislation prohibits discrimination based on disability status and further requires employers to make reasonable accommodations for employees with disabilities. Has the ADA lived up to its stated intent? Has it expanded employment among the disabled?

Thomas DeLeire, a public policy professor at the University of Chicago, wrote his Ph.D. dissertation on the employment effects of the ADA legislation when he was in graduate school at Stanford University. His research shows that the ADA has actually *harmed* the employment opportunities for disabled Americans.[8] By increasing the cost of hiring disabled workers and making it harder to fire them, this legislation has resulted in a reduction in employment among disabled individuals. Prior to the ADA, 60 out of every 100 disabled men were able to find jobs. After the ADA went into effect, however, employment fell to less than 50 per 100 disabled men. After adjusting for other factors, DeLeire concludes that 80 percent of this decline was caused by the bad incentives created by the ADA. While the entire purpose of this legislation was to increase the employment opportunities for the disabled, the data simply do not support this view. Instead, the ADA seems to have made it more difficult and costly for employers to hire disabled workers, resulting in reduced job opportunities for disabled people. If the goal is to expand employment opportunities for disabled Americans, the research suggests that the ADA is not the answer.

Environmental policy often has the most devastating examples of unintended consequences. Under the Endangered Species Act, for example, large areas around the nesting grounds of the red-cockaded woodpecker can be declared 'protected habitats,' which then imposes stringent restrictions on the surrounding property owners (a 'loss of control rights' in the terminology introduced in Chapter 2). When the Federal Fish and Wildlife Service put Boiling Springs Lakes, North Carolina on notice that active nests were beginning to form near the town, it unleashed a frenzy of action on the part of the residents, but not of the type you might expect (Associated Press 2006). Foreseeing the potential future restrictions on their property use, landowners swarmed the city hall to apply for lot-clearing permits. After removing the trees,

---

7   For evidence, see some of the studies complied by the Joint Economic Committee of Congress, available at http://www.house.gov/jec/cost-gov/regs/minimum/case.htm

8   See DeLeire (1997, 2000).

the land would no longer be in danger of being declared an environmentally protected habitat because no future nests could form on the property.

Similar incidents have occurred throughout the range of this bird, and the total habitable nesting area for this species in the United States has fallen dramatically as a result of the poor incentive structure created by the law. The red-cockaded woodpecker has lost a significant portion of its habitat, moving it closer to extinction because of the unintended consequences of the Endangered Species Act.

As these examples illustrate, policy designed with even the best intentions can create unintended consequences that work against the original goal of the policy. The concept of unintended consequences vividly illustrates why having an economic 'captain' can often produce more harm for an economy than not having one.

One additional problem with government regulations mentioned in Chapter 2 is that there is no profit and loss-type system to eliminate bad policies throughout time. In the end, some policies just do not live up to their stated goals, or do so but at too high of a cost. West Virginia, for example, imposed a maximum eight hour operating restriction on taxi drivers.[9] The law was intended to reduce driver fatigue and accidents involving taxis. Policy makers, however, overlooked the unintended consequences resulting from changing the incentives faced by cab drivers. With fewer hours to drive in a day, cab drivers started driving at faster speeds and took fewer breaks. Not only did the law result in a significant reduction in the number of cabs operating in the state, which led to more driving while intoxicated incidents, but it exacerbated the very problem it was designed to reduce. Even though there are *fewer* cabs on the road due to the law, the total number of accidents committed by cab drivers has *increased* in West Virginia since the regulation has been passed. Despite this information being widely-known, state policy makers in West Virginia do not 'have the time to get the law off the books' due to having to deal with too many other, more pressing, current issues. Simply put, government lawmakers just do not have the time to go back and look into the effectiveness of all laws from the past, nor the time to introduce the legislation to repeal them.

This highlights the need for Mississippi to reform its regulatory review process along the lines of the discussion in Chapter 2. Quite simply if a regulation adopted in Mississippi cannot prove, with data, that it is accomplishing its stated goal in a cost effective manner within some period of time, say five years, it should be repealed. Regulations, and other policies, should have to fight to stay in place based on scientific evidence regarding the costs and benefits they create.

Vote Early, Vote Often: Bad People or Bad Incentives?

Economists are of the opinion that government agencies tend to be less efficient than private firms. But the reason has nothing to do with 'bad politicians' or the particular people involved in the government sector. Getting more out of government is not a matter of getting 'better people' in government. Government workers are smart, caring, and devoted to their causes. The problem is that the reward structure—the rules of the game—within their jobs does not provide the right incentives to encourage the best outcomes. Nobel Laureate James Buchanan, with coauthor Gordon Tullock, published a seminal book on this subject called the *Calculus of Consent* (1962). As they pointed out, in government there is no invisible hand. An example will help to illustrate.

Most people know that government budgets are often given as fixed amounts for each fiscal year. At the end of the year, any remaining money in the budget is usually taken back and if money remains the

---

9   See Corey and Curott (2007) for a longer description of this law and its consequences in West Virginia.

next year's funding is likely be reduced because the agency did not need all of the money it was allocated. To avoid this outcome, government agencies are notorious for spending their remaining budgets rapidly at the end of each fiscal year. The point is that even a person who was very careful and frugal with their money at home, or would be at a job in a private corporation, would begin to behave differently under this different set of rules that are present in the government sector. In government, the problem is not the people; it is the incentives they face.

The Nirvana Fallacy

The 'nirvana fallacy' is the logical error of comparing actual things with unrealistic, idealized alternatives.[10] For instance, some might see a problem in the current health care system and propose that because of this failure, we should have a government-run health care system, based on the logic that this ideal government-run system would overcome all of the problems. This tendency to idealize the outcomes of future government policies and programs is a persistent bias in policy making.

In reality, both market and government sector provision have their limitations—neither is perfect, and there will be particular problems under either alternative. To help overcoming this fallacy, there is one simple reminder, or test, that should be remembered when considering new government policies or programs. This is simply asking the question of which *current* government agency do you want running or administering the program. For example, the idealized attractiveness of a government-run health care system is more realistically viewed by imagining the nation's health care system being run by FEMA, the Department of Defense, the Internal Revenue Service, or a state agency such as the Department of Motor Vehicles, Department of Education, or the Department of Social Services.

Only through careful thought about real-world alternatives, by comparing the likely true limitations of both the private and public sectors, can good judgments about policy be made. To be a productive force in an economy, government must do some things (like protect people and their property, enforce contracts in an unbiased manner, and provide a limited set of 'public goods') but refrain from doing others.

Wealth Creation versus Wealth Destruction: Trade and Transfers

As was noted earlier, when Jeff buys corn from Mary for $20, wealth is created. But when the government taxes Jeff $20 and gives it to Mary, this does not create wealth—no corn is produced. When governments do too much of this type of redistribution among individuals, there arises a fierce competition to become a recipient of government funding—another Mary. When business firms in the state think about trying to become more profitable, they too often think about how to secure more government subsidies, favors, or tax breaks. Instead, their efforts should be devoted to doing a better job at whatever it is they produce.

In stressing the role of entrepreneurship in an economy, New York University economist William Baumol notes that entrepreneurial individuals have a choice to devote their labor efforts toward either private-sector wealth creation, or toward securing wealth redistribution through the political and legal processes (e.g., lobbying and lawsuits).[11] This decision is influenced by the corresponding rates of return—or profit rates—of these alternative activities. Capitalist institutions, or institutions providing for secure property rights, a fair and balanced judicial system, contract enforcement, and effective limits on government's ability to transfer wealth through taxation and regulation, reduce the profitability of unpro-

---

10 For a more detailed discussion, and source for this definition, see http://en.wikipedia.org/wiki/Nirvana_fallacy.

11 Spending effort and resources to secure wealth through political redistribution is what economists call 'rent-seeking.' See, for instance, Tullock (1967) and Tollison (1982).

ductive political and legal entrepreneurship. Under this incentive structure, creative individuals are more likely to engage in the creation of new wealth through productive market entrepreneurship.

In areas with weaker capitalist institutions, like Mississippi, these same individuals are instead more likely to engage in attempts to manipulate the political or legal process to capture transfers of existing wealth through unproductive political and legal entrepreneurship—activities that destroy overall wealth. This reallocation of effort occurs because the institutional structure largely determines the relative personal and financial rewards to investing entrepreneurial energies into productive market activities versus investing those same energies instead into unproductive political and legal activities. For example, a steel entrepreneur might react to competition by trying either to find a better way of producing steel (productive entrepreneurship), or by lobbying for subsidies, tariff protection, or filing legal anti-trust actions (unproductive entrepreneurship).

To understand this distinction better, it is useful to consider the difference between positive-sum, zero-sum, and negative-sum economic activities. Activities are positive sum when net gains are created to society. Private market activities are positive sum because both parties gain in voluntary transactions. When you purchase a pizza, you value the pizza more than the money you pay for it, while the pizzeria values the money it receives from you more than it did the pizza. Government actions that transfer wealth, regulate, subsidize, or protect industries from competition are instead zero sum activities. One party's gain (e.g., the subsidy) is offset exactly by another party's loss (e.g., the taxes). However, because the zero-sum transfer requires an investment of resources in lobbying to secure, their overall impact on the economy is negative. Magnifying this is the fact that others will devote resources to political lobbying on the 'defensive side' of transfers to protect their wealth from being seized. The resources devoted toward securing (and fighting against) zero-sum political transfers have a cost; we have more lobbyists and thus fewer scientists and engineers.

Unproductive entrepreneurship is unproductive because it uses up resources in the process of capturing zero-sum transfers and these resources have alternative, productive uses. Baumol's theory is founded in the idea that entrepreneurs exploit profit opportunities not only within private markets but also within the political and legal arenas. Thus, differences in measured rates of *private sector* entrepreneurship are partially due to the different directions entrepreneurial energies are channeled by prevailing economic and political institutions, through the rewards and incentive structures they create for entrepreneurial individuals.

In places like Mississippi, where the state government's large influence over spending encourages individuals to fight over obtaining state government funds, it encourages a high level of unproductive entrepreneurship. As a result, Mississippi has less productive private-sector entrepreneurship.

How much unproductive entrepreneurship is there in Mississippi? While it is hard to derive an exact number, some data can help to illustrate. In 2016, for example, 445 registered lobbyists represented 1,172 companies and organizations in Mississippi.[12] In addition, Mississippi was home to 7,059 resident and active lawyers.[13] Campaign contributions to candidates running for office in 2015 and 2016 Mississippi statewide elections amounted to over $62.6 million, or $32.48 per vote cast in the election.[14] Policy reform that reduces the profitability of initiating lawsuits and lobbying government can create more wealth and prosperity as entrepreneurial efforts are re-channeled into productive uses.

---

12 Mississippi Secretary of State (available at http://www.sos.ms.gov/elec/portal/msel/page/search/portal.aspx).

13 American Bar Association's *National Lawyer Population by State*, 2017 (available at https://www.americanbar.org/content/dam/aba/administrative/market_research/National%20Lawyer%20Population%20by%20State%202017.authcheckdam.pdf).

14 Data for federal offices ($11.4 million) is from www.opensecrets.org and data for state offices ($45.7 million) is from www.followthemoney.org. Voter turnout data (1,209,357 votes were cast in the 2016 general election and 718,180 in the 2015 statewide election) is from the Mississippi Secretary of State, http://www.sos.ms.gov/Elections-Voting/Pages/2016-General-Election.aspx.

Studies that examine the relationship between measures of productive private sector entrepreneurial activity and a state's economic freedom index (measuring institutional quality) have found highly significant results.[15] Higher economic freedom produces higher venture capital investments per capita, a higher rate of patents per capita, a faster rate of sole proprietorship growth, and a higher establishment birth rate (both overall and among large firms) as was seen in Figure 2.7. Capitalism promotes productive entrepreneurial efforts.

But this same research also suggests that states with the worst economic freedom scores have the worst records on lobbying activity and lawsuit abuse—the unproductive types of entrepreneurship. In the ranking of 'net entrepreneurial productivity' where productive entrepreneurship is measured relative to unproductive political and legal entrepreneurship, Mississippi ranks 38th. It has both lower levels of private, productive entrepreneurial activity and higher levels of unproductive activity than fast-growth states with better scores on economic freedom. Mississippi has the 15th highest rate of unproductive entrepreneurial activity among states, while having the 15th *worst* rate of productive entrepreneurship. The relationship between having strongly capitalist institutions (as measured by economic freedom) and the index of net entrepreneurial productivity across states is shown in Figure 3.1.

Figure 3.1: Institutional Quality and Entrepreneurial Productivity

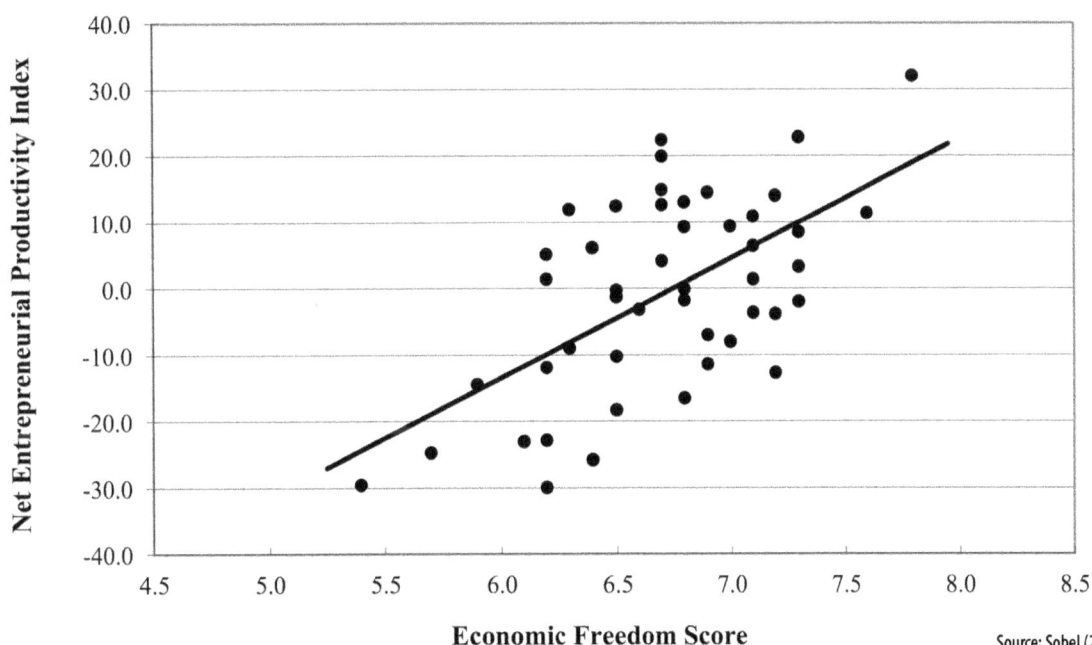

Source: Sobel (2008).

The data in Figure 3.1 suggest that capitalism and limited government promote prosperity not only because they promote productive activities, but also because they discourage unproductive, wealth-destroying activities. While the later chapters of this book are devoted to specific policy reforms for Mississippi, Figure 3.2 gives a general list of state policy reforms that increase net entrepreneurial productivity, thereby generating wealth.

---

15 See, for example, Sobel (2008).

Figure 3.2: Reforms That Increase the Reward to Productive Entrepreneurship Relative to Unproductive Entrepreneurship

- Reduce or eliminate state personal and corporate income taxes

- Eliminate legal minimum and maximum price and wage laws

- Reduce occupational licensing restrictions

- Place constitutional limits on eminent domain and environmental property takings

- Reduce government ownership of productive resources (e.g., land holdings)

- Make broad reductions in government employment, spending, and levels of taxation

- Strive for broadly applied, simplified tax codes that reduce the ability of groups to lobby for specific exemptions, credits, and rate reductions

- Reduce the returns to lobbying by eliminating forms of pork-barrel legislation that use state money to fund local pet projects, and by eliminating business subsidies

- Increase the use of market-based reforms such as medical savings accounts, school vouchers or school choice programs, privatized retirement funds, privatized government services (ambulance, water, garbage)

Source: Based on Sobel (2008).

Conclusion

Chapter 1 made the case for why increasing economic growth should be an important policy goal in Mississippi. Chapter 2 presented evidence that areas relying more heavily on capitalism are wealthier. This chapter examined the underlying reasons why capitalism promotes prosperity.

Capitalism makes people wealthier because it results in higher labor productivity, increased specialization, expansion of markets, increased capital investment, expanded opportunities to trade with others, more entrepreneurial discovery, and a channeling of entrepreneurial efforts toward productive activities. It helps put resources to their most productive uses, generating higher incomes and prosperity in the process.

Despite the overwhelming evidence in favor of increased reliance on capitalism, Mississippi has been reluctant to embrace this ideal in policy. This might be surprising when viewed from the outside as Mississippi is a state who has a Republican governor, and a Republican controlled legislature. However, prior research has shown very little correlation between political party control of the legislature (or other measures of party affiliation) and economic freedom scores.[16]

With the general principles that should guide state policy reform now outlined in detail, the remaining chapters of this book will turn to specific reforms to Mississippi's state policies consistent with economic freedom, growth, and prosperity.

---

16 See Sobel and Leeson (2007).

References

American Bar Association. 2017. *National Lawyer Population by State, 2017* [electronic file]. Chicago, IL: American Bar Association. Online: https://www.americanbar.org/content/dam/aba/administrative/market_research/National%20Lawyer%20Population%20 by%20State%202017.authcheckdam.pdf (cited: June 22, 2017).

Associated Press. 2006. Rare Woodpecker Sends a Town Running for its Chain Saws. *New York Times*. 24 September.

Baumol, William J. 1990. Entrepreneurship: Productive, Unproductive and Destructive. *Journal of Political Economy* 98(5): 893-921.

Buchanan, James M. and Gordon Tullock. 1962. *The Calculus of Consent: Logical Foundations of Constitutional Democracy.* Ann Arbor: University of Michigan Press.

Corey, Joab N. and Nicholas A. Curott. 2007. Lower Business Regulation: Costs and Unintended Consequences, Chapter 9 in Russell S. Sobel (ed.), *Unleashing Capitalism: Why Prosperity Stops at the West Virginia Border and How to Fix It.* Morgantown, WV: Center for Economic Growth, The Public Policy Foundation of West Virginia, pp. 131-143.

DeLeire, Thomas. 2000. The Unintended Consequences of the Americans with Disabilities Act. *Regulation* 23(1): 21-24.

DeLeire, Thomas. 1997. The Wage and Employment Effects of the Americans with Disabilities Act. Ph.D. Dissertation, Stanford University.

Friedman, Milton and Rose Friedman. 1980. *Free to Choose: A Personal Statement.* New York: Harcourt Brace Jovanovich.

Gwartney, James, Richard L. Stroup, Dwight R. Lee, Tawni H. Ferrarini, and Joseph P. Calhoun. 2016. *Common Sense Economics: What Everyone Should Know about Wealth and Prosperity.* New York: St. Martin's Press.

Hayek, F.A. 1967. Studies in Philosophy, Politics, and Economics. Chicago: University of Chicago Press.

Hayek, F.A. 1945. The Use of Knowledge in Society. *American Economic Review* 35(4): 519-530.

Karabegovic, A., McMahon, F., 2005. *Economic Freedom of North America: 2005 Annual Report.* The Frasier Institute, Vancouver

Mississippi Secretary of State. Lobbyist Directory Search [electronic file]. Jackson, MS: Secretary of State. Online: http://www.sos.ms.gov/pages/default.aspx (cited: June 22, 2017).

Read, Leonard E. 1958. *I, Pencil: My Family Tree as Told to Leonard E. Read.* Irvington-on-Hudson: Foundation for Economic Education.

Schumpeter, Joseph A. 1934 [1911]. *The Theory of Economic Development.* Cambridge: Harvard University Press.

Smith, Adam. 1998 [1776]. *An Inquiry into the Nature and Causes of the Wealth of Nations.* Washington: Regnery Publishing.

Sobel, Russell S. 2008. Testing Baumol: Institutional Quality and the Productivity of Entrepreneurship. *Journal of Business Venturing* 23(6): 641-655.

Sobel, Russell S. and Peter T. Leeson. 2007. Why Capitalism Works, Chapter 3 in Russell S. Sobel (ed.), *Unleashing Capitalism: Why Prosperity Stops at the West Virginia Border and How to Fix It.* Morgantown, WV: Center for Economic Growth, The Public Policy Foundation of West Virginia, pp. 37-54.

Sobel, Russell S., and Peter T. Leeson. 2009. Why Capitalism Works, Chapter 3 in Peter T. Calcagno (ed.), *Unleashing Capitalism: A Prescription for Economic Prosperity in South Carolina.* Columbia, SC: South Carolina Policy Council: 49-70.

Sobel, Russell S., J.R. Clark, and Peter T. Leeson. Why Capitalism Works, Chapter 3 in J.R. Clark (ed.), *Freedom and Prosperity in Tennessee.* Chattanooga, TN: The Scott L. Probasco Jr. Chair of Free Enterprise, 2012, pp. 47-68.

Tollison, Robert D. 1982. Rent Seeking: A Survey. *Kyklos* 35(4): 575-602.

Tullock, Gordon. 1967. The Welfare Cost of Tariffs, Monopolies, and Theft. *Western Economic Journal* 5(3): 224-232.

PART 2

Promoting Prosperity
One Issue at a Time

4

Why Are Taxes so Taxing?

Brandon N. Cline and Claudia R. Williamson

4

Why Are Taxes so Taxing?

Brandon N. Cline and Claudia R. Williamson

High taxes are tremendously costly to a state's economy. Countless studies find that higher taxes significantly lower economic growth and reduce standards of living. This is partly due to the fact that the burden taxes place on an economy is not simply the amount of taxes collected. Instead, taxes cost an economy much more than the revenue they generate. These additional costs come in many forms, including enforcement costs, administrative costs, compliance costs, and market inefficiencies. Often overlooked are the resource costs associated with trying to avoid taxes. Individuals, groups, and businesses spend time, effort, and dollars, before a tax is implemented (lobbying) and after a tax is in place (evasion), trying to minimize or avoid paying taxes. This chapter explains the true costs of taxation, reviews the empirical literature on taxation and growth, and examines Mississippi's overall tax burden relative to other states.[1]

Why Taxes Are So Costly

When a tax is levied on one specific group of individuals, such as consumers, this does not mean that they will bear the actual burden of the tax. In economics, this concept is known as 'tax shifting'. A tax imposed on businesses, for example, can lead to higher prices for consumers. If so, consumers may bear more of the burden of the tax even though the tax is levied on businesses. Similarly, a tax imposed directly on consumers of a specific product will reduce demand for that product, shifting some of the tax burden back onto the businesses that produce the taxed product.[2]

We often say 'businesses' or 'groups' pay taxes, but one thing is definite: all tax burdens are paid by *individuals*. Only individuals bear tax burdens since all groups or entities, including businesses, are comprised of individuals. A 'business' does not bear the tax burden; instead, business taxes fall on the owners, suppliers, employees, and customers of those businesses.

---

1 This chapter is based on Ross and Hall (2007), Ross, Hall, and Calcagno (2009), and Hall and Hoffer (2012).

2 For additional information on where the actual burdens of different taxes fall, see Pechman (1985) and Fullerton and Rogers (1993).

In 2013-2014, state and local governments around the country collected over $1.49 trillion dollars in combined tax revenue.[3] Figure 4.1 illustrates that Mississippi's combined state and local government tax revenue amounted to almost $10.5 billion dollars, with over $7.5 billion being levied at the state level. Over 62% of the state tax revenue was generated from sales tax, 22% from individual income tax, and 7% from corporate income tax. Local governments' main revenue source was from property taxes (93.5%). Combined, state and local tax revenue was 46% sales tax, 26% property tax, 16% individual income tax, and 5% corporate income tax.

Figure 4.1: Mississippi 2013-2014 Tax Revenue by Source

	State		Local		Total	
Tax Revenue	$ 7,574,515,000		$ 2,907,640,000		$ 10,482,155,000	
Property	$ 25,103,000	0.33%	$ 2,718,079,000	93.48%	$ 2,743,182,000	26.17%
Sales and gross receipts	$ 4,704,955,000	62.12%	$ 105,911,000	3.64%	$ 4,810,866,000	45.90%
General sales	$ 3,304,632,000	43.63%	n/a	0.00%	$ 3,304,632,000	31.53%
Selective sales	$ 1,400,323,000	18.49%	$ 105,911,000	3.64%	$ 1,506,234,000	14.37%
Motor fuel	$ 409,836,000	5.41%	$ 7,046,000	0.24%	$ 416,882,000	3.98%
Alcoholic beverage	$ 42,402,000	0.56%	n/a	0.00%	$ 42,402,000	0.40%
Tobacco products	$ 146,050,000	1.93%	n/a	0.00%	$ 146,050,000	1.39%
Public utilities	$ 4,384,000	0.06%	$ 56,133,000	1.93%	$ 60,517,000	0.58%
Other	$ 797,651,000	10.53%	$ 42,732,000	1.47%	$ 840,383,000	8.02%
Individual income	$ 1,667,344,000	22.01%	n/a	0.00%	$ 1,667,344,000	15.91%
Corporate income	$ 526,302,000	6.95%	n/a	0.00%	$ 526,302,000	5.02%
Motor vehicle license	$ 154,677,000	2.04%	n/a	0.00%	$ 154,677,000	1.48%
Other taxes	$ 496,134,000	6.55%	$ 83,650,000	2.88%	$ 579,784,000	5.53%

Source: U.S. Census Bureau (2014).

Although these revenue numbers are large, what they actually exclude are the many distortions in economic activity and individual behavior that occur because of taxes. Figure 4.2 highlights these additional costs. The direct cost of taxation is the observable accounting cost—individuals who pay a tax have less money to spend elsewhere. The actual tax revenue collected only measures this reduction in private economic spending. There are, however, other significant indirect costs.

The first hidden cost stems from the political process. The indirect costs of lobbying and rent-seeking (expending resources to capture a 'rent') reflect the resources devoted by individuals attempting to alter tax policy in their favor. Individuals and special interest groups use the political process to fight against the imposition of new taxes, to resist increases in tax rates, and to reduce or repeal specific taxes. They do so by expending substantial time and money to avoid new taxes or rewrite existing tax codes in a way to reduce their tax bill.

To help illustrate this point, let's suppose that the legislature is considering a proposal to levy a new tax on unhealthy fast food. McDonald's calculates this new tax will cost the company $2 million. Clearly, it makes sense that McDonald's would be willing to spend up to $2 million to fight this tax. To do so, McDonald's might hire lobbyists, make campaign contributions, attract media attention, or fight the legality of the tax in court. Even if the tax is imposed, McDonald's will find it beneficial to continue to devote resources toward repealing the tax, reducing it, or securing an exemption. Resources spent in this manner are wasteful. As discussed in Chapter 3, resources used for lobbying are resources that are taken away from productive activities, such as investing in new capital, hiring additional workers, and on the job training. Using the terminology from Chapter

---

3 U.S. Census Bureau, available at: https://www.census.gov/govs/local/.

3, this is 'unproductive entrepreneurship'. It is critical to realize that these hidden costs are present even if the tax is ultimately not imposed. Merely the threat of imposing new taxes creates these indirect costs.

To see the magnitude of tax policy lobbying, one only needs to peruse the Mississippi Department of Revenue's website as it is littered with numerous exemptions to specific taxes.[4] Using Sobel and Garrett's (2002) estimated state-level costs of rent-seeking, between 3.8-5.4% of tax revenue, we can approximate the indirect costs of lobbying. In the 2013-2014 period alone, Mississippi incurred additional indirect costs of $398 to $566 million in wasted resources devoted to altering policy. To reduce such costs, many economists advocate broad-based *uniform* taxes instead of allowing rates and exemptions to vary among individuals, businesses, and different goods and services (Holcombe 2001). With uniform taxes, one particular group or industry is unable to reduce their individual tax bill; hence, any particular group or industry is less likely to expend resources lobbying for tax policy changes. On the contrary, a specific tax that explicitly targets one industry, such as Mississippi's $0.09 per cigarette tax[5] or a soda tax that has been considered in the Magnolia State[6], promotes larger indirect rent-seeking costs.

Figure 4.2: The Cost of Taxation*

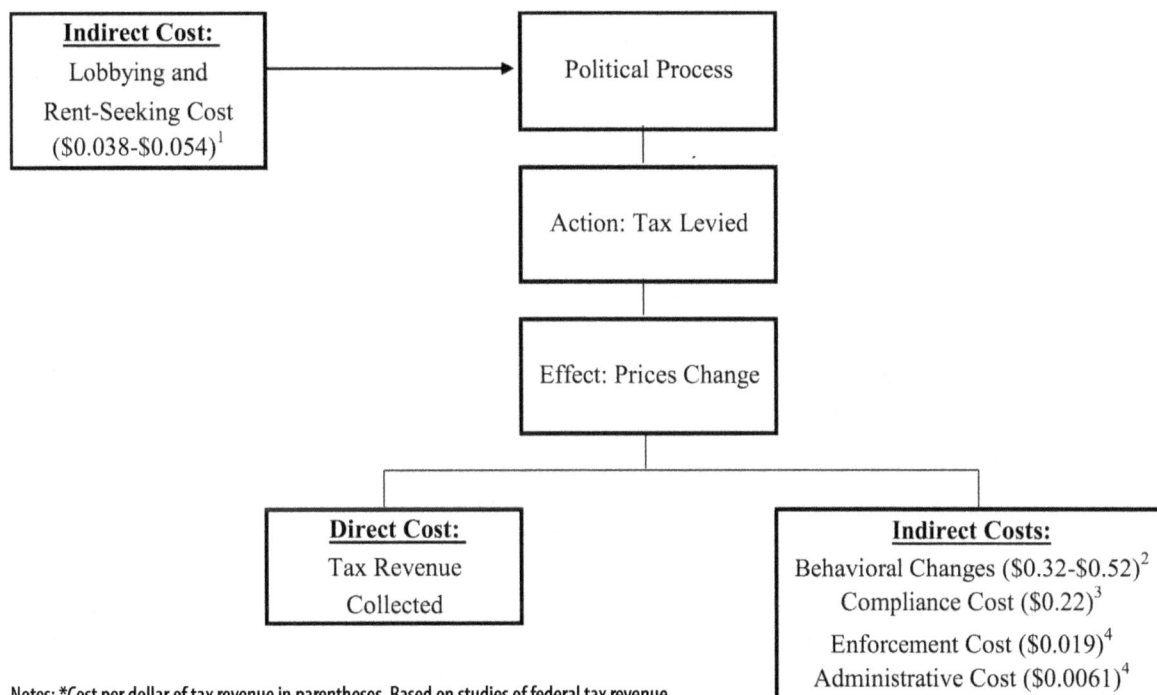

Notes: *Cost per dollar of tax revenue in parentheses. Based on studies of federal tax revenue, except in the case of rent seeking, which is based on the average of all state governments.

Sources: (1) Based on author calculations from estimates of state capital rent seeking in Sobel and Garrett (2002); (2) Feldstein's (1999) estimate of the excess burden from the federal income tax; (3) Moody et al. (2005); (4) Payne (1993).

Moreover, unlike private markets in which you must pay for a good or service in order to receive benefit from it, with government, it is possible to receive benefits from government programs while making *others* pay for them. As a result, there will be additional lobbying costs associated with fighting over which

4 See: http://www.dor.ms.gov/Pages/Tax-Laws.aspx.
5 Source: http://statelaws.findlaw.com/mississippi-law/mississippi-consumer-tax-laws.html.
6 Source: http://www.npr.org/sections/thesalt/2016/11/09/501472007/souring-on-sweet-voters-in-4-cities-pass-soda-tax-measures.

programs will be funded from government expenditures. For example, Continental Tire successfully lobbied state lawmakers for $600 million in incentives to locate in Hinds County (more examples in Chapter 3). In order to secure this funding, they had to compete with other groups who also wanted to receive government funding. The sheer existence of this opportunity to rent-seek and alter tax codes, results in the allocation of government resources to those with the most political power, not those in need. Thus, the political process leads to funding programs that are not always welfare enhancing or helping individuals who are most in need (Holcombe 2001).

So far, we have covered the direct costs of taxation and the indirect lobbying costs associated with the political process. Unfortunately, we are not done. The tax itself creates other indirect costs, as shown in Figure 4.2. These include behavioral changes, compliance costs, enforcement costs, and administrative costs.

The first of these costs, behavioral changes, is the distortions created when producers and consumers respond to the tax. Economists refer to these costs as 'deadweight loss' or the 'excess burden' of taxation—a strange way of saying that taxes cause markets to be inefficient. When an activity is taxed, individuals will substitute away from the taxed activity to other activities that are now relatively cheaper. These inefficiencies can be quite significant, ranging from 32% to 52% of tax revenue.[7]

For example, let's assume that Mississippi imposes a new $100 tax on each candy bar sold in the state, and this results in candy bar sales falling to zero. No tax revenue is collected, but this tax is clearly costly to the state. The producers of candy bars and the consumers who like eating them are now worse off. This tax creates a wedge between producers and consumers who otherwise would be selling and buying candy bars at a price satisfactory to both sides. When these transactions do not take place because of higher prices due to taxes, there is an economic loss to society. The forgone transactions result in unseen market inefficiencies.

Candy bar fanatics may find ways around the tax. Instead of forgoing the purchase of candy bars, these fanatics change where they make their purchase, or if possible, where they live. Mississippians living on the Alabama border will simply drive across the state line to purchase candy bars; real Snickers addicts may move to another state. These reactions to taxes must be included in the costs of taxation. The easier it is for consumers to buy substitute goods, move, or shop in other states, the larger are these indirect costs.

Businesses also have an incentive to change their behavior because of taxes. When a tax reduces the profitability of one particular use of a business's resources, it means that other uses have become relatively *more profitable by comparison*. The business will react accordingly, producing in areas that are not subject to the tax. In our candy bar example, Mississippi candy makers will shift from making candy bars to other tasty treats like fudge, pralines, or caramels. This shift, however, further increases the behavioral costs of taxation. Similar to consumers, firms can also move to other states that impose lower taxes. Again, indirect behavioral costs will be larger the easier it is for businesses to alter their behavior in response to a tax.

The final indirect costs are the compliance, enforcement, and administrative costs. Taxes must be administered and enforced by a taxing authority, which results in additional costs. Ironically, these are typically the least expensive indirect costs, approximately 3% of tax revenue (Payne 2003). Compliance costs, including time spent book keeping, filling out tax forms, hiring accountants to deal with changes in tax laws, etc., are considerably much higher—about 22.2% of tax revenue (Moody et al. 2005).

Collectively, these indirect costs add up to $0.60 to $0.82 for every $1.00 of tax revenue collected. In other words, one tax dollar costs the Mississippi economy between $1.60 and $1.82. These estimates have significant implications when weighing the costs and benefits of undertaking government funded projects. For example, a project with estimated benefits of $150 million that requires $125 million in

---

7 Behavioral costs are estimated to range from $0.32-$0.52 based on Feldstein's (1999) estimate of the excess burden from federal income tax.

taxes appears to be a worthy undertaking; however, once the additional indirect taxation costs are taken into consideration, this project is not an efficient investment.

The true cost to the Mississippi economy to collect $10.5 billion tax dollars is $16.7 to $19 billion.

Comparing Mississippi's Tax Burden

In 2014, Mississippi's total tax bill averaged about $3,500 per person. This was well below the average across all states, which was approximately $4,675 per person. Compared to its neighbors, Mississippi's per capita tax bill is lower than that of Arkansas and Louisiana by $250 and $380, respectively. However, Mississippi's per capita taxes are considerably higher than Alabama ($3,000 taxes per person) and Tennessee ($3,100 taxes per person).[8]

This is not, however, the best measure of the tax burden because some states are wealthier than others. Instead of measuring tax rates or taxes per person, a more appropriate measure of the tax burden is tax revenue as a percent of state income. Individuals or businesses may pay a lower tax dollar amount in Mississippi, but they also receive less income. In order to take this into account, we calculate taxes as a share of personal income.

According to the Tax Policy Center, Mississippi's total tax burden ranks 20th compared to other states. Although Mississippi does better than a little more than half of the states, Mississippi's tax burden is higher than all surrounding states. Alabama, Arkansas, and Tennessee are all in the top ten of states for lower tax burdens, with Tennessee ranking 3rd in the nation.[9] Only New Hampshire and Florida have lower tax burdens as a share of personal income.

Figure 4.3 shows Mississippi's taxes as a share of personal income relative to the overall U.S. average. The first set of columns show state taxes only, while the second set shows state and local taxes combined. A positive number in the difference column indicates that Mississippi's taxes are higher than the U.S. average (in bold).

Figure 4.3: Taxes as a Percent of Personal Income: Mississippi versus the U.S. Average, 2014

	State Only			State and Local		
	MS	U.S. Avg.	Difference	MS	U.S. Avg.	Difference
Tax Revenue	7.41%	5.86%	**1.55%**	10.26%	10.07%	**0.19%**
Property	0.02%	0.10%	-0.07%	2.68%	3.15%	-0.47%
Sales and gross receipts	4.60%	2.78%	**1.82%**	4.71%	3.50%	**1.21%**
General sales	3.23%	1.84%	**1.40%**	3.23%	2.35%	**0.89%**
Selective sales	1.37%	0.95%	**0.42%**	1.47%	1.15%	**0.32%**
Motor fuel	0.40%	0.28%	**0.12%**	0.41%	0.29%	**0.12%**
Alcoholic beverage	0.04%	0.04%	0.00%	0.04%	0.05%	0.00%
Tobacco products	0.14%	0.11%	**0.03%**	0.14%	0.12%	**0.03%**
Public utilities	0.00%	0.09%	-0.09%	0.06%	0.19%	-0.13%
Other	0.78%	0.41%	**0.37%**	0.82%	0.51%	**0.32%**
Individual income	1.63%	2.10%	-0.47%	1.63%	2.30%	-0.67%
Corporate income	0.52%	0.31%	**0.20%**	0.52%	0.37%	**0.15%**
Motor vehicle license	0.15%	0.16%	-0.01%	0.15%	0.17%	-0.02%
Other taxes	0.49%	0.40%	**0.08%**	0.57%	0.58%	-0.01%

Source: U.S. Census Bureau (2014)

---

8 Source: http://www.taxpolicycenter.org/statistics/state-and-local-tax-revenue-capita.
9 Source: http://www.taxpolicycenter.org/statistics/state-and-local-tax-revenue-percentage-personal-income.

According to this measure, Mississippi's state tax burden is 7.41% of income—a difference of 1.55 percentage points, which is significantly higher than the U.S. average. This is a sizeable difference. Mississippi's state taxes are over one-fourth higher than the average state. When examining tax revenue sources, only four fall below the U.S. average, state property taxes, public utilities, income taxes, and motor vehicle license taxes. Corporate income tax, important for economic growth, is higher in Mississippi than the U.S. average.

When local taxes are included, the result is basically the same, with the exception of 'other taxes', which is now slightly below the U.S. average. The total tax burden in Mississippi remains higher than the U.S. average, although the difference is now smaller. This reduction in the difference results from Mississippi's relatively low individual income taxes and residential property taxes, and that many other states impose local sales taxes at higher rates than Mississippi.

Run For The Border

Earlier we described how the behavioral costs of taxation increases the easier it is for individuals and businesses to avoid the tax. According to the U.S. Census, 38.32% of the state's population lives in counties bordering other states. This has increased from 36.43% from the 2000 Census.

Mississippi is a relatively small state (48,430 sq. mi), bordering four other states. Jackson, MS, the state's capital and largest urban center, is located in the middle of the state. However, one can be in Louisiana in about an hour's drive (about 60 miles) or Arkansas in about 2 hours (about 120 miles). In addition, two of Mississippi's four Metropolitan Statistical Areas (MSAs), Memphis and Gulfport-Biloxi-Pascagoula, border or cross over into other states.[10][11] A third MSA, Hattiesburg, is within 30 minutes of either Alabama or Louisiana. This implies that the indirect costs of taxation can be quite large in Mississippi, since the majority of the state's consumers, producers, and workers can easily cross the border to escape the state's high taxes.

We have seen that Mississippi's tax burden is higher than the average state, but let's examine more closely how Mississippi compares to its neighboring states. Figure 4.4 lists taxes as a percent of personal income for Mississippi, Alabama, Arkansas, Louisiana, and Tennessee.

Figure 4.4: Taxes as a Percent of Personal Income: Mississippi versus Neighboring States, 2014

| | State Only | | State and Local | |
	Tax Burden % of Income	Difference from MS	Tax Burden % of Income	Difference from MS
Alabama	5.19%	-2.22%	8.13%	-2.13%
Arkansas	8.01%	0.60%	9.99%	-0.26%
Louisiana	4.99%	-2.42%	9.30%	-0.96%
Mississippi	*7.41%*		*10.26%*	
Tennessee	4.48%	-2.93%	7.68%	-2.57%
Average		-1.74%		-1.48%

Source: U.S. Census Bureau (2014) and Bureau of Economic Analysis (2017)

When only state taxes are included, Mississippi's tax burden is higher than that of three of the four of its neighboring states. Arkansas has a slightly higher tax burden by 0.60. Alabama, Louisiana, and Tennessee all have drastically lower tax burdens, averaging over 2.5 percentage points less than Mississippi. When both state and local

---

10 The purpose of MSA's are to identify areas of high economic and social interaction, where component counties must have either 25 percent of employed residents commuting to the central county or at least 25 percent of the employment filled by a resident of the central county (Hammond 2003).

11 Source: https://www2.census.gov/geo/maps/metroarea/stcbsa_pg/Feb2013/cbsa2013_MS.pdf.

taxes are included, Mississippi's tax burden is higher than all surrounding states. On average, Mississippi's tax burden is 1.48 percentage points higher than neighboring states.

Figure 4.5 summarizes individual income, corporate income, and sales tax rates comparing Mississippi and surrounding states. Mississippi does not have a strict tax advantage in individual income tax rates or sales tax rates. Mississippi's top marginal income tax rate is lower than Arkansas

Figure 4.5: Comparison of 2017 State Tax Rates

State	Individual Income		Corporate Income		Sales	
	Tax Rates	Brackets	Tax Rates	Brackets	Tax Rate	Food Exempt
Alabama	2.0 – 5.0	3	6.5	1	4	No
Arkansas	0.9 – 6.9	6	1.0 – 6.5	6	6.5	1.5^
Louisiana	2.0 – 6.0	3	4.0 – 8.0	5	5	Yes^
Mississippi	3.0 – 5.0	3	3.05 – 5.0	3	7	No
Tennessee	0.0 – 5.0*	1	6.5	1	7	5^

Notes: *Dividends and Interest Income Only. Expected to be phased out by 2022. ^Subject to local food tax.

Source: Federation of Tax Administrators: https://www.taxadmin.org/current-tax-rates.

and Louisiana; however, it ties Alabama at 5%. Tennessee has a clear advantage here as it does not tax earned income and only taxes dividends and interest income at 5% (to be phased out by 2022).

Mississippi ties Tennessee with the highest state sales tax rate of 7%; however, Tennessee allows food to be taxed at a lower rate and Mississippi does not. In fact, Mississippi and Alabama are the only two states in the country that do not allow food tax exemptions. Alabama and Louisiana both have much lower state sales tax rates than Mississippi. State sales tax rates, however, can be misleading due to local sales tax options. Alabama and Louisiana allow local sales tax up to 7% on top of the state sales tax rate. Mississippi caps local sales tax at 1%. Arkansas is capped at 5.1%. All of Mississippi's neighboring states' combined state and local sales tax rate is, on average, over 9%, while Mississippi's is 7.1%. In fact, Louisiana has the highest combined sales tax rate in the country at 10%. This suggest that Mississippi may actually be more competitive in sales tax rates, implying that residents in bordering states, particularly Louisiana, have an incentive to shop in Mississippi.[12]

Mississippi has the lowest top marginal corporate income tax rate (5%) compared to surrounding states. Arkansas starts taxing corporate income at a lower rate than Mississippi (1% compared to 3.05%), but it has a higher top marginal rate of 6.5%. Louisiana has the highest corporate income tax rate of 8%. Only looking at corporate income tax rates can give the impression that Mississippi does not tax businesses too heavily; however, as shown in the next chapter, Mississippi uses other additional businesses taxes that are costly to the state's economy.

Taxation and Economic Growth: The Empirical Evidence

A considerable amount of economic research is devoted to understanding the association between taxes and economic growth. In general, these studies conclude that while some level of government can support capitalism, and in the process generate growth and prosperity, governments almost always expand well beyond the optimal level. This expansion in government increases the tax burden on its citizens and, perhaps worst of all, handicaps economic development.

Vedder and Gallaway (1998), for example, illustrate that the optimal amount of state and local spending to maximize economic growth is 11.42% of Gross Domestic Product (GDP). In 2014, Mississippi state and local spending accounted for almost 27% of Mississippi's GDP, or about $12 million above the opti-

---

12 Source: https://taxfoundation.org/state-and-local-sales-tax-rates-in-2017/.

mal level in that year. This basic analysis highlights that Mississippi's government far exceeds the optimal size to maximize economic growth.[13] Perhaps even more disturbing is the fact that this upward trend in government spending has risen significantly over the past three decades.[14]

Focusing on taxes specifically, a large literature shows a strong negative association between taxes and economic growth. Mullen and Williams (1994) find that higher marginal income tax rates hurt economic growth. Helms (1985) finds that taxation to fund transfer payments significantly retards economic growth. Bartik (1992) concludes that state and local taxes have a consistently negative effect on state and city economic growth.

A study by Holcombe and Lacombe (2004) provides strong evidence of the cross-border effect of taxes. Through a comparison of counties sharing a state border, they control for geographic similarities such as climate, workforce, and proximity to markets, thus leaving only differences in state policy. Not surprisingly Holcombe and Lacombe find that states raising their income tax rates faster than their neighbors had slower economic growth, leading to an average decline in per capita income of 3.4%.

Besci (1996) examines how state and local taxes affect state economic growth. He finds a significant negative relation between state marginal tax rates and state growth from 1961 to 1992. More recently, Poulson and Kaplan (2008) find that higher marginal tax rates have a negative impact on economic growth, and states that rely more on an income tax instead of alternative taxes to generate revenue experience lower growth.

Plaut and Pluta (1983) find high taxes have a negative effect on employment. Interestingly, they find a positive relationship between property taxes and industrial growth. They hypothesize that firms prefer locally-dominated tax systems to state-dominated tax systems (like Mississippi) because the benefits related to the high local property taxes are likely to accrue locally.[15] Conversely, firms may avoid states where most taxes are levied at the state level since the link between taxes paid and benefits received from the firm's perspective is not clear. The link between business taxes and location decisions is explored in Chapter 5.

Taxes not only impact where businesses locate, but also where people locate. If taxes are too high relative to the benefits received from government spending, people will move. Cebula (1974) finds that migrants tend to move to areas with low property tax levels. Conway, Smith, and Houtenville (2001) look at migration by elderly Americans and find that elderly migration is motivated by low personal income taxes and estate taxes. Cebula (2009) updated his earlier work to examine the 2000-2005 period. He finds similar results, namely that individuals during this period 'voted with their feet' and were more likely to move to areas with lower tax burdens.

Conclusion

The purpose of this chapter is to explain the true costs of taxation on the Mississippi economy, and to explore how Mississippi's taxes compare to its neighbors and the country. According to the best economic estimates, each dollar of tax revenue costs the Mississippi economy somewhere between $1.60 and $1.82. In addition, almost every measure of tax burden indicates that Mississippi places itself at a competitive disadvantage in attracting businesses and households when compared to other states.

---

13 State GDP in 2014, according to the Bureau of Economic Analysis (2017), is $104,284,000,000. State and local government expenditures is $27,841,610,000, according to the U.S. Census. For a more recent look at the size of government and growth, see Taylor and Brown (2006).

14 Since 1981, the size of Mississippi's government has increase over 40% (Source: Economic Freedom of North America, online: https://www.fraserinstitute.org/studies/economic-freedom-of-north-america-2016).

15 From Figure 4.1, over 72% of Mississippi's total tax revenue is generated at the state level. This is significantly higher than the U.S. average of 58%, indicating that Mississippi is at a competitive disadvantage.

Empirical studies have a long history of consistently finding that state taxation hinders development and economic growth by constraining the forces of capitalism. To promote economic growth, Mississippi must find ways to significantly lower its overall tax burden. The next chapter will explore several specific tax reforms that can help accomplish this goal.

References

Bartik, Timothy J. 1992. The Effects of State and Local Taxes on Economic Development: A Review of Recent Research. *Economic Development Quarterly* 6(1): 102-111.

Besci, Zsolt. 1996. Do State and Local Taxes Affect Relative State Growth? *Economic Review* 81(2): 18-36.

Bureau of Economic Analysis. 2017. *State Personal Income and Gross Domestic Product by State* [electronic file]. Washington: Bureau of Economic Analysis. Online: https://www.bea.gov/regional/index.htm (cited: July 23, 2017).

Cebula, Richard J. 1974. Local Government Policies and Migration: An Analysis for SMSAs in the United States, 1965-1970. *Public Choice* 19(l): 85-93.

Cebula, Richard J. 2009. Migration and the Tiebout-Tullock Hypothesis Revisited. *American Journal of Economics and Sociology* 68(2): 541-551.

Conway, Karen Smith and Andrew J. Houtenville. 2001. Elderly Migration and State Fiscal Policy: Evidence from the 1990 Census Migration Flows. *National Tax Journal* 54(1): 103-123.

Federation of Tax Administrators. 2017. *Tax Rates/Surveys* [electronic file]. Washington: Federation of Tax Administrators. Online: https://www.taxadmin.org/current-tax-rates.

Feldstein, Martin. 1999. Tax Avoidance and the Deadweight Loss of the Income Tax. *The Review of Economics and Statistics* 81(4): 674-680.

Fullerton, Don and Diane Lim Rogers. 1993. *Who Bears the Lifetime Tax Burden?* Washington: The Brookings Institution.

Hammond, George W. 2003. *What's in a Name? West Virginia Business and Economic Review.* Morgantown: Bureau of Business and Economics Research.

Helms, L. Jay. 1985. The Effect of State and Local Taxes on Economic Growth: A Time Series-Cross-Section Approach. *The Review of Economics and Statistics* 67(4): 574-582.

Hall, Joshua C., and Adam J. Hoffer. 2012. *When It Comes to Taxes in Tennessee: Focus on Competitive Advantage*, Chapter 4 in J.R. Clark (ed.), Freedom and Prosperity in Tennessee. Chattanooga, TN: The Scott L. Probasco Jr. Chair of Free Enterprise, pp. 69-86.

Holcombe, Randall G. 2001. Public Choice and Public Finance. In *The Elgar Companion to Public Choice*, eds. William F. Shughart II and Laura Razzolini. Cheltenham: Edward Elgar: 396-421.

Holcombe, Randall G., and Donald J. Lacombe. 2004. The Effect of State Income Taxation on Per Capita Income Growth. *Public Finance Review* 32(3): 292-312.

Moody, J. Scott, Wendy P. Warcholik, and Scott A. Hodge. 2005. *The Rising Cost of Complying with the Federal Income Tax.* Tax Foundation Special Report SSP No. 138. Washington: Tax Foundation.

Mullen, John K., and Martin Williams. 1994. Marginal Tax Rates and State Economic Growth. *Regional Science and Urban Economics* 24(6): 687-705.

Payne, James L. 1993. *Costly Returns: The Burdens of the U.S. Tax System.* San Francisco: ICS Press.

Pechman, Joseph A. 1985. *Who Paid the Taxes: 1966-1985?* Washington: The Brookings Institution.

Plaut, Thomas R., and Joseph E. Pluta. 1983. Business Climate, Taxes and Expenditures, and State Industrial Growth in the United States. *Southern Economic Journal* 50(1): 99-119.

Poulson, Barry W., and Jules Gordon Kaplan. 2008. State Income Taxes and Economic Growth. *Cato Journal* 28(1): 53-71.

Ross, Justin M., and Joshua C. Hall. 2007. When it Comes to Taxes: Focus on Being Competitive Chapter 5 in Russell S. Sobel (ed.), *Unleashing Capitalism: Why Prosperity Stops at the West Virginia Border and How to Fix It.* Morgantown, WV: Center for Economic Growth, The Public Policy Foundation of West Virginia, pp. 69-79.

Ross, Justin M., Joshua C. Hall, and Peter T. Calcagno. 2009. When it Comes to Taxes in South Carolina: Focus on Remaining Competitive Chapter 4 in Peter T. Calcagno (ed.), *Unleashing Capitalism: A Prescription for Economic Prosperity in South Carolina.* Columbia, SC: South Carolina Policy Council, pp. 73-85.

Sobel, Russell S. and Thomas A. Garrett. 2002. On the Measurement of Rent Seeking and its Social Opportunity Cost. *Public Choice* 112(1-2): 115-136.

Tax Policy Center. 2017. *Statistics State Revenues and Expenditures.* 1977-2014 [electronic file]. Washington: Urban Institute and Brookings Institute. Online: http://www.taxpolicycenter.org/statistics/state-and-local-tax-revenue-capita; http://www.taxpolicycenter.org/statistics/state-and-local-tax-revenue-percentage-personal-income; http://www.taxpolicycenter.org/statistics/state-and-local-tax-revenue-capita (cited: July 23, 2017).

Taylor, Lori L, and Stephen P. A. Brown. 2006. The Private Sector Impact of State and Local Government: Has More Become Bad? *Contemporary Economic Policy* 24(4): 548-62.

U.S. Census Bureau. 2014. *State and Local Government Finances: 2013-14* [electronic file]. Washington: U.S. Census Bureau. Online: https://www.census.gov/govs/local/ (cited: July 23, 2017).

Vedder, Richard K., and Lowell E. Gallaway. 1998. *Government Size and Economic Growth.* Washington: Joint Economic Committee.

5

Make Business Taxes More Competitive

Brandon N. Cline and Claudia R. Williamson

5

Make Business Taxes More Competitive

Brandon N. Cline and Claudia R. Williamson

State and local taxes represent a significant cost for corporations. Location and employment decisions for companies are influenced by the relative tax burdens across states.[1] To become more competitive, Mississippi recently passed the Taxpayer Pay Raise Act of 2016. This bill has several positive tax changes to Mississippi's tax law, most notably the phasing out of the corporate franchise tax.[2] This tax phase out is expected to increase business expansion and attract new companies to the Magnolia State.

Although this is a move in the right direction, Mississippi's tax system needs additional improvements in order to attract new companies and incentivize in-state business expansion. Recall from Chapter 4, the most pro-growth tax systems are characterized by broad-based, low-rate taxes. Unfortunately, Mississippi's tax system fosters an inequitable allocation of the tax burden by varying tax rates across industries, using industry-specific taxes, and providing tax credits to certain companies, an issue more thoroughly explored in Chapter 6. In this chapter, we outline Mississippi's business tax burden and explore several tax reforms that can make Mississippi's tax law more attractive for business growth.

Specifically, in order to promote prosperity, Mississippi should consider 1) reducing business tax rates and apply them equally to all firms, 2) reducing business property tax rates, 3) eliminating the inventory tax and the intangible property tax, and 4) eliminating business tax credits.

---

1 See, Helms (1985), Gupta and Hoffman (2003), Bartik (1985), and Papke and Papke (1986).

2 This bill will reduce the income tax rate for corporate and individual taxpayers. By 2022, no tax will be levied on the first $5,000 of taxable income, the tax rate on income between $5,000 and $10,000 will be 4 percent, and the tax rate on income over $10,000 will be 5 percent. This bill also creates a deduction for self-employed individuals, equal to 17 percent of the federal self-employment taxes in the 2017 tax year, increasing to 34 percent in the 2018 tax year, and 50 percent for tax years beginning after 2018. Source: https://www.grantthornton.com/~/media/content-page-files/tax/pdfs/SALT-alerts-states-M-W/MS/2016/MS-franchise-phaseout-05-17-16.ashx.

Business Tax Burden

Tax competition is an unpleasant reality for state revenue and budget officials, but it provides an effective restraint on state and local taxes. When a state imposes higher taxes than its neighboring states, businesses will cross borders.

Figure 5.1 illustrates that the fiscal constraints placed on businesses operating in Mississippi may be an important factor explaining why Mississippi is unsuccessful at generating business growth. In the first column of Figure 5.1, we report the total effective business tax rate as a percent of private-sector Gross State Product (GSP). Private-sector GSP captures all goods and services created in Mississippi by businesses. This measure reflects the tax burden on companies operating in the private sector, the sector that drives entrepreneurship, job growth, and economic opportunity. Mississippi's effective business tax rate is 6.5%, over 2 percentage points higher than any surrounding state, and 1.9 percentage points higher than the national average. This represents more than a 40% tax burden placed on firms in Mississippi.

The second column paints a similar picture. These statistics show that it costs Mississippi business owners, on average, $6,500 per employee to cover state and local taxes. This is $1,800 more per employee compared to a business in Arkansas or Tennessee and $1,500 more per employee than the average U.S. firm. Mississippi tax laws make it costly to hire additional workers, partially explaining lack of job creation in the state.

The last three columns highlight that Mississippi relies more on business tax revenue at both the state and local levels relative to its neighboring states and the average U.S. state. For example, local businesses in Mississippi contribute over 77% of the local tax revenue. This is 50% higher than the national average and neighboring states. Combined, over 52% of total tax revenue in Mississippi is generated from businesses, which is more than most states in the region. For example, business taxes represent 40% of total tax revenue in Arkansas. On average, business bears 45% of the tax burden across the country.

Figure 5.1: Business Tax Burden, 2014

	Business Tax Burden		Business Share of Total Taxes		
	Total Effective Business Tax Rate (% of private sector GSP)	Business taxes ($ per employee)	Business taxes (% state taxes)	Business taxes (% local taxes)	Business taxes (% total state and local taxes)
Alabama	4.40%	$4,800	42.40%	56.10%	47.30%
Arkansas	4.30%	$4,700	38.70%	46.20%	40.00%
Louisiana	4.00%	$5,500	43.20%	58.00%	49.80%
Mississippi	*6.50%*	*$6,500*	*43.20%*	*77.30%*	*52.50%*
Tennessee	4.20%	$4,700	54.10%	51.20%	52.90%
United States	4.60%	$6,000	40.50%	51.70%	45.00%

Source: Ernst & Young (2015): http://www.ey.com/Publication/vwLUAssets/EY-total-state-and-local-business-taxes-october-2015/$FILE/EY-total-state-and-local-business-taxes-october-2015.pdf.

Mississippi places a much higher tax burden on its businesses, particularly at the local level, discouraging entrepreneurship and small business development. As a result, business minded individuals may never open that new coffee shop, clothing boutique, or hair salon. This results in less job employment in the state and a lack of response to the products and services demanded by Mississippians. These unseen costs, the businesses not opened and the jobs left un-created, are more examples of the indirect costs of taxation discussed in Chapter 4.

State Business Tax Rankings

The Tax Foundation's State Business Tax Climate Index provides an indicator of which states' tax systems are the most hospitable to business and economic growth. States with more competitive tax systems score well in the Index, because they are best suited to generate economic growth.

According to the Tax Foundation's 2017 State Business Tax Climate Index, Mississippi ranks 28th nationally in terms of its overall tax system.[3] This is down 7 spots since 2014. This aggregate ranking indicates that Mississippi is doing well by limiting tax burdens in some aspects, but there is still room for improvement.[4] In fact, there are 27 other states that should be more attractive to a company's location decision. The overall ranking, however, masks significant differences across the diverse types of taxes businesses pay.

As shown in Figure 5.2, Mississippi's overall ranking places it above all neighboring states except Tennessee, which ranks 13th. Tennessee's relatively low tax burden is driven, in part, by its low individual income tax ranking. Alabama comes in at 32nd, mainly due the fact that it ranks 48th for sales tax (which averages over 9% once local sales tax is included). Alabama scores much more favorably than Mississippi on property tax burden. Arkansas also ranks better than Mississippi on property tax, but worse on all other tax measures. Louisiana has the lowest overall rank at 41st, and is last in sales tax (almost 10%, on average, when including local sales tax).[5]

Figure 5.2: 2017 State Business Tax Climate Index

	Overall Rank	Corporate Tax Rank	Individual Income Tax Rank	Sales Tax Rank	Unemployment Insurance Tax Rank	Property Tax Rank
Alabama	32	14	22	48	14	16
Arkansas	38	40	29	44	30	24
Louisiana	41	36	27	50	9	30
Mississippi	*28*	*12*	*20*	*38*	*5*	*35*
Tennessee	13	22	8	46	23	29

Source: 2017 State Business Tax Climate Index: https://taxfoundation.org/2017-state-business-tax-climate-index.

Mississippi ranks higher than its neighbors in the corporate tax category, 12th nationally. This raises an interesting question: if corporate tax rates matter for economic growth, capital accumulation, and entrepreneurship[6], why does Mississippi's economy continue to lag behind nationally and relative to surrounding states? Corporate income tax rates, while important, are only part of the corporate tax burden. Mississippi manages to tax businesses in other ways, discouraging business expansion and deterring new business from locating in the Magnolia State.

---

3 A rank of 1 is best, 50 is worst. The index shows tax systems as of July 1, 2016 (the beginning of Fiscal Year 2017). Thus, Mississippi's ranking does not reflect the phase out of its capital stock/franchise tax, or the reduction of corporate and individual income tax rates, which start in 2018. These changes will be reflected in subsequent editions of the Index. Mississippi's property tax rank should improve once this is incorporated. For example, a company like C Spire, valued at around $600 million, would have to pay an estimated $1.5 million just for the "privilege" of doing business in Mississippi every year.

4 Mississippi does not conform to federal definitions of corporate income or individual income, decreasing its scores in these categories. Mississippi also does not index to inflation, so companies can increase to higher brackets without increasing real income.

5 Source: https://taxfoundation.org/state-and-local-sales-tax-rates-in-2017/.

6 See, Lee and Gordon (2005).

In addition to the basic corporate tax rate, sales and property taxes are significant components of the overall business tax burden. Businesses may pay sales tax on their inputs, for example. Property taxes can be levied on the value of a business's land, office building, machinery, equipment, fixtures, and inventories. Sales and property taxes are Mississippi's two worst categories.

Mississippi ranks 38th in sales tax burden and 35th for property tax burdens. Mark, McGuire, and Papke (2000) show that property taxes and sales taxes have significant negative effects on employment growth. Bartik (1989) further illustrates that high sales taxes, especially sales taxes levied on equipment, have a negative effect on small business start-ups. Unfortunately, Mississippi taxes many business inputs, disguising the tax and creating economic distortions. This highlights one particular aspect of the corporate tax code where Mississippi can make significant improvements. To boost business development and job growth, Mississippi should consider reducing property taxes, cutting sales taxes, and taxing only final goods.

A manufacturing firm, Nissan for example, pays property taxes on the value of the plant including machinery and equipment.

What are Businesses Paying?

It's becoming clear that Mississippi heavily taxes its businesses. To further explore Mississippi's business tax burden, Figure 5.3 breaks down the share of state and local business taxes into seven categories: property, sales, excise (including public utilities and insurance), corporate income, unemployment insurance, pass-through income, and license and other taxes.

Figure 5.3: Share of State and Local Business Taxes, 2014

	Property	Sales	Excise[1]	Corporate income	Unemployment insurance	Pass-through income	License and other taxes
Alabama	27.20%	21.60%	22.80%	5.70%	5.80%	5.40%	11.50%
Arkansas	24.60%	33.70%	10.60%	8.80%	8.10%	5.80%	8.40%
Louisiana	30.70%	30.80%	10.90%	5.40%	2.80%	4.10%	15.20%
Mississippi	*37.10%*	*23.30%*	*13.50%*	*9.30%*	*4.00%*	*3.80%*	*9.10%*
Tennessee	27.50%	30.10%	13.70%	10.70%	5.20%	0.40%	12.40%
U.S. Average	*36.40%*	*20.70%*	*12.20%*	*9.40%*	*7.10%*	*4.90%*	*9.30%*

Notes: [1] Includes public utilities and insurance.

Source: Ernst & Young (2015): http://www.ey.com/Publication/vwLUAssets/EY-total-state-and-local-business-taxes-october-2015/$FILE/EY-total-state-and-local-business-taxes-october-2015.pdf

Mississippi collects over 37% of its business tax revenue from taxing property, making it the category with the largest portion of the tax burden. This is higher than the national average and the highest business property tax burden in the region. This is 12.5 percentage points higher than Arkansas, which means firms in Mississippi pay 50% more in business property taxes compared to firms operating in Arkansas. Mississippi is also 10 points higher than both Alabama and Tennessee and 7 points more than Louisiana.

Sales and excise tax burdens are higher than the national average, but the corporate income tax burden and license and other taxes are slightly lower than the national average. Corporate income, however, has a larger tax share in Mississippi than all neighboring states with the exception of Tennessee. This partially highlights that tax rates can be deceiving as the tax burden can still be high even if the frequently quoted corporate income tax rate appears low.

Business Property Taxes

In order to boost employment and economic growth, Mississippi policymakers should consider reducing business property taxes. But which ones? To help identify business property tax burdens, the Lincoln Institute of Land Policy and Minnesota Center for Fiscal Excellence published a report, *50-State Property Tax Comparison Study*, detailing business property tax burdens. A higher rank represents a higher tax burden.

Based on this study, Figure 5.4 separates business property taxes into commercial property, industrial property, and apartment buildings. Each category specifies the tax rank across all 50 states (higher rank indicates a lower burden), tax rate, and an approximate tax bill.

Figure 5.4: Business Property Taxes, 2015

	Commercial Property			Industrial Property			Apartment Property		
	Tax Rate	Tax Rank	Tax Bill	Tax Rate	Tax Rank	Tax Bill	Tax Rate	Tax Rank	Tax Bill
Alabama	1.45	13	$ 17,400	1.16	12	$ 23,200	1.45	21	$ 9,135
Arkansas	1.436	12	$ 17,231	1.422	24	$ 28,447	1.441	20	$ 9,077
Louisiana	2.106	26	$ 25,274	2.156	41	$ 43,114	1.528	22	$ 9,625
Mississippi	*2.685*	*36*	*$ 32,225*	*2.685*	*48*	*$ 53,709*	*2.685*	*39*	*$ 16,918*
Tennessee	2.838	40	$ 34,061	2.635	47	$ 52,709	2.911	42	$ 18,338
U.S. Average	*2.113*		*$ 25,357*	*1.569*		*$ 31,375*	*1.907*		*$ 12,016*

Notes: Calculated using largest city in each state. To approximate tax bill for commercial and industrial property, land and buildings are valued at $1 million. For apartment property tax bill, the apartment is valued at $600,000.

Source: *50-State Property Tax Comparison Study, June 2016*, http://www.lincolninst.edu/sites/default/files/pubfiles/50-state-property-tax-study-2016-full.pdf.

Mississippi taxes all three categories of business property at a rate that exceeds the national average. Only 14 states tax commercial property, office buildings and hotels, for example, higher than Mississippi, one of which is Tennessee. However, Alabama and Arkansas tax commercial property at much lower rates. For example, Hilton operating a Hampton Inn located in Mississippi with an estimated value of $2 million will pay about $64,450 in property taxes. The same $2 million Hampton Inn located in Alabama will cost Hilton only $34,500 in property taxes. Businesses pay almost double the amount of taxes on commercial property than businesses in Alabama or Arkansas pay.

The story is even grimmer for industrial property taxes, which are levied on manufacturing properties such as machinery and equipment, inventories, and fixtures. Only two states, South Carolina and Michigan, tax industrial property at higher rates than Mississippi. All surrounding states tax manufacturing operations at lower rates, with Alabama and Arkansas taxing below the national average. Mississippi businesses, however, face industrial tax rates that are over 70% more than the national average.

To further illustrate, let's look at a car manufacturing plant located in Alabama, Honda for example. Honda paid a total of $112 million in taxes in 2014[7]; however, if this same car plant were located in Mississippi, its tax bill would increase by over 130%! That means Honda would pay $145.6 million *more* in taxes if it were located in Mississippi. It is no wonder that Honda decided to build their plant in Alabama.

The last three columns highlight Mississippi's tax burden on apartment building owners. Mississippi once again taxes property at a rate higher than the national average (12th highest in the country) and higher than three of four of its neighboring states. For an apartment building valued at $600,000, a Mississippi

---

7 See, https://www.bcatoday.org/hondas-alabama-assembly-plant-contributes-nearly-7-billion-to-states-economy/.

owner pays almost $17,000 in taxes versus an apartment owner in Arkansas who pays around $9,000. Mississippi has several college towns with lots of apartment rentals. These owners pay a substantially higher rate by owning an apartment building in Oxford, MS, for example, versus, Tuscaloosa, AL. In fact, they will pay 85% more in taxes than Alabama apartment owners will. On average, this tax is passed to lower income families and college students.

What drives Mississippi's high business property taxes? Mississippi taxes land, buildings, equipment, and inventory at higher rates than all surrounding states, and is in the minority of states taxing both intangible property and inventory.[8] In fact, Mississippi is only 1 of 10 states that taxes business inventory. Inventory taxes are highly distortionary, because they force companies to make production decisions that are not entirely based on economic demand but rather on how to pay the least amount of tax on the goods produced. Inventory taxes also create strong incentives for companies to locate inventory in states where they can avoid these harmful taxes. Alabama and Tennessee have no inventory tax. Thus, many businesses considering Mississippi may consider these states as lower cost alternatives from which to maintain their operations.

Mississippi is also only 1 of 9 states that tax intangible property, such as stocks, bonds, and other intangibles like trademarks.[9] This tax can be highly detrimental to businesses that hold large amounts of their own or other companies' stock. Perhaps even more detrimental is the fact that trademark value tends to correlate with larger companies employing more people. Taxes on trademark value deters these large firms from locating in Mississippi. As a result, the state may be missing out on significant employment opportunities.

Since property taxes can place a large burden on business, they can have a significant effect on location decisions. Bartik (1989) provides strong evidence that property taxes have a negative impact on business start-ups. Because property taxes are paid regardless of profit, they have the strongest negative effect on the establishment of small businesses since many new businesses are not profitable in their first few years. Bartik estimated that a 10% cut in business property tax rates would increase business activity by 1 to 5%. He further estimated that a 10% decrease would increase the number of new plants opening by 1 to 2%. Mark, McGuire, and Papke (2000) estimate that a tax decrease on business property of one percentage point increases annual employment growth by 2.44 percentage points.

What do these estimates imply for Mississippi property tax rates and business development? Using the numbers in Figure 5.4, if Mississippi were to lower its commercial and industrial property taxes to the national averages, a 20% reduction in commercial property tax and a 40% reduction for industrial property, Mississippi's business activity can be expected to increase by 4 to 20%, new plant establishments can grow between 2 to 8%, and annual employment growth can increase by 1.22 to 2.44 percentage points per year!

Collectively, this tells us that high property tax based systems like Mississippi's will deter new start-ups, decrease employment, and lower overall business activity. States that keep statewide property taxes low better position themselves to attract business investment. Localities competing for business can put themselves at a greater competitive advantage by keeping personal property taxes low. Mississippi should consider reducing property taxes in order to boost business and job growth.

---

8 Tax Foundation's *Location Matters 2015*.
9 Alabama, Louisiana, and Tennessee tax intangible property as well.

Location, Location, Location

So far, we've illustrated figures representing different aspects of business tax rates and tax burdens. By most comparisons, Mississippi does not fare well. However, these figures do not tell business owners what they really want to know before choosing where to locate: how much will our company pay in taxes?

The shortcomings of comparing business tax revenue as a percent of total taxes or business tax rates are that many business taxes are collected in one state but paid by companies in other states. Thus, tax collections do not accurately portray the relative tax burden that real-world businesses incur in each state. In addition, different types of businesses receive tax incentives, such as new job tax credits, new investment tax credits, sales tax exemptions, and property tax abatements. All businesses, however, do not enjoy such incentives. As a result, tax burdens not only vary across states, but also across industries and age of the firm, with older firms facing increased tax rates.

The Tax Foundation published a study, *Location Matters 2015*, to directly tackle these issues. They use seven model firms–a corporate headquarters, a research and development facility, an independent retail store, a capital-intensive manufacturer, a labor-intensive manufacturer, a call center, and a distribution center–and calculated each firm's tax bill in each state. This study accounts for all business taxes: corporate income taxes, property taxes, sales taxes, unemployment insurance taxes, capital stock taxes, inventory taxes, and gross receipts taxes. Additionally, tax rates for 2014 are calculated for a new firm eligible for tax incentives and for a mature firm not eligible for such incentives. In this report, a lower rank represents a lower tax burden.

Figure 5.5 reports the tax cost of doing business in each of the seven industries for mature and new firms for Mississippi and for its neighboring states. Despite its modest corporate income tax rate, Mississippi imposes extremely high tax costs on most businesses, particularly capital and labor-intensive manufacturing operations.

In fact, mature, capital intensive manufacturing faces the second highest tax rate in the country, ranking 49th with an effective tax rate of 17.8 percent! This is 7 percentage points higher, over 68% more, than the national average. Alabama and Arkansas' capital-intensive tax rates are much lower than

Figure 5.5: Tax Costs of Doing Business, 2014

	Capital-Intensive Manufact.			Labor-Intensive Manufact.			Corporate Headquarters			R&D Headquarters		
	Rank	Mature Firm	New Firm	Rank	Mature Firm	New Firm	Rank	Mature Firm	New Firm	Rank	Mature Firm	New Firm
Alabama	19	9.30%	7.10%	24	8.50%	6.70%	20	13.00%	13.30%	44	14.50%	15.80%
Arkansas	44	16.20%	8.60%	39	12.50%	7.30%	24	13.60%	8.90%	39	14.10%	8.10%
Louisiana	16	8.50%	0.10%	9	6.30%	-1.90%	27	13.70%	5.20%	3	1.80%	-10.30%
Mississippi	*49*	*17.80%*	*13.80%*	*35*	*11.20%*	*8.80%*	*29*	*14.10%*	*11.30%*	*28*	*12.40%*	*8.90%*
Tennessee	28	11.10%	8.80%	30	10.20%	11.30%	31	14.50%	17.80%	40	14.10%	16.80%
U.S. Average		10.61%	9.72%		9.24%	9.08%		14.26%	14.16%		11.18%	11.20%

	Distribution Center			Retail Store			Call Center		
	Rank	Mature Firm	New Firm	Rank	Mature Firm	New Firm	Rank	Mature Firm	New Firm
Alabama	3	16.40%	22.30%	8	13.00%	29.00%	7	13.50%	17.20%
Arkansas	17	22.90%	27.90%	21	15.10%	32.20%	30	20.30%	10.90%
Louisiana	34	31.60%	42.40%	25	15.40%	35.40%	26	19.60%	31.20%
Mississippi	*23*	*25.60%*	*20.00%*	*21*	*15.10%*	*34.90%*	*15*	*16.40%*	*11.00%*
Tennessee	27	27.10%	27.00%	30	16.10%	33.70%	24	19.20%	25.50%
U.S. Average		28.18%	34.01%		16.00%	30.88%		19.90%	22.00%

Source: https://files.taxfoundation.org/20170112211359/TF_LocationMatters_2015.pdf

Mississippi's and are below the national average. New firms do receive tax breaks in Mississippi as their effective tax rate is reduced to 13.8%; however, this is still over 4 percentage points higher than the national average (42% increase). Louisiana almost completely eliminates taxes for new, capital-intensive manufacturing firms.

A similar pattern exists for labor-intensive manufacturing. Mississippi ranks 35th in the nation for mature firms, with a tax rate of 11.2% and 8.8% for new firms. Alabama, Louisiana, and Tennessee all tax less than Mississippi does for mature, labor-intensive manufacturing businesses.

As discussed in the previous section, Mississippi's property tax applies to inventory and equipment as well as buildings and land, thus penalizing capital-intensive businesses. Combined, business property taxes comprise 8.4% of the 17.8% tax rate in capital-intensive manufacturing for a mature firm and 7% (of 13.8%) for new firms. Alabama, by comparison, collects less than 2% from property taxes for mature and new capital-intensive firms. Most states tend to treat manufacturing more favorable, not less advantageous as Mississippi does.[10]

Mississippi comes in with about average tax costs for mature corporate headquarters, R&D headquarters, and retail stores. Mississippi is below the national average for a new corporate or R&D headquarter but above the national average for a new retail store, costing a whopping 35%. Alabama is the most retail friendly state in the region for both mature and new firms. Distribution and call centers face lower tax costs in Mississippi compared to the U.S. average, with new firms receiving substantial tax breaks. As a result, Mississippi has the lowest tax burden in the region in these two areas. Call centers represent Mississippi's best tax ranking of 15, illustrating that mature and new call centers face lower tax burdens than call centers located in surrounding states.

Neighboring state Louisiana offers the lowest overall tax burden in the country to new capital- and labor-intensive manufacturing firms, which have tax rates at or under 0.1% due to some of the most generous property tax incentives and withholding tax incentives in the nation. Louisiana also provides hefty tax incentives to new corporate (5.2%) and R&D (-10%) headquarters coming in well below the national average and surrounding states. Mature R&D firms in Louisiana enjoy an effective tax rate of only 1.8 percent, 84% below the median rate nationally.

We are not advocating that Mississippi follow in the steps of Louisiana and pursue more tax incentives. Mississippi already provide generous tax incentives, including job creation tax credits, withholding rebates, capital investment incentives, and research and development (R&D) incentives to qualifying firms. This reduces the tax burdens for many new firms but shifts the burden to established firms. As further described in Chapter 6, this tax strategy not only increases the cost of taxation significantly, it also distorts market activity.

Conclusion and Policy Suggestions

In order to attract more job creation and business development, Mississippi should simplify its tax system, implementing broad-based uniform low tax rates and reducing the administrative and enforcement costs. Recall from Chapter 4, an efficient tax system is one that relies on low rates and uniform application of taxes—the opposite of providing tax incentives for different types of firms and for new versus older operations. In order to attract businesses to locate in Mississippi and promote prosperity, all tax rates need to be reduced, not only for new firms for a specified amount of time, but for all firms in any industry.

---

10 Source: https://taxfoundation.org/location-matters-2015/.

A good starting point is to reduce taxes on manufacturing firms, particularly taxes on capital-intensive industries. This includes repealing property taxes on inventory, machinery, and equipment, and intangible property. This repealing or reducing of business taxes will give new businesses a reason to consider moving to Mississippi, foster entrepreneurship, and encourage expansion of existing businesses.

Policymakers often generate tax credit deals under the umbrella of job creation and economic development. If Mississippi officials need to offer such incentive packages to attract new companies, then this tells us that prior lawmakers created an unfavorable business tax climate that is deterring market activity. Tax credits only cover up a bad business climate. Economic development and job creation tax credits complicate the tax system, narrow the tax base, drive up tax rates for companies that do not qualify, distort the free market, and often fail to achieve economic growth.[11] Indeed, many existing business owners and executives have reason to object to the generous tax incentives enjoyed by some of their direct competitors, and even firms looking to relocate may have cause to be wary of the rates that will ultimately rise once economic development incentives are no longer available. A far more effective approach is the systematic improvement of the state's business tax climate for the long term.

In sum, in order to increase business growth and promote prosperity, Mississippi should 1) reduce business tax rates and apply equally to all firms, 2) reduce business property tax rates, including commercial, industrial, and apartment tax rates, 3) eliminate the inventory and intangible property tax, and 4) eliminate business tax credits.

References

Bartik, Timothy. 1985. Business Location Decisions in the United States: Estimates of the Effects of Unionization, Taxes, and Other Characteristics of States, *Journal of Business and Economics Statistics*, Vol. 3, No. 1., pp. 14-28.

Bartik, Timothy J. 1991. *Who Benefits from State and Local Economic Development Policies?* Kalamazoo, MI: W.E. Upjohn Institute for Employment Research.

Bartik, Timothy J. 1989. Small Business Start-Ups in the United States: Estimates of the Effects of Characteristics of States, *Southern Economic Journal*, pp. 1004-1018.

Ernst & Young LLP. 2015. *Total state and local business taxes State-by-state estimates for fiscal year 2014.* [electronic file]. Washington: Ernst & Young. Online: http://www.ey.com/Publication/vwLUAssets/EY-total-state-and-local-business-taxes-october-2015/$-FILE/EY-total-state-and-local-business-taxes-october-2015.pdf. (cited: July 23, 2017).

Fox, William F. & Matthew N. Murray. 2004. Do Economic Effects Justify the Use of Fiscal Incentives? *Southern Economic Journal*, Vol. 71, No. 78.

Gupta, Sanja and Mary Ann Hoffman. 2003. The Effect of State Income Tax Apportionment and Tax Incentives on New Capital Expenditures, *Journal of the American Taxation Association*, Supplement, pp. 1-25.

Helms, L. Jay. 1985. The Effect of State and Local Taxes on Economic Growth: A Time Series – Cross Section Approach, *The Review of Economics and Statistics*, Vol. 67, Issue 4, November 1985, pp. 574-582.

Lee, Young and Roger H. Gordon. 2005. Tax Structure and Economic Growth. *Journal of Public Economics* 89(5-6): 1027-1043.

Lincoln Institute of Land Policy and Minnesota Center for Fiscal Excellence. 2016. *50-State Property Tax Comparison Study.* [electronic file]. Cambridge: Lincoln Institute of Land Policy and Saint Paul: Minnesota Center for Fiscal Excellence. Online: http://www.lincolninst.edu/sites/default/files/pubfiles/50-state-property-tax-study-2016-full.pdf. (cited: July 23, 2017).

Mark, Stephen T., Therese J. Mc Quire, & Leslie E. Papke. 2000. The Influence of Taxes on Employment and Population Growth: Evidence from the Washington, D.C. Metropolitan Area, *National Tax Journal*, Vol. 53, March 2000, pp.105-123

Papke, James and Lesie Papke. 1986. Measuring Differential State-Local Tax Liabilities and Their Implications for Business Investment Location, *National Tax Journal*, Vol. 39, No. 3, pp. 357-366.

Peters, Alan & Peter Fisher. 2004. The Failure of Economic Development Incentives, *Journal of the American Planning Association*, Vol. 70, No. 27.

Tax Foundation. 2015. *Location Matters: The State Tax Costs of Doing Business* [electronic file]. Washington: Tax Foundation. Online: https://files.taxfoundation.org/20170112211359/TF_LocationMatters_2015.pdf. (cited: July 23, 2017).

Tax Foundation. 2017. *State Business Tax Climate Index.* [electronic file]. Washington: Tax Foundation. Online: https://taxfoundation.org/2017-state-business-tax-climate-index. (cited: July 23, 2017).

Tax Foundation. 2017. *State and Local Sales Tax Rates.* [electronic file]. Washington: Tax Foundation. Online: https://taxfoundation.org/state-and-local-sales-tax-rates-in-2017/. (cited: July 23, 2017).

---

11 See, Peters and Fisher (2004) and Fox and Murray (2004).

6

"Selective Incentives," Crony Capitalism and Economic Development

Thomas A. Garrett and William F. Shughart II

6

"Selective Incentives," Crony Capitalism and Economic Development

Thomas A. Garrett and William F. Shughart II

What is the species of domestic industry which his capital can employ, and of which the produce is likely to be of the greatest value, every individual, it is evident, can, *in his local situation*, judge much better than any statesman or lawgiver can do for him. (Smith, [1776] 1982, vol. 1, p. 456; emphasis added)[1]

Introduction

The answer to the important question of why the economic development trajectories of some U.S. states lag behind those of others is the same as the answer to the question of why some nations are rich and others are poor. The keys to prosperity have been understood for more than two centuries (Smith, [1776] 1982): well-defined and -enforced private property rights, adherence to a rule of law whereby all persons can expect equal treatment, and limited government interference in the lives of responsible men and women, including their interactions within free and open marketplaces. As was discussed in detail in the first three chapters, the evidence supporting that conclusion is overwhelming.

Nevertheless, governors and legislatures in virtually every U.S. state (and many national governments around the globe) seem to think that stimulating economic development requires offering "incentives" to the owners of some business enterprises, especially high-profile corporations, to locate their headquarters, plants, or other facilities within their borders. The reasoning underlying these programs is that most

---

1   Quoted in Hayek ([1960] 2011, p. 225, footnote 16), emphasizing what Hayek in the same volume (pp. 224–225) and elsewhere (e.g. Hayek, 1945) calls the "often unique knowledge of the particular circumstance of time and place" that cannot be comprehended by a single human mind or even by economic development agencies and the consultants who prepare economic impact studies for them.

companies have a menu of geographic options available to them when contemplating relocating existing facilities or building new ones. Incentives in the form special tax breaks and other financial benefits (such as additional public spending on site preparation, infrastructure, and job training programs) therefore are thought necessary to lure them to one place rather than another. The direct benefits claimed for these public "investments" are new (and frequently higher paying) jobs for residents of the state or region, along with more tax revenue for the public sector (both local and state), as the incomes of employees and the businesses that hire them add to the tax base. The indirect effects of the taxpayer-financed incentives, also measured in terms of additional employment opportunities and additional tax receipts, are traced to the activities of suppliers of the new plant that co-locate in the same area. Other businesses (grocery stores, restaurants and dry cleaners, for example) that relocate or expand their operations to cater to the families of the managers and employees who move nearby the new plant are said to be economic development benefits induced by incentive programs.[2]

This chapter evaluates selective incentives in general and for the State of Mississippi in particular. Indeed, as we shall see, Mississippi led the nation (and, perhaps, ignited an interstate incentives' arms' race) by adopting the Balance Agriculture with Industry (BAWI) plan during the Great Depression (Cobb 1993). Our analysis reaches several conclusions.

First, because consumers largely are indifferent about the points of origin of the goods they buy – they're more interested in price and quality (getting a good deal) – whatever time, money and effort are spent by the public sector in attracting a company to one state rather than another are wasted from society's perspective. Taxpayer-financed incentive programs are a form of rent seeking (Tullock 1967) that does not create wealth, but rather redistributes it geographically.[3] Policymakers view this geographical redistribution of wealth to their state as a benefit, but, as discussed in this chapter, because its costs exceed its benefits, such redistribution actually slows economic growth and makes Mississippi less prosperous.

Second, selective incentive programs are very good examples of Frederic Bastiat's (1850) famous essay titled "That Which is Seen, and That Which is Not Seen." The new facilities, infrastructure upgrades and new jobs bankrolled by the incentives are highly visible to voter-taxpayers and, hence, allow politicians to claim credit for attracting them to the state and thereby garnering more political support for themselves on Election Day. As an example, it is often the case even today that all of the workers employed at a new plant are counted as the number of jobs created by targeted incentive programs, despite the fact that many of the new hires already had jobs in the state and moved to the new plant for better pay or better working conditions. A state-sponsored incentive program should be credited only with jobs filled by interstate migrants or by people who previously were unemployed and living in the state (Peavy 2007; Hicks and Shughart 2010).

Furthermore, many people (Bastiat called them "bad economists") fail to see the less visible negative consequences of targeted incentive programs. One of these are the jobs lost or not offered by existing businesses because of the higher taxes required to finance the subsidies, along with a corresponding reduction in private consumption spending. Even if the incentives are paid for in whole or in part by borrowing (public bond issues), other public spending programs necessarily will be shortchanged as present or future tax revenue is redirected to fulfill the promises made to the owners of the new facility. Another

---

2   It is important to recognize that additional tax revenue is at best a zero-sum transfer from the private sector to the public sector. While revenue may be a benefit to the public treasury, it is a cost to taxpaying individuals and businesses.

3   As discussed in chapter 3, selective incentive programs trigger rent seeking – efforts devoted to the pursuit of (usually) artificially created returns in excess of costs – at three levels: (1) governors and state economic development officials compete with one another to lure firms to their own jurisdictions, (2) mayors and other elected politicians, e.g., county supervisors, compete to entice firms to select plant sites in their local area and (3) firms looking for new locations play states and localities off against one another to gain the largest possible incentive package. Existing businesses also seek special treatment from time to time by threatening to move to another jurisdiction unless demands for tax breaks and other benefits are met.

consequence is that selected incentives can harm businesses that do not receive a government subsidy – these firms may lose workers to the incentivized firm (called a displaced worker effect),[4] may have to pay higher wages to those who remain in their current jobs, or both.

Third, while it is unusual for states to evaluate their incentive programs after the fact, that is, to ask whether the estimated benefits in terms of employment and tax revenue gains actually materialized once the subsidized firm is up and running, the evidence we present points strongly to the conclusion that they do not pass a benefit-cost test. In other words, selective incentives are forms of crony capitalism in the sense that, while obvious benefits are provided to the firms receiving them, incentives reduce social welfare overall because non-beneficiaries (taxpayers, the owners of existing businesses) demonstrably are made worse off. Incentive programs may be business-friendly for the recipients of taxpayer-financed largesse, but they are not market friendly. Incentives may change the mix of economic activity in a state (in favor of the firms and industries that the incentives target), but they likely reduce activity in the state's economy as a whole, thereby slowing, not promoting economic development.

Hicks and Shughart (2010) summarize nine previously published peer-reviewed studies of the economic effects of selective incentives to influence the location decisions of private business enterprises. The common finding is that taxpayer-financed subsidies to targeted firms generate either no or quite small (and often temporary) impacts on employment in the county, region or state offering them. When such incentive packages succeed in luring a business to a new location, the cost per job created is extraordinary high, frequently much more than the new employees will earn in a given year. The authors then examine the impact of West Virginia's $35 million grant to Ohio County, announced in 2003, to help attract Cabela's, a well-known retailer of hunting, fishing, and camping gear, to the area. Public funds from the state for infrastructure improvements and other targeted benefits brought the total value of the incentive package to $120 million (Hicks 2007), but no impact on employment in Ohio County could be detected.

This chapter is organized as follows. The next section summarizes Mississippi's adoption of BAWI, its first-in-the-nation attempt to jumpstart economic development in the midst of history's worst economic collapse. Although the Balance Agriculture with Industry program superficially was successful in luring manufacturing firms to relocate to Mississippi from high-wage northern states, it is far from clear that BAWI's costs exceeded its benefits. We turn next to three case studies of incentive packages financed by Mississippi's taxpayers, the first being a public subsidy initiative that convinced Nissan Motor Company to build a new vehicle assembly plant in Canton (Madison County), which opened in May of 2003. We then summarize two more recent selective incentive packages offered to Toyota Motors and Continental AG, a tire manufacturer. We refer along the way to the by-now extensive economics literature, which finds in general that targeted incentive programs rarely deliver their promised benefits or do so only at very high costs per job created.

The chapter's final section recapitulates what has gone before and suggests policy reforms. These reforms include abolishing the Mississippi Development Authority and shifting to a more market-friendly set of economic development initiatives. These may include cutting business and individual income tax rates across the board to encourage capital investment, expansion, and job creation by existing Mississippi firms as well as relocations to the state by out of state firms looking for new places to do business. The hallmark of crony capitalism is cozy relations between politicians and the managers of (often) large, high-profile companies that receive favorable treatment from government officials in return for campaign contributions and other forms of political support for their friends who hold public office. Cronyism breeds corruption

---

4   The people most likely to be hired by the subsidized plant are those who already are employed, who have the skills and on-the-job experience necessary to step into the new position. Individuals who currently are unemployed, especially those who have been for a long time, will find it much more difficult to convince the new employer to put them on the payroll.

because it allows powerful politicians to distribute valuable benefits to a few influential private sector allies; it allows those allies to promote the careers of the hands that feed them at taxpayers' expense. Getting rid of targeted incentive programs means no political favoritism and makes it possible for all business enterprises, be they large or small, old or new, to prosper and promote prosperity in Mississippi.

The Inception of Crony Capitalism in Mississippi

During the Great Depression of the 1930s, the state government of Mississippi for the first time became actively involved in promoting economic growth and industrial development by adopting a Balance Agricultural with Industry (BAWI) plan.[5] That plan, approved by the state legislature in the Mississippi Industry Act of 1936, gave local governments the authority to seek out and entice industrial companies in high-wage northern states to relocate and build new plants in Mississippi (Cobb 1993) through the offer of subsidies, grants, and loans. . BAWI was the first plan of its kind in the nation, and served as the precedent for other state governments' future involvement in their own economic development activities that continues to this day. The goal of BAWI was simple - by taking steps to expand the size of the industrial sector in primarily agrarian Mississippi, legislators could end the state's unacceptably high unemployment rate – the national economy hit bottom in March 1933, with 25 percent of the labor force out of work, just as Franklin Delano Roosevelt entered the White House – as well as permanently alter the composition of the state's economy to lay the foundations for faster economic growth in the long run. Although the BAWI plan lasted only from 1936 to 1940, the history of how the BAWI plan came to be and its lasting impacts on ever more state involvement in economic development from the end of the Second World War to the present cannot be understated.

The BAWI plan was the brainchild of Hugh White, governor of Mississippi from 1936 to 1940. Governor White's conception of the BAWI plan came from his attempt to entice industrial development to his hometown of Columbia, Mississippi, and to Marion County during his tenure as mayor from 1926 to 1936. The so-called Columbia plan, unlike future government-promoted programs like BAWI, did not use taxpayer resources to lure businesses to the area. Rather, the program's funding relied on *voluntary* contributions from wealthy local elites as well as more ordinary citizens. Lester (2008, p. 245) describes that now-unusual financial scheme during White's pursuit of a manufacturing company's potential move to Marion County:

Using his mayoral powers, he [White] declared a two-hour holiday to hold a community meeting and decide the matter. After discussing the proposition, businessmen, secretaries, clerks, school teachers, and farmers signed promissory notes to guarantee the funding for the factory building and construction. With these small pledges from a broad segment of the population, White used his own considerable wealth and influence to obtain a loan from New Orleans bankers for the full amount. Community and investor commitment rather than guarantees from the state were successful in securing the targeted manufacturer's relocation to Marion County.

The Columbia plan was hailed as a triumph in attracting new industry (Hopkins, 1944). White campaigned for the Governor's Mansion touting the success of the Columbia plan. He realized, however, that the local resources and grass-roots efforts used to attract industry to Marion County would not be enough to attract industry statewide; White therefore argued that the state's resources should be used to entice industry to Mississippi. However, moving his plan from an idea to a reality faced a significant legal hurdle, namely, that the Mississippi Constitution explicitly prohibited the state from using credit to finance

---

5   Much of the discussion here is based on Hopkins (1944) and Lester (2008). The reader is referred to these two studies for deeper discussions and analyses of the BAWI plan.

industrial development. To jump over that hurdle, White organized a panel of attorneys to develop legislation that would circumvent the constitutional prohibition of direct state support for industry. Drawing on U.S. Supreme Court decisions as precedent, the panel linked the BAWI plan to the general welfare clause of the Mississippi Constitution. The panel's argument was that employment and economic growth from industrial development enhanced the general welfare of citizens, i.e., that employment itself should be regarded as contributing to the general welfare. In addition, the legislation proposed that local government entities, rather than the state, would oversee any industrial plant built under the BAWI program. Doing so would also require that local elections be held to approve a city or county's subsidy package (tax breaks, grants, and loans) to targeted firms or industries.

The constitutionality of the BAWI plan was upheld in various court cases, and it eventually became a lawful reality in 1936 with the passage of the Mississippi Industry Act. The BAWI plan created a "two tier[ed] plan of 'state sponsorship and control' balanced by 'local finance and operation'" (Lester, p. 247). Specifically, the Act created a three-member State Industrial Commission that was responsible for searching out and ultimately choosing which manufacturing companies would be courted for relocation to Mississippi, whereas local governments would then be responsible for providing the financial incentives necessary to entice the selected firms. For the first time in its history, the state government of Mississippi became involved directly in managing, at least to some degree, the state's economy.

During the program's three-year existence, 12 manufacturing plants relocated to Mississippi and provided several thousand manufacturing jobs. Proponents hailed those statistics as evidence of the plan's success. However, critics at the time argued that BAWI's ballyhooed benefits had been overstated because proponents focused solely on the number of people employed at the new plants and failed to acknowledge several related negative factors, including downplaying (1) the employment displacement effect in the count of new jobs created, (2) the high subsidy cost per worker, and (3) the fact that the roughly 2,700 manufacturing jobs resulting from the BAWI plan accounted for only five percent of the state's manufacturing workforce, which itself represented a small share of total state employment (Hopkins, 1944). In addition, considerable doubt existed that the firms selected for relocation to Mississippi were chosen based on their potential contributions to economic growth rather than having some connection to Commission members. In his comprehensive evaluation of the BAWI plan's success at promoting economic growth in Mississippi eight years on, Hopkins (1944, p. 37) concluded that, "All in all, it cannot be said that the BAWI system was in itself the fundamental or decisive factor in determining many things that were ascribed to it at the outset or that have been ascribed to it since."

The BAWI plan was short-lived, as the state legislature and newly elected Governor Paul Johnson, Sr., canceled the program in 1940. Despite some continued support for BAWI around the state, the small number of jobs created, the costs of administering the plan, and growing doubt about the costs of the subsidies relative to the benefits received all played parts in its demise. Although BAWI had a short life, the plan set the legal precedent for local governments and, eventually, for the State of Mississippi itself to become ever-more involved in managing and attracting businesses to the state by using the public purse (taxpayer-financed subsidies, outright grants, loans and tax relief). Programs similar to BAWI remain active in Mississippi and in many other states despite overwhelming evidence that the vast majority of targeted incentives end up costing taxpayers much more than the benefits created by the subsidized firms.

It turns out that doubts similar to those raised about BAWI's track record continue to be articulated in studies of the targeted incentive programs that followed Mississippi's lead. Companies on the receiving end of selective incentive packages in Mississippi and elsewhere rarely meet the job creation or other economic development targets promised in return for the tax breaks, loans, or grants financed by the public purse. Non-transparent to taxpayer-voters and subject to little accountability, the recipients of taxpayer largesse often pull up stakes and move their operations out-of-state when the subsidies run out. Relocation in search of more generous incentives is a tactic especially popular among "call centers" and high-tech companies that rely on few specialized assets and, thus, can easily abandon one site in favor of another (LeRoy 2005; Hicks and Shughart 2007).

Business Subsidies in Mississippi since BAWI

Since the Balance Agriculture with Industry program ended in 1940, influencing and managing economic development has become an established (and largely unchallenged) function for the state government of Mississippi. Since 2000, the state and local governments in Mississippi have provided nearly $3.8 billion (roughly $1,300 per capita) in taxpayer-funded tax breaks, grants, and loans to hundreds of businesses.[6] The Mississippi Development Authority (MDA) is the lead state government agency that "works to recruit new business to the state and retain and expand existing Mississippi industry and business."[7] On its website, the MDA lists the myriad of taxpayer-funded (state and local) subsidies that are available to existing and prospective business enterprises, as well as promoting those subsidies as testimony to the attractiveness of investing in Mississippi. These taxpayer-funded subsidies fall into one of ten listed categories of incentives, such as tax breaks (temporary relief from sales, property, and income taxes), economic development grants, tourism programs, special programs for movie production companies, and business financing.[8] The category of tax incentives alone lists seven state income tax incentives, seven sales and use tax incentives, three franchise tax incentives, and two property tax incentives. To be sure, recipients consider these incentives to be beneficial (obviously reducing their state and local tax bills), but the benefits are not free because taxes are shifted onto other shoulders (those of unsubsidized firms and individual taxpayers) who must make up the tax revenue forgone by lightening the tax burdens on favorably treated businesses that are enticed to relocate to Mississippi.

A reading of the MDA's *Annual Report* indicates that the main goal of all taxpayer-funded subsidies, and the mission of the MDA itself, is to increase the "number of jobs" in Mississippi.[9] While jobs do provide an economic benefit in terms of employment and wages, if they are "new," in fact, assessing the true net economic gain from subsidizing business should also account for the costs of acquiring these new jobs, including MDA's budget and whatever incentives are offered. The MDA identifies some of the businesses that have taken advantage of its incentives and reports the corporate investment made each company (which doesn't include the cost to taxpayers) as well as the number of jobs created by each of the benefiting companies. As discussed earlier, though, a simple count of new jobs is a poor measure of net economic benefit because it does not consider the employment displacement that occurs (Peavy, 2007).[10] MDA does not attempt to estimate the true cost of these jobs, namely, the actual subsidy amount *plus* the opportunity cost of the subsidy, which the next best use of the resources, as defined earlier in this book). Unfortunately, despite the number of employees at the subsidized plant being a very misleading way of measuring economic development gains, that figure continues to be the most widely publicized evidence supporting the state's continued role in providing taxpayer-funded subsidies.

MDA and other supporters of targeted incentives also do not consider other costs of subsidy packages. When such programs actually lure a new plant to a specific location and thereby expand the local

---

6   See http://subsidytracker.goodjobsfirst.org/prog.php?statesum=MS&order=subsidy&page=1&sort=des (accessed June 13, 2017).

7   https://www.mississippi.org/home-page/about-mda/ (accessed June 13, 2017).

8   The full list of incentives is found here: https://www.mississippi.org/home-page/our-advantages/incentives/ (accessed June 13, 2017).

9   See https://www.mississippi.org/home-page/media-center/annual-report/ (accessed June 13, 2017).

10   To reiterate, a person employed at a facility benefiting from targeted incentives is a net addition to the local and state workforce only if that person was unemployed previously or relocated from out-of-state to take a job there. MDA's job numbers represent double-counting otherwise.

workforce significantly, additional public employees (firefighters, police officers, emergency medical technicians, and public-school teachers) will be needed to serve these households. If the new company on the block has been granted relief from state and local taxes to the point where the favored company's tax bill does not cover those additional costs, the tax burden will fall more heavily on existing businesses and households, reducing after-tax spending and perhaps destroying as many or more jobs than supposedly would be created by the subsidy in the first place (Hicks and Shughart 2007).

Although many of MDA's programs and recipient businesses are not on the public's radar screen, one case attracted a great deal of attention – the construction and operation of a Nissan assembly plant in Canton, Mississippi (Madison County) in 2003. This case was significant owing to the sheer size of the taxpayer-funded subsidies (the largest in Mississippi history) to the company in return for the promise of thousands of new jobs.

The Nissan Plant

Nissan's vehicle assembly plant commenced production of several Nissan models in May of 2003. The current facility occupies 4.7 million square feet and sits on more than 1,000 acres of land in the town of Canton, Mississippi, located in Madison County.[11] Nearly three million vehicles have been manufactured at the plant since it opened more than a decade ago. Nissan reports employing 6,400 workers and an annual payroll of $400 million. A state-commissioned study suggested that the total employment gains associated with the Nissan plant would amount to 16,212 jobs, a figure based on the assumption that nearly 10,000 indirect jobs would be created on top of the Canton plant site's 6,400 employees.[12]

Given that the number of jobs is the predominant evidence used to promote taxpayer-funded corporate subsidies, it is worthwhile looking at actual employment data before and after the opening of the Nissan plant. One surely would expect the Nissan plant to have some positive effect on employment given the absolute number of people filling jobs there, but it also is important to look at the timing of the employment gains in order to determine the extent to which the subsidy to Nissan met its economic development goals.[13] Clearly, crediting the subsidy with all such benefits does not control for other, possibly confounding factors, including employment trends in the region surrounding the new plant and in the Mississippi's economy as a whole.

Figure 6.1 plots employment in Madison County and employment in the region (Madison County and all counties bordering Madison) from 1990 to 2016. As can be seen in that figure, the trend in employment growth in Madison County was not much different after the opening of the Nissan plant (2003) than before. Employment had been rising steadily there since the early 1990s and continued to rise at roughly the same pace beyond 2003. Nissan may have contributed to Madison County's job gains, but other factors clearly are in play, including the exodus of middle and low-income households from the state's high-crime capital in Jackson, located in Hinds County, just to the south.

Considering regional employment, a spike coincident with the Nissan plant's opening in 2003 is obvious. That spike dissipated quickly, though, and total regional employment has varied over the business cycle since then, at times dropping to levels observed before the plant opened. Some, perhaps most, of the regional employment losses after 2004 undoubtedly can be explained by the effects of the financial crisis and the co-called Great Recession, but falling regional employment combined with continued job

---

11 Data on the Nissan plant were obtained from http://www.nissan-canton.com/about-nissan/fact-sheet-vehicle-assembly-plant-canton-mississippi/ (accessed June 16, 2017).

12 See http://siteselection.com/ssinsider/incentive/ti0207.htm (accessed June 23, 2017).

13 All employment data are from the Bureau of Labor Statistics.

Figure 6.1: Employment, 1990 to 2016

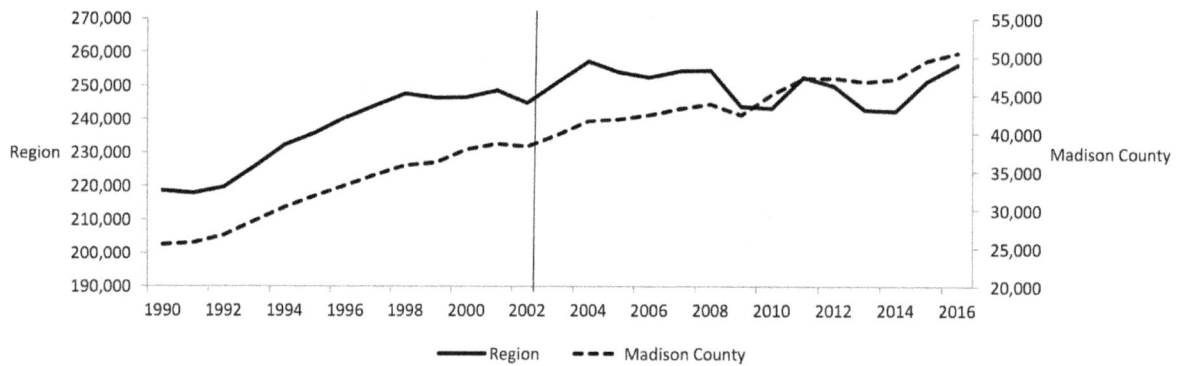

growth in Madison County also is consistent with Peavy's (2007) finding that 90 percent of the Mississippians employed at the Nissan plant lived and worked in the surrounding five-county area. Jobs at Nissan replaced jobs nearby, thus illustrating the displaced worker effect: jobs that should have been deducted from the 6,400 people eventually employed by Nissan to estimate the economic impact of the taxpayer-financed subsidy. In 2016, total employment in the region amounted to about 256,000, roughly 9,000 more than before the plant opened. It is unclear whether this 9,000-person increase in employment can be explained solely by the Nissan plant, but what is clear is that the direct and indirect employment gains were less than the 16,212 suggested by the state-commissioned study.

Relatedly, it is worth pointing out that a similar mistake with respect to tax revenue gains typically is committed by the economic development agencies and the consulting firms they retain to estimate the economic impacts of targeted incentives ex ante. The entire payroll of a new plant ($400 million in Nissan's case) provides the basis for forecasting additions to the income tax base from which state and local governments will generate more revenue. That methodology overstates substantially the income tax revenue gains from a new plant, which properly counts only the increase in wages, if any, received by the people employed there. Ninety percent of Nissan's employees already had jobs when the plant opened (Peavy, 2007) and were paying state income taxes in the five-county region where they then lived and worked (some of them may still reside outside Madison County and commute back and forth). Income tax revenue gains can be attributed to Nissan only for the 10 percent of the plant's employees who either were unemployed previously or moved into Mississippi to take jobs at the plant or at its co-located suppliers. For the other 90 percent of Nissan's employees, revenue gains should be based on the difference between the incomes earned at Nissan and incomes in their last jobs.

To delve more deeply into the employment impacts of the Nissan plant, Figure 6.2 shows Madison County and regional employment as percentages of state-level employment from 1990 through 2016, allowing us to control for trends in the Mississippi economy as a whole. As can be seen in Figure 6.2, Madison County's share of total state employment increased steadily over the 1990–2016 period, with no discernable change occurring in 2003. Regional employment as a percentage of total state employment increased from about 20.5 percent to 21 percent since the plant's opening, thus suggesting that regional jobs began contributing a larger share of total state employment after the Nissan plant's opening than before. The basic conclusion from this analysis is that employment in Madison County tracks employment in the remainder of the state quite well. The opening of the Nissan plant in 2003 cannot be seen in these data at the county level, although some evidence exists that the region led job gains in the state, at least until 2010.

Finally, Figure 6.3 shows that, over the same period, the unemployment rate in Madison County as a percentage of the state unemployment rate and the regional unemployment rate as a percentage of the

Figure 6.2: Employment as a Percentage of Statewide Employment, 1990 to 2016

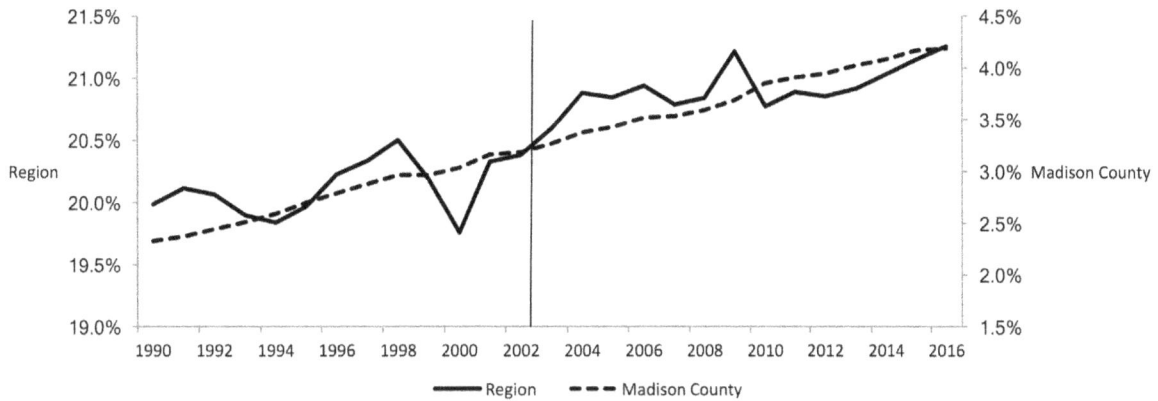

state unemployment rate both have remained relatively unchanged since the plant's opening, with both remaining significantly higher than mid-1990 levels. Why that is so is not clear, but the data suggest that the Nissan plant had no lasting effects on joblessness in central Mississippi, which for a long time has been below the statewide rate, but not so much after 2003 as it was prior to 2000.

In sum, the three graphs point to the conclusion that some employment growth in the central Mississippi region plausibly can be attributed to opening of the Nissan plant in May of 2003, but those employ-

Figure 6.3: Unemployment Rate as a Percentage of Statewide Unemployment Rate, 1990 to 2016

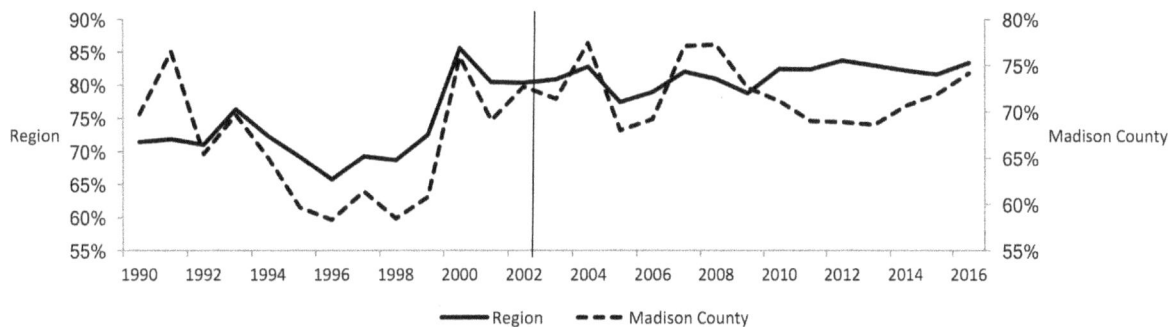

ment gains have been far less than projected ahead of time. Moreover, job growth in Madison County and in the surrounding region has been only slightly faster than the trend in the state as a whole.[14]

Whatever the precise employment effects of Nissan may be, every job created has been subsidized by Mississippi's taxpayers and the size of that subsidy must be taken into account when assessing the incentive package's overall costs and benefits. In total, the state and local governments offered Nissan more than $1.3 billion in return for locating in Canton. Of that total subsidy package, state-financed subsidies (for infrastructure upgrades, job training, business franchise tax relief, and job tax credits) accounted for $1 billion, state borrowing costs accounted for $90 million, and Madison County infrastructure spending and property tax abatements accounted for $235 million (Good Jobs First, 2013). A rough calculation of costs and benefits using Nissan's self-reported data reveals a payroll of $62,500 per worker ($400 million

---

14 These findings generally agree with those of Peavy (2007) and Cardamone (2017).

divided by 6,400) and a taxpayer cost per worker of $203,125 ($1.3 billion divided by 6,400). Despite the large number of people employed at Nissan's Canton facility, the taxpayer cost per worker amounts to more than three times the annual payroll benefit of the average Nissan plant employee. If one also considers claimed indirect employment effects of about 16,212 persons and assumes no job displacement, then the taxpayer cost per worker is $80,188 ($1.3 billion divided by 16,212), which also exceeds Nissan's annual per worker payroll of $62,500.

A full analysis of the costs and benefits of the subsidy package extended to Nissan would take account of the time value of money, namely that the economic benefits in terms of jobs, additional tax revenue, and so on will continue into the future, as will some of the costs (infrastructure maintenance, the salaries and benefits of new local and state government employees), although the bulk of them (site preparation and infrastructure upgrades) were front-loaded and already have been incurred. Some of the package's benefits for Nissan (property and other tax relief) eventually will expire. Nevertheless, the simple accounting presented above suggests a frequently criticized aspect of targeted taxpayer-funded subsidies for luring private business enterprises: the cost to taxpayers of creating one new job often is far greater than the annual income that worker will be paid.

Toyota and Continental AG

Although not as large as the subsidy offered to Nissan, two more recent packages to Continental AG to Toyota Motors were, respectively, the second and third largest taxpayer-funded selective incentives in Mississippi history.

The Toyota plant is located in Blue Springs, Mississippi (Union County) and was a result of the so-called PUL (Pontotoc, Union, and Lee Counties) alliance created by several state constitutional amendments for the purpose of sharing the burden of financing subsidies for the plant, which opened in the fall of 2011. Toyota received a $354 million subsidy package, which included $294 million from the state (for infrastructure improvements, worker training, a 3.5 percent rebate on payroll taxes owed, and a 20-year exemption from state income taxes) and another $60 million from the three allied Mississippi counties.[15] The subsidy package was extended in return for the promise of 2,000 direct jobs at the Toyota plant and an additional 6,300 supplier and indirect jobs by 2013 (Cardamone, 2017).

In her examination of the employment effects of the Toyota plant, Cardamone (2017) finds that the projection of 2,000 indirect jobs was met, but that the actual number of supplier and indirect jobs remains far below the projection of 6,300. This is similar to the experience of the Nissan plant, as was evident in the earlier figures. Cardamone (2017, p. 33) concludes that, "It is unlikely the indirect jobs, which the plant expected to create, were realized as the net employment did not grow to a level that would signify a large increase in employment at the level that was projected by 2013, which is the year when estimates were expected to be met."

The second largest subsidy package in Mississippi history, totaling $600 million, was given to Continental AG in 2016 to build and operate a commercial tire manufacturing plant in Hinds County. The package included $263 million in state borrowing to pay for infrastructure, worker training, and a portion of the factory's construction; roughly $177 million in state income and franchise tax breaks; local property tax breaks of $68 million; and $87.5 million in state income tax rebates.[16] The company is expected to provide 2,500 jobs and thousands more indirect jobs. Although it is too early to determine the economic outcomes of the Continental AG package, the Nissan and Toyota experiences suggest that the Continental

---

15 From http://subsidytracker.goodjobsfirst.org/subsidy-tracker/ms-toyota (accessed June 19, 2017).

16 See http://www.jacksonfreepress.com/news/2016/feb/06/ap-analysis-continental-tire-deal-incentives-600-m/ (accessed June 21, 2017).

AG deal may also fail to meet employment projections and thus leave taxpayers on the hook for hundreds of millions of dollars in wasted resources.

Final Thoughts

Since the inception of the Balance Agriculture with Industry (BAWI) plan, the State of Mississippi has provided private business enterprises with billions of dollars in taxpayer-funded subsidies. The argument advanced by the proponents of selective or targeted incentives is that the benefits of subsidies (i.e., more employment, higher wages, more tax revenue to state and local governments) in luring companies to locate in Mississippi are substantially greater than their costs. As discussed earlier, forecasts of the total economic benefits anticipated from business subsidies are based on projections of employment gains and promises of higher wages paid by the targeted businesses. Through a Keynesian multiplier effect, these employment and wage gains will spill over to other areas of the economy and create even more employment opportunities and higher wages.[17] However, the employment projections rarely become reality because the models used commonly to estimate the multiplier do not account for the job displacement effect, instead assuming contrary to fact that every person employed at the subsidized plant is a new addition to the workforce and that every dollar paid to those employees (the plant's total payroll) adds to the income earned by residents of the state. Our simple graphical analyses in the previous section show clearly that the promised job gains from the Nissan's Canton, Mississippi, plant fell far short of those projected ex ante.

However, even if the benefits of a taxpayer-funded subsidy did outweigh the costs using standard measures of economic impacts, such an outcome would be a necessary, but *not sufficient* condition for concluding that the incentive package passes a benefit-cost test, thereby delivering net economic benefit (benefits > costs) because the analysis fails to consider the subsidy's opportunity cost. One opportunity cost of a taxpayer-funded subsidy is the private-sector economic activity that would have been generated (but is lost) had the subsidy not occurred and the dollars allocated to it remained in the hands of private individuals and commercial businesses.[18] As just explained (see footnote 18), an additional dollar injected into the private sector is exchanged repeatedly in series of market transactions and thus creates economic value greater than the initial dollar. The converse also is true: Every additional dollar of tax revenue taken from the private sector reduces economic activity by more than one dollar.

The true cost of a taxpayer-funded subsidy to business therefore is not just the actual dollar amount of the subsidy, but rather the actual dollar amount of the subsidy *plus* lost private-sector consumption if the subsidy resources were to remain in the private sector. This observation suggests that the true economic cost of a taxpayer funded subsidy is much larger than the subsidy's accounting. So, for example, in the case of Nissan's Canton plant, the true economic cost per worker actually exceeds the $203,125 accounting cost presented earlier because in order to finance the $1.3 billion subsidy, economic activity

---

17 The multiplier idea comes from the observation that some of the income received by one economic actor (an individual or a business enterprise) is spent on goods and services supplied by other actors who, in turn, spend some of the income received from the first actor, on and on ad infinitum. So, a subsidized firm buys inputs from suppliers, suppliers buy from *their* suppliers; the firm's employees spend some of their paychecks at local restaurants and grocery stores, which generates income for their owners, some of which is spent again and money keeps changing hands, generating more economic activity. The size of the multiplier is determined by the marginal propensity to consume (MPC), the fraction of the last dollar of income received that is spent, on average, at each link in the chain of transactions versus how much is saved. In the simplest of Keynesian models, the multiplier is equal to 1/(1-MPC). So, if the MPC is 0.8, that is, 80 cents of the last dollar of income received is spent (20 cents is saved), the multiplier is 5 and $1 of new income eventually generates $5 in new economic activity. The consulting firms that conduct economic impact studies for state and local governments tend to adopt much larger multipliers (sometimes as large as 12) in order to report the results wanted by economic development agencies, namely that a subsidy package passes a benefit-cost test easily.

18 Other possible opportunity costs might include (1) the money that could otherwise have been better spent by lowering taxes on capital investments, or (2) for anyone who likes more government spending, the opportunity cost is the money that could have been spent on roads, schools, or public welfare.

in the private sector will fall by more than $1.3 billion (the multiplier effect working in reverse). The economic criterion for a subsidy to generate a positive net benefit is that those benefits must be greater than the dollar value of the subsidy plus the opportunity cost of the lost private sector consumption.

A business subsidy inherently assumes that every dollar of a taxpayer-funded subsidy is worth more to the economy than if the dollar remained in private sector hands. While this may be true in some cases, the academic research and evidence presented herein suggest that possibility is more the exception than the rule. So, as was discussed in Chapter 3, public officials who advocate for taxpayer-funded subsidies to business are implicitly claiming that they know better than do private individuals and firms interacting in free and open markets how to most effectively allocate resources to their highest valued uses. If that actually were true, then we should allow legislators and public officials to decide all business activity within a state. But, we have seen throughout history (the former Soviet Union, Cuba, Venezuela, and North Korea immediately come to mind) how poorly planned economies perform. Of course, the argument is not being made here that taxpayer-funded subsidies to lure businesses to Mississippi and other states is equivalent to having a planned economy like the aforementioned countries, but the difference is only a matter of degree. Even though less economic planning occurs in the United States than in other nations, planning fails wherever politicians and public officials displace market processes because they lack the information (price and profit signals) and incentives necessary to decide which economic activities merit encouragement and which do not.

Legislators and other public officials who support taxpayer-funded subsidies likely do so with the best intentions — to create greater economic opportunity and a better future for the citizens of their respective cities, counties and states. However, despite these best intentions, it is likely that, in most cases, taxpayer-funded subsidies will do more economic harm than good, in part owing to ignoring the opportunity cost of lost private-sector consumption.[19] That harm is amplified because officials everywhere compete with one another to assemble incentive packages that will entice businesses to their respective jurisdictions. Such competition for business creates ever larger taxpayer-funded subsidy packages that likely will cause even more substantial net economic losses for society as a whole. The only way to stop this race-to-the-bottom is for public officials to stop offering selective incentives to businesses and instead foster a more favorable economic environment for *all* business activity, which includes companies already doing business in a state, whether large or small (e.g., lower taxes on citizens and businesses across the board, control over-excessive and wasteful government spending, promoting a skilled workforce, and minimal regulation). The free market, rather than politicians and bureaucrats, will then decide where business activity will locate.

We think that, in order to promote prosperity, all states and localities should abolish their economic development agencies, thereby saving the budgetary costs of official salaries, benefits and travel expenses to visit and cut deals with companies looking to move or to build new plants. Unilateral disarmament in the vigorous incentives arms' race triggered by Mississippi during the Great Depression may, of course, cause the state to lose opportunities to lure big-name employers in the short or medium term. If an announcement that the Mississippi Development Authority has been shut down is paired with a dramatic cut in state business income taxes, however, the negative impact on revenue will be at most short-lived.

---

19 Even with well-intentioned legislators and public officials, another reason that business subsidies are likely to do more economic harm than good is that there is a disconnect between the evaluation of costs and benefits of a subsidy. The benefits of a successful business relocation are quite visible (e.g., a new plant, greater job numbers, new roads and so on) and thus can easily be touted by public officials as evidence that they are doing good things for their constituents. However, the cost of the business subsidy (the accounting cost plus the opportunity cost) is spread across millions of taxpayers and thus is much less visible than the benefits. Because the benefits are visible and localized whereas the costs are dispersed, public officials have few incentives to weigh the true costs and benefits when deciding on whether to support a taxpayer-funded subsidy. Unlike the private-sector, the disconnect between benefits and costs also results in little punishment of legislators and public officials if the subsidized business is not successful. See the discussion of Bastiat (1850) at the outset of this chapter.

Here's a chance for Mississippi to lead the nation forward with much better effect than its adoption long ago of the Balance Agriculture with Industry program. State officials may then realize that they all are made better off by disarming because selective incentives only shift economic activity around geographically and do not foster prosperity. On the surface, interstate competition for business location is a zero-sum game: one state's gain is another's loss. But, looked at more deeply as we have done in this chapter, the arms' race is a negative-sum game because the ostensible benefits of the competition in terms of job gains, whether direct, indirect or induced, are less than the costs imposed on the private sector, thus hindering economic growth and prosperity in all states, including Mississippi.

References

Bastiat, Frederic. 1850. That Which is Seen, and That Which Not Seen. Available at http://oll.libertyfund.org/pages/wswns; last downloaded 29 June 2017.

Cardamone, Cayla. 2017. Outcomes of FDI in Mississippi: The Cases of Nissan and Toyota. Honor's Thesis, The University of Mississippi.

Cobb, James C. 1993. *The Selling of the South: The Southern Crusade for Industrial Development, 1936–1990*. Urbana: University of Illinois Press.

Good Jobs First. 2013. A Report on Taxpayer Assistance to Nissan in Canton, Mississippi. Washington, D.C: Good Jobs First.

Hayek, Friedrich A. 1945. The Use of Knowledge in Society. *American Economic Review* 35(4): 519–530.

Hayek, Friedrich A. [1960] 2011. *The Constitution of Liberty*. The Definitive Edition. The Collected Works of F. A. Hayek, vol. 17, ed. by Ronald Hamowy. Chicago: University of Chicago Press.

Hicks, Michael J. 2007. A Quasi-Experimental Test of Large Retail Stores' Impacts on Regional Labor Markets: The Case of Cabela's Retail Outlets. *Journal of Regional Analysis and Policy* 37(2): 116–122.

Hicks, Michael J. and Shugart, William F. II. 2007. Quit Playing Favorites: Why Business Subsidies Hurt Our Economy. In Russell S. Sobel, with Joshua C. Hall and Matt E. Ryan (eds.), *Unleashing Capitalism: Why Prosperity Stops at the West Virginia Border and How to Fix It*, Morgantown: The Public Policy Foundation of West Virginia, pp. 119–130.

Hopkins, Ernest J. 1944. Mississippi's BAWI Plan: Balance Agriculture with Industry, An Experiment in Industrial Subsidization. The Federal Reserve Bank of Atlanta, Department of Research and Statistics.

LeRoy, Greg. 2005. *The Great American Jobs Scam: Corporate Tax Dodging and the Myth of Job Creation*. San Francisco: Berrett-Koehler.

Lester, Connie L. 2008. Balancing Agriculture with Industry: Capital, Labor, and the Public Good in Mississippi's Home-Grown New Deal. *Journal of Mississippi History* 70: 235–263.

Peavy, John Patrick. 2007. A Comparison of Two Alternative Models of Economic Impact: A Case Study of the Mississippi Nissan Plant. Ph.D. Dissertation, The University of Mississippi.

Smith, Adam. [1776] 1982. *An Inquiry into the Nature and Causes of the Wealth of Nations*, 2 vols. The Glasgow Edition of the Works of Adam Smith, ed. by R. H. Campbell, A. S. Skinner and William B. Todd. Indianapolis, IN: Liberty Fund.

Tullock, Gordon. 1967. The Welfare Costs of Tariffs, Monopolies, and Theft. *Western Economic Journal* 5: 224–252.

7

Incentive-Based Compensation and Economic Growth

Brandon N. Cline and Claudia R. Williamson

7

Incentive-Based Compensation and Economic Growth

Brandon N. Cline and Claudia R. Williamson

As discussed in Chapter 1, Mississippi ranks poorly across many economic categories. Despite programs to encourage business growth, and the occasional success in convincing large employers to locate or relocate in Mississippi, it is obvious that additional measures could be beneficial. This chapter highlights a potential obstacle to economic growth in Mississippi that could be relatively easy and inexpensive to overcome; one lying outside the usual suspects of administrative costs of doing business, educational system woes, or lack of suitable infrastructure to support technological innovation. Specifically, executive compensation for firms headquartered in Mississippi may not be structured in a way to encourage managers to pursue as many risky, value-enhancing opportunities as they should.

Incentive-based compensation links an employees pay to their performance. Adequately structured incentive pay rewards employees according to their performance and significantly reduces pay when performance is lacking. The basic logic is that employees get paid handsomely only when they perform. Perhaps most importantly, research shows higher sustained economic growth for states and enhanced performance for businesses offering incentive compensation.

The prevalence of incentive-based pay over the last two decades is largely attributable to efforts to minimize agency problems. The generic term "agency problem" refers to any number of scenarios where one party acts on behalf of another. Two common issues often arising from agency problems are shirking and risk-sharing. Shirking takes place when the best interests of the principal and the agent are not aligned, and the principal cannot easily or efficiently monitor the agent's actions. Thus, the agent may take actions that are in his or her best interest but detrimental to the best interests of the principal. For example, employees may spend a little more time checking their phone when the boss is out. Risk-sharing becomes an agency problem when the agent and principal view risk differently. These types of agency concerns are precisely what performance-based payment plans attempt to resolve.

Our purpose in this chapter is to consider how Mississippi firms rank in terms of incentive-based compensation relative to other states. We also consider whether potentially less-than-optimal incentive-compatible contracts may be a contributing factor in the Mississippi's subpar economic performance.[1]

What we find, is that companies headquartered in Mississippi do not emphasize incentive-based compensation as heavily as similar firms headquartered in other states. Thus, an alternative way of enhancing prosperity in Mississippi could include educating Mississippi businesses and policymakers on the benefits of incentive-based compensation and encouraging incentive-based compensation use through state policies.[2]

Incentive-based executive compensation is used to reduce the agency conflicts that result when shareholders, who are the owners of the firm, hire managers to make decisions for the firm. Economic theory suggests that, in the absence of proper incentives, managers make decisions that enhance their own well-being at the expense of others, particularly if their efforts are difficult to observe or costly to monitor. Properly structured employment contracts incentivize managers to take appropriate risks in pursuit of profitable opportunities for the firm.[3] Since shareholders ultimately desire the highest firm value possible, one way to achieve incentive-compatibility between managers and shareholders is by offering managers an equity stake in the firm.

When businesses plan and execute capital expenditures wisely, they in turn experience better company performance and marginal productivity increases. Increasing marginal productivity increases income levels and standards of living for all employees. Therefore, any change that can spur Mississippi businesses to improve performance is ultimately beneficial for all employees of those businesses. It is also beneficial to society in general, as these incentives ultimately lead to the efficient production of the goods and services consumers desire at lower prices resulting in higher standards of living. While the improved income levels and higher standard of living resulting from enhanced business performance are admittedly small in the short-run, even modest gains are valuable. As shown in chapter 1, a one percent increase in the rate of economic growth leads to over $7,000 in additional average income in only one generation. As more gains are made, the common roadblocks to economic growth discussed in the previous chapters can be mitigated.

In addition to general increases in income levels and standards of living for current employees and consumers, there are at least four other reasons better company performance can lead to improved state economic performance. First, better company performance increases corporate income tax payments. Second, new jobs are created for state residents as companies expand. Third, large shareholders tend to be located geographically close to the headquarters of the firms they own.[4] The increased income to shareholders from better firm performance (i.e. a higher stock price) would most likely result in increased income tax revenues for the state and increased consumer or corporate spending. Fourth, as a company's market value increases, it creates additional social value by engaging in corporate social responsibility. For example, Card, Hallock, and Moretti (2008) find that a $100,000 increase in market value for a firm results in an increase of approximately $70 in donations to non-profit organizations in the city of that

---

1 Executive compensation is analyzed purely from a financial research perspective; that is, the study takes no position on whether executives at Mississippi firms are paid too little or too much. Instead, careful attention is given to the ratio of incentive-based compensation to total compensation - allowing for conclusions about the structure, rather than the level, of executive compensation.

2 This chapter is based on Cline and Benefield (2010).

3 Jensen and Meckling (1976).

4 Becker, Cronqvist, and Fahlenbrach (2009).

firm's headquarters. Clearly, the good work done by many non-profit firms can have a very stimulating effect on the state economy.

Incentive–Based Pay

In recent years, executive compensation has become a popular topic among academics, politicians, and members of the popular press. Critics of the route taken in America argue that executives are simply overpaid. The common response to this argument, as voiced by Kay (1998), among others, is that companies have to reward executives fairly in order to attract, retain, and most importantly, motivate high-quality employees. A third group, exemplified by Jensen and Murphy (1990), would argue that the type of compensation is the important factor, rather than the level of compensation.

The statistics reported in this chapter are consistent with the third group. Note that we do not focus on the amount of compensation. We assume that businesses pay what is required to retain valuable employees. Instead, we focus on the proportion of total compensation that is made up of incentive-based pay.

Should evidence be found that Mississippi executives receive less performance-based compensation than executives at similar firms in other states, then it may well be the case that encouraging Mississippi businesses to shift the composition of their executive compensation toward incentive pay results in executives that are better motivated to increase firm performance, which would in turn improve economic growth statewide.

Many firms tie a significant portion of their executives' total compensation to firm performance. Most of these pay-for-performance arrangements connect executive payment and firm performance through the use of stock options or restricted stock. Executive stock options grant executives the right to buy company shares, usually over the next five to ten years, at a specified price that typically equals the market value of company shares on the day of the option award. Restricted stock plans provide an executive with a block of company shares, but disallow the sale of those shares prior to a specified vesting date. Both types of performance-based pay increase incentives for executives to maximize firm value, since executives now profit with rising stock prices through their equity position in the firm.

Although performance-based payment as a primary means of compensating executives is a relatively recent phenomenon, paying executives according to firm performance has been around for quite some time. In fact, executive stock options were authorized as early as the 1950 Revenue Act. For many years after the passage of the Act, executive stock options were granted only to top executives. However, in more recent years, stock options have become increasingly common at all levels of management and have even been granted to non-managerial employees. As documented exhaustively in the mainstream media, and quite regularly in the academic literature, executive pay has increased drastically since the early 1980s. Hall and Liebman (1998), among others, attribute a large part of this rise in executive compensation to increased use of executive stock options, pointing to a 683% surge in the average value of stock option awards during a sample period from 1980 through 1994.

Agency theory predicts that linking executive compensation to firm performance better aligns managerial and shareholder incentives. Research shows that research and development activity, which can be seen as proxies for future positive value project opportunities, are significantly better for firms in which incentive compensation makes up a larger proportion of total compensation. Therefore, it seems that increased executive equity ownership does indeed have a positive influence on firm performance.

Overall, the literature largely supports utilizing performance pay to make executive employment contracts more incentive-compatible with shareholders. In short, using performance-based pay to align the incentives of managers and firm owners is well supported by many rigorous academic studies and should be considered carefully by both government policy-makers and business decision-makers.[5]

Incentive–Based Pay and Taxation

Executive stock options give the holder the right, but not the obligation, to buy a share of stock at a specified price, called the strike price. Executive stock options usually cannot be exercised immediately; rather, some percentage of an option grant will become eligible for exercise each year over a set period of time, often five to ten years. Executive stock options usually make up a substantial proportion of an executive's income; therefore, the tax treatment of executive stock options can have significant implications. Since the income tax treatments for the two types of executive stock options differ greatly, each are discussed separately.

Regardless of the form of compensation, taxes vary primarily along two dimensions. The first dimension is whether the income can be treated as capital gain or as ordinary income for the executive. The second dimension is whether the company can expense the incentive compensation granted and the timing of any such deduction. For non-performance-based executive pay that exceeds $1,000,000, the second dimension is irrelevant, since the federal government prohibits any corporate expense deduction for such payments in an attempt to encourage firms to utilize incentive-based payment plans.

Non-Qualified Stock Options (NQSOs) require that the executive be taxed at his or her personal income tax rate when the options are exercised, and that the firm defers taking a corporate expense deduction for the options granted until exercise. If the executive holds the shares received at exercise beyond the exercise date, any appreciation realized upon sale is taxed as a capital gain. Incentive Stock Options (ISOs) are given much less frequently than NQSOs because the firm can grant only $100,000 worth of ISOs per executive per year, and they also are taxed differently than NQSOs. ISOs are taxed when the executive sells the shares gained from exercise, instead of at the point of exercise. Thus, ISOs require executives to pay only the lower capital gains tax rate, provided they hold the acquired shares for at least one year beyond the exercise date. From the firm's perspective, the drawback to the ISO is the forgone corporate deduction, making ISOs attractive only to firms facing low marginal corporate tax rates. Obviously, a tradeoff exists between the two types of options as to whether the employee or the firm will realize the tax benefit. However, as shown by Hall and Liebman (1998), there is no question that stock options provide greater net tax benefits than straight cash compensation.

Restricted stock awards are a second form of performance-based pay in which the executive is granted ownership of firm shares. However, in the case of restricted stock, the shares cannot be sold until a specified "vesting" date. Interestingly, the Internal Revenue Service (IRS) does not consider restricted stock to be performance-based pay; consequently, it is taxed at the executive's personal income tax rate. Although the IRS does not consider restricted stock to be performance-based, it clearly helps align the interests of managers and shareholders and thus helps mitigate the agency problem. For this reason, restricted stock is included in the incentive-based measure described in the next section.

Although they have not been mentioned as a major part of performance-based compensation to this point, bonuses can also help align managerial and shareholder incentives, if properly structured. Bonuses

---

5   Arguments against the use of performance-based payment exist as well. Most notable is the argument made by Chaudri (2003) that executives are sometimes rewarded or punished for performance that is outside their control. For example, it is quite easy to envision a scenario in which the firm's overall stock performance was quite poor, but the firm actually performed substantially better than its close competitors. Unless the firm's pay-for-performance plan is carefully structured, firm executives might see reduced incentive-based compensation even though they outperformed their peer group.

differ a bit from the other types of incentive-based compensation, as they can be more easily awarded for individual or group performance, while restricted stock or stock options almost by necessity are tied to overall company performance. As for taxation, executive bonuses are taxed as ordinary income and are usually deducted as an ordinary business expense for most companies under Section 162 of the IRS Code. If the bonus was paid in stock grants, then Section 162 limits the corporate expense deduction available to the firm.

Results

The question is whether poorly structured compensation contracts could be one factor contributing to the subpar economic performance in Mississippi. As a first step towards addressing this question, we analyze whether there is in fact a relationship between incentive compensation and state economic performance. To investigate this issue, we examine the association between incentive-based compensation and state economic performance using a relatively standard OLS model of gross state product (GSP). We control for education expenditure, cost of living, median household income, unemployment, and population.[6] The results suggest that the percentage of performance-based compensation relative to overall compensation is a significant predictor of State GSP. This suggests that performance-based pay indeed plays a crucial part in explaining overall growth in a state.

Next, we examine the ranking of performance-based compensation across all states in terms of the proportion of incentive compensation utilized in total compensation packages to determine where Mississippi ranks. Data on executive compensation are obtained from Standard and Poor's ExecuComp database from 2002 through 2016. Following Cline and Benefield (2010), multiple stock option and restricted stock grants within the same year and observations that are missing essential data are eliminated. After these restrictions, the sample includes 152,521 firm-year observations.

Figure 7.1 reports the ranking for all top executives. The mean percentage of total compensation that is performance-based, the mean percentage of total compensation that is option-based, and the mean total executive compensation are reported. However, the focus of the analysis is on the proportion of incentive-based compensation relative to total compensation (i.e. Column 1). Panel A reports results for all executives from all states plus the District of Columbia, while Panel B provides the rankings across all 50 areas sorted by the ratio of incentive-based compensation to total compensation.

Panel A shows that the average executive earns slightly more than $2 million annually over the sample period. Approximately 47% of that $2 million is provided in the form of performance-based pay. Many financial economists argue that stock options are the best tool to align managerial and shareholder incentives due to differences in risk preferences between the two groups. Therefore, the proportion of total compensation attributable to stock option grants is of special interest. Across all states, the average executive receives 20% of their compensation from stock options.

Panel B reveals that Mississippi ranks 47th among these states. Interestingly, only North Dakota, West Virginia, and Montana rank lower. Mississippi corporate executives earn on average $721,360 each year, of which only 30.53% is provided as incentive-based pay. This low percentage differs significantly from the 47% reported for all states in Panel A. Firms in neighboring states such as Louisiana, Tennessee, and Alabama structure the pay for their executives much differently. On average, businesses in these states pay a much higher percentage of total pay in the form of incentive pay (54%, 50%, and 45%, respective-

---

6 The GSP data are obtained from the Bureau of Economic Analysis website. Other independent variables, in addition to the data on percentage of performance-based compensation, are collected from the Department of Education website, the Bureau of Labor Statistics, the Census Bureau, and the Bureau of Economic Analysis website.

Figure 7.1: Rankings by Incentive-Based Compensation for all Executives

	Mean% performance comp (median)		Mean% option based comp (median)		Mean total executive comp (median)		Number of Obs.
Panel A: All States							
All States	47.11	(52.62)	20.24	(11.86)	2,092,780	(1,078,040)	152,521
Panel B: State Rank							
RI	62.26	(64.11)	24.89	(22.91)	3,153,709	(2,088,428)	338
DE	56.68	(61.06)	27.21	(22.80)	2,746,536	(1,415,929)	327
ME	54.76	(54.03)	26.19	(30.41)	1,370,644	(916,609)	135
LA	54.08	(62.91)	13.41	(0.00)	1,535,202	(1,092,532)	756
WY	53.33	(66.20)	17.14	(14.84)	1,333,037	(1,072,373)	47
AZ	52.53	(57.23)	18.88	(0.00)	2,041,665	(1,043,101)	1,266
CA	52.20	(60.23)	23.36	(13.54)	2,618,605	(1,211,090)	14,564
NC	51.17	(57.54)	13.94	(0.00)	2,272,316	(1,282,322)	2,350
MO	50.98	(55.71)	19.09	(8.90)	1,847,513	(1,168,769)	2,318
MA	50.48	(56.13)	21.01	(10.12)	1,901,891	(960,111)	5,312
NH	50.34	(51.12)	3.94	(0.00)	1,161,345	(778,751)	232
TN	50.25	(56.92)	22.06	(14.90)	1,799,591	(1,147,147)	2,241
CT	50.11	(55.57)	20.28	(10.02)	2,370,428	(1,257,987)	2,902
KY	50.00	(55.23)	22.48	(19.08)	1,904,881	(1,152,341)	811
IL	49.21	(54.35)	21.30	(16.26)	2,023,444	(1,240,225)	7,113
NJ	49.01	(55.13)	20.44	(13.77)	2,448,122	(1,392,797)	3,565
MN	48.99	(54.10)	25.15	(21.96)	1,911,638	(945,238)	3,141
TX	48.62	(55.16)	18.18	(4.10)	2,002,483	(1,106,588)	11,699
WI	48.39	(52.41)	21.85	(18.84)	1,565,536	(1,013,896)	2,290
PA	48.14	(53.95)	21.83	(17.36)	1,899,883	(1,098,029)	5,055
FL	48.07	(53.31)	16.03	(0.00)	2,121,821	(1,250,770)	3,801
ID	47.98	(50.77)	16.73	(0.00)	1,429,602	(647,939)	336
MI	47.85	(51.30)	17.66	(11.40)	2,072,197	(1,098,326)	2,406
CO	47.83	(56.44)	17.95	(5.62)	1,835,580	(1,057,133)	2,520
VA	47.53	(54.21)	17.21	(7.14)	2,222,255	(1,318,591)	3,553
GA	47.47	(51.46)	16.53	(6.87)	2,013,964	(1,081,287)	3,426
OK	47.38	(53.51)	13.88	(0.00)	2,206,953	(1,054,080)	954
OH	47.35	(52.12)	18.45	(14.31)	1,944,839	(1,139,293)	5,223
MD	47.27	(55.52)	20.29	(6.75)	2,491,060	(1,371,300)	1,531
NY	46.94	(52.15)	17.99	(7.60)	3,564,452	(1,575,180)	9,769
WA	46.14	(52.38)	18.91	(0.00)	1,941,191	(915,336)	1,875
IN	45.03	(50.34)	15.93	(2.05)	1,778,119	(970,069)	1,923
AL	44.78	(50.35)	17.06	(0.00)	1,298,091	(903,200)	763
DC	43.72	(53.08)	12.74	(0.00)	2,605,112	(1,486,347)	413
AR	42.64	(43.86)	14.35	(0.00)	2,407,791	(859,629)	896
KS	42.39	(50.65)	9.15	(0.00)	1,940,676	(769,269)	549
NV	41.12	(45.30)	22.15	(12.55)	2,306,932	(1,257,500)	805
OR	41.07	(44.26)	18.05	(0.00)	1,251,617	(672,538)	802
SC	41.07	(43.16)	13.45	(5.67)	1,176,772	(761,171)	711
NM	40.75	(41.82)	10.03	(9.58)	832,894	(546,952)	79
HI	39.06	(44.15)	11.91	(0.00)	935,378	(695,674)	418
AK	38.24	(40.15)	11.80	(0.00)	1,054,681	(844,641)	82
UT	37.72	(39.94)	24.56	(12.14)	1,155,420	(685,603)	711
NE	33.45	(36.29)	15.93	(0.00)	1,773,921	(888,521)	557
SD	32.56	(33.11)	10.12	(0.00)	555,617	(452,778)	297
IA	31.16	(32.15)	17.76	(14.14)	1,285,156	(745,790)	777
MS	**30.53**	**(32.51)**	**4.39**	**(0.00)**	**721,360**	**(528,585)**	**404**
ND	29.55	(40.44)	0.00	(0.00)	851,014	(672,185)	90
WV	21.35	(20.32)	6.07	(0.00)	488,342	(353,750)	181
MT	6.43	(4.94)	6.14	(4.84)	330,522	(305,907)	53

ly). Executive stock option grants account for an average of only 4.39% of total executive compensation at Mississippi firms, which is also significantly lower than the 20% of total compensation from options reported for the full sample.

Figure 7.2 reports this ranking for Mississippi for each year of the sample period. It illustrates that Mississippi's average rank of 47th is driven from the fact that Mississippi has consistently ranked among the lowest states year in and year out in terms of performance based executive compensation. With the exception of 2003 through 2006, Mississippi records a rank of 44th or worse in every year.

Figure 7.2: Mississippi Performance Pay Rank over Time

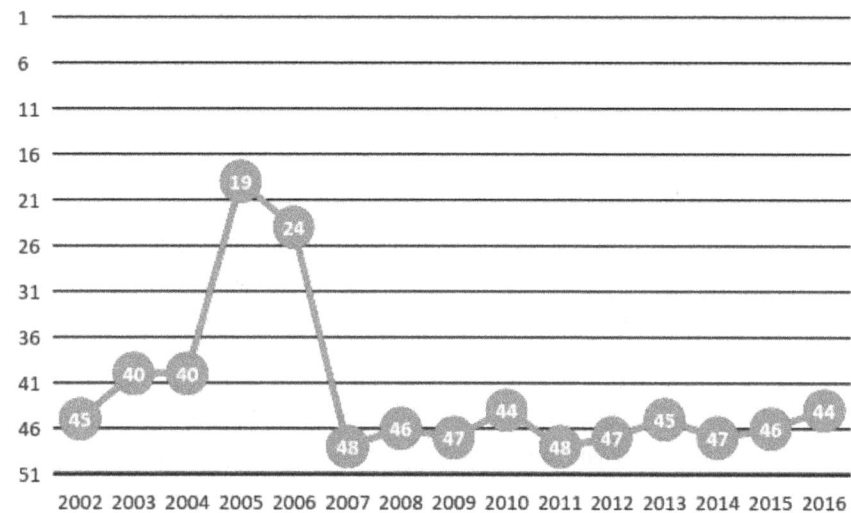

Figure 7.3 plots the percentage of performance-based compensation for Mississippi during each year of the sample period and the mean percentage-based compensation for all other states. Consistent with the pattern in Figure 7.2, we see that with the exception of a short period in the mid-2000s, Mississippi firms have consistently offered low performance-based pay relative to firms headquartered in other states.

Figure 7.3: Mississippi Performance Pay vs. Other States over Time

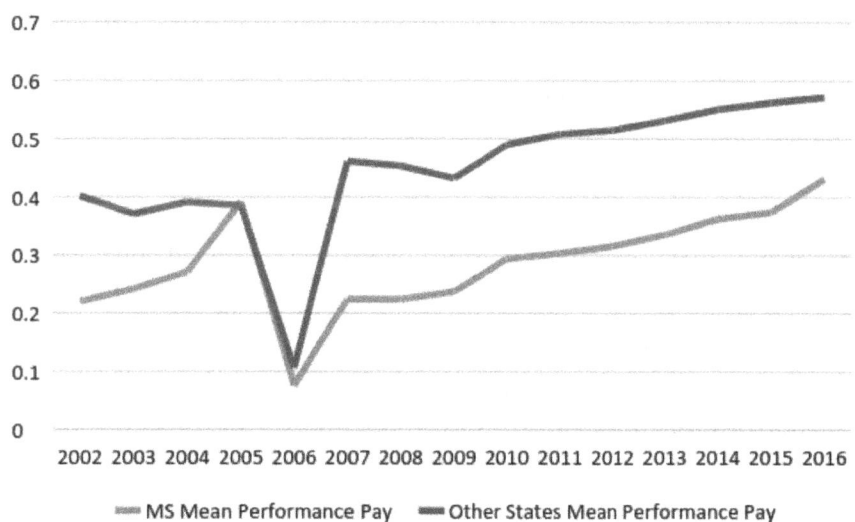

MS Mean Performance Pay   Other States Mean Performance Pay

A number of studies argue that the structure of CEO compensation has the largest influence on firm performance. We therefore make a similar comparison for a sample including only CEOs in Figure 7.4. The results in Panel A demonstrate that the average CEO earns slightly more than $3.8 million annually. Of that $3.8 million, on average 55% is provided as incentive-based pay, with an average of 21% of total compensation being paid in the form of stock options.

The rankings by state in Panel B are very similar to the rankings provided by Panel B of Figure 7.1. Most important to us is that Mississippi ranks 48th, with West Virginia and Montana being the only states where CEOs receive a lower percentage of their compensation in the form of performance-based compensation. The results show that on average Mississippi CEOs earn just under $1.4 million per year with an average of 33.56% of total compensation coming from incentive-based payment plans. This 33.56% average is statistically significantly less than the average 55% of total compensation from performance pay for all CEOs across all states. Panel B also shows that Mississippi CEOs earn only 4.04% of total compensation from stock option grants, which again is statistically significantly lower than the 21% for all CEOs across all states.

Multivariate Analysis

Figures 7.1 and 7.4 clearly indicate that Mississippi firms on average rank low relative to other states with regard to their percentage of incentive-based compensation. But couldn't other factors be contributing to this? There are a number of factors that might influence the average percentage of incentive-based compensation provided by firms in a particular state. For example, firms from a particular industry that eschew the usage of performance pay may be more highly concentrated in a certain state, or the majority of firms in a particular state may be small enough to believe complicated incentive-based compensation schemes are too costly and unnecessary. It's entirely possible that Mississippi firms naturally concentrate in these industries or have characteristics that are associated with firms that offer less performance-based pay for a reason. Hence, an additional test is needed that takes these other factors into account.

In the brief analysis that follows, we control for these other factors in multivariate regressions and discuss the results. Specifically, the percentage of performance-based pay is estimated using ordinary least squares (OLS) regression, while controlling for other factors known to affect executive compensation.

In the regression model, the dependent variable, Mean % performance comp, is the same variable used in developing the rankings in Figures 7.1 and 7.4. Other factors include firm size, book-to-market, leverage, dividend yield, prior 5-year stock performance, stock return variance, CEO indicator, CEO tenure, CEO age, CEO gender, director indicator, rural indicator, urban indicator, industry controls, and year control.[7]

The final term in the model, the regression residual, represents the portion of incentive-based compensation that remains unexplained by the variables included in the regression.[8] Viewing the regression residual in this way, you can think of the residuals as the unexplained portion of compensation. Using the average regression residuals for each state, we can then determine in which states firms are offering performance-based pay above or below the percentage expected. States that rank lowest are paying less than the amount suggested from the model after taking into account the other factors that predict performance-based compensation.

Although the rankings change considerably for a number of states, the results suggest that Mississippi firms pay less in the form of incentive-based compensation when considering these additional factors. Using multiple specifications, Mississippi continues to rank in the lowest six states with respect to incentive pay. These results are consistent with the analysis in Figures 7.1 and 7.4. Collectively, the evidence suggests that Mississippi firms on average offer less performance pay relative to other states and less than optimally predicted by the compensation model. Thus, considerable support is offered for the notion that

---

7   A number of additional variables were considered; however, due to data limitations, these variables are not included.

8   For a detailed description of variables and the model see Cline and Benefield (2010).

Figure 7.4: Rankings by Incentive-Based Compensation for CEOs

	Mean% performance comp (median)		Mean% option based comp (median)		Mean total executive comp (median)		Number of Obs.
Panel A: All States							
All States	54.91	(64.47)	21.33	(10.34)	3,808,650	(2,204,780)	21,321
Panel B: State Rank							
Panel B: CEOs by State							
NH	76.74	(77.14)	2.12	(0.00)	2,994,363	(2,948,333)	29
RI	75.45	(78.65)	24.83	(26.47)	6,817,136	(5,568,168)	51
DE	64.45	(76.41)	18.94	(14.91)	4,767,715	(4,036,345)	30
LA	64.11	(71.10)	16.95	(0.00)	2,840,182	(2,040,151)	126
ME	63.54	(59.22)	35.18	(35.32)	2,805,784	(2,602,251)	26
MN	62.70	(72.09)	29.39	(27.34)	3,710,600	(2,614,201)	392
NC	61.79	(69.78)	16.47	(0.00)	3,895,943	(2,446,122)	357
MO	61.59	(64.57)	21.54	(8.11)	3,511,422	(2,315,000)	347
ND	60.74	(65.63)	0.00	(0.00)	1,762,241	(2,070,135)	5
AZ	60.39	(67.21)	18.95	(0.00)	4,280,386	(2,089,637)	177
WY	60.23	(74.99)	18.06	(17.71)	2,921,393	(2,959,986)	9
MI	59.31	(64.34)	20.39	(13.99)	3,626,709	(2,089,631)	310
IL	59.08	(66.34)	23.78	(18.01)	3,842,396	(2,488,700)	927
CA	58.16	(70.10)	22.73	(0.00)	4,408,159	(2,490,497)	2066
MD	58.01	(71.88)	22.36	(6.71)	4,810,110	(2,766,463)	257
CO	57.82	(69.58)	20.64	(9.30)	3,685,510	(2,259,454)	337
CT	57.77	(67.19)	20.59	(4.21)	3,935,641	(2,477,897)	425
MA	57.44	(68.13)	19.45	(0.00)	3,367,294	(1,691,109)	704
OK	57.17	(64.30)	14.03	(0.00)	2,872,049	(1,978,872)	118
TN	57.01	(66.39)	22.86	(14.72)	3,287,550	(2,192,854)	312
NY	56.99	(66.96)	18.91	(0.00)	6,616,727	(3,557,756)	1264
NM	56.87	(63.97)	4.40	(0.00)	1,826,449	(2,063,956)	10
OH	56.73	(65.61)	19.63	(16.35)	3,334,873	(2,478,894)	639
WI	56.69	(65.97)	22.92	(20.09)	2,676,778	(2,076,425)	290
GA	56.66	(63.98)	15.61	(0.00)	3,761,223	(2,249,799)	499
FL	56.31	(69.63)	16.04	(0.00)	4,245,151	(3,012,865)	573
PA	56.13	(64.77)	22.42	(16.33)	3,065,727	(1,897,535)	688
NJ	55.77	(64.17)	22.13	(16.09)	4,483,377	(2,677,820)	504
TX	55.45	(67.07)	17.74	(0.00)	3,411,125	(2,190,212)	1594
KY	55.37	(66.86)	18.93	(8.04)	3,337,579	(2,271,281)	98
ID	54.99	(61.83)	19.19	(0.00)	2,048,113	(1,283,936)	58
IN	53.99	(59.22)	17.59	(4.14)	3,238,045	(1,633,950)	292
DC	53.71	(69.06)	14.60	(0.00)	3,018,754	(1,858,500)	55
OR	53.70	(61.55)	17.81	(0.00)	2,448,618	(1,191,307)	113
AL	52.24	(55.48)	17.89	(0.00)	2,177,808	(1,375,404)	130
VA	51.35	(64.52)	15.35	(0.00)	4,065,810	(2,225,717)	440
WA	50.61	(63.08)	18.56	(0.00)	3,378,706	(1,722,084)	260
SC	50.61	(62.43)	15.78	(0.00)	2,383,922	(2,023,396)	87
AR	50.25	(54.85)	12.81	(0.00)	3,122,800	(1,501,460)	114
KS	46.23	(64.28)	2.50	(0.00)	2,746,120	(1,647,305)	67
HI	44.99	(50.30)	9.35	(0.00)	1,601,722	(1,128,084)	68
UT	44.99	(51.31)	26.48	(14.02)	1,991,693	(1,507,000)	118
NV	43.96	(53.75)	23.52	(17.52)	3,293,446	(2,708,461)	112
SD	42.60	(47.56)	12.96	(0.00)	967,023	(984,886)	49
AK	37.91	(38.67)	12.36	(0.00)	1,653,924	(1,521,776)	15
NE	37.74	(49.49)	17.43	(0.00)	2,598,609	(1,939,445)	97
IA	34.05	(32.03)	20.04	(16.10)	2,169,295	(1,266,258)	118
MS	**33.56**	**(46.24)**	**4.04**	**(0.00)**	**1,394,293**	**(1,153,543)**	**54**
WV	27.06	(18.32)	6.89	(0.00)	1,041,943	(1,010,988)	36
MT	5.64	(4.16)	4.54	(1.78)	468,752	(449,547)	14

top executives at firms headquartered in Mississippi receive less performance-based pay than top executives at firms headquartered in other states.

Conclusion

Literature offers considerable evidence that linking executive compensation to firm performance helps align managerial and shareholder incentives. Properly structured employment contracts provide top executives with the motivation necessary to encourage efficient corporate risk-taking and desirable pursuit of value-enhancing projects. Mississippi rates poorly across a wide range of economic indicators. This study provides evidence that one contributing factor to the condition of Mississippi's economy might be the failure by Mississippi businesses to properly motivate executives by providing enough performance-based income.

The results of this study illustrate that, over the sample period of 2002 through 2016, Mississippi ranks poorly relative to other states in terms of the proportion of incentive-based compensation. Pay-for-performance on average makes up only 30% of total compensation for top five executives in Mississippi firms, compared to 47% nationally. Likewise, performance-based compensation makes up only 33%, on average, of total compensation to CEOs for firms headquartered in Mississippi, compared to a national average of 55%. Relative rankings for Mississippi firms fare no better after controlling for firm-specific features that might influence the prevalence of incentive compensation within a firm. This leaves only state-specific characteristics as the culprit behind low performance-based compensation utilization in Mississippi. Additional analysis highlights that the proportion of incentive-based pay has a significantly positive impact on state level gross domestic product.

The state-specific characteristics preventing further use of incentive-based compensation can be addressed by increasing awareness on the part of firms regarding the benefits of these compensation plans and by adjusting the state tax code to more closely resemble the federal tax code described above, which is designed to encourage incentive-based compensation. As long as executives at the largest firms in Mississippi remain inadequately motivated to maximize shareholder value, residents of Mississippi will not enjoy as much positive economic spillover from these firms as they otherwise could. Given the condition of the state economy, every small percentage increase in economic growth helps and shifting policy to encourage more incentive-based executive compensation can be one of the factors to help produce this growth.

References

Becker, Bo., Cronqvist, Henry., and Fahlenbrach, Rudiger. 2009. Estimating the Effects of Large Shareholders Using a Geographic Instrument. Harvard Business School working paper.

Card, David., Hallock, Kevin F., and Moretti, Enrico. 2008. The Geography of Giving: The Effect of Corporate Headquarters on Local Charities. Cornell University working paper.

Chaudri, Vivek. 2003. Executive Compensation: Understanding the Issues. *Australian Economic Review* 36: 300-305.

Cline, Brandon., and Benefield, Justin, D. 2010. Incentive-Based Executive Compensation and Economic Growth in the Southeast: Encouragement or Disincentive? *Southern Business and & Economic Journal* 33(1/2): 51-79

Hall, Brian. and Liebman, Jeffrey. 1998. Are CEOs Really Paid Like Bureaucrats? *Quarterly Journal of Economics* 113: 653-691.

Hall, Brian. and Murphy, Kevin. J. 2000. Optimal Exercise Prices for Executive Stock Options. *American Economic Review* 90: 209-214.

Jensen, Michael, C. and Meckling, William. 1976. Theory of the Firm: Managerial Behavior, Agency Costs and Ownership Structure. *Journal of Financial Economics* 3: 305-360.

Jensen, Michael. and Murphy, Kevin, J. 1990b. CEO Incentives: It's Not *How Much*, but *How*. *Harvard Business Review* 68: 138-149.

Kay, Ira, T. 1998. *CEO Pay and Shareholder Value: Helping the U.S. Win the Global Economic War*, London: St. Lucie Press.

Murphy, Kevin, J. 1985. Corporate Performance and Management Remuneration: An Empirical Analysis. *Journal of Accounting and Economics* 7:11-42.

Murphy, Kevin, J. 1999. Executive Compensation. in O. Ashenfelter and D. Card (eds.). *Handbook of Labor Economics, Vol. 3b*, Amsterdam: Elsevier Science North Holland.

8

Mississippi Shadow Economies: A Symptom of Over-Regulated Markets and Measure of Missed Opportunities

Travis Wiseman

8

Mississippi Shadow Economies: A Symptom of Over-Regulated Markets and Measure of Missed Opportunities

Travis Wiseman

Here, I turn the economic lens toward Mississippi's regulatory landscape. Other chapters in this book document Mississippi's poor economic performance and low rankings in many common measures of state-level prosperity and economic well-being – such as Mississippi's low income per capita, slow economic growth, and low level of economic freedom. This chapter highlights a feature of Mississippi's regulatory environment that helps explain the state's poor positioning – a cumbersome habit of maintaining outdated and burdensome regulation, in many cases for far longer than other states. I revisit concepts introduced in Chapter 3, with emphasis on the perverse incentives that regulations often create, which not only include incentives for individuals to engage in less productive activity, or more unproductive (or worse, *destructive* and criminal) activity, but also for businesses and entrepreneurs to hide their economic activity from tax authorities and other public officials – that is, to engage in the *shadow* economy. In this chapter, I discuss several sensible and low-cost reforms to the state's regulatory process that can help to promote prosperity in Mississippi.

Institutions and The Economic Underworld

Institutions are 'rules of the game,' formal and informal, that govern human action and social interaction (North, 1991). Formal rules are those found, for example, in constitutions and statutory law – codified political and legal frameworks. Informal rules include social norms, customs, and culture that are not codified or enforced by the formal structure – religion, for example, is one subset of informal institutions. William Baumol (1990), first introduced in Chapter 3, suggests that productive entrepreneurs are guided by institutions that reward wealth creation; and unproductive entrepreneurs by institutions that reward zero- or negative-sum activities – e.g., rent-seeking and frivolous lawsuits.[1]

A question that arises concerning Baumol's productive and unproductive entrepreneurship hypothesis is: *How do productive individuals respond to rule changes that decrease the relative rewards to productive activities?* Productive individuals in the legal sector of the economy may of course choose to bear the full cost of an unfavorable institutional adjustment – that is, for example, if a tax policy targeted at their industry reduces entrepreneurs' disposable incomes, they may simply carry on their productive activity, only with lower incomes. However, there are other plausible options. They may migrate to more favorable institutional conditions – such as other states with fewer regulatory burdens; or re-focus their efforts toward legal, unproductive activity. They may simply choose to give up entrepreneurship entirely. Alternatively, they may move their efforts *underground* to engage in productive, unproductive, and destructive – e.g., theft, murder, etc. – activity. These latter activities are defined as *shadow* economic activity.[2] In the next section, I will discuss shadow economies – how they come to fruition, how they relate to measures of economic performance discussed here and in other chapters, and what can be done to reduce the size of the shadow economy in Mississippi, and promote prosperity moving forward.

The Shadow Economy

The phrase "shadow economy" often summons thoughts of prostitution rings and illicit drugs sales. But shadow economies, while they most certainly involve these risky businesses, include much more. They include *all* exchanges that are intentionally kept from the government's purview – whether to evade tax or other legal authorities. An unlicensed hairdresser, styling hair for cash and not reporting it on her taxes, is one example. Shadow economies often provide goods and services that consumers demand, but are not available (or affordable) in the formal sector.

Many of the same barriers to market entry discussed throughout this book, that discourage productive entrepreneurship, simultaneously *encourage* participation in underground economies. For example, occupational licensing (Chapter 10) effectively restricts supply of goods and services in the market. With licensed protection from potential competitors, license-holders can raise prices on the goods and services they provide. This works to discourage both consumers and future producers from entering the market – that is, the *legal* market. Entrepreneurs and consumers excluded from the legal sector, will often undertake transaction illegally.

Corporate incentive programs (Chapter 6) produce similar results. Financially favored firms who win special privilege – in the form of tax breaks, credits, and exemptions, for example – through the political process effectively secure a competitive advantage in the market. This is neither beneficial for consumers nor firms denied such privilege. Un-favored firms may only be able to obtain similar privileges in the shadow economy; or are forced to downsize legal sector production, or leave the market entirely, creating unemployed workers, who themselves may turn to underground activities to maintain their livelihoods.

---

1   Several studies investigate this hypothesis. See, for example, Sobel (2008), and Wiseman and Young (2013). Additionally, Wiseman and Young (2014) examine productive and unproductive outcomes in the context of informal, religious institutions.

2   The shadow economy has many synonyms – e.g., underground economy, second economy, black markets, informal sector, extra-legal sector, off-the-books, under-the-table, etc.

High taxes tend to increases underground activity. Taxes increase the cost of producing goods and services, raise prices that consumers pay for final products, and reduce disposable income. This heightens the incentive for buyers and sellers to bargain off-the-books. You may have had direct experience with this phenomenon if you ever been offered a discount on your purchase for paying in cash.

Welfare programs also generate perverse incentives that encourage shadow economic activity. According to economists Friedrich Schneider and Dominik Enste:

> The social welfare system leads to strong negative incentives for beneficiaries to work in the official economy, since their marginal tax rate often approaches or equals 100 percent. [...] Such a system provides disincentives for individuals receiving welfare payment to even search for work in the official economy, since their overall income is higher if they receive these transfers while working in the underground economy. (2000, pp. 86)

The 100 percent marginal tax rate that Schneider and Enste reference, is inherent in the welfare program. Many welfare programs are designed to reduce the dollar amount of benefits as recipients earn more income from their own formal employment. As a result of this tax – economists sometimes refer to it as an *implicit marginal tax rate* – many people get trapped inside the welfare program. For example, if a welfare recipient finds formal sector work and her income from work rises by $6,000, but her welfare benefits are reduced by $4,000, she gains only $2,000 in disposable income. This amounts to a substantial marginal tax rate of approximately 67 percent.

$$Implicit\ Marginal\ Tax\ Rate\ = 1 - \frac{Change\ in\ Disposable\ Income}{Change\ in\ Income\ Earned\ from\ Formal\ Employment}$$

$$1 - \frac{\$6,000\text{-}\$4,000}{\$6,000} = 1 - 0.33 = 0.67\ or\ 67\%$$

Suppose that, in addition to welfare transfers, this person is also earning an off-the-books income of $3,000 that she would have to give up when she accepts the legal sector position. This amounts to $7,000 in combined welfare benefits ($4,000) and underground income ($3,000) that she would forego, while earning $6,000 at her new job.

$$1 - \frac{\$6,000\text{-}\$4,000\text{-}\$3,000}{\$6,000} = 1 - (\text{-}0.16) = 1.16\ or\ 116\%$$

In this case, the welfare beneficiary experiences negative returns (an implicit tax rate of 116 percent), which makes her *worse off* for choosing to pursue legal employment. She may choose, rationally, to remain both in the welfare program and the shadow economy. The important point here is that income earned in the shadow economy is not reported and therefore does not affect the benefits received from government programs – in contrast to the income earned from legal employment. Therefore, high implicit marginal tax rates make participation in the shadow economy relatively more attractive.

Any policy or regulation that raises the cost of doing business – whether as a sole proprietor or larger business entity – in a legal setting or discourages searching for formal employment, will invariably lower the cost of doing business in the shadow economy. Underground exchanges make up a not-so-insignificant portion of total U.S. economic activity. Studies suggest that the value of total U.S. shadow economy transactions, in recent years, rests between $1 trillion and $2 trillion, annually (Wiseman, 2013; Cebula and Feige, 2011). This is clear indication that shadow economies have important policy implications. Shadow economic activity amounts to potentially billions in lost tax revenue.

If you've ever paid cash to the neighbor for mowing your lawn or babysitting your children[3], chances are that you've taken part in an underground exchange. A recent study of U.S. shadow economies documents Mississippi's shadow economy as the largest among the 50 states (Wiseman, 2013). On average, estimates place Mississippi's shadow economy size at 9.54 percent of the state's economy. What this means is that for every ten dollars of income generated in the state's legal sector, nearly one additional dollar is earned in the shadow economy and unreported. In terms of value, based on a 2016 estimate of real GDP in Mississippi totaling $95.3 billion, the state's shadow economic activity amounts to approximately $9.1 billion during 2016. That amounts to approximately $3,044 per person.[4]

Shadow economies are largest where states rely less on capitalism, and more on government. Figure 8.1 illustrates the relationship between economic freedom, from the *Economic Freedom of North America* index, and shadow economy size in the U.S. states.

Large shadow economies are an indication of just how difficult it is to create wealth in the formal, legal economy. Moreover, this difficulty produces a number of downsides affecting nearly everyone. For policy makers, one downside is the lost tax revenue from unreported transactions. However, the downsides to the actual buyers and sellers of underground goods and services may be even worse. Transactions undertaken off-the-books expose parties of the exchange to the risk of being swindled in a number of ways. The purchaser of an underground good or service might end up with a faulty product – we've all heard stories of the unlicensed handyman who destroyed more than he fixed or left the job unfinished, then fled the scene – or the seller of services left with a bad check, or no payment at all. These risks are high because in the underground world there is little legal recourse for bad outcomes.

Figure 8.1: Shadow Economy Size and Economic Freedom

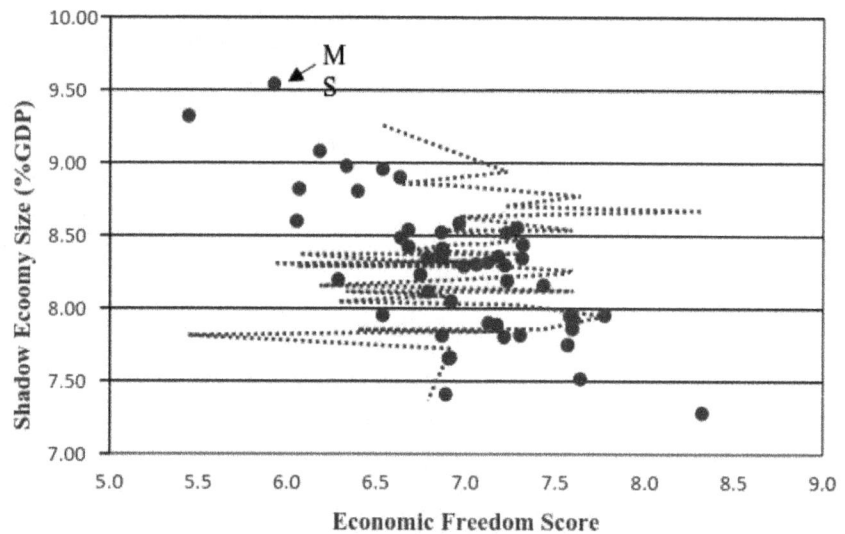

Source: Wiseman (2015), average shadow economy size versus average EFNA score, 1997-2008.

The situation is more ominous in the market for goods that are at all times illegal – i.e., prohibited goods. Prohibitions encourage a lot of bad behavior. Drug markets provide great examples. Since drug suppliers lack legal recourse to, say, the theft of their product, they often take the law into their own hands or purchase protection services from others willing to risk their lives in the underground. History reveals

---

3   http://www.nytimes.com/1993/05/02/nyregion/nannygate-for-the-poor-the-underground-economy-in-day-care-for-children.html?pagewanted=all

4   Shadow economy value estimates based on the author's own calculations. Real GDP and real GDP per capita estimates come from the Bureau of Economic Analysis (www.bea.gov), and shadow economy size (9.54%) comes from Wiseman (2013). The value of shadow economic activity is derived as ($real GDP_{2016} x 9.54\%$), or ($95.3 billion x 0.0954) = $9.1 billion. Similarly, shadow economy value per capita is measured as ($real GDP per capita_{2016} x 9.54\%$) = ($31,881 x 0.0954) = $3,044.

that large underground protection agencies tend to develop around prohibited products for which there remains a very high demand. We know these protection and supply agencies as gangs, mafias, and cartels. When exchanges in these markets go wrong, these problems simply cannot be reported to the legal authorities for restitution. Imagine a drug buyer calling the police to report the drugs he purchased were tainted, or to report a theft that occurs in the transaction.

It is no coincidence that entrepreneurs who are excluded from the formal sector – by prohibitive occupational licensing, or other policies and regulations that make it difficult to secure a job – often turn to underground markets. Moreover, working off-the-books is illegal to begin with, and prohibited goods – e.g., illicit drugs – command higher prices. Those prices are tempting to many who work in the underground.

In a recent study published by the Institute for Justice, *License to Work*, the authors (Carpenter, et. al, 2012, p. 84) assert:

> *"Only four states license more occupations than Mississippi, which has erected barriers to entry in 55 of the 102 low- and middle-income occupations studied. That places Mississippi in the second tier of most broadly and onerously licensed states ..."*

"Low- and middle-income" amount to low- and middle-skill sets – that is, individuals who are *limited in their education and training*. In other words, licensing in Mississippi is aimed disproportionately at those who might benefit most from a job, but simultaneously have the most difficulty obtaining such a job because they lack the competitive skill sets and the income that would give them an advantage in the labor market.. Though licensing doesn't tell the entire story of Mississippi's shadow economy, barriers like these keep the poorest of the population locked in precarious situations – unable to get their footing on the first rung of the economic ladder to prosperity.

For comparison, Figure 8.2 shows the record of 3 states with the largest shadow economies in the nation, and the 3 smallest. Averages of all estimates are provided to demonstrate the remarkable differences in important indicators of wealth and well-being, including the state's real GDP per capita (of legally re-

Figure 8.2: Shadow Economy, Income, Entrepreneurship and Education

	Shadow Economy Size (% GDP)[1]	Real GDP Per Capita[2]	Productive Entrepreneurship Score[3]	% Population with Bachelor Degree or More[4]
3 Largest Shadow Economies				
Mississippi	9.54	$31,881	16.33	20.8
West Virginia	9.32	$36,315	7.85	19.6
New Mexico	9.08	$41,348	23.05	26.5
Averages:	**9.31**	**$36,515**	**15.74**	**22.3**
5 Smallest Shadow Economies				
Colorado	7.52	$52,795	41.06	39.2
Oregon	7.41	$50,582	30.82	32.2
Delaware	7.28	$63,664	37.09	30.9
Averages:	**7.40**	**$55,680**	**36.32**	**34.1**

Sources: 1. Wiseman (2013); 2. Bureau of Economic Analysis; 3. Wiseman (2014); 4. Census Bureau, 2016

ported activities), productive entrepreneurship scores, and educational attainment at the bachelor degree level or higher. The states with smaller shadow economies have, on average, a higher educated population (34.1% with bachelor degrees versus 22.3%), experience more formal sector productive entrepreneurship (an average score of 36.32 versus 15.74), and realize a higher real per capita gross domestic product ($55,680 versus $36,510).

Taking aim at reducing the size of the underground economy in Mississippi would vastly improve the human condition of Mississippians. But how should the state approach it's shadow economy? Research suggests that decreases in tax and social welfare burdens, as well as labor market regulations, are associated with large decreases in shadow economic activity (Schneider and Enste, 2000). For example, a recent study of U.S. underground economies (Wiseman, 2013) suggests a one percentage point decrease in burdens from taxes and charges (e.g., licensing fees) is associated with approximately a 0.3 percentage point decrease in shadow economy size, on average.[5] This may not sound like much, but consider the value of 0.3 percent of Mississippi's 2016 real state-level GDP. At a little over $95 billion, a 0.3 percent reduction in shadow market activity amounts to approximately $286 million, annually. Much of that might be captured in the formal sector once barriers to market entry have been reduced. Most shadow market participants would prefer to do business on the up and up, and they will as long as operating in the legal economy is not prohibitively costly.

Alternatively, the same study suggests that direct attempts to identify and regulate the shadow economy – e.g., increasing police forces to combat underground activity – are associated with much smaller decreases in shadow economic activity. Increasing state expenditures (as a percent of GDP) for shadow market task forces by one percentage point amounts to about a 0.05 percentage point reduction in shadow economy size, on average. Compare this to the aforementioned effect of reducing burdens from taxes and charges (0.3 > 0.05). Moreover, task force measures put additional pressure on taxpayers to fund such initiatives. It is plausible that the increased tax burdens might simply crowd out the efforts of task forces – that is, as task forces reduce shadow economic activity, the taxes required to fund those forces incentivize more participation in the underground – creating a vicious cycle. Furthermore, entrepreneurs and firms already operating in the shadow economy have an increased incentive under pressure from task force initiatives to innovate new methods to avoid detection.[6] Pushing shadow participants deeper underground only increases costs to maintaining an effective task force.

Mississippi Should Provide Shadow Market Participants Incentive to Join the Official Economy

The following is a summary of suggested reforms.

- *Reduce tax and other social welfare burdens.* Reducing sales, corporate, and personal income taxes lowers the cost of formal, legal economic activity. Also, simplifying the tax code to constrain wealth redistribution would leave lobby groups with less to demand, and bureaucrats less to supply. Delaware hosts one of the nation's most inviting tax environments for business – low, fixed corporate income taxes, and no sales tax. It also hosts the smallest shadow economy.

- *Reduce or eliminate occupational licensing requirements.* Hotels, cabs, beauty salons, mail delivery, etc. In the formal sector these industries all profit in a big way from exclusive trade licensing. Unfortu-

---

5   Wiseman (2013) measures both taxes and charges as a percent of GDP.

6   Recent examples of such innovations include the dark web – a peer-to-peer web platform that houses many services designed to maintain user anonymity in exchanges. Silk Road is one dark web exchange forum where anonymous buyers and sellers exchange illicit goods and services, typically using a crypto-currency (such as Bitcoin) as a store of monetary value.

nately, such licensing keeps many would-be practitioners and customers from engaging in the formal economy. Licensing laws are responsible for many relatively harmless underground industries that states' task forces focus their limited resources on – see, for example, the cases of illicit hair braiders[7] and Uber drivers in Mississippi.[8]

- *Reconsider prohibition.* Undoubtedly, there is substantial shadow economic activity associated with goods that are outright illegal to produce and consume. Choice to outlaw a good necessarily forces its remaining production and consumption underground. For example, with the legalization of marijuana for recreational use in Colorado, Washington, and other states, consumption and production has become more visible. The good is taxed, and producers and consumers have recourse to the legal system and experience workplace and quality standards that go along with the aboveground economy.[9]

Prohibitions are possibly the most troublesome regulations imposed in any one place. They are often based on common misperception that if the good or service is outright prohibited, social ills and anxieties associated with consumption of the good or service will simply go away. However, history tells a different story.

In his autobiography, published one year before his death, famed Spanish filmmaker, Luis Buñuel, declared "*I never drank so much in my life as the time I spent five months in the United States during Prohibition*" (Buñuel, 1982, p. 45). The next section discusses the historical record of America's Alcohol Prohibition, 1920-1933, and explores the shadow economies that developed during the period to provide evidence of policymakers' failure to achieve their stated goals. Importantly, I highlight a feature of Mississippi's regulatory environment that helps explain the state's poor positioning in all measures of freedom and prosperity: a cumbersome habit of maintaining outdated and burdensome regulation for far longer than other state.

Mississippi's Hold-Out Problem

In the July 1, 2016 issue of *The Clarion-Ledger*, a leading publication in Jackson, Mississippi, columnist Michael Rejebian lamented:[10]

> Among America's 50 states, Mississippi is "Juror 3."
>
> You remember Juror 3 from the classic courthouse drama, "12 Angry Men," the story of an all-male jury deciding the fate of a young, poor Puerto Rican man accused of murder. Beginning with a single juror convinced of the man's innocence, the rest of the panel slowly and agonizingly comes to the same conclusion. Juror 3 – like Mississippi – proves to be the last stubborn holdout, finally breaking down in tears at the realization that he is without a foundation with which to continue standing.
>
> Mississippi has always been that juror – the final holdout.

The author goes on to list a number of Mississippi holdout cases. For example, Mississippi was the last state to ratify the Thirteenth Amendment to abolish slavery (in 2013); the last state to ratify the Nineteenth Amendment, which granted women the right to vote (in 1984), and the last state to repeal alcohol prohibition in 1966. The first two bear no real economic consequences – slavery was abolished

---

7   http://ij.org/client/melony-armstrong/

8   http://www.wlox.com/story/29570549/uber-likely-to-leave-south-mississippi

9   For readers interested in more details about the impacts of marijuana legalization on crime, public health, traffic fatalities, etc., see: https://www.cato.org/blog/common-myths-about-marijuana-legalization. Also, Bradford and Bradford (2016) demonstrate that prescription drug dependency and Medicare program spending is reduced in states that permit medical marijuana use.

10 http://www.clarionledger.com/story/opinion/columnists/2016/07/01/mississippi-last-holdout/86527622/

nationwide in 1865, and women across the country gained voting rights in 1920 after their respective constitutional amendments were ratified by the required 36 states in those years. The very late Mississippi ratifications were more or less expressions of social solidarity – a 'we're on your side' proclamation of sorts – and each fell on an anniversary of the respective amendments' ratifications.[11] The last repeal, however, *did* have economic consequences, as Mississippians weren't legally permitted to produce alcohol between 1908 and 1966.

First to Prohibit, Last to Permit: Mississippi's Brewing Industry

The ratification of the 18th Amendment to the U.S. Constitution, on January 16, 1919, ushered in a nationwide alcohol prohibition. Mississippi was the first state to ratify the Amendment – having already issued a state-wide ban on alcohol production in 1908, 10 years prior to the federal mandate. Prohibition had a devastating effect on the brewing industry in the United States, and sponsored a monstrous underground economy of beer and alcohol production, and brutal mafia violence, as mobsters fought for underground market share of the liquor trade.[12] Figure 8.3 illustrates the decline and rise of total breweries in the United States across the period 1890 to 2009.

Ratification of the 21st Amendment would later repeal federal prohibition – though not fully – and return decision-rights, concerning intoxicating drink, to the states. Mississippi was the last state to ratify the 21st Amendment in 1933, and would remain the state with the longest lasting outright prohibition on alcohol production, until regulatory repeal in 1966 (Holder and Cherpitel,

Figure 8.3: Total U.S. Breweries, 1890-2009

Source: Gohmann (2015)

1996). Today, 33 of Mississippi's 82 counties – approximately 40 percent of the state's counties – prohibit liquor sales in all or part of their jurisdictions.[13]

In 1978, President Jimmy Carter signed Bill H.R. 1337 – an Act that, among other things, repealed the federal prohibition holdover on home production of beer. The law went into effect on February 1, 1979,

---

11 These very late expressions should not be entirely discounted as meaningless, however. Important to note, is that these slow expressions of solidarity are also possibly indications of very slow cultural shift in Mississippi. Studies show that informal institutions – such as culture, religion, etc. – play no small role in economic development, and when used to inform policy decisions can lead to negative, unintended consequences (Williamson, 2009). Wiseman and Young (2014) show that states with larger religious networks tend to experience less productive entrepreneurial activity – possibly as a result of more onerous regulations in states with high levels of religiosity.

12 Ken Burns and Lynn Novick recently directed a three-part documentary series that outlines many of the unintended consequences of Prohibition – including increased fatalities due to poisoning from poor quality underground alcohol, mafia wars, etc.: http://www.pbs.org/kenburns/prohibition/

13 Most counties in Mississippi allow beer, wine and alcohol sales in restaurants, and beer sales in grocery stores and convenience stores. Counties designated as "dry" prohibit liquor and wine sales outside of restaurants. "Wet" counties permit sales of wine and spirits in designated storefronts. Some dry counties contain wet cities, also known as "moist" counties – e.g., Newton County, MS is a dry county, but the city of Newton, located within Newton County, permits liquor and wine sales in designated storefronts.

making homebrewing legal at the federal level – again, returning decision-right to the states. Figure 8.3 above shows remarkable growth in the number of U.S. breweries thereafter. Carter's signature prompted the rebirth of an industry. Prior to 1978, homebrewing supplies had to be moved quietly to the basements of aspiring brewers, and brewing carefully undertaken so that neighbors wouldn't catch on and alert the authorities. The following poem captures the spirit of the time:[14]

> *Mother's in the kitchen, washing out the jugs; Sister's in the pantry, bottling the suds; Father's in the cellar, mixing up the hops, Johnny's on the porch, watching for the cops.*

After 1978, a legal network of homebrewers and homebrew suppliers began to develop, and the experienced among them began slowly putting their skills to the test in professional production facilities. Not in Mississippi, however. Mississippi would be the last state in the nation to legalize homebrewing – in *2013*!

As other states led a craft brewing revolution, Mississippians sat on the sidelines, missing out on millions in profit opportunity. In the year prior to homebrewing legalization in Mississippi, the national craft brewing scene contributed $34 billion to U.S. gross domestic product.[15] With only 3 breweries in the state in 2012, Mississippi made only a small, marginal contribution to this total. Today Mississippi continues to lag behind in the brewing industry as a result of onerous state regulations governing the distribution of beer, and relatively heavy tax burdens.[16]

Figure 8.4 shows the 5 U.S. states with the most breweries per adult (age 21+) and the bottom 5, or fewest breweries per adult. A number of measures are highlighted, including economic impact per

Figure 8.4: Breweries Per Capita – Top 5 and Bottom 5 States

	Breweries Per Number of Adults (Age 21+)[1]	Per Capita Economic Impact[2,3]	Industry Jobs as a Percent of Total Labor Force[2,4]	Average Industry Wages[2]	Beer Tax Burden[2]	Total Breweries in 2016[5]
Top 5 States						
Vermont	9.4	$1820	2.48%	$38,602	25.1%	73
Oregon	7.6	$1814	2.19%	$45,560	17.5%	304
Colorado	7.2	$2764	2.38%	$54,421	21.8%	386
Montana	6.5	$1295	1.93%	$35,297	19.2%	79
Maine	5.9	$1748	2.46%	$39,541	25.4%	102
Averages:	**7.32**	**$1888**	**2.29%**	**$42,648**	**21.8%**	**189**
Bottom 5 States						
Alabama	0.7	$581	1.02%	$38,715	30.1%	37
Georgia	0.6	$822.	1.09%	$45,203	28.9%	69
Louisiana	0.6	$961	1.60%	$40,989	22.2%	34
Oklahoma	0.5	$723	0.98%	$41,928	30.0%	26
Mississippi	0.4	$147	0.23%	$37,814	32.1%	14
Averages:	**0.56**	**$647**	**0.90%**	**$40,930**	**29.0%**	**36**

Sources: 1. The Brewer's Association; 2. The Beer Institute; 3. Census Bureau (population data); 4. Bureau of Labor Statistics (labor force population); 5. U.S. Department of Treasury, Alcohol and Tobacco Tax and Trade Bureau

---

14 The poems author remains unidentified, only reported as a "Poem by a New York state Rotary Club member" and published in the September 21, 1928 issue of *Collier's Weekly*. Sourced from Noon (2007, pp. 103).

15 The Brewers Association: https://www.brewersassociation.org/

16 Until July 1, 2017, Mississippi breweries were not permitted to sell their product on-site – a regulation which made beer production very costly. Breweries would essentially have to brew large batches of beer and distribute it in kegs, bottles, and cans (which added additional labeling and advertising costs to the process) before they knew whether or not their product had a potential consumer base in the market. https://mississippitoday.org/2017/03/03/senate-passes-bill-allowing-on-site-craft-brewery-sales/

person, percent of the state's labor force employed in an industry related to brewing,[17] average wages for all brewing-related jobs (direct and indirect), state-level tax burden on beer, and total brewery establishments. Again, averages of all estimates are provided for quick comparison. The 2016 economic impact of Mississippi breweries is $147 per capita, and pales in comparison to all other states – including Alabama, which legalized homebrewing just one month prior to Mississippi. Mississippi also hosts the fewest jobs as a percent of the state's total labor force, and imposes a higher tax rate on beer than any other state listed. At the national level, Mississippi hosts the fewest breweries - both total, and on a per capita basis.

Onerous regulations like the ones imposed on the brewing industry in Mississippi keep Mississippians locked in last place. To promote prosperity in the state, policy makers must move quicker to free up productive entrepreneurs to engage in wealth creation through the profit and loss system. While it is instructive to look to other states for examples of wealth creation where there are fewer regulatory burdens, it is important for Mississippi to one day *be that state* to set the example.

Conclusions

This chapter introduces the reader to the shadow economy – what it is, what causes it, what can be done to reduce its size – and highlights Mississippi as the largest shadow economy in the United States. Mississippi's tax and regulatory environments are largely to blame. Onerous occupational licensing, burdensome tax policies and incentive programs, and outdated prohibitions all work against Mississippians by hindering their path to prosperity. Productive entrepreneurs thrive in places where barriers to market entry are low – where they participate less in the shadow economy, and more in the legal sector. This means also that they commit fewer crimes, dedicate less effort toward unproductive rent-seeking activity, and instead focus their efforts towards wealth creation. Mississippians must recognize that government will not pave the state's path to prosperity with wasteful spending initiatives and burdensome regulation. To expand economic opportunities, Mississippians should work to eliminate the government's role in picking who gets to participate in the market and who doesn't. Instead let the free-enterprise system determine that. Unleashing capitalism and promoting productive entrepreneurship in the state is the only way to forward to promoting prosperity!

References

Baumol, William. 1990. "Entrepreneurship: Productive, Unproductive and Destructive," *Journal of Political Economy*, 98, pp. 893-921.

Buñuel, Luis. 1982. *My Last Sigh: The Autobiography of Luis Buñuel*, Random House: New York.

Bradford, Ashley, and David Bradford. 2016. "Medical Marijuana Laws Reduce Prescription Medication Use in Medicare Part D," *Health Affairs*, 35(7), pp. 1230-1236.

Carpenter II, Dick M., Lisa Knepper, Angela C. Erickson, and John K. Ross. 2012. *License to Work: A National Study of Burdens from Occupational Licensing*. Arlington, VA: Institute for Justice.

Cebula, Richard J., and Edgar L. Feige. 2011. "America's Unreported Economy: Measuring the Size, Growth and Determinants of Income Tax Evasion in the U.S.," *Crime, Law and Social Change*, 57(3), pp. 265-258.

Gohmann, Stephan. 2015. "Why Are There So Few Breweries in the South?" *Entrepreneurship Theory and Practice*, 40(5), pp. 1071-1092.

Holder, Harold D. and Cheryl Cherpitel. 1996. "The End of U.S. Prohibition: A Case Study of Mississippi," *Contemporary Drug Problems*, 23(2), pp. 301-330.

Noon, Mark. 2007. *Yuengling: A History of America's Oldest Brewery*, Jefferson, NC: McFarland & Company, Inc. Publishers.

North, Douglas. 1991. "Institutions," *Journal of Economic Perspectives*, 5(1), pp. 97-112.

Schneider, Friedrich, and Dominik Enste. 2000. "Shadow Economies: Size, Causes, and Consequences," *Journal of Economic Literature* 38, pp. 77-114.

Sobel, Russell. 2008. "Testing Baumol: Institutional Quality and the Productivity of Entrepreneurship," *Journal of Business Venturing*, 23(6), pp. 641-655.

---

17 In addition to brewing, wholesaling, and retail jobs directly related to the industry, this measure also includes indirect employment in other sectors such as agriculture, construction, business and personal services, etc.

Stansel, Dean, José Torra, and Fred McMahon (2016). *Economic Freedom of North America 2016*, Fraser Institute.

Williamson, Claudia. 2009. "Informal Institutions Rule: Institutional Arrangements and Economic Performance," *Public Choice,* 139, pp. 371-387.

Wiseman, Travis, and Andrew Young. 2013. "Economic Freedom, Entrepreneurship & Income Levels: Some U.S State-level Empirics," *American Journal of Entrepreneurship,* 6(1), pp. 100-119.

Wiseman, Travis, and Andrew Young. 2014. "Religion: Productive or Unproductive," *Journal of Institutional Economics,* 10(1), pp. 21-45.

Wiseman, Travis. 2013. "U.S. Shadow Economies: A State-level Study," *Constitutional Political Economy,* 24(4), pp. 310-335.

Wiseman, Travis. 2015. "Entrepreneurship, Corruption, and the size of U.S. Underground Economies," *Journal of Entrepreneurship and Public Policy,* 4(3), 313-330.

9

Occupational Licensing in Mississippi

Daniel J. Smith

9

Occupational Licensing in Mississippi

Daniel J. Smith

Occupational licensing is the regulation of individual entry to a profession through mandated professional requirements. While these professional requirements vary by industry, they often include registration, educational requirements, exams, and background checks set by industry boards comprised primarily of industry practitioners. Since occupational licensing laws explicitly prohibit an individual from practicing in an industry if they have not met the requirements set forth by the licensing board, these requirements often represent substantial barriers to individuals attempting to enter a profession. Individuals caught practicing in these professions without a license can face cease and desist orders, fines, and even jail time.

The stated purpose of occupational licensing laws is to protect the safety and well-being of consumers, especially when it comes to goods and services with asymmetric information problems. An asymmetric information problem is when one party to an exchange has more information than the other party. For instance, the seller of a good or a service is often much better informed about the good or service they are selling than the buyer. This is particularly the case with credence goods, which are complex goods that consumers find difficult to properly evaluate.

Consumer safety and well-being can be compromised in two primary ways in the presence of information asymmetries. First, consumers can be sold goods or services they don't really need. For instance, most consumers ordered to get an x-ray by a physician, dentist, chiropractor, etc., are unable to judge whether an x-ray is appropriate or not, given their lack of medical training and experience. In addition, they are also often unqualified to read an x-ray to assess whether the subsequent medical recommendation is appropriate or even necessary. Second, consumers' safety could be put at direct risk in the presence of information asymmetries. For instance, in the face of information asymmetries, a consumer may not be able to ascertain whether a tattoo artist is utilizing adequate health and safety precautions.

To supplement overarching fraud, misrepresentation, and false advertising laws already in place to protect consumers, as well as to supplement remedies available through civil courts, occupational licensing is often advanced as a method to protect consumers using goods and services with information asymmetries. Occupational licensing can be implemented to help ensure that practitioners in a profession with information asymmetries are properly qualified, trained, and monitored to mitigate the exploitation of consumer ignorance.

Occupational licensing is often implemented through legislation that creates an industry board composed of industry practitioners, oftentimes with nominal consumer representation, tasked with designing, implementing, and verifying the education, experience, and professional conduct requirements of industry practitioners. To ensure compliance, these boards are given the legal power to mandate these requirements and are tasked with initiating action against practitioners found to be unlicensed, improperly qualified, or engaged in professional misconduct.

While there are examples of federal occupational licensing, such as an aircraft pilot licensing administered through the Federal Aviation Administration, and local occupational licensing laws, such as barbering in some Alabama countries prior to its state-wide licensing in 2013,[1] most occupational licensing occurs at the state level. Across the United States, over 1,000 different occupational categories are now licensed.[2] While around one in twenty workers needed a license to work in 1950, current estimates suggest that many more U.S. workers, around one in five, must now obtain a license to work.[3]

The requirements set forth by state licensing boards often vary drastically between states. For instance, educational requirements for licensure for an embalmer range from a 12-month mortuary school to a four-year B.S. degree in mortuary science.[4] Not only do occupational licensing requirements vary drastically between states, but even whether an occupation is licensed or not varies widely between states. For instance, the vast preponderance of the over 1,000 occupations licensed across the United States are not licensed in every state.[5]

In practice, industry practitioners themselves, not consumers seeking safety and quality assurance, have been the advocates for occupational licensing. Professional practitioners advocate for occupational licensing in the name of consumer safety, health, and protection, but stand to benefit from the artificially higher wages that often emerge when entry to the profession is restricted and competition is reduced. The information asymmetries enable industry practitioners to potentially impose unnecessarily complicated or costly requirements to restrict entry to the profession.[6] The variety of occupations licensed and the variety of requirements suggests that occupational licensing laws are primarily driven by industry groups seeking professional cartelization, not by consumers concerned about health and safety, as it is difficult to surmise why barbers without licenses would have represented a threat to consumers in Mississippi but not Alabama. Thus, occupational licensing can reduce the choices available to consumers, raise prices for consumers, and may even put low-income consumers at more safety risk if reduced choice and increased prices forces them to home-production or black markets as was highlighted in Chapter 8. The costs of occupational licensing can be substantial. The estimated cost to U.S. consumers ranges from $127 to $203 billion.[7] As licensing is extended to increasingly more industries, even in the absence of evidence of

---

1 Bureau of Labor Statistics (available at: https://www.bls.gov/opub/mlr/2015/article/the-de-licensing-of-occupations-in-the-united-states.htm).
2 See Summers (2007).
3 Bureau of Labor Statistics (available at: https://www.bls.gov/cps/certifications-and-licenses.htm).
4 See Smith and Trudeau (2016).
5 See Carpenter, Knepper, Erickson, and Ross (2012).
6 See Gellhorn (1976) and Kleiner (2006).
7 See Furth (2015, November 23) and Kleiner (2011).

information asymmetries that pose real threats to consumers, it gives unlicensed industries the ability and incentive to organize and lobby for professional licensure.[8]

Perhaps even more of a concern, cost prohibitive and unnecessarily complex occupational licensing requirements can reduce occupational choice and mobility for U.S. workers. This is particularly a concern when it comes to occupations that would, without occupational licensing, provide a low-cost professional opportunity for even low-income entrepreneurs. For instance, in the absence of occupational licensing laws, occupations, such as a barber or manicurist, requiring little startup capital, enable access to the American dream. In the absence of overtly stringent and oftentimes unnecessary licensing requirements, low-entry cost occupations often provide important avenues for occupational choice and economic mobility to individuals on the lower rungs of the economic ladder. While most occupational licensing falls on educated workers, such as physicians and lawyers, a total of 8.3 percent of employed people in the United States with less than a high school degree are currently required to obtain a license.[9] This, of course, doesn't capture the individuals who, in the absence of occupational licensing, would have entered these professions as entrepreneurs.

There is substantial evidence to suggest that workers receive artificial wage premiums when they successfully restrict entry to their profession through occupational licensing.[10] Especially in the absence of documented threats to consumer safety and health, this provides an explanation for why occupational licensing has rapidly expanded across the United States. For instance, Edward Timmons and Robert Thornton find that barber licensing provisions may be responsible for a wage premium between 11 and 22 percent.[11] A more general analysis of all occupational licensing laws across the United States, finds that licensing raises industry wages by 11 percent on average.[12]

While often restricting labor market mobility, reducing competition, and raising prices, occupational licensing doesn't necessarily always achieve its stated objective of advancing the public interest in terms of consumer safety and protection.[13] In some occupations, such as K-12 teaching, strict licensure laws may actually discourage quality applicants from even attempting to enter the profession.[14] Even if occupational licensing does perceivably increase quality, it may produce quality enhancements that exceed a cost-benefit analysis, especially when factoring in the effects of reduced competition.[15] This is because industry practitioners have the incentive to impose unnecessarily complex or costly requirements to restrict entry to the profession. Thus, while licensing requirements may serve to improve quality, the marginal improvements may exceed the benefits produced.

Often, the most harmful and troubling effects of occupational licensing fall on low-income individuals. In addition, while the evidence is mixed, occupational licensing may disproportionately harm minorities.[16] Occupational licensing falls hardest on low-income individuals for five reasons.[17] First, occupational licensing can render what would otherwise be low-cost professions prohibitively expensive

---

8   See Maurizi (1974) and McMichael (2017).

9   Bureau of Labor Statistics (available at: https://www.bls.gov/cps/certifications-and-licenses.htm).

10 See Adams, Ekelund, Jr., and Jackson (2003), Carroll and Gatson (1983), Hogan (1983), Gross (1986), and Morris (2000).

11 See Timmons and Thornton (2010).

12 Kleiner and Vorotnikov (2017).

13 See Adams, Ekelund, Jr., and Jackson (2003), Angrist and Guryan (2008), Carroll and Gatson (1983), Hogan (1983), Goldhaber and Anthony (2007), Gross (1986), Kleiner (2000), Levine, Oshel, and Wolfe (2011), Svorny (2004), and Wolfe (2000).

14 See Boyd, Goldhaber, Lankford, and Wyckoff (2007) and Larson (2015).

15 See Shilling and Sirmann (1988) and Young (1986).

16 See Dorsey (1983), Freeman (1980), Klein, Powell, and Vorotnikov (2012), Law and Marks (2009 & 2012), Wheelock (2005), Williams (1982 & 2011), and Young (1985).

17 See Smith (2017).

for low-income individuals. Second, for those practitioners with the resources to meet the occupational licensing requirements, the costs of occupational licensing can be passed on to consumers in the form of higher prices. Low-income individuals thus must sacrifice a relatively larger portion of their more limited budgets to pay for services from industries with occupational licensing. Third, unreasonably high standards often set by occupational licensing boards restrict the price and quality tradeoff available to consumers. Low-income individuals can either pay top-dollar for premium services (the so-called "Cadillac effect") or resort to often-dangerous home-production or black-market purchases. Due to this Cadillac effect, occupational licensing for a wide range of industries, including electricians, dentists, medical doctors, optometrists, pharmacists, veterinarians, plumbers, and real estate brokers have actually experienced reductions in quality for low-income individuals in some contexts.[18] Fourth, occupational licensing boards often impose stringent or even prohibitive requirements on rehabilitated prisoners, making it difficult for convicted felons to obtain honest employment after having served their mandatory sentences.[19] Fifth, occupational licensing laws often disproportionately affect the spouses of military service members as well as veterans, already facing the problems associated with transitioning from the military to the civilian section, including PTSD. The frequent inter-state moves required for military service members means those military members with spouses in licensed professions must often go through the licensing process, pass state jurisprudence exams, and pay an assortment of application or reciprocity fees every time they move out-of-state to a new military base.[20] Veterans themselves often face complicated licensing requirements and costs to enter the workforce after their military service despite their extensive training and experience.[21]

It is important, then, to carefully monitor licensed occupations to ensure that licensing requirements serve to protect consumer safety by maintaining only reasonable entry costs and requirements. Especially important, is ensuring that occupational licensing is limited to industries with demonstrated asymmetric information problems and thereby not extended to cover occupations with no demonstrated need for occupational licensure. For instance, licensing for occupations such as florists, casket sellers, auctioneers, and hair braiders have increasingly been challenged, and often successfully removed, due to the lack of consumer safety and health concerns. States, such as Mississippi, concerned with the costs of occupational licensing in terms of higher consumer prices and reduced occupational choice and mobility, can also explore alternative methods to help ensure consumer safety, even in those occupations where asymmetric information problems are found. For instance, private certification, advertising, second opinions, reputation, and consumer reviews are a few possible mechanisms that often operate successfully in markets to ensure consumer safety without imposing occupational licensure.

This chapter provides an in-depth investigation of occupational licensing in Mississippi, including estimates of the extent of occupational licensing, the costs of occupational licensing, and a detailing of some of the more egregious abuses of occupational licensing in Mississippi. I then offer a few possible avenues for reforming occupational licensing in Mississippi.

---

18 See Carroll and Gaston (1978 & 1981), Anderson, Halcoussis, Johnston, and Lowenberg (2000), Bond, Kwoka, Jr., Phelan, and Whitten (1980), Friedman (2002), Kleiner and Kudrle (2000), and Svorny (2008).

19 See Bromberger (1971-2), Dale (1976), Lucken and Ponte (2008), May (1995), and Pager (2006).

20 U.S. Department of Treasury and U.S. Department of Defense (available at: http://www.militaryonesource.mil/footer?content_id=279115).

21 See Kleiner (2015).

Occupational Licensing in Mississippi

I provide a detailed estimate of the costs imposed by occupational licensing laws in Mississippi, supplementing some national studies looking at certain aspects of Mississippi's occupational licensing regime. Most notably, the Institute for Justice estimated in 2012 that Mississippi licensed 55 low-income occupations, tied fifth worse in the nation with Nevada, substantially suppressing occupational choice and economic mobility for low-income Mississippians.[22] A recent survey by Heritage Institute's Salim Furth estimates that occupational licensing costs the average household in Mississippi over $800.[23]

The first step in compiling an estimate of the costs of occupational licensing in Mississippi is first identifying what occupations are licensed within the state. While occupational licensing in theory is easy to identify, in practice it is often difficult to detail all the occupations within a state bearing the restrictions necessary to be labeled occupational licensing, especially when it comes to distinguishing between commercial licensing and occupational licensing. For instance, while not considered a traditional licensed occupation, commercial fishing licenses in Mississippi, required for operating, for instance, a commercial fishing boat, require a license obtained through fees, a certificate from the Coast Guard, drug screening, and proof of identification and registration.[24] Child care facilities in Mississippi, while licensed extensively as businesses, do not have official occupational licensing.[25] Since child care facilities are often sole proprietorships, however, the business licensing requirements for child care facilities may create some of the same adverse side effects of occupational licensing.[26] Similarly, while tanning booth operators do not have an occupational license requirement in Mississippi, new tanning facilities must be licensed as a business, which includes a training certification requirement.[27] Some occupations had both individual licenses and business licenses. For instance, technicians, installers, salespersons, and helpers for electronic protection systems all have to be individually licensed (costing $150 for a license fee, $50 for a fingerprinting fee, and $279 to $299 for examinations required for technicians and installers), each contracting company needs to be also licensed (for a $450 license fee).

Mississippi has at least 118 different occupational categories with occupational licensing restrictions, and these are listed in Figure 9.1. While this chapter attempted to include every category of occupational licensure found in Mississippi, this list may not be comprehensive due to the inherent difficulties in compiling such a list. For instance, while hair braiders in Mississippi were freed from much stringent licensing requirements, they still maintain minor fee and licensing requirements. I excluded, however, many business licensures, such as those related to childcare facilities and fishing mentioned above, that may also operate, in practice, as a form of occupational licensure. In addition, we excluded some within-industry subcategories. For instance, pest control licensing in Mississippi contains 13 separate licenses, ranging from agricultural to wood destroying insect control. Cosmetologists, estheticians, and manicurists also separately license regular practitioners, master practitioners, and instructors, which are not included separately in this calculation. I also excluded temporary and emergency occupational licensing categories. This included emergency independent adjusters, emergency public adjusters, temporary elevator mechanics, temporary modular home installers/transporters, temporary insurance providers, and temporary limited lines insurance producers.

---

22 See Carpenter, Knepper, Erickson, and Ross (2012).

23 See Furth (2016).

24 Mississippi Department of Marine Resources (available at: http://www.dmr.ms.gov/images/regulations/Licensing/2016-Commerical-License-Requirements.pdf).

25 Mississippi Department of Health (available at: http://msdh.ms.gov/msdhsite/_static/30,0,183,225.html).

26 See Thomas and Gorry (2015).

27 Mississippi Department of Health (available at: http://msdh.ms.gov/msdhsite/_static/30,0,401.html).

Figure 9.1: Occupational Categories with Licensing Restrictions in Mississippi

Acupuncturists
Architect
Art Therapist
Athletic Agent
Athletic Trainer
Audiologist
Audiologist Aide
Automobile Club Agent
Bail Agent
Bail Enforcement Agent
Bail Soliciting Agent
Body Piercing Artist
Broker-Dealer / Investment Adviser
Broker-Dealer Agent / Investment Adviser Representative
Burial Agent
Certified Interior Designer
Certified Public Accountant
Chiropractic Assistants
Chiropractic Radiological Technologist
Chiropractor
Contracting - Commercial Builder
Contracting - Commerical Carpenters
Contracting - Commercial Electricians
Contracting - Commercial HVAC
Contracting - Commercial Masonry
Contracting - Commercial Mechanical
Contracting - Commercial Painters
Contracting - Commercial Plumbing
Contracting - Commercial Roofers
Contracting - Tile and Marble
Contracting - Commercial Welding
Contracting - Residential Builder
Contracting - Residental Remodeler
Contracting - Residential Roofer
Cosmetologist
Crematory Operator
Dental Hygienists
Dentist
Developer of Factory-Built Homes
Developer of Factory-Built Modular Homes
Dietitian
Electronic Protection Systems - Class B (System Installer)
Electronic Protection Systems - Class B (System Technician)
Electronic Protection Systems - Class D (System Salesperson)
Electronic Protection Systems - Class H (helper)
Elevator Contractor
Elevator Inspector
Elevator Mechanic
Engineer
Esthetician
Eye Enucleator
Foresters
Funeral Director
Funeral Service Manager (Embalming)
Geologist
Hair Braiding
Hearing Aid Specialist
Hemodialysis Technicians
Independent Adjuster

Insurance Producer
K-12 Educator
Land Surveyor
Landscape Architect
Lawyer
Legal Agent
Licensed Clinical Social Worker
Licensed Master Social Worker
Licensed Practical Nurse
Licensed Social Worker
Limited Elevator Contractor
Limited Elevator Mechanic
Limited E-Ray Machine Operator
Limited Line Credit Insurance Producer
Limited Lines Insurance Producer
Managing General Agent (Individual)
Manicurist
Manufacturers of Factory-Built Homes
Marriage and Family Therapist
Marriage and Family Therapist Assistant
Massage Therapy
Medical Radiation Technologist
Modular Home Contractor
Modular Home Installer / Transporter
Motor Vehicle Dealer or Representative
Motor Vehicle Salesman
Nursing Home Administrator
Occupational Therapist
Occupational Therapy Assistant
Pomologist
Pest Control
Pharmacist
Pharmacist Student
Pharmacist Technician
Physical Therapist
Physical Therapist Assistant
Physician Assistants
Physicians (MD, DO)
Podiatrist
Polygraph Examiner
Psychologist
Public Adjuster
Radiologist Assistant
Real Estate Appraiser
Real Estate Broker
Real Estate Salesperson
Registered Nurse
Reinsurance Intermediary Manager or Broker (Individual)
Respiratory Care Practitioner
Risk Retention Agent
Speech Language Aide
Speech Language Pathologist
Supervising General Agent (Individual)
Surplus Lines Insurance Producer
Tattoo Artist
Tree Surgeon
Veterinarian
Viatical Settlement Representative or Broker (Individual)
Wigologist

I also excluded intern, student, and trainee licensures from this total. Chiropractors, engineers, geologists, funeral services, funeral directors, independent adjusters, nursing home administrators, pharmacists, polygraph examiners, public adjusters, real estate appraisers, and surveyors all required intern, student, or trainee licenses. These licenses came with fees ranging from $25 (engineer intern) to $225 (Nursing Home Administrator-in-Training).

Finally, this chapter also excluded occupations such as bus and taxi drivers and gaming workers, that are not officially licensed, but still require a mixture of education, background, and certification requirements.[28] These, and related regulations, often operate effectively as occupational licensing. For instance, regulations prevented some Mississippians from working for ridesharing companies such as Uber and Lyft as discussed in Chapter 8.

Over 250,000 Mississippians—nearly 20 percent of Mississippi's labor force—works in an industry which requires an occupational license.[29] Individuals attempting to enter these occupations with licensing requirements face an assortment of different fees, examination requirements, educational requirements, drug screenings, background checks, and other requirements. The direct costs associated with applying for licensure in these occupations included application, board processing, criminal background, membership (in national professional organizations) verification (not to mention the membership fees for joining that professional organization), examination, fingering printing, licensure, and certificate fees. For example, an art therapist in Mississippi must pay an application fee of $100, an examination fee of $235, and an annual renewal fee of $75 to practice in Mississippi. In total, based on our estimates of the total number of current active practitioners in these licensed occupations, the total estimated cost of these initial licensing costs in Mississippi totals over $48 million.[30] Estimated annual renewal costs add up to over $13.5 million. The occupations with the highest estimated costs of initial occupational licensing in Mississippi included Occupational Therapists ($765), Occupational Therapist Assistants ($715), Commercial Contractors (minimum of $520), and Radiologist Assistant ($500). Also of note are Acupuncturists ($400), Athletic Trainers ($400), Massage Therapists ($350), Art Therapists ($335), Auctioneers ($300), and Tattoo Artists ($300).

Commercial contracting licensing in Mississippi was particularly difficult to include in the estimates. Per the Mississippi State Board of Contractors, the license and application fees amount to $400 plus $100 for each additional specialty area. There are over 180 commercial contracting minor specialty areas in Mississippi, including sign erection, painting, and landscaping, under seven major commercial construction classifications. Over 40 of these specialties indicate that exams were also required, in addition to the Business & Law Management Exam which is required for every specialty. The Builders License and Training Institute lists these exam prices as $120 per portion, in addition to offering courses to prepare for the exam ranging from $69 to $229.[31] In addition, each applicant for a commercial contracting licensing must submit CPA prepared and audited financial statements demonstrating a

---

28 Mississippi Department of Motor Vehicles (available at: http://www.dmv.org/ms-mississippi/special-licenses.php and Mississippi Gaming Commission (available at: http://www.msgamingcommission.com/index.php/forms_procedures/casino_gaming).

29 This is a conservative estimate since, 1) the list of licensed occupations isn't comprehensive, and 2) I was unable to obtain the number of active practitioners in the following licensed occupations: audiologist aide, chiropractic assistants, chiropractic intern, chiropractic radiological technologists, commercial crab trappers, cosmetologist instructors, cosmetologist masters, crematory operators, funeral service trainees, funeral director trainees, geologists in training, hemodialysis technicians, independent adjustor trainees, K-12 educators, limited e-ray machine operators, marriage and family therapist assistants, motor vehicle dealers, motor vehicle salesmen, nursing home administrators-in-training, pharmacist students, polygraph examiner interns, real estate appraiser trainees, speech language aides, surveyor interns, and temporary modular home installers.

30 To be conservative, to the extent possible, I excluded out-of-state practitioners holding licensure in Mississippi to estimate the costs falling on Mississippi residents. It is possible, however, that out-of-state practitioners in Mississippi may pass along these licensing costs to Mississippi consumers, thereby rendering the estimate conservative.

31 Builders License and Training Institute (available at: https://www.licensetobuild.com/mississippi/).

minimum of $50,000 in net worth to obtain a major classification and at least $20,000 in net worth to obtain a specialty classification. Several commercial contracting licensing requirements also have other occupational licensing requirements issued by other agencies, including the Department of Insurance (alarm systems, access systems, and security equipment, conveyor systems), the Department of Environmental Quality (elevators and escalators, lead base paint abatement, tanks and vessels, demolition, underground storage tanks, well driving), the Bureau of Plant Industry (landscaping, grading and beautification), and the Department of Agriculture (herbicide application). Thus, depending on the specialty area(s) a commercial contractor elects to provide, the total licensing costs ranges upwards from a minimum around $520.

Reforming Occupational Licensing in Mississippi

Given the substantial costs of occupational licensing in Mississippi, especially when factoring in the evidence that occupational laws are often used to restrict consumer and occupational choice without enhancing quality along dimensions valued by consumers, policymakers in Mississippi can consider reforming occupational licensing laws along several dimensions to promote prosperity in Mississippi, especially for those Mississippians struggling at the lower ends of the economic ladder.

One possible initial step in reforming occupational licensing laws is setting up uniform standards of transparency to publicly list all licensed occupations in Mississippi to enable policymakers to properly gauge the extent and burden of occupational licensing within the state. These licensed occupations and their requirements and fees can then be compared to other states, especially neighboring states, to judge whether occupational licensing requirements are overly burdensome, costly, or even unnecessary. For instance, some occupations licensed in Mississippi, such as art therapists (licensed directly by only five other states and indirectly by five additional states)[32] and wigologists (licensed by no other state), are not widely licensed across the United States.[33]

Mississippi has recently taken a step in this direction with the passage of the 2017 Occupational Board Compliance Act, which will provide an important legislative vehicle to monitor and rein in excessive and oftentimes unnecessary occupational licensing provisions. Mississippi has also recently overseen the relaxation and even elimination of occupational licensing restrictions considered to be unnecessary in terms of protecting consumer safety and health. For instance, hair braiders, now licensed in only three other states,[34] were recently freed from the more onerous requirements preventing them from practicing in Mississippi. After a 2000 court case, Mississippi was also required to repeal their licensing requirements on casket sellers, an occupation with little apparent need for occupational licensing, demonstrated by the fact that it is licensed in only eight remaining states.[35]

Voluntary certification offers one avenue of reform to help ensure consumer safety. Voluntary certification enables private third-parties to set standards for individuals to voluntarily subscribe providing quality assurance for consumers. This enables unrestricted entry to the profession, within the confines of overarching existing fraud, misrepresentation, and negligence laws, while enabling consumers to determine the appropriate quality/price tradeoff that best meets their budgetary circumstances. Mississippi already has experience with voluntary certification, for example, EMTS, paramedics, EMT drivers,

---

32 American Art Therapy Association (available at: http://myaata.arttherapy.org/Public/Public_Policy___Advocacy/Licensure_by_State.aspx?WebsiteKey=6a9efc36-907a-40a4-8509-f336f5815d92).

33 America Association of Cosmetology Schools (available at: http://beautyschools.org/licensing-hour-requirements/).

34 America Association of Cosmetology Schools (available at: http://beautyschools.org/licensing-hour-requirements/).

35 See Smith and Trudeau (2016).

nurse aides, and orthotists and prosthetists in Mississippi all use voluntary certification. Additional market mechanisms, including advertising, contracting, liability clauses, insurance, brand names, chain stores, leasing, warranties and guarantees, reputation, pre-purchase inspections, second options, performance or maintenance history reports, and consumer reviews, often emerge successfully in markets with information asymmetry problems to supplement voluntary certification in assuring consumers of quality and protecting consumer safety and health.[36] The Institute for Justice and the American Legislative Exchange Council both provide model legislation for states to better protect consumers and occupational choice.[37]

Occupational licensing reform can also be considered when it comes to the process for extending occupational licensing to new occupations in Mississippi. Reasonable requirements, such as the demonstration of a realistic and verifiable risk to consumer safety that broader civil and criminal codes do not apply to, an analysis that compares all the costs and benefits of the proposed licensing requirements, and a comparison to the licensing regimes of other states, can help curb the expansion of occupational licensing to industries without the apparent need for it. Such a reform can protect Mississippians from the cost and diminished occupational choice associated with the expansion of occupational licensing.

Conclusion

While often advanced under the pretenses of protecting consumer safety, the evidence suggests that occupational licensing often benefits industry practitioners by helping industry practitioners cartelize their profession. This is a concern in Mississippi for three primary reasons. First, occupational licensing often artificially raises the wages of industry practitioners by raising the prices of goods and services that require occupational licensing. Second, occupational licensing reduces the occupational choice and mobility of low-income Mississippians. Third, occupational licensing reduces consumption choice for Mississippians, sometimes forcing low-income residents, faced with the high prices required for the high "Cadillac" quality mandated by licensing requirements, to home-production or black markets. To the extent that occupational licensing does push low-income residents to home-production or black markets, it can even decrease the quality of the good or service and increase their risk exposure.

These problems are especially harmfully economically when occupational licensing is either unnecessary, due either to the lack of information asymmetries or the availability of private mechanisms such as consumer reviews, or unnecessarily onerous. Higher prices and reduced occupational mobility are a particular concern in Mississippi where the average income is below the national average.

With over 100 occupations licensed in Mississippi, representing over 20 percent of its labor force, reforming occupational licensing laws is an important policy reform necessary to promote prosperity in Mississippi. To promote prosperity in Mississippi, policymakers can explore avenues for reforming occupational licensing laws in Mississippi. First, they can create more transparency when it comes to the extent and full burden of occupational licensing in order to better compare occupational licensing regimes in Mississippi to other states, especially neighboring states. Second, policymakers can remove particularly burdensome and unnecessary occupational licensing requirements, including removing occupational licensing altogether for professions with no apparent need for it. Finally, Mississippi policymakers can put

---

36 See Akerlof (1970), Bond, Kwoka, Jr., Phelan, and Whitten (1980), Bonray, Lemarie, and Tropeano (2013), Dulleck, Kerschbamer, and Sutter (2011), Emons (1997), Hahn (2004), Hey and McKenna (1981), Holcombe and Holcombe (1986), Kihlstrom and Riordan (1984), Klein and Leffler (1981), Klein (1998 & 2002), MacLeod (2007), Milgrom and Roberts (1986), Sanford (2013), Schmalensee (1978), and Sultan (2010).

37 The Institute for Justice (available at: http://ij.org/activism/legislation/model-legislation/model-economic-liberty-law-1/) and the American Legislative Exchange Council (available at: https://www.alec.org/model-policy/occupational-board-reform-act/).

better processes in place to scrutinize legislation that seeks to expand occupational licensing to additional professions in order to curb the extension of occupational licensing to a larger portion of Mississippi's labor force.

References

Adams, Frank A. III, Robert B. Ekelund Jr., and John D. Jackson. 2003. Occupational Licensing of a Credence Good: The Regulation of Midwifery," *Southern Economic Journal* 69(3): 659-675.

Akerlof, George A. 1970. The Market for 'Lemons': Quality Uncertainty and the Market Mechanism. The *Quarterly Journal of Economics* 84(3): 488-500.

Anderson, Gary M., Dennis Halcoussis, Linda Johnston, M.D., and Anton D. Lowenberg. 2000. Regulatory Barriers to Entry in the Healthcare Industry: The Case of Alternative Medicine. *The Quarterly Review of Economics and Finance* 40(4): 485-502.

Angrist, Joshua D. and Jonathan Guryan. 2008. Does Teacher Testing Raise Teacher Quality? Evidence from State Certification Requirements. *Economics of Education Review* 27(5): 483-503.

Bond, Ronald S., John E. Kwoka Jr., John J. Phelan, and Ira Taylor Whitten (1980). Effects of Restrictions on Advertising and Commercial Practice in the Professions: The Case of Optometry. Staff Report, Bureau of Economics, Federal Trade Commission, Washington, D.C. Online: https://www.ftc.gov/sites/default/files/documents/reports/effects-restrictions-advertising-and-commercial-practice-professions-case-optometry/198009optometry.pdf (cited August 14, 2017).

Bonray, Olivier, Stephane Lemarie, and Jean-Philippe Tropeano. 2013. Credence Goods, Experts, and Risk Aversion. *Economics Letters* 120: 464-467.

Boyd, Donald, Daniel Goldhaber, Hamilton Lankford, and James Wyckoff. 2007. The Effect of Certification and Preparation on Teacher Quality. *The Future of Children* 17(1): 45-68.

Bromberger, Brian. 1971-2. Rehabilitation and Occupational Licensing: A Conflict of Interest. *William & Mary Law Review* 13: 794.

Carpenter, Dick M., Lisa Knepper, Angela C. Erickson, and John K. Ross. 2012. License to Work: A National Study of Burdens from Occupational Licensing. Retrieved June 6, 2017. Online: http://www.ij.org/licensetowork (cited August 14, 2017).

Carroll, Sidney L. and Robert J. Gaston. 1978. Barriers to Occupational Licensing of Veterinarians and the Incidence of Animal Disease. *Agricultural Economic Review* 30: 37-39.

Carroll, Sidney L. and Robert J. Gaston. 1981. Occupational Restrictions and the Quality of Service Received. *Southern Economic Journal* 47 (1981): 959-76.

Carroll, Sidney L. and Robert J. Gatson. 1983. Occupational Licensing and the Quality of Service. *Law and Human Behavior* 7(2/3): 139-146.

Dale, Mitchell W. 1976. Barriers to the Rehabilitation of Ex-Offenders. *Crime & Delinquency* 22: 322-337.

Dorsey, Stuart. 1983. Occupational Licensing and Minorities. *Law and Human Behavior* 7(2/3): 171-181.

Dulleck, Uwe, Rudolf Kerschbamer, and Mattias Sutter. 2011. The Economics of Credence Goods: An Experiment on the Role of Liability, Verifiability, Reputation, and Competition. *The American Economic Review* 101(2): 526-555.

Emons, Winand. 1997. Credence Goods and Fraudulent Experts. *The RAND Journal of Economics* 28(1): 107-119.

Freeman, Richard B. 1980. The Effect of Occupational Licensure on Black Occupational Attainment. In, Simon Rottenberg (Ed.), *Occupational Licensure and Regulation*, 264-284. Washington, D.C.: American Enterprise Institute.

Friedman, Milton. 2002. *Capitalism and Freedom*. Chicago, IL: University of Chicago Press.

Furth, Salim. 2016, April 15. The Hidden Tax That Costs Households Up to $1,600 a Year. *The Daily Signal*. Online: http://dailysignal.com/2016/04/15/the-hidden-tax-that-costs-households-up-to-1500-a-year/ (cited August 14, 2017).

Furth, Salim. 2015, November 23. Costly Mistakes: How Bad Policies Raise the Cost of Living. The Heritage Foundation *Backgrounder* No. 3081. Online: http://www.heritage.org/government-regulation/report/costly-mistakes-how-bad-policies-raise-the-cost-living (cited August 14, 2017).

Gellhorn, Walter. 1976. The Abuse of Occupational Licensing. *The University of Chicago Law Review* 44(1): 6-27.

Goldhaber, Dan and Emily Anthony. 2007. Can Teacher Quality be Effectively Assessed? National Board as a Signal of Effective Teaching. *The Review of Economics and Statistics* 89(1): 134-150.

Gross, Stanley J. 1986. Professional Licensure and Quality: The Evidence. CATO Institute *Policy Analysis* No.79. Online: https://www.cato.org/publications/policy-analysis/professional-licensure-quality-evidence (cited August 14, 2017).

Hahn, Sunku 2004. The Advertising of Credence Goods as a Signal of Product Quality. *The Manchester School* 72(1): 50-59.

Hey, John D. and Chris J. McKenna. 1981. Consumer Search with Uncertain Product Quality. *Journal of Political Economy* 89(1): 54-66.

Hogan, Daniel B. 1983. The Effectiveness of Licensing: History, Evidence, and Recommendations. *Law and Human Behavior* 7(2/3): 117-138.

Holcombe, Randall G. and Lora P. Holcombe. 1986. The Market for Regulation. *Journal of Institutional and Theoretical Economics* 142(4): 684-696.

Kihlstrom, Richard E. and Michael H. Riordan. 1984. Advertising as a Signal. *Journal of Political Economy* 92(3): 427-450.

Klein, Daniel B. 1998. Quality-and-Safety Assurance: How Voluntary Social Processes Remedy Their Own Shortcomings. *The Independent Review* 2(4): 537-555.

Klein, Daniel B. 2002. The Demand for and Supply for Assurance. In, Tyler Cowen and Eric Crampton's (Eds.), *Market Failure or Success: The New Debate*. Oakland, CA: The Independent Institute, pp. 172-192.

Klein, Benjamin and Keith B. Leffler. 1981. The Role of Market Forces in Assuring Contractual Performance. *Journal of Political Economy* 89(4): 615-641.

Klein, Daniel H., Benjamin Powell, and Evgeny S. Vorotnikov. 2012. Was Occupational Licensing Good for Minorities? A Critique of Marc Law and Mindy Marks. *Economic Journal Watch* 9(3): 210-233.

Kleiner, Morris M. 2000. Occupational Licensing. *Journal of Economic Perspectives* 14(4): 189-202.

Kleiner, Morris M. 2006. *Licensing Occupations: Ensuring Quality or Restricting Competition?* Kalamazoo, MI: W.E. Institute for Employment Research.

Kleiner, Morris M. 2011. Occupational Licensing: Protecting the Public Interest or Protectionism? W.E. Upjohn Institute for Employment Research Policy Paper No. 2011-009. Online: http://research.upjohn.org/cgi/viewcontent.cgi?article=1008&context=up_policypapers (cited August 14, 2017).

Kleiner, Morris M. 2015, March. Reforming Occupational Licensing Policies. The Hamilton Project Discussion Paper 2015-1. Online: https://www.brookings.edu/wpcontent/uploads/2016/06/THP_KleinerDiscPaper_final.pdf (cited August 14, 2017).

Kleiner, Morris M. and Robert T. Kudrle. 2000. Does Regulation Affect Economic Outcomes? The Case of Dentistry. *Journal of Law and Economics* 43(2): 547-582.

Kleiner, Morris M. and Evgeny Vorotnikov. 2017. Analyzing Occupational Licensing Among the States. *Journal of Regulatory Economics* 1-27.

Larson, Bradley. 2015. Occupational Licensing and Quality: Distributional and Heterogeneous Effects in the Teaching Profession. SSRN Working Paper. Online: https://papers.ssrn.com/sol3/papers.cfm?abstract_id=2387096 (cited August 14, 2017).

Law, Marc T. and Mindy S. Marks. 2009. Effects of Occupational Licensing Laws on Minorities: Evidence from the Progressive Era. *Journal of Law & Economics* 52(2): 351-366.

Law, Marc T. and Mindy S. Marks. 2012. Occupational Licensing and Minorities: A Reply to Klein, Powell, and Vorotnikov. *Economics Journal Watch* 9(3): 234-255.

Levine, Alan, Robert Oshel, and Sidney Wolfe. 2011. State Medical Boards Fail to Discipline Doctors with Hospital Actions Against Them. Online: http://www.citizen.org/documents/1937.pdf (cited August 14, 2017).

Lucken, Karol and Lucille M. Ponte. 2008. A Just Measure of Forgiveness: Reforming Occupational Licensing Regulations for Ex-Offenders Using BFOQ Analysis. *Law & Policy* 30(1): 46-72.

MacLeod, W. Bentley. 2007. Reputations, Relationships, and Contract Enforcement. *Journal of Economic Literature* 45(3): 595-628.

Maurizi, Alex. 1974. Occupational Licensing and the Public Interest. *Journal of Political Economy* 82(2): 399-413.

May, Bruce E. 1995. The Character Component of Occupational Licensing Laws: A Continuing Barrier to the Ex-Felon's Employment Opportunities. *North Dakota Law Review* 187: 71.

McMichael, Benjamin J. 2017. Political Spending on Occupational Licensing Laws. *Southern Economic Journal*, forthcoming.

Milgrom, Paul and John Roberts. 1986. Price and Advertising Signals of Product Quality. *Journal of Political Economy* 94(4): 796-821.

Morris M. 2000. Occupational Licensing. *Journal of Economic Perspectives* 14(4): 189-202.

Pager, Devah. 2006. Evidence-Based Policy for Successful Prisoner Reentry. *Criminology & Public Policy* 5(3): 505-514.

Sanford, Jeremy. 2013. Competition and Endogenous Impatience in Credence-Good Markets. *Journal of Institutional and Theoretical Economics* 169(3): 531-565.

Schmalensee, Richard. 1978. A Model of Advertising and Product Quality. *Journal of Political Economy* 86(3): 485-503.

Shilling, James and C. Sirmann. 1988. The Effects of Occupational Licensing on Complaints Against Real Estate Agents. *Journal of Real Estate Research* 3(2): 1-9.

Smith, Daniel J. 2017. Occupational Licensing in Alabama. *Labour & Industry*, forthcoming.

Smith, Daniel J. and Noah J. Trudeau. 2016. The Undertaker's Cut: Challenging the Rational Basis for Casket Licensing. SSRN Working paper. Online: https://papers.ssrn.com/sol3/papers.cfm?abstract_id=2781971 (cited August 14, 2017).

Sultan, Arif. 2010. Lemons and Certified Pre-owned Cars in the Used Car Market. *Applied Economics Letters* January-February 17(1-3): 45-50.

Summers, Adam B. 2007. Occupational Licensing: Ranking the States and Exploring Alternatives. *Reason*. Online: http://reason.org/files/762c8fe96431b6fa5e27ca64eaa1818b.pdf (cited August 14, 2017).

Svorny, Shirley. 2004. Licensing Doctors: Do Economists Agree? *Economic Journal Watch* 1(2): 279-305.

Svorny, Shirley. 2008. Medical Licensing: An Obstacle to Affordable, Quality Care. CATO *Policy Analysis* No. 621. Online: http://www.cato.org/sites/cato.org/files/pubs/pdf/pa-621.pdf (cited August 14, 2017).

Thomas, Diana and Devon Gorry. 2015. Regulation and the Cost of Child Care. Mercatus Working Paper. Online: https://www.mercatus.org/publication/regulation-and-cost-child-care (cited August 14, 2017).

Timmons, Edward J. and Robert J. Thornton (2010). The Licensing of Barbers in the USA. *British Journal of Industrial Relations* 48(4): 740-757.

Wheellock, Darren. 2005. Collateral Consequences and Racial Inequality. *Journal of Contemporary Criminal Justice* 21(1): 82-90.

Williams, Walter E. 2011. *Race & Economics*. Stanford, CA: Hoover Institute Press.

Williams, Walter E. 1982. *The State Against the Blacks*. McGraw-Hill Book Co.

Wolfe, Sidney M. 2000. Survey of Doctor Disciplinary Information on State Medical Board Web Sites. *Health Letter* 16(3): 1-3. Online: http://www.citizen.org/documents/HL_200003.pdf (cited August 14, 2017).

Young, David. 1985. Licensing and Minorities: A Question of Fairness. *Business and Professional Ethics Journal* 4(3/4): 185-193.

Young, S. David. 1986. Accounting Licensure, Quality, and the "Cadillac Effect". *Journal of Accounting and Public Policy* 5(1): 5-19.

10

Prosperity Districts: A Ladder Out of Last Place

Trey Goff

10

Prosperity Districts: A Ladder Out of Last Place

Trey Goff

It is well known throughout popular culture and illustrated in the opening chapters of this book that Mississippi is not exactly an economic powerhouse. However, most people are unaware of how bad Mississippi's economic malaise truly is: Mississippi has had the lowest per capita personal income (PCPI) in all but two years since 1929.[1] Mississippi is and has always been at the bottom of the economic ladder in the United States. However, it doesn't have to be that way.

An innovative, unique policy reform to address Mississippi's economic woes can be found in prosperity districts. Prosperity districts are geographically self-contained areas that reduce or eliminate unnecessary government restrictions on business activity, including regulation, taxation, and private subsidization. These districts allow for radical policy transformation by those who consent to it without the necessity of reform in the whole state, rendering their realization more politically feasible. These districts also allow for policy experimentation to better figure out what works best for a local area. Imagine the pure theoretical definition of economic freedom, discussed in Chapter 2, turned into reality through prosperity districts in Mississippi.

Prosperity district analogs have been utilized with massive success in China and Singapore, and they could have a powerful impact here in Mississippi. No American state has yet adopted prosperity district legislation, but Mississippi could finally be ahead of, rather than behind, the curve by being the first state to take this step toward economic freedom with prosperity districts.

---

1 BEA, SA1 Personal Income Summary: Personal Income, Population, Per Capita Personal Income, 2016

Mississippi Works Hard for the Money

Mississippi's economic woes would be hard to overstate. As stated previously, Mississippi's PCPI is and has nearly always been 50th. Many government actions like occupational licensing (see Chapter 9) and excessive regulation create perverse incentives for individuals to attain gainful employment. This could play a large part in explaining the economic malaise of Mississippi.

Take, for example, the labor force participation rate (LFPR). LFPR is the percentage of those eligible to work (i.e. those who aren't disabled, in school, too young, or too old) who are, in fact, working. Mississippi's labor force participation rate is currently 54.6%, which is significantly less than the national average of 62.7%.[23] Mississippi is behind all of its surrounding states with Alabama at 54.9%, Arkansas at 56.6%, Louisiana at 58.8%, and Tennessee at 57%. Moreover, Mississippi's labor force participation rate is lower today than it was in 1976. Fewer individuals working can perhaps explain Mississippi's low income per capita. Taken together, Mississippi's PCPI and LFPR indicate that too few Mississippians are working relative to other states, and that those who are working are earning less than their counterparts.

A possible explanation for Mississippi's economic gap is that Mississippians simply work fewer hours. The data, however, paints the exact opposite picture: Mississippians employed full time work, on average, 39.3 hours per week, which is more than individuals in other states.[4] This puts Mississippi at 9th in the nation for average hours worked per week. Compared to surrounding states, Mississippians work longer than most. The exception is Louisianans who average 39.5 hours. Louisiana outpaces Mississippi in terms of PCPI, with the average worker in Louisiana earning almost $10,000 more than the average Mississippi worker.[5] An increase of a mere 0.2 hours worked per week cannot possibly explain this massive income gap between Mississippi and Louisiana. Even the number 49th ranked state in PCPI, West Virginia, works fewer hours, on average, than Mississippians.

Mississippi is, however, ranked first in one labor category: percentage of the population earning minimum wage.[6] Mississippi is tied with Idaho, Kentucky, Louisiana, and South Carolina for first place in that category, with 5% of the labor force earning the minimum wage.

In summary: Mississippians who work full-time work more hours than workers in other states, yet earn far less money from it. Mississippi does not have a disproportionate share of individuals working part-time, but it does have a low labor force participation rate. Overall, too few Mississippians are working, and those that are working are not making nearly enough money to close the gap between Mississippi and everyone else.

Why might this be so? Government policies could create the lack of incentives to work and the ability to find high wage jobs. For example, transfer payments, such as welfare, alter the incentives for individuals to work, especially in a state as poor as Mississippi. Mississippi has almost 651,000 food stamp recipients, which is 21.74% of the entire state's population.[7] In fact, transfer payments in Mississippi total to 26.3% of total state GDP.[8] As such, these large amounts of benefits distort incentives to work.

These large benefit levels create what is known as a "welfare cliff." At certain income levels, most welfare programs fall off. This means that the higher one's income rises, the lower one's welfare benefits

---

2   Local area employment statistics, Bureau of Labor Statistics, April 19, 2017

3   Labor Force Statistics from the Current Population Survey, Bureau of Labor Statistics, June 13, 2017

4   Geographic Profile of Employment and Unemployment 2015, Bureau of Labor Statistics

5   BEA, SA1 Personal Income Summary: Personal Income, Population, Per Capita Personal Income, 2016

6   "Characteristics of Minimum Wage Workers, 2016," BLS reports, Bureau of Labor Statistics, April 2017

7   "States with the Most People on Food Stamps," USA Today, January 17, 2015

8   "13 Things You Need To Know About the State Economy," Clarion Ledger, February 16, 2016

become. Sometimes, this can create an income "cliff" wherein a small pay raise is more than offset by a concomitant large loss in welfare benefits. In order to keep from falling off of this welfare-induced income "cliff," some individuals may choose to forgo the pay raise and maintain welfare benefits so as to keep a higher overall income level. This can clearly dissuade people from attempting to move up the economic ladder and earn more, or dissuade them from taking a potentially more lucrative job.

Mississippi has the 4th highest government spending per capita of any state in the US. It is not hard to illustrate that government spending does not equate to prosperity. Government spending is often absorbed by the myriad of bureaucracies, bureaucrats, and technocrats that make up a state government, as well as disseminated through the variety of government-related private contractors. It is unclear how much of this expenditure actually benefits Mississippians. Very little government expenditure has a tangible, meaningful impact on the day-to-day lives of the citizens of a state. As illustrated throughout this book, government spending can detract, not add, to individual wellbeing with its burdensome costs and labor market distortions created by bad policies. Rather than continual reliance upon ineffectual government policies, removal of cumbersome and growth suppressing institutions, such as onerous taxation and regulation, may stimulate growth and unleash the productive capacities of Mississippians.

Prosperity Districts Framework

In order to lift Mississippi up out of last place economically, more Mississippians need to be working, and those that do work need to be earning more money. Prosperity districts offer a potential way to do both. A prosperity district is, in its most basic and ideal form, simply an exemption from most regulation and taxation within a small, given geographic area. However, the ideal prosperity district has a number of other unique features that make it the optimal form of special jurisdiction creation.[9]

First and foremost, a prosperity district is consent-based. All residents of a given area must consent to the creation of the district for it to become a reality. This makes it such that a prosperity district cannot be foisted upon a population that does not desire one, and it gives the district a sense of political legitimacy that few other entities can claim. The governance to which they will be consenting is one of ultimate individual liberty to pursue economic prosperity. These districts will act as a "reset" to state law. All legislation above the foundation of the state constitution, common law, and mens rea criminal law, will be invalid within these districts. This is the primary mechanism by which prosperity districts can encourage accelerated economic growth: they clear away the labyrinthine and oppressive scheme of state regulation and replace it with a "regulatory best practices" regime, a regime where only absolutely essential and low cost regulations are kept. Prosperity districts will operate as the "sole governing political subdivision" within that geographic area.[10] Think of a prosperity district as a new city government, but with far less authority than an actual city government would ordinarily be expected to have.

The limitation of the prosperity district's authority is as follows:

- No eminent domain or civil forfeiture power (see Chapter 17);

- No taxing power (see Chapters 4 and 5);

- Police powers restricted to criminal law, common law of least restrictive regulation (see Chapter 16);

- No subsidization of private enterprise (see Chapter 6);

---

9   Prosperity States Fact Sheet, Compact for America, 2017
10 Ibid.

- Municipal services limited to competitively contracted public-private partnerships;

- Borrowing capacity limited to net assets and no possibility of state or federal bailout;

- Regulatory authority limited to impede cronyism (see Chapters 8, 9).

This means that prosperity districts are given a "clean slate" from which to craft public institutions completely free from the burden of decades of already extant legislation. Because of these limitations, a prosperity district is guaranteed to have far more business and entrepreneur-friendly institutions than the rest of the state within which it is located. Although the prosperity district will be exempted from most all state taxation, it will tailor a revenue agreement with the state that is at least equal to the district's state tax revenue prior to its creation.

Better Institutions for a Better Economy, One District At a Time

The theory behind prosperity districts is a simple one: crafting better economic institutions will result in accelerated economic growth and a flourishing economy. Recall the discussion of economic institutions in Chapter 2. The most important of these institutions are private property rights. The French economist John-Baptiste Say (1880) put it most succinctly: "Political economy recognises the right of property solely as the most powerful of all encouragements to the multiplication of wealth."[11]

It is only through private property institutions that the price system may be born, and it is only through the price system—the spontaneous ordering of the disparate, specific, and specialized knowledge of all individuals pursuing their own self-interest[12]—that the wide scale coordination and adaptability required to create anything, even something as simple as a wooden pencil, can possibly occur.[13] The magnificence and beauty of such seemingly magical emergent order can only occur, and indeed does occur, within the institutional framework of private property rights. Property rights institutions are the foundation upon which the wealth of civilization is constructed.

There is more than theoretical support for this assertion. Chapter 2 provides an overview of the relevant empirical research, which overwhelmingly indicates that both in the U.S. and across the world, stronger property rights institutions cause economic growth and prosperity. Nearly every conceivable measure of human well-being is improved with a higher degree of property rights protection and economic freedom. Simply put, no matter how one cares to parse the data, strong property rights institutions and general human prosperity are inextricably intertwined. The Cato Institute puts it succinctly in their 2015 Economic Freedom of the World report:

> Nations in the top quartile of economic freedom had an average per capita GDP of US$38,601 in 2013, compared to US$6,986 for bottom quartile nations. Moreover, the average income of the poorest 10% in the most economically free nations is about 50% greater than the overall average income in the least free nations. Life expectancy is 80.1 years in the top quartile compared to 63.1 years in the bottom quartile, and political and civil liberties are considerably higher in economically free nations than in unfree nations.[14]

It is thus incontrovertible that increases in human well-being increase concomitantly with increases in economic freedom in a given jurisdiction. Recall the discussion from Chapter 2 that Mississippi is at

---

11 *A Treatise on Political Economy*, pg. 127, Jean-Baptiste Say, Augustus M. Kelly Publishers, 1971

12 *Individualism and Economic Order*, F.A. Hayek, pg. 77-92, The University of Chicago Press, 1948

13 See *I, Pencil*, Leonard Read, Foundation for Economic Education for more on the marvel of interconnectivity

14 "Economic Freedom of the World 2015," Cato Institute

least 40th or lower on nearly any measure of economic freedom and institutional quality. Thus, there is much room for improvement in Mississippi's economic institutions. This begs the obvious question: how can Mississippi improve its economic freedom in order to improve its poor economic performance?

Prosperity districts represent an opportunity for Mississippi to greatly improve its institutional environment by carving out an enclave of maximal economic freedom within the state. Within a prosperity district, all state taxation would effectively be removed and replaced with one simple fee to the prosperity district's governing entity, as outlined in a revenue agreement with the state government. Thus, this particular region would avoid the costliness of taxation, as discussed in Chapter 4. Furthermore, increases in economic activity will follow as businesses flood into the area to take advantage of the elimination of the income tax, property tax, payroll tax, and inventory tax, just to name a few (see Chapter 5). By relying on one fee to generate public revenue, prosperity districts eliminate many of the indirect costs of taxation, such as lobbying costs, behavioral changes, and enforcement and administrative costs. The district begins anew, free of the constraints of state tax policy and traditional local taxes, and as such can craft a tax regime that maximizes economic activity while minimizing compliance costs and overall tax levels.

Prosperity districts likewise strengthen property rights institutions and economic freedom by stripping all state regulation from the region. Government regulation increases the costs of doing business by inducing compliance costs which, in turn, can keep new competitors out of the marketplace; this type of regulation can even be encouraged by larger firms within an industry, effectively allowing large firms to dictate regulations to their own advantage–a phenomena known as "regulatory capture."[15] Regulation also weakens property rights institutions by enacting barriers and qualifications to how property owners may utilize their property, thus diminishing economic freedom and economic prosperity in the process.[16] These 'regulatory takings' are discussed in Chapter 17.

Prosperity districts will avoid the growth-crushing impact regulations can have by ensuring that only a minimal level of absolutely necessary regulation is enacted within the district. It will recraft business oversight by creating its own "regulatory best practices."[17] The regulatory best practices model is a framework wherein only the absolutely necessary and least costly regulations survive.

Regulations within the district will be enacted at the behest of an independent regulatory authority stipulated in the prosperity district legislation. This regulatory authority takes full responsibility for all regulation in the district. However, it is heavily restricted in the scope of its regulatory activities. It can never, under any circumstances, exercise eminent domain authority, which strengthens property rights institutions. It may not authorize any monopoly or cartel for the provision of any good or service, and it may not accept any gifts or grants whatsoever, effectively safeguarding it from regulatory capture. It cannot, under any circumstances, subsidize any private enterprise, further protecting it from rent-seeking and the encroachment of regulatory capture. Any regulation it promulgates must protect a measurable, tangible threat to the life, liberty, or property of a resident of the prosperity district.

Any potential regulation must be subject to thorough regulatory impact statements, both before and after adoption. These impact statements must consider all the costs and benefits of the regulation, including unintended consequences. Further, the authority must "demonstrate consideration of a wide variety of alternate and less restrictive or burdensome regulatory approaches consistent with the hierarchy of regulation contemplated, including, but not limited to, expressly assessing whether the regulation has

---

15 "The Theory of Economic Regulation," George Stigler, *Bell Journal of Economics and Management Science*, 1971

16 According to the most accurate modelling procedures, if US federal regulation were to have been frozen in the year 1980, the "model predicts that the economy would have been nearly 25 percent larger by 2012 (i.e., regulatory growth since 1980 cost GDP $4 trillion in 2012, or about $13,000 per capita)." Source: "The Cumulative Cost of Regulations," Coffey et al., Mercatus Center, April 2016.

17 "Cut the Red Tape," Adrain Moore, Compact for America Policy Brief, December 5, 2016. This entire section borrows heavily from that article and should be accredited in its entirety to her.

a negative effect on competition, whether the regulation can be modified to reduce its anti-competitive effects, and determining whether and how private voluntary action can reduce the risks addressed by the regulation."[18] Finally, if it is decided that the benefits of the regulation outweigh the costs of doing nothing at all, then the authority must demonstrate that it is pursuing the least costly, least intrusive way to enact the regulation. All regulation promulgated by the regulating authority has an automatic sunset provision of five years. Thus, all regulation expires in 5 years from the time it is enacted and must again go through the entire process outlined here to become law once more.

This onerous and lengthy process is created to ensure that no unnecessary, costly regulations will be enacted within the district, and that those which are enacted will only be the most effective and necessary regulations possible. The combination of such a regulatory regime coupled with tax abatement will ensure that property rights institutions are as strong as possible, economic freedom is maximized, and the associated economic growth and prosperity can occur unfettered by state intervention.

Another advantage of prosperity districts lies in their governance flexibility. Prosperity district governance institutions can take a variety of experimental forms contingent upon the desires of the citizens organizing the district. In this way, prosperity districts can have adaptable governance structures that can be tailored to the individual constituency and geography. For example, a small district with an active citizenry may opt for a model of democracy resembling the direct democracy of ancient Athens, while others may opt for a more representative style of governance. This is similar to economist Paul Romer's idea of a charter city.[19] Charter cities work in approximately the same fashion as prosperity districts in that they are able to evolve and develop governance institutions however they please underneath the umbrella of the foundational law of the country wherein they are located. For this reason, it is hypothesized that charter cities, much like prosperity districts, could have a powerful impact on the alleviation of poverty wherever they are implemented, and some have even argued on these grounds that they are a moral imperative.[20]

Evidence of Success

Up to this point, the discussion here has primarily centered on a theoretical explanation of how and why prosperity districts would bolster the Mississippi economy. Now, I will lay out evidence to show that prosperity districts and their analogues have a proven track record of success in unleashing economic growth and prosperity.

Although a prosperity zone has yet to be instituted anywhere in the United States, the potential impact of such a district on Mississippi's economy has been estimated.[21] In order to do so, economist Mark Lutter determined what the economic freedom index rating would be for a proposed prosperity district, then plugged that number into an equation which estimated—with statistical rigor—the impact of economic freedom on economic growth amongst the 50 states.[22] The results are persuasive:

> I find that an individual in state level Prosperity Districts with an annual income of $35,000 would see, over a five-year period, their income increase by $1,330 - $,1729 more than the increase of the national average. I additionally find that, compared to a

---

18 Ibid.

19 "Technology, Rules, and Progress: The Case for Charter Cities," Paul Romer, Center for Global Development, March 2010

20 "Cosmopolitanism Within Borders: On Behalf of Charter Cities," Christopher Freiman, Journal of Applied Philosophy, 2013

21 "Mississippi Prosperity District Economic Impact Estimate," Mark Lutter, unpublished manuscript, November 28, 2016

22 "Panel Evidence on Economic Freedom and Growth in the United States," Compton, Giedeman, and Hoover, *European Journal of Political Economy*, January 2011

comparable city, Prosperity Districts with 100,000 residents would see 2,800 new jobs added over a decade, Prosperity Districts with a population of 400,000 residents would see 11,000 new jobs added over a decade, and Prosperity Districts with a population of 2 million residents would see 56,000 new jobs created over a decade.

State level Prosperity Districts with 100,000 residents would have an annual spillover between $134 million and $175 million more GDP at the end of a five-year period. The annual spillover of Prosperity Districts with 400,000 residents would be between $537 million and $699 million more GDP at the end of a five-year period. The annual spillover of Prosperity Districts with 2,000,000 residents would be between $2.7 billion and $3.5 billion more GDP at the end of a five-year period.[23]

These estimates show that the impact of a prosperity district could produce real, effective levels of economic growth in Mississippi. According to these estimates, a prosperity district of 400,000 residents could get Mississippi out of last place in income rankings in less than 7 years. Furthermore, this doesn't account for the potential impact of other districts forming in the wake of the success of the original, meaning that the impact of the spread of prosperity districts across the state could be even greater than the estimate above.

Although the evidence of a prosperity district's impact in America specifically rests on a foundation of sound theoretical predictions, there is ample direct, empirical evidence of the astounding successes of prosperity district's closely related cousin, special economic zones. Special economic zones are analogous to prosperity districts in that they exempt certain geographic regions from a high degree of taxation and regulation.[24] Much like a prosperity district, special economic zones exist as an oasis of economic freedom in an otherwise (relatively) unfree country. The economic successes of special economic zones have been nothing short of incredible.

Shenzen, China's first special economic zone, was founded in 1980 and has seen its GDP per capita grow by an unimaginable 24,569%.[25] Its population has boomed from 30,000 to nearly 12 million. This mind boggling economic growth was due to the fact that Shenzhen was given exemptions to a wide range of taxation and regulation, massively strengthening property rights institutions and economic freedom in the process.

Or consider the story of Hong Kong. Although not a directly intentional prosperity district or special economic zone, it has been roughly equivalent to one since WWII as a result of it being a British colony possessing institutions with high degrees of economic freedom.[26] Recall from Chapter 1 the discussion of Hong Kong's growth from a small, impoverished rock island to the wealth levels of the United States in a matter of 40 years.

To further illustrate this point, let's look at Singapore. Singapore gained its independence in 1965, enabling it to enjoy political and economic autonomy. At that time, Singapore was as poor as any developing nation with a GDP almost half that of the world average. Singapore has utilized its autonomy to pursue economic freedom in much the same way as Hong Kong (the two jurisdictions often take turns at the number 1 and 2 spots on economic freedom indices). Because of this, the World Bank rates Singapore as one of the best places in the world to conduct business.[27]

---

23 "Mississippi Prosperity District Economic Impact Estimate," Mark Lutter, unpublished manuscript, November 28, 2016

24 *Special Economic Zones,* Thomas Farole and Gokhan Ekinci, The World Bank, 2011

25 "China's New Special Economic Zone Evokes Memories of Shenzhen," Frank Holmes, *Forbes,* April 21, 2017

26 "The Hong Kong Experiment," Milton Friedman, The Hoover Institution, July 1998

Such a commitment to economic freedom has yielded astonishing results for the small island nation. Singapore went from having a GDP per capita less than 20% of the US in 1965 to over 100% of the US in 2015, or an increase from $3,905 in 1965 to $51,855 in 2015 (in constant 2010 USD).[28] However, even this magnitudinous growth understates what Singapore has accomplished because the small island's population has ballooned from 1.7 million in 1960 to 5.6 million today. This means that over the very time period in which its population more than tripled, Singapore's GDP per capita multiplied by a factor of over 13. Likewise, Singapore's unemployment rate hovers near 2%, while their labor force participation rate is nearly 70% (recall from above that Mississippi's numbers are 5.6% and 54.6%, respectively).[29]

Singapore went from being a place of destitute poverty to the wealth level of the United States in a mere 40-year time span by embracing private property, free enterprise, and voluntary exchange to the utmost degree. Hong Kong and Shenzhen also stand as shining examples of the kind of economic growth that can be catalyzed by improving institutions of property rights and economic freedom as a prosperity district aims to do.

Figure 10.1 displays this astoundingly rapid wealth growth graphically, with GDP per capita on the vertical axis and year on the horizontal axis. Notice how rapidly both Singapore and Hong Kong grew, as well as how powerfully their growth path diverged from the world average.

Figure 10.1: Hong Kong, Singapore, United States, and World Average, GDP per capita 1965-2015

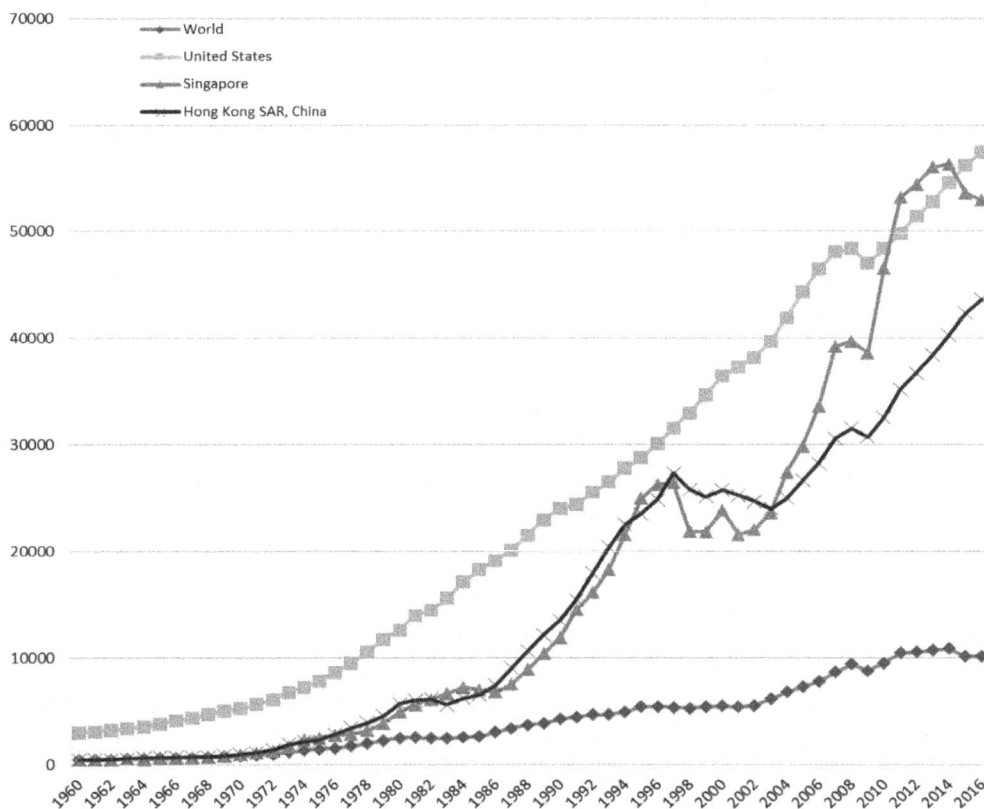

Note: GDP per capita in current US$

Source: WorldBank national accounts data, and OECD National Accounts data files: http://data.worldbank.org/indicator/NY.GDP.PCAP.CD?locations=SG-HK-US-1W

---

27 "Doing Business," World Bank, 2016

28 World Bank national accounts data, and OECD National Accounts data files

29 Singapore Department of Statistics

The impact such a massive degree of economic growth has on human prosperity and wellbeing in these two locations would be difficult to overstate. Residents of Singapore and Hong Kong have seen their countries go from destitute, developing world living conditions to decadent, ostentatious wealth in the short duration of a single lifetime. Such is the power of economic freedom and voluntary exchange, buttressed by strong property rights institutions, and unfettered, unshackled, and unrestricted by the weighty chains of state action. This is the power that prosperity districts seek to unleash.

Conclusion

Mississippi ranks either last or almost last among the 50 states in nearly every metric of economic growth and well-being. Fewer Mississippians are working than surrounding states, and those who are working are earning less money. Clearly, something has to change in order for Mississippi to ascend out of last place economically.

The answer can be found in prosperity districts. Prosperity districts will give Mississippians the opportunity to unburden themselves of the weight of state taxation and regulation, greatly improving their economic freedom in the process. Such a strategy has deep roots in sound economic theory and has been proven an effective strategy for unimaginable growth, prosperity, and wealth all over the globe. This radical economic reform strategy has the unique advantage, however, of also being politically feasible because of the small geographic size of a prosperity district.

Rather than begrudgingly accepting its last place station in the world as an inevitability, Mississippi should take a bold step forward by unleashing the creative and productive capacities of its people with prosperity districts. Prosperity districts could provide the solution that Mississippi needs to promote prosperity.

References

Bureau of Economic Analysis. 2016. SA1 Personal Income Summary: Personal Income, Population, Per Capita Personal Income. Washington, D.C.: Bureau of Economic Analysis.

Bureau of Labor Statistics. 2017. Characteristics of Minimum Wage Workers, 2016. Washington, D.C.: Bureau of Labor Statistics.

Bureau of Labor Statistics. 2017. Current Population Survey. Washington, D.C.: Bureau of Labor Statistics.

Bureau of Labor Statistics. 2015. Geographic Profile of Employment and Unemployment. Washington, D.C.: Bureau of Labor Statistics.

Bureau of Labor Statistics. 2017. Local Area Employment Statistics. Washington, D.C.: Bureau of Labor Statistics.

Coffey, Bentley, Patrick McLaughlin, Pietro Peretto. 2016. The Cumulative Cost of Regulations. Washington,D.C.: Mercatus Center Online: https://www.mercatus.org/system/files/Coffey- Cumulative-Cost-Regs-v3.pdf

Compact for America. 2017. Prosperity States Fact Sheet. Washington, D.C.: Compact for America.

Compton, Ryan, Daniel Geideman, Gary Hoover. 2011. Panel Evidence on Economic Freedom and Growth in the United States. *European Journal of Political Economy* 423-435.

Farole, Thomas, and Gokhan Ekinci. 2011. Special Economic Zones. Washington, D.C.: World Bank. Online: https://www.cgdev.org/publication/technologies-rules-and-progress-case-charter-cities.

Freiman, Christopher. 2013. Cosmopolitianism Within Borders: On Behalf of Charter Cities. *Journal of Applied Philosophy* 40-52.

Friedman, Milton. 1998. The Hong Kong Experiment. Hoover Digest web. Online: http://www.hoover.org/research/hong-kong-experiment.

Hayek, F. A. 1948. Individualism and Economic Order. Chicago: The University of Chicago Press.

Holmes, Frank. 2017. "China's New Special Economic Zone Evokes Memories of Shenzen." Forbes, April 21: web. Online: https://www.forbes.com/sites/greatspeculations/2017/04/21/chinas-new-special-economic-zone-evokes-memories-of-shenzhen/#3498987776f2.

James Gwartney, Robert Lawson, Joshua Hall. 2016. Economic Freedom of the World 2015. Washington, D.C.: Cato Institute. Online: https://www.cato.org/economic-freedom-world

Lutter, Mark. 2016. Mississippi Prosperity District Economic Impact Estimate. Washington, D.C.: unpublished manuscript.

Moore, Adrain. 2016. Cut the Red Tape. Washington, D.C.: Compact for America.

Pender, Geoff. 2016. 13 Things You Need to Know About the State Economy. Clarion Ledger, February 16. Online: http://www.clarionledger.com/story/news/politics/2017/02/16/state-economic-briefing/97993092/.

Rawes, Erika. 2015. States with the Most People on Food Stamps. USA Today, January 17. Online: http://www.singstat.gov.sg/statistics/browse-by-theme/population-and-population-structure.

Read, Leonard. 2010. I, Pencil. Atlanta: Foundation for Economic Education.

Romer, Paul. 2010. Technology, Rules, and Progress: The Case for Charter Cities. Washington, D.C.: Center for Global Development. Online: https://www.cgdev.org/publication/technologies-rules-and-progress-case-charter-cities.

Say, Jean-Baptiste. 1971. A Treatise on Political Economy. New York: Augustus M. Kelly Publishers. Online: https://mises.org/sites/default/files/A%20Treatise%20on%20Political %20Economy_5.pdf

Stansel, Dean, Jose Torra, Fred McMahon. 2016. Economic Freedom in North America 2015. Washington, D.C.: Fraser Institute. Online: https://www.fraserinstitute.org/sites/default/files/efna-2015-na-post.pdf

Stigler, George. 1971. The Theory of Economic Regulation. *Bell Journal of Economics and Management Science* 3-21.

World Bank. 2016. Doing Business 2016. Washington, D.C.: World Bank.

11

Promoting Prosperity in Mississippi through Investing in Communities

Ken B. Cyree and Jon Maynard

11

Promoting Prosperity in Mississippi through Investing in Communities

Ken B. Cyree and Jon Maynard

Recent publicity surrounding industrial recruitment in Mississippi gives the impression that industrial recruitment is the key to economic success and prosperity in Mississippi. As discussed in the previous chapter, elected officials and state agencies often use selective tax incentives or other attractive terms to entice employers to enter the state. An Associated Press analysis quoted in the Jackson Free Press newspaper found the incentives package offered to locate Continental Tire in 2016 in Hinds County totaled approximately $600 million.[1] The State of Mississippi expects the payback for this investment to be roughly $220 million by the year 2040 – 24 years after the initial pledge of $600 million to one company. The return on investment being less than the initial incentive package, as well as the lengthy and potentially uncertain time frame for this deal, display in concrete terms some of the dangers of engaging in large-scale industrial recruiting through selective incentives that were discussed in previous chapters.

Mississippi's traditional model of economic development focuses primarily on industrial recruitment. As illustrated in the Continental Tire Case, industrial recruitment such as this often brings with it large costs to the state, local governments, and taxpayers. Further complicating matters, the overall benefits and terms of deals are often private or difficult to disentangle, making efforts to analyze the overall benefits and costs of these investments extremely difficult and costly. This difficulty and uncertainty for determining the return on investment for large-scale industrial recruiting further decreases the probability that such strategies can be effective policies for economic growth in Mississippi. Although

---

1 Source: http://www.jacksonfreepress.com/news/2016/feb/06/ap-analysis-continental-tire-deal-incentives-600-m/ The Associated Press; Saturday, February 6, 2016 8:53 p.m. CST

much about the risks of large-scale industrial recruiting is well established in academic literature, unfortunately the measure of success for Mississippi policy makers still seems to be landing the "big deals."

Even if industrial recruiting in this manner did not have the associated risks and counterproductive effects on economic growth, it would still be an inappropriate and impractical growth policy strategy for Mississippi for purely logistical reasons. At present, most counties in Mississippi simply cannot afford the cost of industrial recruiting. Lowndes County, MS spent over $200 million in infrastructural improvements to attract industrial firms, an investment that is simply unfeasible for many of Mississippi's smaller counties with more limited revenues. What's more, little of Lowndes County's investment in infrastructural improvements directly benefitted the general public and taxpayers who paid for these improvements in the first place. Instead, it primarily benefitted only these specific industrial firms rather than the individuals whose incomes it was derived from.

Across Mississippi, economic indicators such as population growth, total employment growth, manufacturing employment growth, retail sales growth, county assessed value growth, and school ranking are largely stagnant or negative for the most recent 16 year period. Some of these trends are demonstrated in Figure 11.1 for the 82 counties in Mississippi and the State of Mississippi as a whole.

The left end of each spectrum represents positive growth. Unfortunately, very few counties are consistently experiencing high growth across these key economic indicators. The counties that are experiencing growth in these indicators have successfully developed their economy based on the quality of their place rather than the recruitment of large manufacturers into their community. Lafayette and Madison are two of the counties experiencing more success. While both communities have large manufacturers in their local economy, these manufacturers represent a small percentage of total economic activity in these regions, as both counties' ratios of manufacturing employment to total employment are relatively low. What is clear in these bar charts is that in Mississippi, a few counties are experiencing growth, but the majority of counties are not. This wide discrepancy in county economic success justifies investigation into of some of the possible reasons that may account for the difference between Mississippi's highest and lowest performing counties.

Other Methods to Promote Prosperity in Mississippi

An unbiased evaluation of the economic strength of a community can be located at policom.com. This organization ranks all micropolitan areas and all metropolitan statistical areas (MSA's) in the United States annually. Micropolitans are defined as communities with at least 10,000 population but less than 50,000. Oxford, MS is ranked by policom.com as one of the highest ranked micropolitans in the US since the study was formed in 2007. These rankings are for economic strength, and Oxford is ranked number 36 out of 551 micropolitans nationwide. Therefore, we use Oxford as an illustration to discuss alternative methods to promote prosperity in Mississippi.

When Oxford is measured against other communities in Mississippi, the economic indicators favor Oxford. The economic development strategy in Oxford has been counterintuitive to the traditional assumptions of large scale industrial recruitment. Oxford has concentrated on the quality of the community and the recruitment of people over large manufacturers. The cost for this has been quite low compared to the cost of most other economic development programs throughout the state. The budget for the Oxford-Lafayette County Economic Development Foundation (EDF) is roughly $300,000 per year, in contrast with comparably sized communities in Mississippi where the budgets are two to three times higher. The Oxford EDF focuses heavily on creating the ecosystem for business start-ups to thrive in Lafayette County. They have had success with several technology start-ups as well as a proliferation of local small businesses.

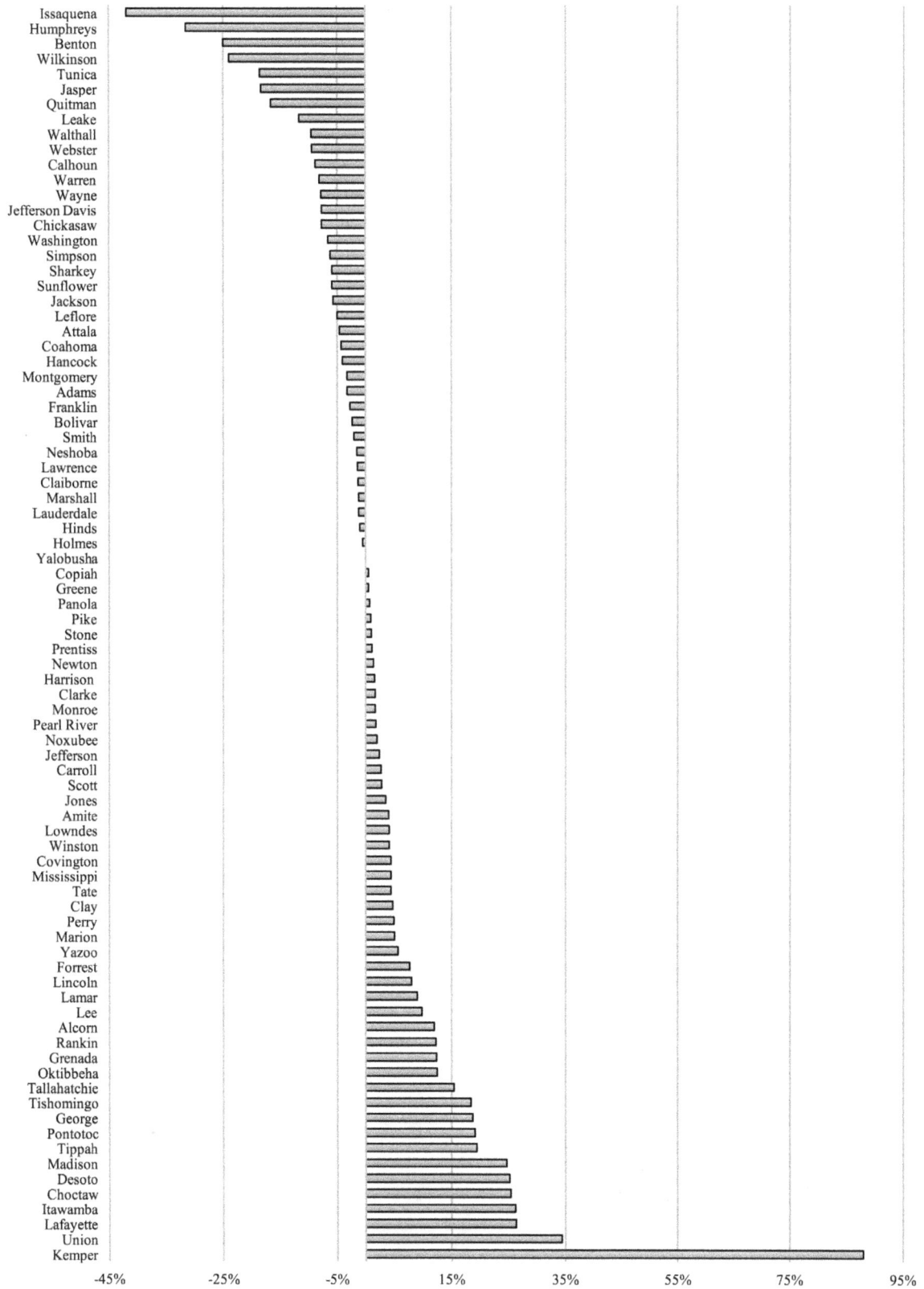

Figure 11.1 continues on the next page

Figure 11.1: County Level Economic Indicators: 2000-2016 Percent Change in Total Retail Sales, All Counties in Mississippi

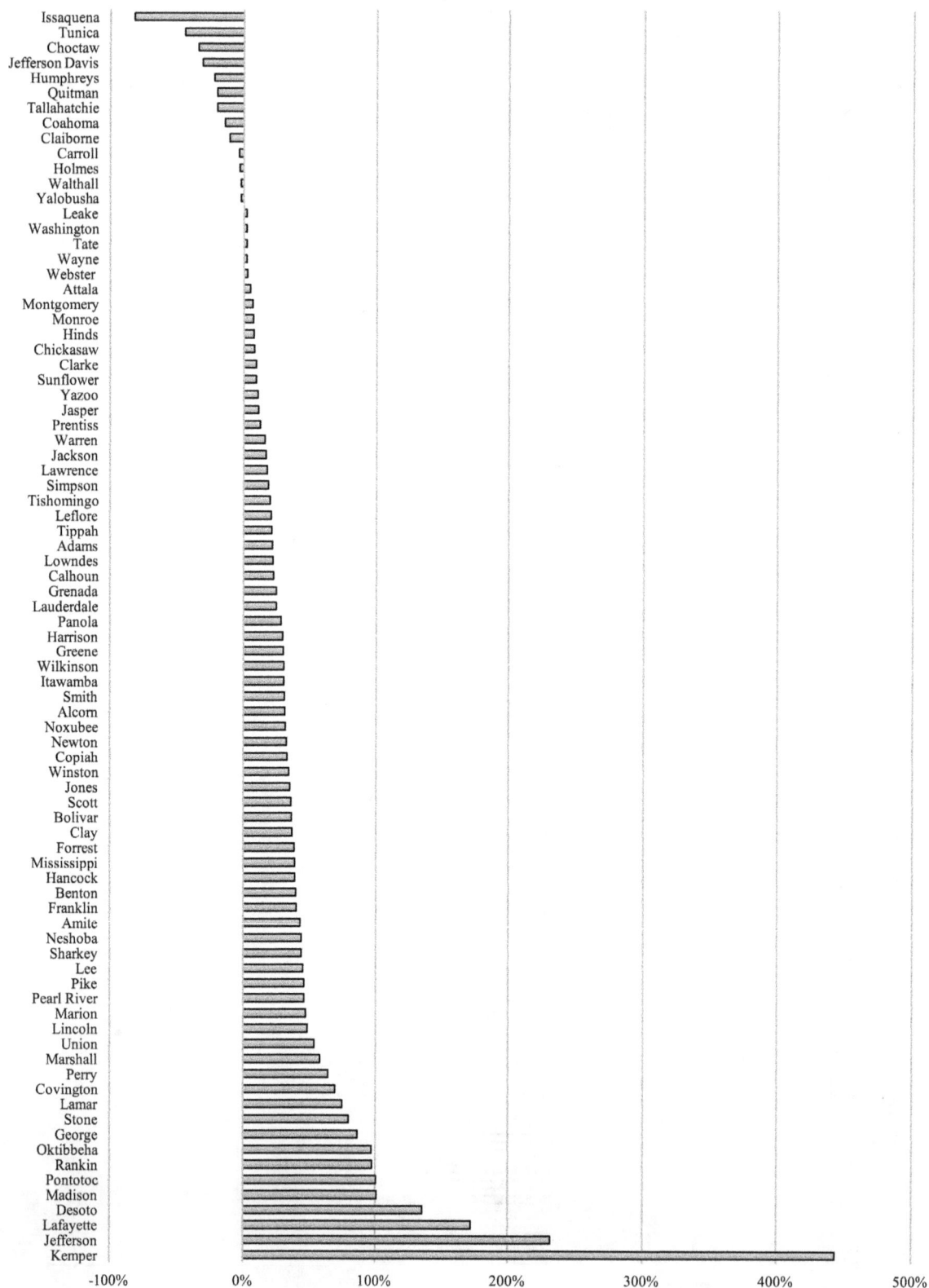

Figure 11.1 continues on the next page

Promoting Prosperity in Mississippi

Figure 11.1: County Level Economic Indicators:
2000-2016 Percent Change in Manufacturing Employment, All Counties in Mississippi

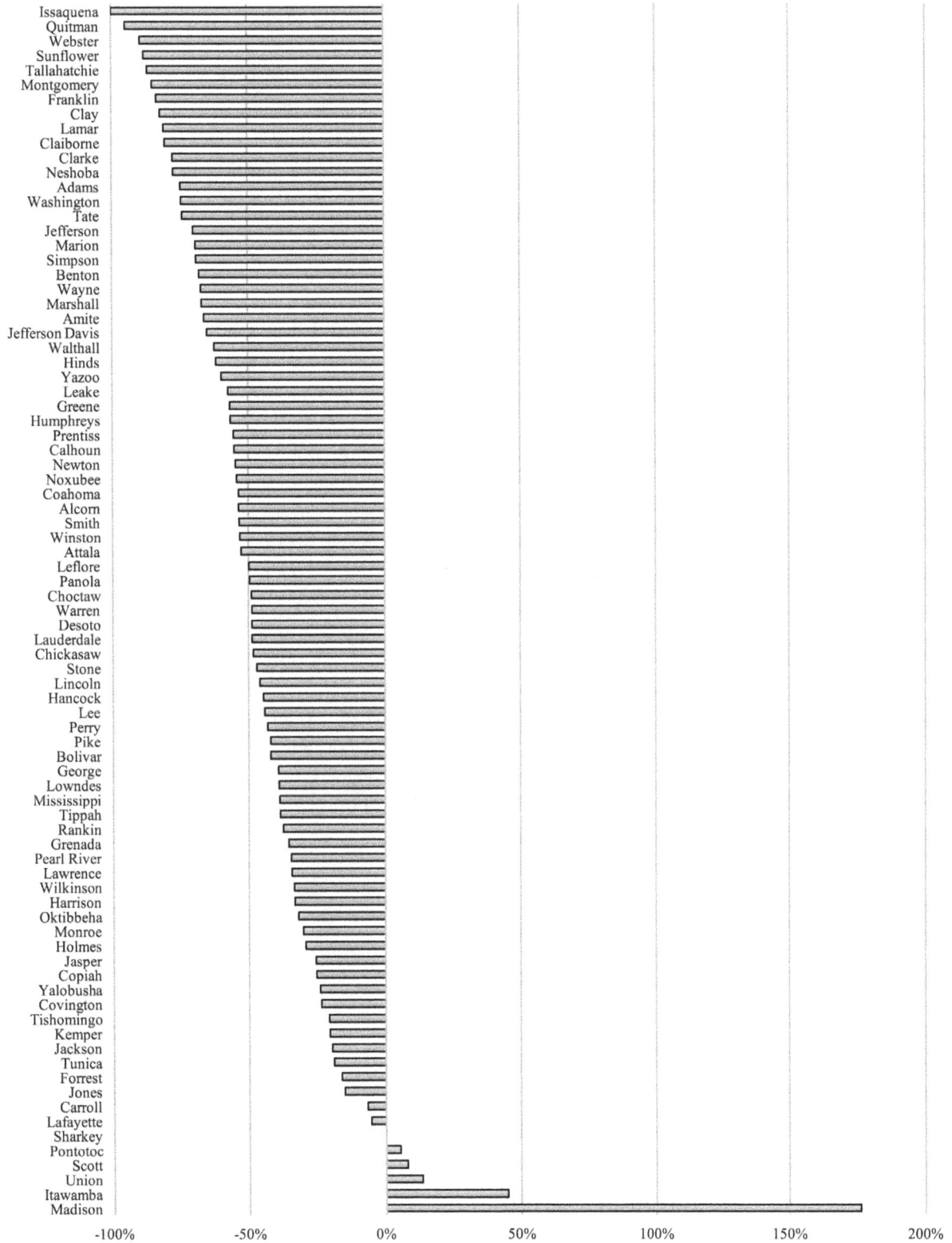

Issaquena
Quitman
Webster
Sunflower
Tallahatchie
Montgomery
Franklin
Clay
Lamar
Claiborne
Clarke
Neshoba
Adams
Washington
Tate
Jefferson
Marion
Simpson
Benton
Wayne
Marshall
Amite
Jefferson Davis
Walthall
Hinds
Yazoo
Leake
Greene
Humphreys
Prentiss
Calhoun
Newton
Noxubee
Coahoma
Alcorn
Smith
Winston
Attala
Leflore
Panola
Choctaw
Warren
Desoto
Lauderdale
Chickasaw
Stone
Lincoln
Hancock
Lee
Perry
Pike
Bolivar
George
Lowndes
Mississippi
Tippah
Rankin
Grenada
Pearl River
Lawrence
Wilkinson
Harrison
Oktibbeha
Monroe
Holmes
Jasper
Copiah
Yalobusha
Covington
Tishomingo
Kemper
Jackson
Tunica
Forrest
Jones
Carroll
Lafayette
Sharkey
Pontotoc
Scott
Union
Itawamba
Madison

-100%   -50%   0%   50%   100%   150%   200%

Chapter 11: Promoting Prosperity in Mississippi through Investing in Communities

The goal of this chapter is to study the competing model of economic development by investing in the quality of the community to attract people and impact employment through growth from within the community. Establishing a "growth from within" policy places a priority on growing and expanding those small businesses and entrepreneurs in the communities in which they began. This recruitment of people is both active and passive. Active recruitment involves marketing and other direct interactions that bring in tourists and residents to the community. Examples of active recruitment are a retirement attraction program, tourism marketing, and advertising the community in various publications. Passive recruitment is defined as making noticeable improvements to the quality of the community such as school ranking, local amenities such as retail shopping and restaurants, design and quality guidelines for construction, healthcare and increased affordable housing. We study the effects of passive recruiting by relating the growth in total employment to the local school ranking, the change in wages, the change in retail sales per capita, and the change in assessed property value. If passive recruiting is effective, then there would be some statistical relation to total employment.

Further, this model of economic development could promote prosperity in many more counties in Mississippi than large scale industrial recruitment where most counties find it difficult to compete. Also, the growth is driven by market forces to meet local business needs as they arise organically, without intervention through subsidies or other incentives. For many communities, such as in the Mississippi Delta region, growth from within is the only feasible path to economic success available. Because of the lack of infrastructure and shrinking workforce, areas like the Delta will have little chance at industrial recruitment. For example, having families grow marketable fruits and vegetables in small plots can add to the family income and give them a sustainable economic future. The expertise and ability to get their products to market are offerings that local, regional and state economic developers can deliver with very little cost.

Other areas are embracing a shift to growth from within. For example, Kansas City, MO has publicly announced that they will no longer incentivize large scale economic development projects. Instead they are offering individual entrepreneurs $50,000 and two years of free rent in a business incubator. The cost to the city is much lower. The Kauffman Foundation, located in Kansas City was instrumental with helping to shape this shift in economic development policy. Similarly, Pittsburgh, PA has elevated access to innovation and quality of place to the top of their current marketing points for economic development. Pittsburgh was known as a manufacturing and steel city for many decades. However, for the past dozen or so years, they have focused heavily on entrepreneurship and placemaking. The website www.pittsburghregion.org has placed the traditional assets of location, workforce and cost of doing business at the bottom of their list of business investment advantages.

Hypotheses and Data

We use total employment as a measure of prosperity. We investigate total employment to see if it is related to new business starts, local school ranking, the change in wages, the change in retail sales per capita, and the change in assessed property value all Mississippi counties with at least 5,000 in total employment from 2007-2016. Thus, our hypothesis is that investing in "growth from within" through schools, retail amenities, and increasing property values and wages impacts the change in total employment, and therefore promotes prosperity.

The data are from publicly available sources. Mississippi Departments of Revenue, Employment Security and Education have all provided the data that we will analyze in our study. School rankings, known as Accountability Results by the Mississippi Department of Education, follow Mississippi's grading system (A, B, C, D and F), but we use their numerical points assigned where higher points indicates a better performing school system. This system considers a variety of factors including students' performance on state tests, improvement from the previous year and whether or not high schoolers are graduating within four years. The aggregated information for all 82 counties and the State of Mississippi as a whole were gathered and analyzed, however the final sample includes 53 counties with at least two yearly observations that meet the 5,000 total employment threshold.[2] As shown in Figure 11.2, the trend in total employment is largely negative since 2008. And, the bulk of this fall in employment is due to a decline in manufacturing employment.

Figure 11.3 contains the descriptive statistics for the sample of Mississippi counties that have at least 5,000 total employees. Total employment ranges widely with a minimum of 5,000 (by design) and a maximum of over 139,000. Importantly, the change in total

Figure 11.2: Mississippi Total Employment 2000-2016

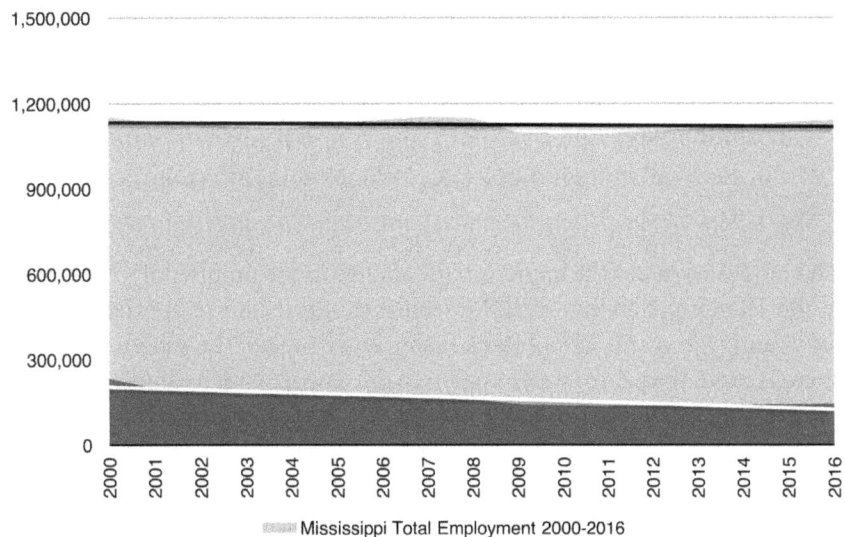

Mississippi Total Employment 2000-2016

Figure 11.3: Descriptive Statistics

Variable	Mean	Maximum	Minimum	Median	Std Dev
Total Employment (000's)	20.4875	139.9300	5.0000	11.4700	23.7295
Change in Total Employment	-0.0019	0.1443	-0.1249	-0.0007	0.0339
Service Employment (000's)	17.8981	134.5900	3.1300	9.6500	22.4855
Change in Service Employment	0.0012	0.1373	-0.1355	0.0017	0.0285
Change in Manufacturing Empl.	-0.0231	0.4479	-0.5490	-0.0140	0.1006
New Business Applications	0.1727	14.7143	-0.8818	0.0385	0.8608
Wages ($000's)	31.8834	48.0540	23.9170	31.1770	4.0897
Change in wages	0.0185	0.3138	-0.1943	0.0187	0.0274
Change in Sales per capita	0.0067	0.4709	-0.3257	0.0100	0.0685
Change in Property Assessments	0.0449	10.1664	-0.9002	0.0176	0.4556
School Ranking Points	567.8	694.5	464.0	565.5	57.77

employment is -0.19% and the change in manufacturing employment is -2.31%. Thus, the positive change in service employment, defined as total employment minus manufacturing employment, almost offsets the drop in manufacturing employment across the whole sample, but not quite. The average change in new business applications is over 17 percent, indicating lots of new businesses being created during the sample period.[3] The changes in wages, per capita retail sales, and assessed property values are all positive, and each show wide ranges of variation. Collectively, these statistics show that our sample is representative and varies widely across Mississippi counties, and that employment in Mississippi has declined over our sample period.

---

2   Only Attala, George, Wayne, and Winston counties are not in the sample every year.

3   Note that these business start statistics contain each application with the Secretary of State, thus a construction project that created 10 LLC's would be counted as 10 new businesses in the database. However, we believe this feature is repeated throughout the sample such that it averages out over time and should not cause any statistical issues.

Regression Model to Estimate Total Employment

To investigate whether total employment is related to livability factors in Mississippi counties with at least 5,000 in total employment we estimate the following model:

$$\Delta \text{TotalEmployment}_{i,t} = \alpha + \sum_{t=08}^{16} \pi_t Y_t + \beta_{i,t} \Delta \text{NewBusinessApplications} + \theta_{i,t} \text{SchoolRankingPoints} + \rho_{i,t} \Delta \text{Wages} + \mu_{i,t} \Delta \text{PerCapitaSales} + \gamma_{i,t} \Delta \text{AssessedValue} + \varepsilon_{i,t}$$

The model estimates the impact on the change in the number of total employees using economic variables at the Mississippi county level. New Business Applications are the number of new business applications for County i in year t. School Rank Points is the rank of the school system(s) in the county in 2016. When there is more than one school system in the district with a ranking, we average them together. Change in Wages is the change in the mean wage in the county for year t. Change in Sales per Capita is the change in per-capita sales for each county in year t. The Change in Assessed Value variable accounts for the changes in local market conditions for property, which has many determinants, but is largely a measure of the desirability to live in the area. All of these variables are used to estimate the relation between the local economic and community conditions and prosperity through total employment.

Our variables of interest as related to total employment are the changes in business starts, school ranking, and the changes in wages, per capita income, sales per capita, and assessed value. If adding new business increases total employment, then we would see a positive and significant coefficient on New Business Applications, all else equal. This variable is an indication of new businesses in the county, but does not account for businesses that exit or fail. The School Ranking Points variable is based on grades given by the Mississippi Department of Education and is an indication of the quality of schools in the system where more points indicate more favorably rated school systems. Thus, if the quality of schools is important to the change in total employment, then we would see a positive and significant sign for School Ranking Points. The Change in Wages, Change in Sales per capita, and Change in assessed value variables are our measures of quality of life in the county, with higher wages and higher retail sales per capita assumed to be positively associated with livability through purchasing power and purchasing options on a relative population basis, and assessed value an indication of desirability of property in the county. If quality of life and livability are important for promoting prosperity, we would see a positive relation between these variables and the change in total employment.

Figure 11.4 contains the results of the OLS regression model estimation with a dependent variable of the change in total employment in each Mississippi county with at least 5,000 in total employment.[4] The results indicate that the statistically significant factors in this model for the change in total employment in Mississippi counties are school ranking, the change in wages, and the change in retail sales per capita. These estimates indicate that being in a highly ranked school is important; a one standard deviation increase in school ranking (57.77 points) translates into about a 0.80% change in total employment in these Mississippi counties.[5] If a school system raised their ranking by 100 points, the change in employment would be 1.4%. Similarly, one standard deviation in wages is about 2.74%, thus a one-standard deviation increase in wages would increase employment by 0.57%. Additionally, a one standard deviation increase in retail sales per capita of 6.85% translates into about a 0.44% increase in the change in total employment.

---

4   For robustness, we also exclude Mississippi counties with less than 2,500 and the main results are similar.

5   We also estimate a model with the change in total employment, and separately change in wages as the dependent variables. Results indicate a strong positive relation between WAGECHG and EMPCHG showing that rising wages and increasing employment are statistically related in these data.

These calculations show the level of school ranking carry the greatest impact for a one standard deviation change.

Our findings support the hypothesis that the quality of life and community is an important factor in promoting prosperity through increased employment, at least for school ranking, and the change in sales per capita. Similarly, the change in wages is likewise a measure of the quality of life in a community, but it could also be caused by increased demand as total employment rises, thus we do not classify it as strictly a quality of life variable. In effect, these results indicate that employment increases in communities that have growing economic outcomes, although not necessarily through an increase in business starts. In other words, the lack of significance with new business applications indicates there is no relation between business starts and change in total employment. We conjecture that this measure of new business activity is too crude since it does not take into account the size or scope of the business, but rather treats all business starts as equal. Regardless, this coefficient is not significant, indicating no statistical relation with the change in employment for Mississippi counties in our sample.

Figure 11.4: Parameter Estimates for Dependent Variable Change in Total Employment by County

Variable	Parameter Estimate	t Value	Pr > |t|
Intercept	-0.0815	-6.30	<.0001
Y08	-0.0178	-3.20	0.0015
Y09	-0.0462	-8.19	<.0001
Y10	-0.0049	-0.85	0.3932
Y11	-0.0025	-0.45	0.6542
Y12	-0.0007	-0.13	0.8944
Y13	-0.0011	-0.20	0.8426
Y14	0.0088	1.59	0.1134
Y15	0.0058	1.04	0.2974
Y16	0.0118	2.10	0.0362
New Business Applications	-0.0002	-0.11	0.9108
School Ranking Points	0.00014	6.50	<.0001
Change in wages	0.2093	4.32	<.0001
Change in Sales per capita	0.0638	3.17	0.0016
Change in assessed value	0.0016	0.59	0.5567

Notes: The total number of counties and years is 505. The R^2 of the regression is 33.76%.

Conclusion and Policy Implications

Our anecdotal evidence as well as statistical analysis indicates that promoting prosperity through "growth from within" is a viable alternative to the traditional model of attracting large industrial companies. As shown, manufacturing employment has declined in Mississippi, despite attracting large employers during our sample period. While we do not compare the costs and benefits of incentivizing industrial firms to locate in Mississippi to our "growth from within" model directly, it is clear that creating livability and quality of place is related to more employment in a broad sample.

In particular, our results indicate that having higher ranked schools, larger changes in wages, and higher changes in per capita retail sales increase total employment. These results support our hypothesis of livability being related to promoting prosperity through more employment. We cannot directly link causality of our results to emphatically say that "if you build it they will come," but regardless of the causality of the growth in employment, having more livable communities reasonably creates places people want to both live and work, therefore, employment increases. We conjecture that these things quite likely happen at the same time, but it is clear that without quality of place that economic development does not appear to be working. Human nature tells us that people will work where they want to live. Current trends in millennial migration indicate that future generations will choose a location first and a career path second. This trend suggests that creating quality places will be the natural economic growth engine to promote prosperity for the next generation.

Our current economic development practices and expectations are over 70 years old. We are working hard to apply old solutions to new problems. This old formula appears to have declining success rates in the growth of Mississippi's economy. For policy, our suggestions are that legislators and government officials consider more investment in quality of place, which our analysis shows promotes prosperity as measured by larger increases in employment. We acknowledge that this is a change in focus for policy-makers. For example, the Mississippi Development Authority (MDA), the lead economic development organization in the state, spends a large proportion of its time and money working on industrial recruitment projects for Mississippi. They do have business retention and expansion, workforce and entrepreneurship in their agency, but these are not funded at the same level as industrial recruitment. If MDA inverted their approach to asset allocation, focusing more on the small and local businesses in Mississippi, and an emphasis on place making, then we might see a shift in the economically burdensome areas such as the Delta region. This policy reform would not be an overnight process. It will take a tremendous amount of collaboration and education to be accepted broadly. Quite likely, this sort of inversion would require large amounts of political capital and influence to convince policymakers that these efforts will yield better long term outcomes than the current approach.

Our findings are consistent with the free market of allocating resources within desirable markets and through entrepreneurship and organic growth. This fosters the creation livable communities by letting the marketplace dictate the growth. Statewide resources that have traditionally gone toward funding large deals could be re-directed to smaller and more numerous business ventures. This will have a cumulative impact on the state as a whole. The role of the economic developer would shift from being an external marketer to an internal agent for quality control at local, regional and state levels. Encouraging local growth with start-up companies, creating quality growth standards that supersede political terms and focusing on educational achievement at the local level would be the new role of economic development. Changing this dynamic would encourage a stronger free-market approach to economic development and give communities in Mississippi that are not competitive under the current practice to promote prosperity again in the future.

12

Local Governments Run Amok? A Guide for State Officials Considering Local Preemption

Michael D. Farren and Adam A. Millsap

12

Local Governments Run Amok? A Guide for State Officials Considering Local Preemption

Michael D. Farren and Adam A. Millsap

State governments often overrule local government ordinances. For example, Mississippi—along with Alabama, Louisiana, Tennessee, and fifteen other states—bars municipal governments from setting a minimum wage higher than the state's minimum. The act of overruling municipal law with state law is known as preemption, which is a legal doctrine asserting that state laws take precedence over local laws. The recent Mississippi laws preempting local control of minimum wages and Transportation Network Companies (TNCs) have reasserted the authority of state government to overrule local regulations. This raises the question: What circumstances should motivate the use of state authority to interfere with local rule-making?

This chapter provides a framework to guide state officials who are considering local preemption. We use this framework to analyze four issues that are relevant in Mississippi: 1. The sharing economy, including TNC regulations; 2. Labor market regulations, such as minimum wage laws; 3. Land use regulations; and 4. Tax and expenditure limits (TELs). We conclude that state preemption is warranted in situations where local governments enact non-general policies interfering with free exchange via price controls or similar restrictions.

To Preempt or Not to Preempt?

City officials tend to push back against preemption, arguing that those with local knowledge should determine local policy. This argument has some merit. Many advocates of free enterprise, such as Nobel Prize winning economist Friedrich Hayek, have also extolled the value of local knowledge.[1]

But a counter argument is that local policy makers and voters often fail to incorporate local knowledge into their decision making, implementing policies based on dubious economic reasoning. Furthermore, local influential special interest groups are often more interested in accomplishing their narrow goals rather than supporting broad economic growth. In order to appease them, local politicians—who are often focused on winning re-election—enact popular yet economically inefficient policies.

For example, the popular Fight for $15 campaign supports a $15 minimum wage in cities from San Francisco to Minneapolis despite the differences between local labor markets. Even economists who support higher minimum wages, such as Arindrajit Dube, caution that they should be based on local conditions, yet this is rarely acknowledged by sympathetic policymakers at the local level.[2] The result is ill-fitting policy that creates unintended consequences.[3]

Mississippi's preemption of local minimum wage laws and its more recent preemption of local ride-sharing ordinances, along with similar preemption in other states, raises the question of when state preemption of local authority is appropriate. In the next section, we explore the legality of state preemption.

State Sovereignty Over Local Government

In the United States, government generally operates at three levels: federal, state, and local. Each layer of government provides certain goods and services for its constituents, and most people believe that the different layers, while perhaps not completely separate, are largely distinct from one another. Using cake as metaphor, this depiction of government would take the form of a layer cake, with the federal layer at the top and the local layer at the bottom.

But in reality, the layers are not so well-defined. Both the federal and state government play some role in providing local goods and services. For example, Medicaid is largely a federally-funded program that is administered by the states (see Chapter 14). Federal and state governments also provide resources to local governments for K–12 schools, road construction and repair, police and fire provision, and parks and public housing. Instead of a layer cake with three distinct layers, government in the United States is better imagined as a marble cake in which the upper layers often overlap the lower layers.

More importantly, only the federal and state governments have governing authority according to the U.S. constitution, which is the supreme law of the land. Well-established legal precedents have declared local governments, whether they be counties, cities, villages, school districts, etc., to be creations of the state and ultimately subject to state control. This relationship is clearly exemplified in county governments, which were created for state government administrative purposes.[4] In short, local governments wield power only at the state's discretion and have no independent authority.

However, the administrative decentralization of state authority gives the *illusion* of local autonomy, stemming from local governments exercising rulemaking authority such as levying taxes and implement-

---

1 See Hayek (1945).
2 See Dube (2014) and Matthews (2013).
3 Refer to Chapter 3 for a detailed discussion of how seemingly good policies can lead to unintended, negative consequences.
4 See Marando and Reeves (1991).

ing economic regulations. Additionally, in many cases this quasi-independence is established by state legislation or by a state constitutional amendment.

While all local governments in all states are ultimately subservient to state law, states that follow "Dillon's Rule" adhere to a strict interpretation of state authority. Under Dillon's Rule local governments only have the powers expressly granted to them by the state. The map below shows which states follow Dillon's Rule.

Figure 12.1: Map of U.S. States Using Dillon's Rule

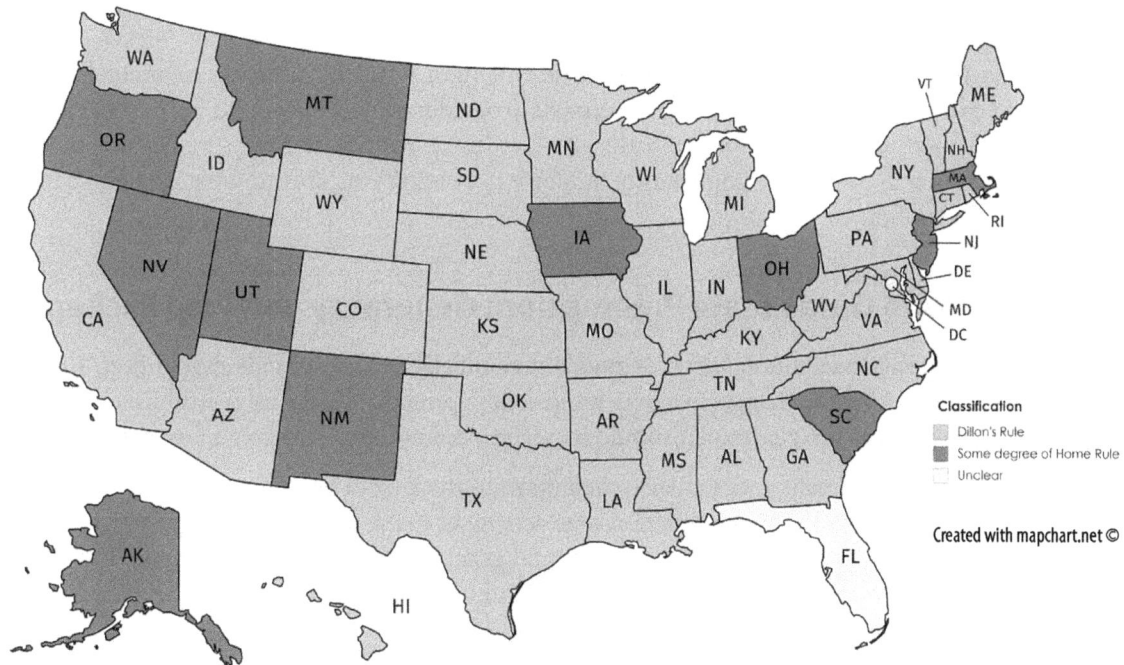

Source: Richardson, Gough, and Puentes, (2003)

The alternative to Dillon's Rule is a spectrum of policies combining the strict interpretation of state authority with various degrees of what is commonly called Home Rule. Home Rule grants local governments greater freedom to determine policy as long as local laws and regulations do not contradict state law. There is wide variability in how Home Rule is granted: Some states grant Home Rule to counties but not cities, others grant Home Rule to large cities but not small ones, as well as other arrangements.

Mississippi is typically categorized as a Dillon's Rule state, though the state legislature has granted municipal governments some degree of local discretion.[5] Relative to other states, however, Mississippi grants local governments little power to set policy.[6] As stated by Mills:

"While the 1985 passage of the "home rule" statute did away with the general legal principle that a specific grant of power was necessary for a municipality to take an action,

---

5   In 1985 the Mississippi Legislature granted municipalities limited home rule with the adoption of § 21-17-5 of the Mississippi Code of 1972. See Mills (2014).

6   See Richardson, Gough, and Puentes (2003).

it contained numerous exceptions as set out above. With regard to the levy of taxes, issuance of bonds, procedures for elections, change of municipal boundaries, change in the form of government, sale of alcoholic beverages, donations, or rent control, the rule remains the same. In each of these instances, state law must be followed."[7]

Furthermore, as is standard in states with even the most laissez-faire Home Rule, municipal ordinances in Mississippi must not clash with state law. In a 2010 ruling, the Mississippi Supreme Court stated that:

> "If a county or municipality passes an ordinance which stands in opposition to the law as pronounced by the legislature, the ordinance, to the extent that it contradicts state law, will be found void by this Court, as the laws of this state supersede any and all local ordinances which contradict legislative enactments."[8]

In practice, the difference between "Home Rule" and "Dillon's Rule" is often not clear cut. However, it is clear that Mississippi's state government ultimately decides which powers to grant local governments and can supersede local ordinances with state law. In the next section we discuss how the state should exercise such power. Most importantly, under what conditions and to what degree should it exercise local preemption?

Two Principles to Guide State Preemption: Generality and Free Exchange

When making decisions about local preemption, state officials in Mississippi should keep the principles of 'generality' and 'free exchange' firmly in mind. These principles serve as guardrails: if municipal policy bumps up against either guardrail it should be scrutinized and perhaps preempted by the state.

The first principle, "generality," is similar in definition to the rule of law—the same laws and regulations should apply to all persons engaged in the same activity or living under the same government. Any deviation from generality likely constitutes governmental granting of privilege to some people over others.[9] Such privileges often arise from lobbying by special interest groups for political favoritism.

While public condemnation is the common reaction to such lobbying, it's important for policymakers—as well as the public—to understand that seeming perversions of government authority are an inherent aspect of all forms of government. James Madison recognized this in Federalist No. 10 when he said that "the latent causes of faction (special interests groups) are thus sown in the nature of man" and that "the *causes* of faction cannot be removed [...] relief is only to be sought in the means of controlling its *effects*."[10]

In other words, it is precisely the unavoidable problem of special interest groups lobbying for privileges that requires government to put limiting structures on itself. Because municipal governments serve as local wardens of state authority—and because it can be easier for special interest groups to sway local policymakers[11]—it's appropriate for state government to limit the ways in which municipalities can grant privileges.

The argument in favor of restrictions on government-granted privilege can be made on the basis of equality and fairness, but such favoritism also harms economic growth, as described in Chapters 2 and 3. Giving some industries or businesses a competitive advantage in the marketplace through subsidies,

---

7   See Mills (2014).

8   Ryals v. Bd. of Sup'rs of Pike County, 48 So. 3d 449 (Miss. 2010) from Mills (2014, 48).

9   For a discussion of government-granted privilege, see Mitchell (2015).

10 See Hamilton, Jay, and Madison (2001).

11 See Farren (2017).

beneficial tax treatment, or regulations that raise their rivals' costs reduces customers' ability to decipher which companies serve their needs best.[12]

Under a system of free enterprise, competition to attract customers pushes businesses to provide the best value-for-cost product, and customers reward those companies with repeat business and word-of-mouth advertising. These incentives lead to long-run economic growth as companies constantly seek to find new ways to provide better products for lower cost. But government-granted privileges throw sand in the gears of this system because they protect businesses from competition, removing some of the focus to satisfy customers. As a result, regulations that violate generality decrease long-run economic growth.

The second guiding principle, "free exchange," emphasizes the importance of creating an environment that encourages people's natural inclination to "truck, barter, and exchange."[13] This includes developing effective contract law and providing public safety to support market transactions. However, this principle also means that governmental interference in individual market transactions should be minimized. The extent to which people can trade determines the degree of specialization in the economy, and greater specialization makes people more productive. Therefore, economic growth is directly tied to people's ability to freely exchange.

Economist and historian Deirdre McCloskey describes the amazing growth in living standards over the last 200 years as the result of "trade-based-betterment," emphasizing that both current and future generation's well-being is dependent on social and legal rules facilitating exchange.[14] Furthermore, the ability of entrepreneurs to experiment with new ideas in order to discover innovative ways to satisfy customers and solve social problems is critical for achieving the greatest possible growth, as discussed in Chapter 3.

Cities, which are simply clusters of people living and working in proximity, are the result of such specialization and trade and thus are the drivers of economic growth. However, when cities pass laws or regulations that inhibit free exchange, they limit the degree of economic growth that can occur by limiting the degree of specialization. In the following sections we discuss the ways that government policies can violate the principles of generality and free exchange and provide a framework public officials can use to avoid these problems.

Violations of Generality and Free Exchange

Violations of generality and free exchange can be grouped into three general types: barriers to entry, price controls, and business practice mandates. The same policy can fall into multiple categories, however, because some kinds of business practice mandates can create barriers to entry or price controls, and some price controls can create barriers to entry.

Barriers to entry limit who can offer goods and services to other people. A common example of a barrier to entry is Jackson, Mississippi's requirement that a taxi company obtain a Certificate of Public Necessity and Convenience (CPNC). CPNCs require new companies to demonstrate that there is unmet customer demand before they can legally start providing service. Furthermore, it allows existing companies to try to keep out new competition by testifying to regulators that they are providing sufficient service.[15]

Price controls are restrictions on the terms of exchange between customers and producers. They limit how much the producers of goods and services can charge, and how much customers are allowed to pay

---

12 See Chapters 5 and 6 for additional discussion of tax policy and "crony capitalism."
13 See Smith (1976).
14 See McCloskey (2006).
15 The harm caused by occupational licensing is further discussed in Chapter 9.

for those goods and services. Continuing the taxi example, a customer who is late to a job interview would likely be willing to pay a premium for priority service, but Jackson, like most cities, sets a maximum legal fare. This decreases the incentive to supply taxi service, meaning less service is available to those who value it the most. Similarly, price minimums prevent prices from falling *below* the mandate, limiting customer access to low-cost goods and services.

As described in Chapter 2, prices are important in a market economy since they reflect the relative scarcity of resources and incentivize entrepreneurs to alleviate such scarcity. For example, a high price of housing in one neighborhood relative to another sends a signal to developers that housing is relatively scarce in the high-price neighborhood and incentivizes developers to build there. Rent control, which is a type of price control, interferes with the proper functioning of the housing market and prevents resources, in this case building materials, from being used where they are valued the most, hindering economic growth.

Other policies create implicit price controls by mandating a certain quality or quantity of a good. For example, land-use regulations that mandate a minimum lot size increase the price of housing.[16]

Business practice mandates are restrictions on how, when, or where goods and services can be offered to customers. Common examples of such mandates are the regulations that many cities have regarding the color, quality, and age of taxicabs (and sometimes even the dress code of the driver!). In 2013, Washington, D.C. mandated that all taxicabs be painted in a new red and gray color scheme, costing upwards of $600 per vehicle. Regulations like these increase the cost of providing service, which can eliminate low-cost service to low-income neighborhoods. Similarly, mandated practices preclude entrepreneurs from experimenting with new products and services in the regulated area, reducing innovation and long-run economic growth.

Framework to Guide Policymakers in Preempting Local Authority

In order to maximize economic growth, and the higher quality of life that comes with it, state policymakers should consider preempting local policy in situations where it violates generality or free exchange. The framework discussed below (and summarized in Figure 12.2) can help guide officials' decisions on whether to preempt.

The first step is to start with a blank slate. State officials should explicitly approach the situation from the perspective of a blank slate to avoid status quo bias from influencing their thinking. This is important because the economy and society are constantly changing due to new entrepreneurial discoveries or shifting social preferences. Regulations are often an implicit attempt on the behalf of special interest groups to freeze the current state of the world in place, intrinsically limiting the potential for economic growth. Starting from a blank slate makes it more likely that state officials will consider solutions that are unlikely to be enacted at the local level due to the influence of local special interests.

The second step is to define the nature of the problem. State officials should explicitly identify what the local policy is trying to accomplish. Importantly, they should determine whether this goal lies within the purview of local government. If it does not, then there may be reason for the state to preempt the policy. Alternately, the problem might be better addressed by entrepreneurs because social problems often create profit opportunities for those who can solve them. Lastly, in some cases *ex post* solutions via the

---

16 See our case study on local housing regulations later in this chapter for a more detailed discussion on how regulations can create implicit price controls.

courts are a more effective and less intrusive way of addressing a situation that might or might not cause future problems.

Step three is to determine whether the policy violates generality or free exchange. State officials can use the litmus test of asking whether the policy imposes barriers to entry, affects prices via strict or implicit controls, or creates business practice mandates. However, local policies can violate these principles in other ways than these three main avenues, so state officials should be alert to any policy which appears to go outside the guardrails of generality and free exchange.

The final step is to decide to preempt or require revisions. State officials should preempt existing local policies or require them to be revised when they violate generality or free exchange. In cases where policies would inherently violate generality or free exchange, as in the case of strict price controls, state officials should proactively preempt them. For example, Mississippi precluded municipalities from implementing rent control in 1985. State officials should also consider proactive preemption when there is good historical evidence that local policy tends to violate these principles. Taxi regulations are an example of this because their history is rife with examples of regulatory capture and subsequent anticompetitive regulations.[17]

Importantly, any regulations at the local *or* state level should focus on the goal to be achieved rather than mandating the method to solve the problem. This allows for innovation in compliance and encourages entrepreneurs to find better and lower cost means of satisfying the regulation, leading to greater economic growth.

Figure 12.2: Framework to Guide Local Preemption

Step 1: Start with a Blank Slate	State officials should explicitly approach the situation from the perspective of a blank slate to avoid status quo bias from influencing their thinking. This method helps state officials to consider solutions that are unlikely to be enacted at the local level due to the influence of local special interests.
Step 2: Define the Nature of the Problem	State officials should explicitly identify what the local policy is trying to accomplish. Importantly, they should determine whether this goal lies within the purview of local government.
Step 3: Determine Whether the Policy Violates Generality or Free Exchange	State officials should consider preemption when the policy violates generality or free exchange. They can use the litmus test of asking whether the policy imposes barriers to entry, affects prices via strict or implicit controls, or creates business practice mandates.
Step 4: State Preemption or Required Revisions	State officials should preempt existing local policies or require them to be revised when they violate generality or free exchange. Importantly, any regulations left in place should focus on the goal to be achieved rather than mandating the method to solve the problem.

---

17 See Farren, Koopman, and Mitchell (2016).

Applying The Framework To Mississippi

There are multiple ways in which state officials can apply this framework. The process of reviewing local policy can take place in the legislature itself or by a separate oversight committee. Importantly, there should be a process through which citizens can submit policies for review. To encourage transparency and accountability, any recommendations for preemption should be published in an official report justifying the determination. Additionally, regardless of the process used, it should be codified and clearly communicated to local officials and voters.

Approaching local policies that violate generality and free exchange on a case-by-case basis is a lesser hurdle than full state preemption of all municipalities. It also encourages experimentation since local officials often have the best information on problems facing their communities and therefore can craft properly nuanced policy. A case-by-case approach also limits the unintended consequences that arise from one-size-fits-all state policies and respects those municipalities which have not violated the key principles.

In order to demonstrate usage of the framework, we apply it to four policies of interest to Mississippi lawmakers: transportation network company regulations, local labor market regulation, local land use regulation, and local taxes.

Transportation Network Company Regulations

Transportation Network Companies (TNCs), like Uber and Lyft, entered the mainstream transportation services market in 2012 and 2013. TNCs use smartphones to connect passengers with drivers and manage the exchange, reducing the transaction cost[18] in multiple ways, thereby vastly expanding the potential market for transportation services. The emergence of TNCs motivated taxi special interest groups around the United States to try to use local governmental authority to protect their industry from this new competition. In response, Uber and Lyft lobbied state legislators to preempt local regulation of TNCs.

Mississippi enacted HB 1381 into law in 2016, creating a statewide regulatory standard for TNCs and preempting municipalities from enacting their own taxes, licenses, and regulations on TNC operations. This overruled Jackson, Mississippi, which had just passed an ordinance licensing and regulating TNCs, and other cities which had disallowed operations.

Taxi regulations are commonly enacted at the municipal level and are quite literally the textbook definition of how anticompetitive regulations harm customers.[19] They are a perfect example of local policy historically creating barriers to entry (through limits on taxicab licenses), price controls (through maximum and minimum legal fares), and mandated business practices (requiring specific costly equipment and service standards). Because the transportation service industry is rife with regulatory capture that violates generality and free exchange, starting from a blank slate is the only way that policymakers can hope to enact appropriate reform.

The largest problem facing transportation service markets is the anonymity between the driver and passenger. This anonymity in the past has created a public safety problem due to drivers extorting higher fares from passengers or else using the seclusion of a taxi ride to assault them. Similarly, though less emphasized, drivers are at the mercy of criminally-minded passengers, with the result that taxi drivers face the highest on-the-job murder rate for any profession in the U.S.

---

18 Transaction costs are the sum of monetary and non-monetary costs that must be paid to enable a transaction to take place. Examples include credit card processing fees, uncertainty of payment or product quality, and the distance (whether the distance is the result of physical or social separation) between the buyer and seller.

19 See Kahn (1988) and Viscusi, Harrington, and Vernon (2005).

Laws created in the interest of public safety are an appropriate function of local government. However, many times special interest groups use the guise of public safety to argue for regulations that protect them from competition. For example, although mandating that taxicabs have bulletproof partitions between the driver and passenger would protect the driver from thieves, they are a costly piece of equipment that can create a barrier to entry for entrepreneurs. Furthermore, many other taxi regulations have explicitly limited entry by new drivers or companies, as well as creating price controls and business practice mandates that have nothing to do with public safety. In short, there are many clear violations of the principles of generality and free exchange.

Because most taxi regulations violate generality and free exchange, there is good reason to believe that municipal-level TNC regulations would have the same effect. Thus, Mississippi appears to have acted correctly in preempting local regulation of TNCs. In fact, the argument could be made that Mississippi did not go far enough and should have preempted local regulation of taxis and limousines as well, following Michigan's example.

Local Labor Market Regulations

Since 2012, there has been an accelerating trend in municipalities enacting local labor market regulations. By 2017, 39 different cities and counties had passed minimum wage laws. Similarly, by mid-2016, twenty cities had passed ordinances mandating that employers provide employees a minimum amount of paid leave.[20]

Simultaneously, states began explicitly preempting local governments' ability to set minimum wages or create other labor market regulations. By early 2017, at least 24 states had preempted the possibility of local minimum wages either by explicit legislation or implicitly via Dillon's Rule legal constraints. Seventeen states have passed legislation limiting how local governments can otherwise regulate the labor market, in particular by preempting municipal mandates on paid leave requirements. In addition, ten states have preempted local regulations on other kinds of employment benefits.[21] Mississippi proactively preempted local governments from implementing these labor market regulations in 2013 via HB 141.

It should be fairly easy for Mississippi policymakers to start from a blank slate on minimum wages because Mississippi is one of five states which does not have a state-specific minimum wage—the only minimum wage in effect is the federal minimum wage. Similarly, Mississippi does not have any state-level mandates requiring employers to offer paid leave as part of a worker's compensation.

The problem addressed by labor market regulations, as it relates to the core functions of government, is uncertain. Rather, labor market regulations appear to be an attempt by special interest groups to ensure a better quality of life for low-skilled workers. While this goal is laudable, minimum wage and paid leave mandates are a blunt instrument and are poorly targeted to achieve this end. More importantly, government interventions into the prices of goods and services inherently distort the economy, leading to less economic growth and therefore decreased quality of life for future generations.

Minimum wages are explicit price controls, while paid leave requirements are a business practice mandate that requires part of a worker's wage or salary be converted into guaranteed paid leave. As such, these labor market regulations violate free exchange, since they preclude some compensation options which both workers and employers would find agreeable. Therefore, restricting local governments' authority to affect the cost of employing a worker is an appropriate use of preemption.

---

20 Paid leave includes vacation, sick, family, and medical leave.
21 See DuPuis et al. (2017), Doroghazi (2017), and Center for Labor Research and Education (2017) for local and state ordinances.

Local Land Use Regulations

Mississippi grants local governments the power to construct a comprehensive plan to guide economic development and maintain some influence over an area's quality of life.[22] Such plans are implemented via zoning and other land-use regulations, most of which violate both generality and free exchange.

Zoning commonly divides an area into residential, commercial, and industrial uses, prohibiting the land from being used in ways that do not conform to its designated use. Zoning violates free exchange by preventing property owners from fully utilizing their land, thereby artificially decreasing its value.[23] For example, home-based businesses often violate zoning ordinances because they are located in areas zoned for residential but not commercial use. In such cases, zoning creates a barrier to entry that inhibits new economic activity.

Zoning ordinances also violate free exchange because they create implicit price controls. Common restrictions such as minimum lot sizes, maximum building heights, minimum parking requirements, and restrictions on the number of dwelling units combine to limit the supply of housing and lead to correspondingly higher prices.[24]

The restrictions created by zoning ordinances are generally recognized and local governments often attempt to maintain flexibility in order to deal with unforeseen circumstances. Rezoning, which amends the existing zoning ordinance to allow uses previously prohibited, and spot zoning, which rezones a single property, are two ways of modifying a zoning ordinance. Variances and special uses are additional ways of dealing with peculiarities and are determined on a case-by-case basis.

However, relying on case-by-case discretion, spot zoning, variances, and special uses can result in a government-granted privilege by violating generality. Because of the potential for abuse, Robert Barber, Sr., Hernando, Mississippi's city planner, argues that officials should explain the rationale behind any special-use or spot-zoning accommodation.[25] Making the rationale public and subject to scrutiny can reduce the danger of favoritism, but unfortunately it cannot eliminate it.

In his book *Zoning Rules!*, economist William Fischel persuasively argues that zoning is largely the result of a bottom-up process that starts because locals demand it.[26] Local residents, especially homeowners, want zoning because it protects their enjoyment of their neighborhoods and their home values. For example, in 2011 Jackson's city council changed an industrial zone to a mixed-used zone despite the current industrial tenant's concerns about the effects on its business. One council member who voted for the change cited the wishes of nearby residents who "don't want the kind of dust and noise that comes with expanded industrial use."[27]

Because only current residents—not future or potential residents—can vote in local elections, it is difficult to get local politicians to internalize the broader costs that zoning imposes on the state economy. Starting from a blank slate enables state officials to consider policies that local governments typically dismiss due to the influential interests of local homeowners/voters.

---

22 See Barber, Sr. (2014).
23 See Ihlanfeldt (2007).
24 Jackson's zoning ordinance includes many of these restrictions. Also see Ikeda and Washington (2015) and Zabel and Dalton (2011).
25 See Barber, Sr. (2014).
26 See Fischel (2015).
27 See Lynch (2011).

Zoning attempts to address the problem of urban disorder so that a city does not become an unpleasant place to live, but state officials need to balance the desire of residents who favor zoning as a means of controlling their environment with the widely held desire for a thriving state economy.

Since many zoning policies violate free exchange and generality via barriers to entry, implicit price controls, and case-by-case exceptions, further scrutiny from the state is warranted.

Local land-use regulations take a variety of forms and some provide more flexibility for residents and businesses than others. Therefore, the best preemption approach might be to overrule specific ordinances on a case-by-case basis. Also, once local government officials see examples of the kind of land use ordinances the state is preempting, they may proactively change their policies to be in compliance.

Municipal Tax and Expenditure Limits

State intervention should always be exercised with caution, and it should be done to promote rather than hinder economic freedom. So far, we have discussed examples where some degree of state preemption is warranted, but there are instances where local control is best. One such instance is local government spending and taxation.

Some states interfere with local government finances by imposing tax and expenditure limits, or TELs, on municipalities. Proposition 13 in California, which limits property tax rates and the growth of assessments, is one notable example.

Mississippi grants municipalities the power to raise revenue through various fees and an ad valorem tax on property. It also imposes a modest TEL on property taxes, which limits revenue growth to no more than 10% over prior year tax collections, with some exceptions.[28]

In terms of our framework, local property taxes usually do not violate free exchange or generality. As long as the tax is levied on all property of the same type in a consistent manner, it is sufficiently general. And as long as the tax is not so high as to essentially prohibit an activity, it does not violate free exchange.

TELs are also different than the previous case studies of justifiable preemption because taxes are largely the result of residents' demand for public goods and services, especially at the local level. Municipal taxes fund many public and quasi-public goods and services such as roads, police and fire protection, schools, and parks. The quantity and quality of these goods is a function of the preferences of the local population, and while no level of government can have complete information about the preferences of its constituents, local officials are likely better informed than state officials.

Since local knowledge is important for making effective decisions about the proper amount of public goods and services, local funding mechanisms should not be curtailed by state policymakers who lack such knowledge. Restrictions on both property tax rates and assessments are a common feature of local TELs, and they force communities that want to improve or expand public goods and services to employ alternative, often less efficient means of funding.

For example, there is evidence that local governments circumvent TEL prohibitions on property tax increases by raising revenue via higher user fees, short-term debt, or asset securitization.[29] Thus, instead of limiting taxes, TELs instead may simply change the revenue-raising mechanism. More importantly, this change likely degrades local economic efficiency.

---

28 See Smith (2014).
29 See Jimenez (2017).

In some cases, property taxes and other local taxes may have a negative effect on local economies—as discussed in Chapter 4—but this burden is largely shared by all members of the community. In contrast, minimum wage laws, land-use regulations, and restrictions on the sharing economy tend to disproportionately affect certain groups, such as less-skilled, lower-income people. If citizens want to restrict government spending, a locally imposed TEL is more appropriate than a state-level TEL since the local polity is collectively choosing to bind its own spending.

Conclusion

The growth in state preemption has made it a popular topic for discussion and research. Unlike the federalist relationship between the federal and state governments that is enshrined in the Constitution, local governments are creations of the state, meaning the state can preempt local authority. The degree to which state governments preempt local governments varies across states, and in this chapter we presented two guiding principles and a framework to help state officials decide when preemption is appropriate.

State officials should consider preemption when local rules violate generality or free exchange. Specifically, officials should preempt local policies that impose price controls, create barriers to entry, or mandate business practices, since these are common means of violating these principles. We have discussed three examples where preemption is appropriate from the perspective of our framework: TNC regulations, labor market regulations, and land-use regulations. Such policies violate one or both guiding principles and have harmful effects on economic growth because they inhibit economic activity and the efficient allocation of resources. Humans' natural inclination to trade means local government officials can best promote prosperity by providing public safety, maintaining local infrastructure, and enforcing contracts, rather than interfering with the local economy.

However, state-level preemption needs to be done prudently. Local knowledge is important for effective governance, and thus some authority is best left in the hands of local officials. We provided one such example regarding local tax and government expenditure limits (TELs).

Ultimately, the nature of state preemption is the prerogative of each state's officials and voters. We hope that the principles and framework presented in this chapter will serve as a useful guide for state officials considering preemption and for reevaluating prior preemption.

References

Barber, Sr., Robert L. 2014. Planning, Zoning, and Subdivision Control, Chapter 8 in Sumner Davis and Janet P. Baird (eds.), *Municipal Government in Mississippi*, 5th ed. Mississippi State University, Mississippi: Center for Government & Community Development, Mississippi State University Extension Service: 127–138.

Center for Labor Research and Education. 2017. *Inventory of US City and County Minimum Wage Ordinances*. Center for Labor Research and Education, UC Berkeley Labor Center, Berkeley, CA. Online: http://laborcenter.berkeley.edu/minimum-wage-living-wage-resources/inventory-of-us-city-and-county-minimum-wage-ordinances/ (cited: May 8, 2017).

Doroghazi, Lauren. 2017. Heat Between Cities and States Rises as Local Preemption Continues. *MultiState*. 18 April. Online: https://www.multistate.us/blog/heat-between-cities-and-states-rises-as-local-preemption-continues (cited: August 17, 2017).

Dube, Arindrajit. 2014. Proposal 13: Designing Thoughtful Minimum Wage Policy at the State and Local Levels, in *Policies to Address Poverty in America*. Brookings Institution, Washington, D.C.

DuPuis, Nicole, Trevor Langan, Christiana McFarland, Angelina Panettieri, and Brooks Rainwater. 2017. *City Rights in an Era of Preemption: A State-by-State Analysis*. National League of Cities, Center for City Solutions, Washington, D.C.

Farren, Michael D. 2017. Nirvana's Nightwatchman: A Response to Adam Thierer, in *Capitol Hill, State House, or City Hall: Debating the Location of Political Power and Decision-Making*. Mercatus Center at George Mason University, Arlington, VA.

Farren, Michael D., Christopher Koopman, and Matthew D. Mitchell. 2016. *Rethinking Taxi Regulations: The Case for Fundamental Reform*. Mercatus Research. Mercatus Center at George Mason University, Arlington, VA.

Fischel, William A. 2015. *Zoning Rules!: The Economics of Land Use Regulation*. Cambridge, MA: Lincoln Institute of Land Policy.

Hamilton, Alexander, John Jay, and James Madison. 2001 [1818]. *The Federalist*. Edited by George W. Carey and James McClellan. Gideon ed. Indianapolis: Liberty Fund.

Hayek, F. A. 1945. The Use of Knowledge in Society. *The American Economic Review* 35(4): 519–530.

Ihlanfeldt, Keith R. 2007. The Effect of Land Use Regulation on Housing and Land Prices. *Journal of Urban Economics* 61(3): 420–435.

Ikeda, Sanford, and Emily Washington. 2015. *How Land-Use Regulation Undermines Affordable Housing*. Mercatus Research. Mercatus Center at George Mason University, Arlington, VA.

Jimenez, Benedict S. 2017. Institutional Constraints, Rule-Following, and Circumvention: Tax and Expenditure Limits and the Choice of Fiscal Tools During a Budget Crisis. *Public Budgeting & Finance* 37(2): 5–34.

Kahn, Alfred E. 1988. *The Economics of Regulation: Principles and Institutions*. Cambridge, MA: MIT Press.

Lynch, Adam. 2011. Council Battles Over Zoning. *Jackson Free Press*. 17 May.

Marando, Vincent L., and Mavis Mann Reeves. 1991. Counties As Local Governments: Research Issues and Questions. *Journal of Urban Affairs* 13(1): 45–53.

Matthews, Dylan. 2013. "A $15 Minimum Wage Is a Terrible Idea." *Washington Post*, June 22, sec. Wonkblog. https://www.washingtonpost.com/news/wonk/wp/2013/06/22/a-15-minimum-wage-is-a-terrible-idea/.

McCloskey, Deirdre N. 2006. *The Bourgeois Virtues: Ethics for an Age of Commerce*. Chicago: University of Chicago Press.

Mills, Jerry L. 2014. The Nature of the Municipal Corporation, Chapter 5 in Sumner Davis and Janet P. Baird (eds.), *Municipal Government in Mississippi*, 5th ed. Mississippi State University, Mississippi: Center for Government & Community Development, Mississippi State University Extension Service: 43–96.

Mitchell, Matthew D. 2015. *The Pathology of Privilege: The Economic Consequences of Government Favoritism*. 2nd ed. Mercatus Center at George Mason University, Arlington, VA.

Richardson, Jesse J., Meghan Zimmerman Gough, and Robert Puentes. 2003. *Is Home Rule the Answer?: Clarifying the Influence of Dillon's Rule on Growth Management*. Center on Urban and Metropolitan Policy, Brookings Institution, Washington, D.C.

Smith, Adam. 1976 [1776]. *An Inquiry into the Nature and Causes of the Wealth of Nations*. Chicago: University of Chicago Press.

Smith, Edward W. 2014. Financial Administration, Chapter 9 in Sumner Davis and Janet P. Baird (eds.), *Municipal Government in Mississippi*, 5th ed. Mississippi State University, Mississippi: Center for Government & Community Development, Mississippi State University Extension Service: 139–151.

Viscusi, W. Kip, Joseph Emmett Harrington, and John M. Vernon. 2005. *Economics of Regulation and Antitrust*. 4th ed. Cambridge, MA: MIT Press.

Zabel, Jeffrey, and Maurice Dalton. 2011. The Impact of Minimum Lot Size Regulations on House Prices in Eastern Massachusetts. *Regional Science and Urban Economics* 41(6): 571–83.

School Choice:
How To Unleash
The Market
In Education

Brett Kittredge

13

School Choice: How To Unleash The Market In Education

Brett Kittredge

More than six decades ago, Nobel-prize winning economist Milton Friedman first proposed the idea of giving parents the opportunity to use the public funds associated with their child's education to pay for private school, if they desired.[1] As he stated, "The way to bring back learning into the classroom; the way to make sure that schools are responsive to the needs of the children they have in their classroom is to give parents more power and more control over their own child's schooling."[2] Friedman's solution? The simple, yet life-altering voucher plan that would do just that.

It would take more than three decades before this idea became law anywhere in the United States[3], but Friedman believed that by providing options to parents for the first time, all schools would now be competing on the same level, and district schools would be incentivized to increase student performance to ensure parents remain enrolled in their schools. For the first time, if parents were not happy, they could go somewhere else.

---

1   See, Friedman (1955).

2   See, Friedman (1980).

3   The Milwaukee Parental Choice Program was enacted and launched in 1990 is considered the nation's first modern private school choice program. It provides vouchers to low-income Milwaukee students.

Mississippi should follow the model put forth by Friedman over 60 years ago and open district schools to competition by empowering parents to direct the funding of their child's education to the setting that they believe is right for their child, whether that is public, private, charter, home school, or some combination of various educational services.

Choice is A Daily Part of American Lives

Parents make countless choices every day. If a parent is not happy with his or her child's pediatrician, he or she can look elsewhere. This remains as true for patients who pay through a government funded program such as Medicaid or the state Children's Health Insurance Program (CHIP). Once again, this option of choice applies to families receiving government assistance via the Supplemental Nutrition Assistance Program (SNAP), more commonly known as food stamps, or the Temporary Assistance for Needy Families (TANF) program.

In these two very important areas that will impact a child's health and well-being, the government has made the decision that families, even those receiving government assistance, can make their own choices for their own children. Not only that, it is then up to parents to decide if those choices are working out for their family with the freedom to shop around if they are displeased. Because doctors and grocery stores know families have options and are making these choices of their own free will, they must be responsive to families or risk losing their money and patronage. If one grocery store does not provide a family with the food options their child needs, they can go to the next grocery store. There are no district lines. There are no bureaucrats who need to approve your switch.

We generally love having choices, even if it is difficult to decide between more than 50 different types of breakfast cereal. Markets enable individuals to have choices, and through choice individuals are able to improve their lives as they see fit, as discussed in Chapters 2 and 3.

But the one area of our lives where a government monopoly exists with rare opportunities to choose differently is education in the United States. For more than a century, most children have attended an assigned district school based on two factors that have little to do with ensuring a child receives the education he or she needs to be successful in their career and life.

For one, children are assigned a school based on the location of their parent's home. In most instances, a five-digit zip code that a child will never choose will be the determining factor in the quality of education a child receives. Additionally, children are assigned to a grade based on the year they were born – a practice grounded in the belief that all students of the same age progress at roughly the same pace. This model is designed for some imaginary "median child," who holds high-achieving students back while leaving students who are struggling behind.

Despite the noble efforts of Milton Friedman starting in the 1950s to education reformers across the country today, America has stubbornly refused to allow citizens to choose when it comes to education

Learning From Other Countries

More than 25 years ago, another nation was dealing with failing district schools and looking for solutions to improve academic outcomes. Parents in Sweden were unhappy and concerned about what the poor academic performances might mean for the nation's future. So Sweden took decisive action by adopting a universal voucher program in 1992. Under this program, every student receives a voucher for a district school or private school, including religious schools and for-profit private schools, whichever the parents choose:

> Independent schools, like the public schools, get a voucher payment for each child. They compete vigorously with one other because the money follows the child to the school of his or her choice. Schools must satisfy their customers, or lose them.[4]

As a result, Swedes today enjoy a market-based approach to education where families are free to choose the school they like best. In regard to education, a family living in Sweden has more freedoms than a family living in the United States.

Not surprisingly, this program has resulted in a high level of satisfaction among parents and children. More than 4,500 miles away in Eastern Asia, South Korea also stands out as a model for a high-tech, free market approach to education. Private after-school tutoring academies called "Hagwons" are a $17 billion market that have made teachers millionaires and turned the academic performance of the country around:

> Hagwons, in this sense, are like professional sports teams, constantly on the prowl for top tutoring talent. The more highly-regarded the tutor – whose reputation is linked to how his or her students perform on standardized tests and whether they are accepted into top colleges – the more the hagwon can charge. Moreover, since students sign up for specific tutors, the better a tutor's reputation, the more money that tutor makes.[5]

South Korea has adopted a model that rewards top-performing tutors with a limitless salary, capped only by their abilities. South Korea has now gone from a country that was mostly illiterate to one that ranks second on the Programme for International Student Assessment, or PISA, a global test of academic excellence. Moreover, the nation's high school graduation rate stands at 93 percent, far outpacing both Mississippi and the United States.

From a Scandinavian country in Northern Europe, to the East Asian country of South Korea, there are unique examples of market-based education that are providing options to families, letting schools innovate and compete, and helping to improve academic outcomes for students- and countries.

The State of Education

Every nine seconds a student in America drops out of school, often rendering that young adult unemployable and relegating him or her to a life with few opportunities and necessary skills.[6] This has a real cost not just for one individual, but for his or her family and every taxpayer in the country.

Consider this: High school dropouts are nearly three times more likely to be unemployed than college graduates. Additionally, among those who are employed, they will earn, on average, about $8,000 a year less than high school graduates and $26,500 less than college graduates.[7]

Additionally, two-thirds of the prison population in state, local, and federal prisons are made up of high school dropouts. The nation could save as much as $18.5 billion in annual crime-related costs if the high school male graduation rate increased by just five percent. If the number of dropouts was cut in half, the nation could save $7.3 billion annually in Medicaid savings, $12 billion in heart disease-related sav-

---

4   See, Butler (2009).
5   See, Crotty (2013).
6   See, Lehr (2004).
7   See, Alliance For Excellent Education (2014).

ings, $11.9 billion in obesity-related savings, $6.4 billion in alcoholism-related savings, and $8.9 billion in smoking-related savings.

On the other hand, increasing the graduation rate to 90 percent for one year would create more than 65,000 new jobs and boost the economy by nearly $11 billion. And the graduation rate has been increasing over the past several years. Both Mississippi and the United States saw record high four-year graduation rates for the 2014-2015 school year of 78 and 83 percent, respectively. [8]

But what does this mean? More people are graduating from high school, but is the United States lowering the bar rather than improving academic performance? The Organization for Economic Co-Operation and Development recently reported that American students ranked 25th out of 72 countries when tested on topics in science.[9] A Pew Research study found that American students ranked 38th out of 71 countries when tested in math, reading, and science.[10]

The National Assessment of Educational Progress, or NAEP, which bills itself as the nation's report card, found that only 40 percent of fourth-graders, 33 percent of eighth-graders, and 25 percent of 12th-graders are "proficient" or "advanced" in math.[11]

Mississippi has seen some recent progress as it was the only state in the nation to show significant increases in both 4th grade math and reading in 2015 on the NAEP, which arguably offers the best apples-to-apples comparison for student performance across the country. However, Mississippi still generally falls among the bottom five states in all measures as the state performed significantly lower than the National public average in 4th and 8th grade math and science.

In fact, *Education Week's* Quality Counts report rated Mississippi as having the worst education system in the country, ranking it 51st in educational quality in 2014; even putting Washington, D.C. ahead of the Magnolia State.[12] It is clear that something is not working and dramatic improvements need to be made. Indeed, the United States has much work to do to catch up with the rest of the world, and Mississippi has much work to do to catch up with the United States.

Is Money The Issue?

When the debate about education woes arises, a large contingent is guaranteed to make one, popular argument: District schools need more money. Many claim that lack of funding is the root of all problems and if schools had more money the results would follow. Yet Mississippi and the United States have been throwing more money at the problem for more than four decades.

In Mississippi, more than 50 cents for every dollar collected in the state's general fund is spent on public education.[13] In 2015, the state spent over $9,700 per student when including state, local, and federal dollars. This is an uptick from around $8,000 just a few years prior and is part of a larger trend. Adjusted for inflation, spending on education in Mississippi has increased by 54 percent since 1992. This large increase occurred while student enrollment decreased by 3 percent and teacher salaries increased by only 2 percent.

---

8   See, National Center for Education Statistics (2017).

9   See, Hunt (2016).

10 See, Desilver (2017).

11 See, The Nation's Report Card (2015).

12 See, Education Week (2014).

13 See, Legislative Budget Office (2016).

Similar increases have occurred nationwide. Going back to 1970, inflation-adjusted spending on education has increased by 192 percent. However, the scores for 17-year-olds on the Long-Term Trend NAEP Assessments have remained flat.[14] A 2016 report from the United States Department of Education showed that a School Improvement Grants (SIG) program over the past decade pumped $7 billion into education with zero impact on student achievement.

Designed to help failing schools, the SIG provided no academic gains for the students it was intended to help, and failing schools that received multi-year grants ended with results that were no better than similar schools that did not participate in the program.[15] Only the federal government can spend $7 billion with nothing to show for their effort. The country is spending considerably more while showing little in the way of academic progress.

The Best Schools Are Often Off Limits

This, however, does not mean that no child is receiving a high quality education in a district school in Mississippi, or in the United States. Indeed, there are district schools throughout the country that rival the academic output of any in the world. Likewise, Mississippi has a share of district schools that regularly produce high ACT scores and graduation rates, a healthy number of national merit finalists, and generally do a good job at preparing their students for success in college and life.

Madison Central High School, in Madison, Mississippi, is one of those schools. Families are flocking to Madison. Over the past ten years, the city's population has increased by about 25 percent while the population for the state of Mississippi has been stagnant, and they are moving for good reason. In 2016, Madison Central had an average ACT score of 22.4, a full four points higher than the state average and almost two points above the national average.[16]

However, the city of Madison, like many other neighborhoods with highly successful district schools in the United States, has a high bar for access due to a cost of living that makes these desirable neighborhoods unattainable for many. Yes, these schools are "public" meaning a family does not pay tuition as they would at a private school. However, they pay in other ways, such as such as higher home costs and property taxes. Since students are assigned schools based on district lines, only those who live within the coveted districts have access.

If a family cannot afford to live in Madison, they may choose to live in nearby Ridgeland. Unfortunately, Ridgeland High School's ACT scores are three points less, on average, than those of Madison Central and their graduation rate trails Madison Central by almost 13 points. If that family is not in Ridgeland, they may be in Canton, another option just north of Madison. The graduation rate of Canton High School was a tragic 52 percent in 2015 and their average ACT score is a little over 14.

Only 18 miles separates Canton High School from Madison Central High. Just four miles separates Ridgeland High School and Madison Central High School. However, a student's education achievement will be radically different depending on which side of the line he or she lives.

The story in Madison County is not different than many other places in Mississippi or around the nation. High-performing free, district schools are available, but only for families who can afford to purchase real estate within the district lines. As education quality rises, so does demand to move into the right

14 See, Burke (2016).

15 See, Smarick (2017).

16 See, Madison County Business League (2017).

neighborhood, which increases housing costs. The estimated home value in Madison is $238,000 compared to $177,000 in Ridgeland and $125,000 in Canton. Additionally, just six percent of Madison residents rent compared to 52 percent in Ridgeland and 37 percent in Canton. Housing costs are an indirect way of paying for higher quality education. The arbitrary lines that destine some children to success and others to failure serve as an invisible, but very real, wall between a good education and a poor education.

What Options Are Currently Available

If a family in the United States is not satisfied with their assigned district school, they do have options besides moving to a different school district, but these options are not available to everyone or even most. These options include public charter schools, magnet schools, private schools, and homeschooling.

Charter schools are public schools that receive government funding but are given the flexibility to innovate while being held to a high academic standard. Like traditional district schools, they are open to all children (though that is often limited based on capacity and district lines), they do not charge tuition, and they do not have special entrance requirements.

Charter schools are approved by an authorizing entity, which in some instances may be the local school district, and are run by either non-profit or for-profit entities.[17] Each charter school has a "charter" that can be revoked by the authorizer after a certain period of time if that school is not producing the academic outcomes agreed upon. The authorizing board provides one level of accountability. Parents provide additional accountability. No family is assigned to a charter school; rather families must choose to enroll their children, or "opt-in," and they can leave at any time.

Charter schools are relatively new in the United States. The first charter law passed in Minnesota in 1991 and City Academy in St. Paul, Minnesota became the nation's first charter school to open its doors the following year. After the first school, the charter school movement soon began to spread. Numerous states quickly followed Minnesota's lead and by 2016, 44 states including Mississippi had approved charter schools on some level.

For the 2016-2017 school year, more than 6,900 charter schools are serving an estimated 3.1 million students. In a ten-year period, enrollment in charters has tripled from 1.2 million since the 2006-2007 school year.[18] Figure 13.1 illustrates this trend. The current numbers represent about 6 percent of total public school enrollment today.

In many urban areas that have long suffered from having the worst district schools in the country, the charter movement has flourished. During the 2016-2017 school year, 17 districts across the country had 30 percent or more of "enrollment share," the percentage of public school students attending a charter school," with New Orleans being the nation's first nearly all-charter district. Figure 13.2 list these 17 districts along with their share of enrollment.

However, charter schools are not readily available to every family who may wish to enroll their child. This may be due to either new laws, restrictive laws, or lack of school options and availability. That is certainly the case in Mississippi where the school districts in which a charter school can be located and the number of charter schools that can be authorized each year is limited.

---

17 In Mississippi, charter school operators must be non-profit.

18 See, National Alliance For Public Charter Schools (2017).

Figure 13.1: Charter school enrollment trends from 2006 through 2017

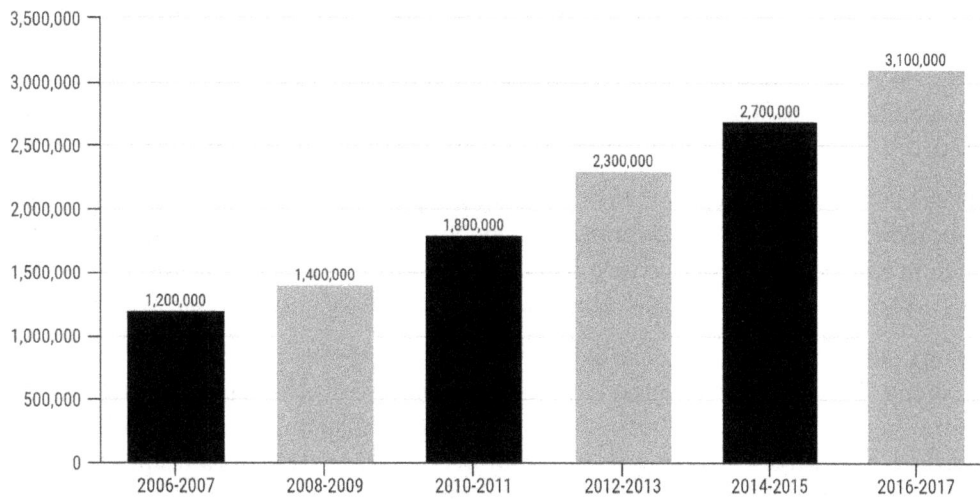

Source: National Alliance for Public Charter Schools

Another option is magnet schools. Magnet schools are public schools run by the local school district, usually specializing in a field not found in a traditional district school. These schools are usually among the highest performing locally and nationally, but in many cases they are select admission public schools. This means, as opposed to charter schools (or district schools), a student needs to test-in to be admitted.

Figure 13.2: School Districts with Large Charter School Enrollment Share

School District	State	Charter School Enrollment Share
New Orleans	LA	92%
Detroit	MI	53%
Flint	MI	53%
District of Columbia	DC	45%
Gary	IN	43%
Kansas City	MO	40%
Camden	NJ	34%
Philadelphia	PA	32%
Indianapolis	IN	31%
Dayton	OH	31%
Cleveland	OH	31%
Grand Rapids	MI	31%
Victory Valley Union	CA	31%
San Antonio	TX	30%
Natomas Unified	CA	30%
Newark	NJ	30%
St. Louis	MO	30%

During the 2010-2011 school year, there were about 3,000 magnet schools in the United States, including 20 in Mississippi.[19] While magnet schools are an option for parents, they are run by a local school district and therefore do not apply any pressure on a school district to improve academic outcomes for their other students as there is no risk of lost revenue.

A third option is private schools, or non-public schools, which are privately funded schools that operate independently of the government. Private schools are funded by tuition and fees a child pays to attend the school, as well as private financial support. During the 2013-2014 school year, there were more

---

19 See, National Center for Education Statistics (2012).

than 33,000 private schools in the country serving over 5.3 million students.[20] This is a decline from 6.3 million students in 2001, and estimates show enrollment is projected to decrease to 5.1 million by 2015.

The decline in private school enrollment is due to, in some part, competition from free charter schools, particularly in urban areas where charters are at their strongest. This has been particularly true for Catholic schools as their share of the private school market declined from 54.5 percent in 1989 to 41.3 percent in 2011.

Mississippi had 177 private schools in operation during the 2013-2014 school year. While there are instances of private schools in Mississippi that are donor funded and provide scholarships to every student, the tuition and fees necessary to run a school, which averages around $5,300 per student but can reach $10,000-$15,000 at certain schools, often make private school cost prohibitive for many families.

Educating a child at home, either done by the parent or as part of a local co-op, is another educational option for parents. However, participation is also limited because of the costs associated with providing the education, since one parent will likely stay home.[21] Approximately 1.8 million students were home-schooled in the United States in 2012, an increase from 850,000 in 1999. As a result, the percentage of students who are homeschooled makes up 3.4 percent of school-age children across the nation.[22]

All of these choices in education provide options for some, but for the most part, they do not shake the market share of enrollment enjoyed by district schools. Charter schools have been successful in doing so in some cities, but even their impact is limited and localized. Private school and homeschooling, because of the costs associated with each, are also unable to match the market share of district schools, and therefore district schools receive little market pressure.

As a result, district schools have been able to enjoy an unparalleled government monopoly and have not had to improve their academic performances to please their consumers: parents.

What A Market Based Education System Would Look Like

Putting parents firmly in control of their child's education and forcing all education sectors to compete for students will help improve and unleash the academic potential of American students.

There is no perfect system that has ever been designed that will always produce high quality results. Every child is different and with different needs comes the necessity to educate children in their unique learning style. The goal should not be a top-down approach that dictates one education model, but one that provides incentives to meet an individual's learning needs where schools are directly accountable to parents.

What programs might be shaped to provide universal school choice and options for every child? The most common type of school choice programs include vouchers, education savings accounts, and tax credit scholarships.

Vouchers direct money from the state to a private school of the parent's choice. There are currently 26 voucher programs available nationwide in 16 states, including two small programs in Mississippi for students with dyslexia and speech language therapy needs.[23] The programs in Mississippi mirror those

---

20 See, National Center for Education Statistics (2017).

21 There have been several articles written about parents who work full-time and homeschool their child, but there is no data to determine just how many parents are doing this. See, for example, Laura Vanderkam, "How These Parents Work And Homeschool Too," Fast Company, January 2016, https://www.fastcompany.com/3055528/how-these-parents-work-and-homeschool-too

22 See, National Center for Education Statistics (2016).

of many other states in that they are limited in reach and eligibility. Just two voucher programs, the John McKay Scholarship for Students with Disabilities in Florida and the Indiana Choice Scholarship Program, have more than 30,000 students enrolled.

Education Savings Accounts, or ESA's, have been called vouchers 2.0 or the new frontier in education choice. Similar to vouchers, ESA's allow families to utilize public education dollars to pay for the education they determine is best for their child. However, the funds flow directly from the state to the parent, rather than the school. The parent can then decide how those funds are spent from an array of educational options including not just private school tuition, but also tutoring, therapy, textbooks, online curriculum, transportation, etc. Mississippi passed the nation's third ESA in 2015 for students with special needs. Funding for the program has been limited to 425 students, resulting in a waiting list for the program during the 2016-2017 school year.

Tax credit scholarships allow individuals and corporations to make donations to a scholarship granting organization that then provides private school scholarships. Donors then receive up to a dollar-for-dollar tax credit on their state income tax. There are currently 21 tax credit scholarship programs available in 17 states, but not Mississippi. This includes one of the nation's largest single school choice programs, the Florida Tax Credit Scholarship Program, which has approximately 100,000 students participating.

Regardless of the specific type of program, there are certain parameters that need to be in place if a program is going to be universal, have the potential to reshape the education system, and offer meaningful change. These include broad eligibility standards, limited regulations, and equal funding.

A school choice program needs a critical mass of potential students to pave the way for new private schools and education providers and to have a true impact on the broader education system. The goal should be universal, or near universal, eligibility.[24] Too often these programs are limited to certain demographics, such as students with special needs, students in failing schools, or low-income students. This is what Mississippi has done with both public charter schools and private school choice programs. It is certainly a laudable goal to provide these populations who for too long have been left behind with new education options, but limiting the populations who are eligible in any regard will likely not cause the market to expand.

School choice programs should let private schools maintain their autonomy and let parents judge the performance of the school they choose. When school choice programs place burdensome regulations on private schools, two things generally happen: The best schools choose not to participate and families are left to choose among low-performing schools that are simply looking for new revenue

This is exactly what happened in Louisiana where, even though it was well-intentioned, their voucher program required all participating private schools to alter their admissions process, accept the scholarship as payment in full, administer state tests, and provide mountains of paperwork to the state. The schools that were the most successful passed on the program because they did not need it to survive. As a result, parents' choices were severely diminished and it became the first private school choice program where students' academic outcomes decreased after entering a private school. However, by the third year the negative impact of the program has been removed.

Funding for a school choice program should mirror what the state is already paying for education. For example, New Hampshire has a tax credit scholarship program which is light on regulations and even

---

23 See, EdChoice (2017).

24 For funding purposes, states often limit school choice programs to only students who are currently enrolled in a district or charter school. This will ensure a program does not have a negative "fiscal note."

allows homeschool families to participate, but the maximum scholarship amount is just $2,655, much less than the average cost of tuition to a private school. As a result, just 178 students participated in the 2015-2016 school year. In New Hampshire and elsewhere, too often school choice programs offer scholarship amounts that are just a fraction of what is spent in district schools, which prevents many students from being able to participate.

What Options Are Currently Available In Mississippi?

Mississippi is relatively new to the school choice arena, passing the state's first private school choice program in 2012 and authorizing charter schools for the first time in 2013. For the 2016-2017 school year, 1,125 Mississippi students participated in a school choice program out of more than 490,000 students enrolled in a district school.[25] This is a modest number, far behind many states, but it is a sharp increase from just 32 students in the 2013-2014 school year.[26] (See Figure 13.3.)

Mississippi's school choice programs take several forms. Mississippi had three charter school open in the 2016-2017 school year, serving 528 students in the city of Jackson. Mississippi was one of the last states to join the charter school movement. The state's first charter schools opened for the 2015-2016 school year.

The current law created a state authorizing board who is the sole authorizer of charter schools in the state. If a charter wishes to open in a school district rated "A," "B," or "C," they first need to get approval from the local school board. That has yet to occur, and the focus has instead been on failing school districts. Students who wish to attend a charter school

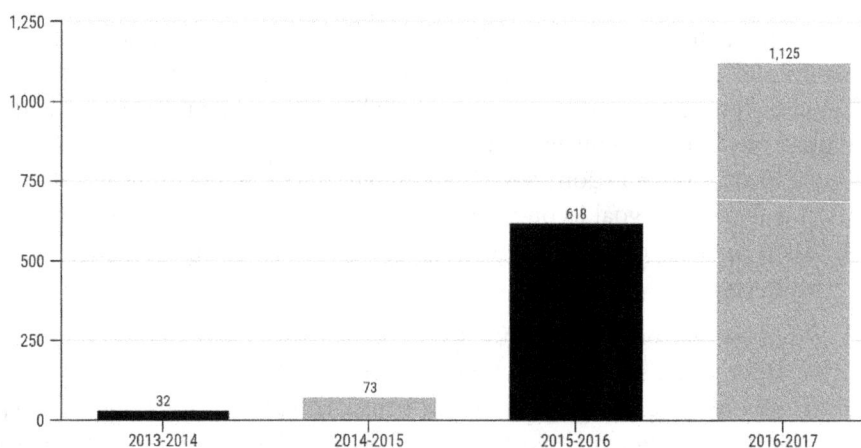

Figure 13.3: School choice enrollment in Mississippi

Source: Mississippi Dept. of Education

must either reside in the school district where the charter is opening, or they can cross district lines if they attend a school district rated "C," "D," or "F."

Mississippi's first private school choice program was designed exclusively for students with dyslexia, which was the only program of its kind in the nation. This program has been serving students since the 2012-2013 school year. For the 2016-2017 school year, 159 students participated in the program. Every eligible student receives a scholarship equal to the base student cost calculated through the state's funding formula, the Mississippi Adequate Education Program (MAEP). While this program has steadily grown, it

---

25 This number is based off enrollment in Mississippi's charter schools and three private school choice programs detailed on the next page. This does not include enrollment in private school (except for those receiving an ESA or voucher), students in magnet schools, or those who are homeschooled.

26 See, Kittredge (2016).

is limited in its reach because of a requirement in the law mandating participating schools be accredited by the Mississippi Department of Education. As a result, just five schools are currently participating.

Mississippi also has a speech language therapy scholarship. This allows students with speech language impairments to receive a voucher equal to the base student cost of MAEP. This program was enacted in 2013, but has never served more than 14 children a year. Very few schools qualify because they not only must be accredited by the state, but they must have speech language therapy as their primary purpose for the school. This restricts schools that would otherwise meet the needs of students who qualify for the scholarship but serve students with multiple types of disabilities.

Mississippi became the third state in the nation to approve a Special Needs Education Scholarship Account in 2015. Scholarships were initially worth $6,500, but that number fluctuates with increases or decreases to the base student cost in the state. Because parents are able to customize their child's education, the scholarship can be used on a number of educational services, including private school, tutoring, therapy, textbooks, curriculum, district school classes, transportation, and testing fees. Unlike the Dyslexia Scholarship and Speech Language Therapy Scholarship, which place heavy burdens on participating schools, this program only requires schools be accredited.

For a student to be eligible, they must have received an Individualized Education Plan (IEP) in the past five years. For the 2016-2017 school year, all 425 slots in the program were filled with many more on the waiting list. In fact, the greatest limitation to this program has been level funding that has not allowed the program to grow as it was authorized to in its first three years.

While this program is limited in eligibility and funding, it put a platform in place to truly revolutionize education for Mississippi students if expanded broadly. Until then, Mississippi will have a long way to go before the state nears any type of market-based approach to education for every family.

What Does The Data Show?

The empirical data on school choice shows that it has a history of improving not only the academic outcomes of participants but of students that remain in public schools as well.

- Fourteen of the 18 random assignment studies show choice participants' academic scores improved as a result of participating in a private school choice program. Two of the studies showed no visible effect on test scores and two showed a negative effect.[27]

- The two studies that showed negative results were both from Louisiana. This chapter previously referenced the government regulations imposed on participating private schools in the Louisiana Scholarship Program, and the negative effect it had in the first two years of the program.

- Thirty-one of 33 studies found that the market effects from a school choice program led to academic improvements in local district schools, including schools in Louisiana.

- Every study conducted on the fiscal impact of school choice has found that such programs either save tax dollars, or have no visible effect. Twenty-five studies have shown that school choice programs have a positive fiscal impact, while three have shown no visible impact. A review of school choice programs found a cumulative savings ranging from $1.7 billion to $3.4 billion through the 2013-2014 school year.

---

27 See, Forster (2016).

Lawmakers today do not need to wait for a study to determine if school choice works. They do not need to act on speculation on what may or may not happen, whether positive or negative. Twenty-six years after the first modern school choice program, the empirical evidence shows that everyone involved—participants, district schools, and taxpayers—benefits from school choice.

Parents are the Ultimate Accountability Measure

A universal school choice program puts parents in control and allows them to make the best education decisions for their child. While there are numerous accountability measures in place to determine the quality of education a child is receiving, such as standardized test scores, school grades, or graduation rate, the most important and most overlooked measure is parental satisfaction.

Parents are attuned to their child's unique learning needs and educational progress in ways that may not be measured accurately by a standardized test. And every survey that has measured parental satisfaction has one underlying point: Parents are more satisfied with their child's school if they are free to choose that school.[28]

That correlates with the findings of Empower Mississippi's report on parental satisfaction in Mississippi's Special Needs ESA program. *The Special Needs ESA: What Families Enrolled In The Program Are Saying After One Year* tested parental satisfaction with the program, with a child's new educational setting, and with the ease of using the program and receiving reimbursements.[29]

The survey found that 91% of ESA parents are highly satisfied with the ESA program, with 63% reporting being very satisfied and another 28% being somewhat satisfied. The survey also found that 98% of respondents were satisfied with the school or educational program they chose for their child. This contrasts sharply with the parents' levels of satisfaction at their child's previous assigned district school, where 38% were very unsatisfied and an additional 29% were somewhat unsatisfied with the school or program in which their child was educated before enrolling in the ESA program. Overall, 67% were not satisfied with the previous program, while 24% were satisfied and only 5% were very satisfied. Figure 13.4 summarizes these findings.

Making decisions today is easier than it has ever been with crowd sourcing and user generated reviews. Just as Yelp has provided user generated reviews on hotels and restaurants, websites like Private School Review, School Digger, Great Schools, and Niche allow anyone to read reviews from parents and students on the schools in their community.

Many families utilize private outlets like Forbes, Princeton Review, and U.S. News & World Report for perspectives on choosing the right college and websites like Rate My Professors offer peer review options for students. Why is K-12 any different? State run accountability systems are far from the only- or even best- means of evaluating education options.

Market Based Education Works

Arizona is the closest model to a free market education setting in the United States. Today they have five private school choice programs serving nearly 70,000 students. That number is likely to increase in the coming years after the legislature expanded the state's ESA to universal (but capped) eligibility over

---

28 See, Stewart (2014).
29 See, Kittredge (2016).

Figure 13.4: Satisfaction level among ESA participants

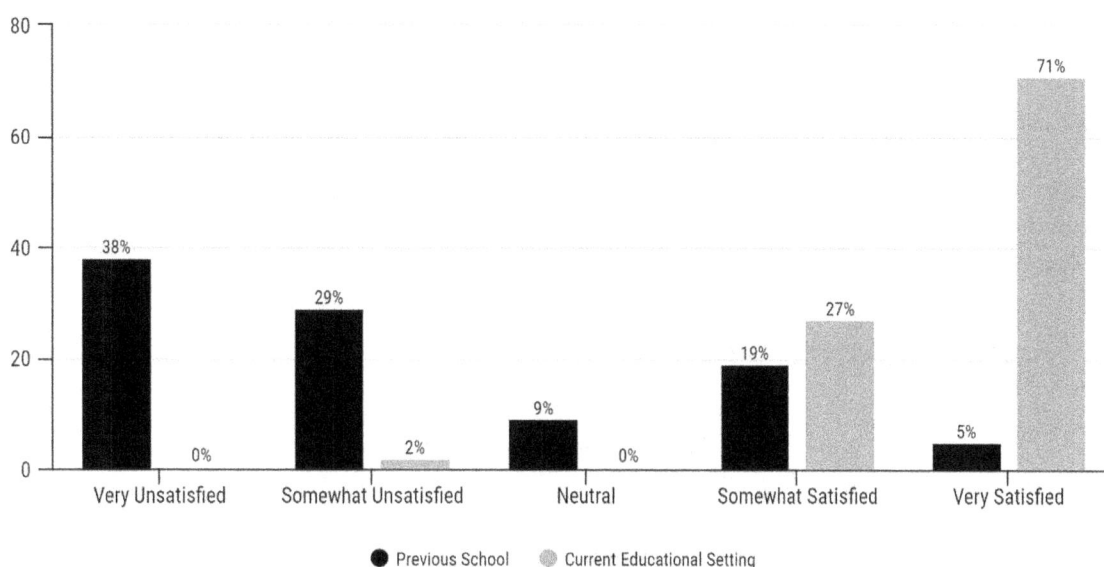

Source: The Special Needs ESA: What Families Enrolled In The Program Are Saying After One Year

a several year phase-in period. They also have more than 15 percent of public school students attending a charter school.

Arizona has over 600 charter schools with more than 200 charters opening since 2010 alone. Yet at the same time 100 charter schools were also closed.[30] Remarkably, most of these failing schools have not being closed by the state, but rather by parents. If parents believe their child is not getting a great education, they are voting with their feet. Those schools that closed lasted, on average, just four years and had an average of 62 students their final year. Parents in Arizona enjoy school choice, and they are able to make immediate decisions about their child's future. If a school is not performing at a level they believe it should, they do not have to wait for it to improve. They can simply move on.

Figure 13.5 shows that charter schools in Arizona are now competing with the most highly regarded district schools in the country. The 2015 National Assessment of Educational Progress (NAEP) scores show charter students in Arizona are nearly even with Massachusetts and ahead of New Hampshire, Minnesota, and New Jersey, which are states that spend among the most in the country per student.

At the same time, students in traditional district schools have experienced similar gains. In fact, Arizona led the nation in growth on the NAEP science test from 2009 to 2015. While Arizona has spent two decades providing families access to public and private school choice, all students have seen a benefit.

Figure 13.5: 2015 NAEP Scores, 8th Grade Math

State	8th Grade Math Scores	Spending per student
Massachusetts	297	$15,087
Arizona (charter schools)	296	$7,528
New Hampshire	294	$14,335
Minnesota	294	$11,464
New Jersey	293	$17,907

---

30 See, Ladner (2016).

It turns out, when parents are given the opportunity to choose the best school for their children, children in both schools of choice and traditional district schools do better.

In a small way, Mississippi has seen the market effects of a school choice program. The 3-D School in Petal, MS is a specialty school that provides comprehensive dyslexia therapy services for students. Many of the families receive either the Dyslexia Scholarship or Special Needs ESA to help cover the cost of tuition. Because very few schools offer the services they provide, some families travel up to four hours per day roundtrip for their children to attend the school. The school is now opening a second location on the Gulf Coast due to this demand created by the school offering a high quality product and the scholarship programs that make the school more affordable for families.

What About The Supply Side?

The first part of the school choice battle, and the area that has drawn the most attention, is passing a law that provides every parent with the option to choose the right educational setting for their child. What if Mississippi passed a universal school choice bill tomorrow? Parents need to have options, thus, the second part of the discussion involves the supply side of a market based education.

If parents suddenly had the ability to receive a scholarship from the state to choose the best school for their child, new schools would open and current, high quality schools would expand due to demand from parents. As the program matures, parents would be able to judge the viability of all schools, whether public or private. In this scenario, parents have the ability to choose and schools must work to attract students and prove they are the best choice for that child. For the first time, all schools would be competing on the same playing field, and each school would have an incentive to develop the best product for their consumers: Mississippi families. District schools today can generally ignore the small population that is in a school choice program because it has not affected their educational market share. Therefore, they are not incentivized to meet the demands of parents. In this scenario, they would not enjoy that luxury, and families would expect schools to perform the way they expect any product they purchase to perform.

Education is not, and should not be, different than any other sector of our economy.

Conclusion

There is no one answer that will solve every education woe overnight. In fact, those top-down proposals have often been the problem. For too long, lawmakers have concentrated on well-minded, but small and administration centric reforms that do not move the needle as it relates to real choice, accountability, or academic improvements.

In reality, the goal is simple: Schools should be permitted to innovate, and parents should be free to choose in order to provide every child access to a quality education, regardless of the provider.

School choice programs should have universal eligibility, providing all parents with the ability to make the best decision for their child's unique learning needs. Private schools should be allowed to maintain their autonomy, free of government regulations that often stifle academic growth, and parents should be able to judge the performance of their child's school while being able to compare one school to another.

In this model, new schools would open and expand to meet the demands of families and all schools would finally be competing on a level playing field for students and would be incentivized to produce an excellent product that appeals to their consumers.

Mississippi has started in this direction. And while lawmakers should be commended for approving any type of school choice proposal thus far, if they want to see fundamental change, they need to begin thinking on a larger scale.

To promote prosperity, Mississippi needs to develop a truly market based approach to education where every parent has the options to personalize their child's education, and private schools are permitted to maintain the autonomy that has allowed them to flourish. Anything short of that is not market based, and will not help Mississippi, or the United States, achieve the goal of providing every child with a high quality education.

References

Alliance For Excellent Education. 2014. The High Cost of High School Dropouts: The Economic Case for Reducing the High School Dropout Rate. [electronic file]. Washington, DC: Alliance For Excellent Education. Online: https://all4ed.org/take-action/action-academy/the-economic-case-for-reducing-the-high-school-dropout-rate/

Burke, Lindsey and Bedrick, Jason. 2016. Recalibrating Accountability: Education Savings Accounts As Vehicles Of Choice And Innovation. [electronic file]. Washington, DC: The Heritage Foundation. Online: http://www.heritage.org/education/report/recalibrating-accountability-education-savings-accounts-vehicles-choice-and

Butler, Stewart. 2009. Learning From Sweden's School Voucher Success. [electronic file]. Washington, DC: The Heritage Foundation. Online: http://www.heritage.org/education/commentary/learning-swedens-school-voucher-success

Crotty, James Marshall. 2013. South Korean Tutor Makes $4 Million A Year. Can You? [electronic file]. New York City, NY: Forbes. Online: https://www.forbes.com/sites/jamesmarshallcrotty/2013/08/11/south-korean-tutor-makes-4-million-a-year-can-you/#2333d62c697c

Desilver, Drew. 2017. U.S. Students' Academic Achievement Still Lags That Of Their Peers In Many Other Counties. [electronic file]. Washington, DC: Pew Research Center. Online: http://www.pewresearch.org/fact-tank/2017/02/15/u-s-students-internationally-math-science/

EdChoice. 2017. School Choice In America. [electronic file]. Indianapolis, IN: EdChoice. Online: https://www.edchoice.org/school-choice/school-choice-in-america/

Education Week. 2014. Quality Counts 2014. [electronic file]. Bethesda, MD: Editorial Projects In Education. Online: http://www.edweek.org/ew/toc/2014/01/09/index.html

Forster, Greg. 2016. A Win-Win Solution: The Empirical Evidence On School Choice, Fourth Edition. [electronic file]. Indianapolis, IN: EdChoice. Online: http://www.edchoice.org/wp-content/uploads/2016/05/A-Win-Win-Solution-The-Empirical-Evidence-on-School-Choice.pdf

Friedman, Milton. 1955. The Role Of Government In Education. [electronic file]. Austin, TX: The University of Texas. Online: http://la.utexas.edu/users/hcleaver/330T/350kPEEFriedmanRoleOfGovttable.pdf

Friedman, Milton. 1980. Putting Learning Back In The Classroom. Online: https://youtu.be/Syp_jR4BNBk

Hunt, Katie. 2016. Singapore Teens Top Global Education Ranking As U.S. Lags. [electronic file]. Washington, DC: CNN. Online: http://www.cnn.com/2016/12/06/world/pisa-global-education-rankings/

Kittredge, Brett. 2016. Education Choice Enrollment Grows 80 Percent In One Year. [electronic file]. Ridgeland, MS: Empower Mississippi. Online: http://empowerms.org/education-choice-enrollment-grows-80-percent-in-one-year/

Kittredge, Brett and Bedrick, Jason. 2016. The Special Needs ESA: What Families Enrolled In The Program Are Saying After Year One. [electronic file]. Ridgeland, MS: Empower Mississippi. Online: http://empowerms.org/wp-content/uploads/2016/12/ESA-Report-final.pdf

Ladner, Matthew. 2016. Arizona Parents Put Charter Schools Out Of Business Early And Often. [electronic file]. Jay P. Greene's Blog. Online: https://jaypgreene.com/2016/08/12/arizona-parents-put-charter-schools-out-of-business-early-and-often/

Legislative Budget Office. 2016. State of Mississippi Budget Bulletin, Fiscal Year 2017. [electronic file]. Jackson, MS: Joint Legislative Budget Committee. Online: http://www.lbo.ms.gov/pdfs/fy17_bulletin.pdf

Lehr, C.A. et al. 2004. Essential tools: Increasing rates of school completion. [electronic file]. Minneapolis, MN: National Center on Secondary Education and Transition. Online: http://www.ecs. org/html/Document.asp?chouseid=6649

Madison County Business League. 2017. Madison County Academic Scores of 2016. [electronic file]. Canton, MS: Madison County Business League. Online: http://madisoncountybusinessleague.com/_literature_147002/Madison_County_Academic_Scores_2016

National Alliance For Public Charter Schools. 2017. Estimated Charter Public School Enrollment, 2016-17. [electronic file]. Washington, DC: National Alliance For Public Charter Schools. Online: http://www.publiccharters.org/wp-content/uploads/2017/01/EER_Report_V5.pdf

National Center for Education Statistics. 2016. Homeschooling In The United States. [electronic file]. Washington, DC: U.S. Department of Education. Online: https://nces.ed.gov/pubs2016/2016096rev.pdf

National Center for Education Statistics. 2012. Numbers And Types Of Public Elementary And Secondary Schools. [electronic file].

Washington, DC: U.S. Department of Education. Online: https://nces.ed.gov/pubs2012/pesschools10/tables/table_02.asp

National Center for Education Statistics. 2017. Private School Universe Survey. [electronic file]. Washington, DC: U.S. Department of Education. Online: https://nces.ed.gov/surveys/pss/

National Center for Education Statistics. 2017. Public High School Graduation Rates. [electronic file]. Washington, DC: U.S. Department of Education. Online: https://nces.ed.gov/programs/coe/indicator_coi.asp

Smarick, Andy. 2017. The $7 Billion School Improvement Grant Program: Greatest Failure in the History of the US Department of Education. [electronic file]. Washington, DC: American Enterprise Institute. Online: https://www.aei.org/publication/greatest-failure-in-history-us-department-of-education/

Stewart, Thomas and Wolf, Patrick. 2014. The School Choice Journey: School Vouchers and the Empowerment of Urban Families. New York, NY: Palgrave Macmillan. P. 31.

The Nation's Report Card. 2015. State Performance Compared To The Nation. [electronic file]. Washington, DC: U.S. Department of Education. Online: https://www.nationsreportcard.gov/profiles/stateprofile?chort=1&sub=RED&sj=AL&sfj=NP&st=MN&year=2015R3

14

Medicaid:
A Government
Monopoly That
Hurts the Poor

Jameson Taylor

14

Medicaid:
A Government Monopoly
That Hurts the Poor

Jameson Taylor

Government: If you think the problems we create are bad, just wait until you see our solutions.

DESPAIR, INC.

Medicaid is a microcosm of what's wrong with American health care. It is subsidized, expensive, and inefficient, spending vast sums to obtain marginal benefits. It is too focused on health insurance, instead of quality of care. As a government-sponsored monopoly, Medicaid is also crowding out better products and policies.

At the state level, health care policy revolves around Medicaid. It constitutes the single largest expenditure in Mississippi's budget, far outstripping K-12 education. It is also among the largest, if not the largest, purchasers of health care in Mississippi. At the same time, the state has little control over its Medicaid program. In theory, Medicaid is a voluntary federal-state partnership. In practice, the federal government funds much of the program, leaving few opportunities for reform. Medicaid is a conundrum. Mississippi cannot afford to leave the program, even as it increases costs for taxpayers and leads to poor outcomes for patients.

The road to a free-market health care system in Mississippi cannot go through Medicaid, but must go around it. Disruptive innovation, focused on the power of pricing and direct payment models, is the best strategy for salvaging the system. Many of these improvements, however, must be undertaken at the federal level. Still, state policymakers can implement a handful of concrete ideas that will inch us toward a free market for health care.

What is Medicaid?

Many people do not really understand what Medicaid is, often confusing it with Medicare. Here is a list describing what Medicaid is and is not:

First, Medicaid is not health care. Created in 1965, Medicaid is a government-subsidized health insurance program for low-income families. As an insurance product, Medicaid essentially provides financial protection from medical bankruptcy. In turn, the Mississippi Division of Medicaid is not a health care provider, but a purchaser of health care. A person may have Medicaid insurance, but still be unable to see a doctor who accepts Medicaid. In addition, even people who have no insurance at all are guaranteed emergency care under a federal law known as EMTALA.

Second, Medicaid is not Medicare. Medicare is a (mostly) single-payer, national insurance program that covers people aged 65 and older and some disabled populations. Medicare is fully funded by the federal government whereas Medicaid requires cost-sharing between the federal government and the states. "Dual eligibles" are people eligible for both Medicaid and Medicare. Nineteen percent of Mississippi's population is on Medicare.

Third, Medicaid is a large and costly program. Medicaid is the largest health insurer in the United States. It covers 71 million people while Medicare covers 57 million. The federal agency that runs both programs, the Centers for Medicare and Medicaid Services (CMS), is the single-largest purchaser of health care in the world. One-quarter of Mississippi's population is on Medicaid.

As a share of U.S. health care expenditures, combined Medicaid/Medicare spending (37 percent) exceeds private health insurance spending (33 percent). Over the next 10 years, federal Medicaid spending is projected to exceed $5 trillion. For Mississippi, combined federal/state appropriations for 2015-2016 were $6.396 billion with total state appropriations of $1.59 billion.[1] With average monthly enrollment of 779,298, Medicaid insurance costs federal/Mississippi taxpayers roughly $8,207.26 per beneficiary per year.[2]

Fourth, Medicaid is optional, as underscored by the U.S. Supreme Court in *NFIB v. Sebelius* (2012). That said, the financial incentives are so great every state participates.

Why is Medicaid Important?

Medicaid has an ideological and practical significance that makes reforming the program very difficult and eliminating the program extremely unlikely. The ideological significance derives from the Left's desire to use Medicaid and Medicare as a vehicle for creating a single-payer health insurance system in which the government pays all costs: "Medicare-for-all." The "insurer" in this case is present and future taxpayers and debt holders. What is left out of the fantasy, is that under this system the government will control (and ration) everything: health care providers, medical equipment, hospital construction, etc.

Advocates of socialized medicine have been largely successful owing to the mixture of sympathy and confusion many voters feel about health care. On the one hand, most Americans are uncomfortable at the prospect of someone "dying in the street" because that person cannot afford care. On the other, many

---

1 These figures include a $51.6 million midyear deficit request.

2 This total includes both Medicaid and Medicare DSH payments and Mississippi Hospital Access Payments (MHAP); it also includes agency administrative costs. The latest data available (2013-2014) records Medicaid spending for a full-benefit enrollee at $6,780 per person for Mississippi, with a high of $21,087 for seniors and a low of $2,568 for children. The estimate provided here is more comprehensive and also includes CHIP enrollment.

people do not understand how health insurance works and do not know how much health care costs. This ignorance has been used to transform Medicaid (and, even more so, Medicare) into a "third-rail": a program that is politically untouchable, however defective it may be.

When many voters hear "Medicaid," they think "health care for the elderly and the disabled." They do not realize Medicaid is health insurance, and they do not realize anyone may obtain emergency care, regardless of ability to pay. They are also not familiar with direct-payment models that bypass traditional insurance. The reason for this misunderstanding is beyond the scope of this chapter, but the government is largely to blame.

The practical significance of Medicaid, especially for Mississippi, is that many, many entities benefit: hospitals, insurance companies, doctors and patients. Best of all, most of the costs are paid for by someone else: federal and state taxpayers and federal debt holders. For the average politician, Medicaid brings in billions of dollars of "free money."

Federal Medicaid funding for each state is determined by a formula called the federal medical assistance percentage (FMAP), correlated against state per capita income. In exchange for this funding, each state agrees to the federal government's rules, in particular, minimum eligibility and benefit requirements.

As the poorest state, Mississippi has the highest FMAP: 74.63 percent for 2016-2017. This means the federal government contributes 75 cents of every dollar Mississippi spends on Medicaid. By contrast, for every dollar in cuts Mississippi makes to its Medicaid program, it saves only 25 cents. If the state wanted to save $10 million in state Medicaid funding, it would have to reduce its overall Medicaid budget by $40 million.

In addition, Mississippi has almost no incentive, and little authority, to limit Medicaid enrollment and spending. Medicaid is an open-ended entitlement, which means anyone eligible for the program has a legal right to enroll. Federally mandated coverage groups include: children, very low-income parents, pregnant women, and aged, blind and disabled individuals receiving SSI (Supplemental Security Income). Income eligibility is generally correlated against the federal poverty limit (FPL), with Mississippi's categories ranging from $27,168/year for a family of three with children aged 6 to 18 to $42,684 for a family of three enrolled in the Children's Health Insurance Program (CHIP).[3] States may cover optional services and populations, and many do so in order to drawdown even more federal funds.[4] At the same time, states are prohibited from implementing enrollment caps or individual spending caps.[5] The only real limit on Medicaid spending is demonstrated need. Consequently, Medicaid is "a market perpetually in a state of excess demand."[6]

In Mississippi, total Medicaid appropriations for 2017-2018 were $6.015 billion, consuming 32 percent of an $18.531 billion budget. By comparison, total K-12 appropriations were $3.448 billion. Excluding federal funding, state General Fund appropriations for Medicaid were $853 million, with every expectation the Division would go over budget and request additional funding by midyear.

---

3   CHIP covers children with family income that exceeds Medicaid limits. Passed in 1997 by a Republican-majority Congress, the program was a fallback plan after the failure to enact "Hillarycare." CHIP has some features, such as a capped block-grant allotment, that would help control Medicaid spending.

4   For a list of mandatory and optional services, see: https://www.macpac.gov/subtopic/mandatory-and-optional-benefits/. For a list of mandatory and optional populations, see: https://www.medicaid.gov/medicaid-chip-program-information/by-topics/waivers/1115/downloads/list-of-eligibility-groups.pdf.

5   By contrast, TANF (Temporary Assistance for Needy Families) is a cash welfare program funded by a block grant, meaning states receive a fixed amount of funding per year and so have incentives to reduce costs.

6   Graboyes (2014), 180.

Who Benefits from Medicaid?

While Medicaid seems indispensable, its value has come under additional scrutiny since the passage of the Affordable Care Act (otherwise known as Obamacare). The Affordable Care Act (ACA) attempted to force states to provide Medicaid coverage to able-bodied, childless adults earning less than 138 percent FPL: $16,642.80 for an individual in 2017. The U.S. Supreme Court struck down this mandate, making it optional. As a result, some states have engaged in robust debates over whether to expand Medicaid. To date, 19 states, including Mississippi, have declined to expand Medicaid to include able-bodied, childless adults. Much of the wrangling over the ACA repeal and replace effort is over how long to continue to fund this expansion in the other 31 states.[7]

If Medicaid were such an advantageous program, more states would be eager to expand. As indicated above, hospitals, insurance companies, doctors, and patients are the primary beneficiaries, but each group benefits to varying degrees.

As far as hospitals go, institutional participation in Medicaid and Medicare is voluntary, but virtually all hospitals participate. Nonprofit hospitals are also encouraged under the terms of their tax-exempt status to care for Medicaid/Medicare patients. Accordingly, such patients account for 60 percent of all hospital care provided in the United States.

Not unlike private insurance companies, Medicaid negotiates discounted prices with providers. In Mississippi, provider reimbursements for Medicaid fee-for-service procedures are set at 90 percent of Medicare fees. The national average is 72 percent. It would seem Mississippi Medicaid pays providers relatively well, except providers complain that Medicare does not pay enough.

Whether hospitals lose money on Medicaid/Medicare is a contentious issue. Many hospitals claim they do and demand government backstop payments, referred to as Disproportionate Share Hospital (DSH) payments and Upper Payment Limits (UPL), to cover losses. Hospital pricing, though, is notoriously inflated, leading to questions over whether "uncompensated care" costs are as high as reported.[8]

For all their handwringing, most hospitals profit from Medicaid.[9] Notes a recent study in *Health Affairs*:

> It is generally believed that most hospitals lose money on Medicaid admissions. The data suggest otherwise. Medicaid admissions are often profitable for hospitals because of payments from both the Medicaid program and the Medicare program, including payments for uncompensated care and from the Medicare disproportionate-share hospital program.[10]

Not coincidentally, hospitals around the country also strongly supported the Obamacare Medicaid expansion. Thus, we find the president of the Mississippi Hospital Association declaring:

> The Mississippi Hospital Association supports Medicaid expansion and we have consistently said we are for Medicaid expansion. ... We also support expansion because of the financial realities our hospitals now face.

---

7   The Medicaid expansion population is eligible for a 90 percent federal match, which is larger than any state's FMAP and a larger match than for any other population, including the disabled.

8   Gruber and Rodriguez (2007) argue the value of uncompensated care is vastly overstated, accounting for less than 1 percent of physician revenue.

9   "Many hospitals receive Medicaid payments that may be in excess of cost. Understanding how much Medicaid pays hospitals is difficult because there is no publicly available data source that provides reliable information to measure this nationally across all hospitals." See Cunningham et al. (2016).

10   The authors note that the Medicare DSH formula incentivizes Medicaid admissions and discourages charity care. For the last several years, observers have been waiting for CMS to amend this formula. Stensland et al. (2016).

Oddly enough, private insurance companies also earn significant profits from Medicaid through a payment model known as managed care. Under managed care, Mississippi pays private insurance companies a monthly payment to insure Medicaid recipients. Mississippi's program is called MississippiCAN and enrolls about 500,000 individuals with annual spending estimated at $3 billion and an average monthly payment of $473 per member. Notably, MississippiCAN excludes the most expensive Medicaid recipients – nursing home residents, for example, but includes the least expensive – children.

Medicaid's benefit to physicians and providers who do not directly work for a hospital is less predictable.[11] Because states cannot cap enrollment or per person funding, they have few options when it comes to reducing costs. They can eliminate or reduce optional coverage categories or services, but this risks alienating some voting blocks, such as the disabled. They can also cut payments to providers. By and large, physicians are the easiest target.[12]

While some health care providers are willing to take a loss on Medicaid patients, others are not. Presumably still others are able to profit, likely by reducing the time spent with each patient, thus increasing volume. In any event, a significant number of doctors in Mississippi do not accept Medicaid insurance. A 2014 survey by the Social Science Research Center at Mississippi State found that between 26 percent and 50 percent of primary care physicians are not accepting new Medicaid patients, compared to 7 percent not accepting new patients with private insurance and 15 percent not accepting new Medicare patients. National studies have found a 58 percent non-acceptance rate, suggesting the upper bound of 50 percent is more likely.

Finally, patients who have Medicaid insurance obviously benefit from having their insurance paid for by other people. This benefit is of dubious value, though.

Who is Harmed by Medicaid?

Medicaid is often said to be a "good deal" by Mississippi policymakers boasting that the program brings in $3 in federal funding for every $1 Mississippi contributes. Even so, the state's capacity to fund Medicaid is limited by competing priorities. Even assuming a net fiscal impact for Mississippi, Medicaid is a harmful program that results in poor health outcomes and crowds out innovation.

It might sound strange that patients with Medicaid insurance are harmed by it. What we mean is that while Medicaid functions like any insurance product by providing a measure of financial protection, it does so at the expense of good health outcomes. In fact, in terms of health care quality, having Medicaid insurance is generally worse than having no insurance at all.

Several studies show that health outcomes for Medicaid beneficiaries are very poor. A University of Virginia study reviewed nearly 900,000 surgical procedures finding that mortality rates for Medicaid patients were far higher than for any other group, including the uninsured, who have similar risk factors. Similarly, economists at the University of Missouri-Columbia calculated that Medicaid recipients have a 32 percent higher mortality rate than the uninsured.[13]

---

11 As Medicaid expands, physicians may be forced to participate. See http://www.illinoisattorneygeneral.gov/pressroom/2009_04/20090427.html.

12 See Holgash (2017).

13 See Kim and Milyo (2011). A note of caution: the study uses these findings to invite skepticism regarding other studies using observational methods that purport to show the opposite – namely that being uninsured (and, conversely, remedying this problem with Medicaid insurance) correlates with high mortality rates. See also Chris Conover's entertaining analysis, which specifically questions the methodology used in the Medicaid expansion study by B. Sommers (2012); https://www.forbes.com/sites/theapothecary/2017/06/30/reality-check-the-obamacare-medicaid-expansion-is-not-saving-lives-part-i/#3bc57511100a.

One reason Medicaid patients have higher mortality rates than the uninsured is because some health care providers would rather treat an uninsured patient, not to mention a patient with private insurance. "At least with uninsured patients, there is some prospect of high reimbursement," explain Gruber and Rodriguez. As a result, even though a patient may have Medicaid, he may still be unable to obtain care in a timely manner. A 2011 survey published in the *New England Journal of Medicine* observed that "children with Medicaid/CHIP were significantly more likely to be denied an appointment than privately insured children", and that "on average, children with public insurance waited 42 days for an appointment with a specialist, whereas privately insured children waited 20 days."

The best study we have on Medicaid outcomes is called the Oregon Health Insurance Experiment (OHIE). The OHIE compared uninsured, low-income, able-bodied adults that were randomly selected by lottery to participate in Medicaid against a statistically similar control group not selected in the lottery. After two years, they found that Medicaid increased the use of health care services. Medicaid also "decreased financial strain ... and virtually eliminated catastrophic out-of-pocket medical expenditures." The study, however, found "no statistically significant effect on physical health outcomes." As health policy guru Avik Roy chastised, "If Medicaid were a new medicine applying for approval from the Food and Drug Administration, it would be summarily rejected."

Faced with the sobering conclusion that Medicaid's functional value is equivalent to a very expensive catastrophic health insurance plan, the Oregon researchers pivoted toward evaluating the program as a "redistributive tool." They found that Medicaid primarily benefits hospitals, not patients. Most importantly, the researchers observed that Medicaid recipients do not value Medicaid as much as other welfare programs, and that they would rather be uninsured if they had to pay for their own Medicaid coverage. "A substantial portion of the government's Medicaid spending – about 60 cents on the dollar – represents a transfer to the providers," concluded the study, "rather than a direct benefit for Medicaid recipients."[14]

Setting aside the question of whether health care is a right that places a claim on others, most people would agree that if we are going to have government-subsidized health care, it should be cost-effective. As indicated, the estimated cost of Mississippi Medicaid is $8,207 a year per enrollee. Compared to what Obamacare defines as a "Cadillac" plan, this cost is fairly low. The cost is also somewhat lower than the average price of an individual unsubsidized insurance policy in Mississippi.[15] The OHIE, however, found that the value of Medicaid to the average recipient is only 40 percent of the total cost, meaning that, relative to the perceived value it provides, Medicaid is way overpriced.

Even if Medicaid costs were lower, the program perpetuates massive inefficiencies and opportunity costs. First, Medicaid is displacing other spending priorities, consuming resources that could otherwise be used to stabilize the state employee retirement system, maintain roads, or cut taxes. Second, Medicaid is crowding-out private insurance coverage. Recall from Chapter 3, crowding out is what happens when government spending displaces private investment and activities. Gruber and Simon estimate Medicaid/CHIP crowds-out private coverage at a rate of 60 percent to 81 percent. This means that for every 100 families who enroll in Medicaid/CHIP, 81 families stop purchasing private insurance. Third, Medicaid is increasing the cost of private insurance. One prominent study conservatively pegs the increase at between $21.1 billion and $42.2 billion, roughly 2.3 percent to 4.6 percent of private health insurance costs.

---

14 The authors take great pains to clarify how the various models they use affect the results. See Finkelstein, Hendren, and Luttmer (2015).

15 The average age of purchasers of individual plans on ehealthinsurance.com was 37 years old; obviously, Medicaid covers a population ranging from the very young to the very old. This makes apples-to-apples comparisons difficult. See http://news.ehealthinsurance.com/_ir/68/20169/eHealth%20Health%20Insurance%20Price%20Index%20Report%20for%20the%202016%20Open%20Enrollment%20Period%20-%20October%202016.pdf.

Fourth, Medicaid increases the price of health care overall. Medicaid patients tend to over-utilize certain forms of care (such as emergency rooms), but lack access to and may postpone seeing a specialist. They are also more likely than patients with private insurance to require nonelective/urgent surgery, resulting in higher costs and longer hospital stays.

Taken together, the benefits of Medicaid do not outweigh the costs. For patients, Medicaid either does not improve physical health outcomes, or correlates with worse outcomes, compared to the uninsured and those with private insurance.[16] Likewise, physicians are significantly less likely to see Medicaid patients because Medicaid pays less, or in some cases not at all. It also imposes time-consuming and expensive administrative burdens on health care providers. Medicaid even fails as a mechanism for funding hospital uncompensated care liabilities: a direct subsidy would cost far less in the end.

The Problem with Medicaid

It is tempting to presume Medicaid could be fixed by increasing provider payments.17 This would boost physician participation, but it would not encourage patients to become more proactive about their health, as discussed in Chapter 15 regarding how to fight obesity. The root problem is incentives.

Medicaid facilitates poor lifestyle decisions by shifting the consequences of these decisions to others. Even as Medicaid may give patients more access to some health care services, it insulates them from the financial consequences of poor health care decision-making. In turn, these poor choices translate into worse health care outcomes and mortality rates than Medicaid patients might otherwise have under a system with better incentives.

For example, the OHIE researchers found that Medicaid insurance recipients, in comparison to the uninsured control group,[18] used more health care services: 50 percent more office visits; 40 percent more emergency room visits; 30 percent more hospital admissions. Medicaid recipients also used more prescription drugs and obtained more preventative care and screening. Most telling, being on Medicaid increased the likelihood of being diagnosed with diabetes and using diabetes medication, but did not result in a significant change in the marker (glycated hemoglobin) that indicates effective treatment. It seems these patients simply didn't follow their physicians' advice. Because they are not paying for their care, Medicaid recipients use more health care, at least whenever it is readily available. But, perhaps, because they do not feel responsible for their care, Medicaid recipients are not able to leverage this access to obtain better health.

As Congress continues to struggle over how to fix Obamacare, the White House is encouraging states to use (Section 1115) waivers to innovate within their Medicaid programs. Some of the options include: work requirements for able-bodied adults; lifetime caps; participation time limits; meaningful cost-sharing; and Health Savings Accounts (HSAs). That said, most of the ideas are punitive in nature, aimed at reducing Medicaid dependency; and HSAs have not been proven to work in a Medicaid context.[19]

What is most needed is a global waiver that would allow states to opt out of Medicaid altogether

---

16 Still, the causal relationship between any form of insurance coverage and health outcomes, not to mention mortality, is very difficult to verify. There are too many factors to control for; although that doesn't stop health policy advocates from trying. Second, and for the same reason, the causal relationship between even health outcomes and health care access is difficult to verify.

17 Roy (2013) notes that even though Oregon pays providers significantly more than the national average, the OHIE still did not find improved health outcomes, as compared to the uninsured; although it may well account for the increase in health care utilization.

18 After one year, the lottery group was 25 percent more likely to have insurance (i.e., Medicaid) than the control group.

19 Seema Verma and Don McCanne debate the pros and cons of Indiana's Medicaid HSA here: http://www.pnhp.org/news/2016/august/indiana%E2%80%99s-phony-medicaid-health-savings-accounts. Other attempts – Florida, South Carolina, West Virginia – at incorporating consumer-directed accounts into Medicaid invite skepticism.

if they can show how to use reduced funding to produce similar, if not better, results. Such a revolution is not without precedent. Romneycare, the Massachusetts program that laid the groundwork for Obamacare, was partially a product of an 1115 waiver. A state pilot program that went in the opposite direction, allowing for innovation outside of the broken Medicaid construct, would be a good first step. Second that, Congress will continue to debate giving states block grants that could be used to make existing Medicaid programs more efficient.[20]

Medicaid reform is a doubtful proposition because it is very difficult to fix the incentives (for instance, by charging higher copays) without essentially replicating a private insurance program. This would be a step in the wrong direction because Medicaid's number one problem is that it functions too much like a typical American insurance policy in that it detaches recipients from health care pricing. Improving aspects of Medicaid insurance coverage, such as expanding networks or increasing provider payments, will not necessarily produce better health outcomes. Instead, policymakers should be clear about the actual goal: delivering quality care to low-income families.

Create Healthcare Customers

One reason we have Medicaid is because most Americans believe insurance coverage is necessary to obtain health care. The ACA reinforces this bias by penalizing employers who do not offer insurance and fining individuals who do not obtain insurance. While there is a place for third-party insurance in health care, employer-based insurance, in particular, has almost completely undermined the U.S. health care market by training Americans not to approach health care with a consumer mentality that balances price against quality.

Above we noted that hospital pricing is nontransparent. Health care pricing, in general, is nontransparent because insurance companies (along with Medicaid and Medicare) are the largest purchasers of health care. Most individual consumers simply do not care how much their health care costs because their insurance provider is paying the bill. Those few who do pay out-of-pocket are often charged exorbitant prices, with one recent study finding charges more than 10 times the amount allowed by Medicare, with "a markup of more than 1,000 percent for the same medical services." "Because it is difficult for patients to compare prices, market forces fail to constrain hospital charges," conclude the authors.[21]

Fixing health care will require creating a market that incentivizes quality care at a lower price. Lawmakers should promote policies that encourage consumers to pay cash for health care, or to at least begin to ask about price. Three policy reforms, in particular, can unleash the power of pricing in health care: Large Health Care Savings Accounts (HSAs); direct primary and surgical care; and comparative shopping incentives.

An HSA is a tax-advantaged medical savings account that, under federal law, must be paired with a high-deductible health insurance policy. Because HSA holders have high deductibles, they tend to pay cash for minor services. If HSA contribution limits were higher, more consumers could use their HSA to pay for major medical procedures. While Mississippi can't increase the federal limit, it can increase its own. Much like Singapore, federal policymakers could also create subsidized HSAs as an alternative to Medicaid.[22]

---

20 A somewhat similar reform is the Rhode Island Global Waiver, an 1115 waiver granted in 2009 by the Bush administration. The program used the concept of a "medical home" in an attempt to lower costs by better managing and coordinating care, but critics charge the program reduced state spending by shifting costs to the federal government.

21 Bai and Anderson (2015).

22 As Bartholomew (2016) observes, there is no free-market health care system anywhere. Singapore, though, does an admirable job of reducing the distortions caused by government subsidies. See pp. 67-70.

State lawmakers should also incentivize direct surgical care. In 2015, Mississippi became one of the first states to protect the contractual right of physicians to provide direct primary care, also known as "concierge care." Concierge care patients pay a monthly fee to a physician in exchange for a predefined set of benefits, such as unlimited doctor visits. The next step is to expand the direct payment model to surgical care, as is being done at the Surgery Center of Oklahoma. At least one public health plan (Oklahoma County) and numerous private employers are bypassing the traditional insurance model and partnering with the center, which bills itself as a "free-market loving, price displaying, state-of-the-art facility." The center lists on its website all-inclusive prices for hundreds of procedures, attracting customers from around the world. It does not accept insurance. The center's prices are about 1/6 that charged for comparable procedures at local nonprofit hospitals and lower than what Medicare or Medicaid would pay.[23]

Finally, even people with traditional insurance can be encouraged to comparison shop. Some states have experimented with mandatory pricing transparency without much success. The missing element is to provide an incentive for consumers to actually shop around. New Hampshire is seeing success by using an app that enables state employees to compare health care pricing. If an employee elects to use a less expensive provider, he gets to keep some of the savings. The rest accrues to the state. In three years, the New Hampshire State Employee Health Plan has saved $12 million, with $1 million going back to shoppers. In 2017, Maine also instituted incentivized shopping for small-group health plans.

The reforms described above would benefit all consumers by using the power of pricing to deliver affordable, quality care. But what about families who cannot afford health care? As indicated, the reason we have Medicaid is because policymakers have fallen into the trap of confusing health insurance with health care access. Not everyone who is uninsured in America is unable to afford health care. A 2008 study by Pfizer found 7 percent of the uninsured earn more than $75,000 annually while 30 percent earn more than $50,000. Likewise, not all of the uninsured are uninsured for very long. According to a pre-ACA Congressional Budget Office report, 71 percent of the uninsured regained insurance within a year.

Instead of treating the uninsured, or the poor, for that matter, as a victim class, policymakers should approach them as customers. From a market perspective, Medicaid is a niche product created for low-income consumers. Its value should be judged against similar "products" in the same sector. The primary nongovernmental competitors in this market are nonprofit hospitals and charity care clinics.

Nonprofit hospitals – in Mississippi, there are 31 – receive significant federal and state tax breaks in return for offering a "community benefit." Prior to 1969, federal law required every nonprofit hospital to provide "to the extent of its financial ability, free or reduced-cost care to patients unable to pay for it."[24] According to a 2015 IRS report, community-benefit activities for nonprofit hospitals accounted for about 10 percent of total expenses, with just over 5 percent of total expenses actually being used on charity care and uncompensated care. Public hospitals didn't do much better. Mississippi lawmakers could encourage nonprofit hospitals to provide more charity care by strengthening the state's "community benefit" provisions; otherwise, they should eliminate the targeted tax breaks for these hospitals.

By contrast, dozens of private charity care clinics around the state are providing free and low-cost care to indigent persons. Based on the experience of other states, policy reforms aimed at deregulating charity care could incentivize $27 million in free care for Mississippi. Another way to expand charity care is to provide a corporate and individual tax credit for donated time and money.

Still, other would-be competitors to Medicaid have been regulated out of existence. One such alter-

---

23 See https://surgerycenterok.com/blog/lets-discuss-pricing/.
24 James (2016).

native is mandate-light insurance coverage that costs less, but includes fewer "essential health benefits," such as contraception or chiropractic. Prior to the ACA, it was estimated that such mandates increased the cost of insurance by at least 30 percent. Obamacare's essential health benefits provisions have increased premiums even more.

Worst of all, Medicaid's insurance monopoly has stifled the development of new insurance products and health care services that could better serve low-income Americans.[25] Free-market entrepreneurs are not naturally attracted to the health care sector because the government is such a large purchaser and regulator of health care. Likewise, Medicaid has stifled the ability of states to develop a better safety net for low-income families. The promise of Medicaid was to help states improve upon their existing charity care infrastructure. Instead, Medicaid undermined this infrastructure, leading to the closure of charity wards and other centers for indigent care.[26]

Conclusion

Medicaid is the federal government's attempt to deliver better health care to low-income families. Poor health outcomes for Medicaid patients demonstrate the program has not met this objective. In addition, Medicaid has crowded out the private sector from developing innovative products that would deliver high-quality, affordable care to low-income consumers. It has also handicapped the public sector in developing better policies. If we want to promote good health – and prosperity – in Mississippi, we must disrupt Medicaid's deadly monopoly.

References

American Hospital Association. Dec. 2016. Underpayment by Medicare and Medicaid Fact Sheet. Online: http://www.aha.org/content/16/medicaremedicaidunderpmt.pdf (cited August 25, 2017).

Bai, Ge and Gerard F. Anderson. 2015. Extreme Markup: The Fifty US Hospitals with the Highest Charge-to-Cost Ratios. *Health Affairs* 34(6): 922-928, June 24. Online: http://content.healthaffairs.org/content/34/6/922.abstract[content.healthaffairs.org (cited August 26, 2017). See also: Some Hospitals Marking Up Prices More than 1,000 Percent. 2015. Johns Hopkins School of Public Health. June 8. Online: http://www.jhsph.edu/news/news-releases/2015/some-hospitals-marking-up-prices-more-than-1000-percent.html (cited August 26, 2017).

Bartholomew, James. 2016. *The Welfare of Nations.* Washington, D.C.: Cato Institute.

Bisgaier, Joanna and Karin V. Rhodes. 2011. Auditing Access to Specialty Care for Children with Public Insurance. *New England Journal of Medicine* 364: 2324-2333. Online: http://www.nejm.org/doi/full/10.1056/NEJMsa1013285#t=articleTop (cited August 25, 2017).

Congressional Budget Office. May 2003. How Many People Lack Health Insurance and for How Long? Washington, D.C.: Congress of the United States. Online: http://www.cbo.gov/sites/default/files/cbofiles/ftpdocs/42xx/doc4210/05-12-uninsured.pdf (cited August 26, 2017).

Cossman, Ronald E. et al. Feb. 2014. Access to Primary Care Physicians Differs by Health Insurance Coverage in Mississippi. Southern Medical Association. 107(2): 87-90. Online: http://nemsahec.msstate.edu/wp-content/uploads/Access-to-Primary-Care-Differs.pdf (cited August 25, 2017).

Couglin, Teresa A., John Holahan, Kyle Caswell, and Megan McGrath. 2014. Uncompensated Care for the Uninsured in 2013: A Detailed Examination. Cost Shifting and Remaining Uncompensated Care Costs. The Henry J. Kaiser Family Foundation, May 30. Online: http://www.kff.org/report-section/uncompensated-care-for-the-uninsured-in-2013-a-detailed-examination-cost-shifting-and-remaining-uncompensated-care-costs-8596/ (cited August 26, 2017).

Cunningham, Peter et al. 2016. Understanding Medicaid Hospital Payments and the Impact of Recent Policy Changes. Henry J. Kaiser Family Foundation. June 9. Online: http://www.kff.org/report-section/understanding-medicaid-hospital-payments-and-the-impact-of-recent-policy-changes-issue-brief/ (cited August 25, 2017).

---

25 One option might be to connect EITC payments with incentivized HSAs. Public-private partnerships, similar to the "Alzira Model" of Spain, might also show promise.

26 See "Before Medicaid, how did doctors treat the poor?" for a brief discussion of how some physicians approached charity care prior to Medicaid. https://www.centerforhealthjournalism.org/fellowships/projects/medicaid-how-did-doctors-treat-poor.

Finkelstein, Amy, Nathaniel Hendren and Erzo F.P. Luttmer. June 2015. The Value of Medicaid: Interpreting Results from the Oregon Health Insurance Experiment. Working Paper 21308. Cambridge, MA: National Bureau of Economic Research. Online: http://www.nber.org/papers/w21308 (cited August 25, 2017).

Graboyes, Robert F. 2014. Medicaid and Health, Chapter 9 in Jason J. Fichtner (ed.), *The Economics of Medicaid*. Arlington, VA: Mercatus Center at George Mason University: 173-190.

Gruber, Jonathan and David Rodriguez. Nov. 2007. How Much Uncompensated Care Do Doctors Provide? Working Paper 13585. Cambridge, MA: National Bureau of Economic Research. Online: http://www.nber.org/papers/w13585.pdf (cited August 25, 2017).

Gruber, Jonathan and Kosali Simon. Jan. 2007. Crowd-Out Ten Years Later: Have Recent Public Insurance Expansions Crowded Out Private Health Insurance? Working Paper 12858. Cambridge, MA: National Bureau of Economic Research. Online: http://www.nber.org/papers/w12858 (cited August 26, 2017).

Haislmaier, Edmund F. and Drew Gonshorowski. 2015. Responding to *King v. Burwell*: Congress's First Step Should Be to Remove Costly Mandates Driving up Premiums. *Issue Brief* No. 4400, May 4. Washington, D.C.: Heritage Foundation. Online: http://thf_media.s3.amazonaws.com/2015/pdf/IB4400.pdf (cited August 26, 2017).

Henry J. Kaiser Family Foundation, 2016. State Health Facts: Medicaid-to-Medicare Fee Index. Online: http://www.kff.org/medicaid/state-indicator/medicaid-to-medicare-fee-index/?currentTimeframe=0&sortModel=%7B%22colId%22:%22Location%22,%22sort%22:%22asc%22%7D (cited August 25, 2017).

Holgash, Kayla. 2017. State Medicaid Responses to Fiscal Pressures. Washington, D.C.: MACPAC, March 2. Online: https://www.macpac.gov/wp-content/uploads/2017/03/State-Medicaid-Responses-to-Fiscal-Pressures.pdf (cited August 25, 2017).

Internal Revenue Service. Jan. 2015. Report to Congress on Private Tax-Exempt, Taxable, and Government-Owned Hospitals. Washington, D.C.: Department of the Treasury. Online: https://www.vizientinc.com/-/media/Documents/SitecorePublishingDocuments/Public/Report_to_Congress_on_Hospitals_Jan_2015.pdf (cited August 26, 2017).

James, Julia. 2016. Health Policy Brief: Nonprofit Hospitals' Community Benefit Requirements. *Health Affairs*, Feb. 25. Online: http://healthaffairs.org/healthpolicybriefs/brief_pdfs/healthpolicybrief_153.pdf (cited August 26, 2017).

Kim, Jenny and Jeffrey Milyo. 2011. Health Insurance and Mortality in US Adults: A Cautionary Tale. Working paper. Online: http://web.missouri.edu/~milyoj/files/AJPH_Brief_Draft.pdf (cited August 25, 2017).

LaPar, Damien J. et al. 2010. Primary Payer Status Affects Mortality for Major Surgical Operations. 130th Annual Meeting of the American Surgical Association 252(3): 544-551. Online: https://www.ncbi.nlm.nih.gov/pmc/articles/PMC3071622/ (cited August 25, 2017).

Mississippi Hospital Association. 2013. Medicaid expansion rally at the Capitol, March 27, 2013: Remarks of Sam W. Cameron. Online: http://mhanewsnow.typepad.com/pressroom/mha_official_statement/ (cited August 26, 2017).

Oregon Health Insurance Experiment. Cambridge, MA: National Bureau of Economic Research. Online: http://www.nber.org/oregon/ (cited August 25, 2017).

Pfizer Medical Division. 2008. Pfizer Facts: A Profile of Uninsured Persons in the United States. Online: http://www.pfizer.com/files/products/Profile_of_uninsured_persons_in_the_United_States.pdf (cited August 26, 2017).

Roy, Avik. 2013. Oregon Study: Medicaid Had 'No Significant Effect' on Health Outcomes vs. Being Uninsured. *Forbes*, May 2. Online: https://www.forbes.com/sites/theapothecary/2013/05/02/oregon-study-medicaid-had-no-significant-effect-on-health-outcomes-vs-being-uninsured/#bbb274d60430 (cited August 25, 2017).

Sanger, Jeffrey A. Fall 2014. "No Discharge: Medicaid and EMTALA." *Regulation* 37(3): 52-57.

Stensland, Jeffrey, Zachary R. Gaumer and Mark E. Miller. December 2016. Contrary to Popular Belief, Medicaid Hospital Admissions Are Often Profitable Because of Additional Medicare Payments. *Health Affairs* 35(12): 2282-2288. Online: http://content.healthaffairs.org/content/35/12/2282 (cited August 25, 2017).

Younger, Charles and Shane Aguirre. 2016. Bill will let good Samaritans donate to poor Mississippians. *The Clarion-Ledger*, March 13. Online: http://www.clarionledger.com/story/opinion/columnists/2016/03/13/bill-let-good-samaritans-donate-poor-mississippians/81653274/ (cited August 26, 2017).

15

Tipping the Scales: Curbing Mississippi's Obesity Problem

Raymond J. March

15

Tipping the Scales: Curbing Mississippi's Obesity Problem

Raymond J. March

In 2013, Mississippi Governor Phil Bryant enacted legislation banning counties from passing legislation to restrict portion sizes and require nutritional labeling for food retailers. Bryant's conviction, "it is simply not the role of the government to micro-regulate citizens' dietary decisions" received significant criticism.[1] Several outlets have satirically described the legislation as "Anti-Bloomberg".[2] More critically, former New York City Mayor Michael Bloomberg referred to Bryant's legislation as "ridiculous".[3] Executive Director of the Center for Science in the Public Interest, Michael Jacobson, expressed, "If I were a member of the Mississippi legislature, I would be much more concerned with the money the state shells out to treat obesity".[4] The University of Mississippi Medical School is also concerned with the growing prevalence of obesity in Mississippi. The University has declared obesity to be "the most important threat to the health of Mississippians" which could, "overwhelm our health-care system" resulting in, "a tidal wave of disease, disability, and premature death".[5]

A person is considered obese when their Body Mass Index exceeds 30. For most, obesity is the result of an unhealthy diet and insufficient physical activity, which leads to more calories consumed than

---

1 Yan (2013, p. 5).

2 Other states including Florida, Ohio, Arizona, and Alabama have enacted similar legislation. However, Mississippi legislation goes farther than other states that only restrict efforts to regulation the restaurant industry while Mississippi specifically limits portion size and required nutritional labeling.

3 (Pettus 2013, pp.5).

4 (Neporent 2013, pp. 17).

5 See https://www.umc.edu/Research/Centers-and-Institutes/Mississippi-Center-for-Obesity-Research/Home-Page.html.

burned. It is preventable and reversible. Most efforts, including government policy, to combat obesity revolve around diet and nutrition instead of physical activity. Thus, this chapter focuses on how Mississippi's food and nutrition policies affect obesity.

The concerns regarding obesity in Mississippi are justified. As of 2015, Mississippi ranks 2nd among all US states in adult obesity where approximately 36% of the adult population is considered obese. Children and teens are also affected. According to the Mississippi State Department of Health (MSDH), in 2013 approximately 20% of high school students and 22% of children from kindergarten to 5th grade are considered obese. Obesity commonly leads to increased risk for heart attacks, heart disease, diabetes, liver and kidney disease, and certain forms of cancer. Obesity is also associated with increased health care costs. The United Health Foundation finds the average obese patient spends 42% more on healthcare expenditures than the non-obese patient. The organization also estimates approximately 21% of annual medical spending (including household and government spending) in Mississippi goes to treating obesity or obesity related health issues.

Policymakers, including Bryant, agree on the seriousness of Mississippi's obesity. The fundamental disagreement is regarding what method works best to reduce it—private individuals working at the local level versus public actors using governmental effort to enact policy and regulation.

The recent trend across US cities and states is to use government regulation of food products and distribution in order to influence consumer choices. For example, New York City bans food retailers from selling soft drinks and other sweetened drinks larger than 16 ounces. Philadelphia taxes soda at 1.5 cents per liter. San Francisco forbids toys from being distributed in fast-food meals. Fast-food restaurants are not allowed in certain Los Angeles neighborhoods. In 2010, California became the first state to ban the use of artificial trans-fats. Following suit, legislation to ban trans-fats has been introduced in Massachusetts, Maryland, and Vermont.

Mississippi, although less intrusive than the previous examples, engages in similar legislation. Each year the MSDH develops a State of Obesity Action Plan. This plan details the state government's efforts to reduce and prevent obesity by implementing programs in schools, businesses, and other public outreach centers. The most recent plan calls for approximately $10 million in state funding to reduce the prevalence of adult and childhood obesity by the year 2020.[6]

Widespread obesity in the US and Mississippi is often described as an epidemic. The analogy implies a sudden, unanticipated, and pervasive increase in body fat content. However, obesity does not occur quickly. Rather, it is the result of countless choices made by millions of individuals. Examining the obesity issue in terms of choice rather than contamination recasts the question from what factors prevent obesity to what factors contribute to it.

This chapter examines contributing factors to Mississippi's obesity through the lens of economic analysis. Despite the best of intentions, Mississippi's regulatory and policy efforts play a considerable role in bolstering obesity rates in the state. Furthermore, state policy efforts provide little promise of preventing or reducing future obesity rates. Instead, local level private interests frequently provide an effective means to combat obesity. Entrepreneurs often provide healthy products, services, and information on how to live healthier lives to health-conscious consumers. The evidence provided in this chapter indicates private and local efforts, instead of state-led efforts, are significantly more likely to successfully address Mississippi's obesity problem.

---

6   The plan does not provide any specific measurable goals (i.e. reduce overall obesity by 10%, etc.)

What Does Economics Have to do With It?

Economics is the study of choices. If we reframe obesity as stemming from a series of food consumption choices, economics can be used to understand the nature of such choices. When viewing choices through an economic lens, individuals choose by responding to their incentives while attempting to make themselves better off. This applies whether people choose to consume healthy or less healthy food items. Which item is picked stems from different incentives and desires. Thus, widespread obesity, including obesity in Mississippi, is the result of individuals facing incentives to consume comparatively less healthy food items.

These incentives are divided into internal, cognitive incentives and external, market conditions with different prescriptions recommended based on which incentives are believed to be more relevant. Internal conditions include an understanding of how food choices affect obesity risk. A common explanation of wide-spread obesity is that people over-consume less healthy food options due to cognitive and psychological factors.[7] It is argued that most underestimate the impact food consumption choices have on their health. If true, obesity is a result of cognitive biases that are beyond the consumer's control. Self-discipline is incapable of fixing these psychological contributors. Thus, government intervention is necessary to limit access to unhealthy food options or directly influence consumer choices.[8] This perspective partially explains recent government regulation preventing the sale of certain foods, restricting portion sizes, and implementing specific taxes on unhealthy foods. Governments also fund educational programs on healthy dietary habits and proper nutrition as an attempt to alter mental biases.[9]

Although consuming relatively less healthy food can raise the risk of becoming obese, wide-spread obesity is not fully explained by limited mental capacity to make "better" choices. Lack of awareness does not explain why obesity rates affect different regions and income levels differently. Limited cognition also does not explain why obesity rates are increasing despite consumers holding more knowledge of proper diet and nutrition than in any previous time period.[10]

Thus, understanding the underlying factors of wide-spread obesity is incomplete without examining external conditions. External conditions include market, financial, and regulatory factors that influence food consumption. The primary external condition, therefore, is food prices. Consumers, particularly those with limited income, must consider price when making food choices. When certain food items become more expensive, consumers purchase less of them and substitute to comparatively cheaper foods. Conversely, consumers purchase more of the less expensive food and substitute away from comparatively more expensive products.

Unfortunately, studies find that cheaper food items tend to contain higher sugar and fat content; thus, individuals are incentivized to consume unhealthier foods because they are relatively cheaper.[11] This, in turn, raises the risk of obesity.

Government policies and regulations frequently affect food prices, which makes some food items artificially more expensive than others.[12] Since this affects the entire population, the result is population wide substitutions into different food items. Those most price sensitive to changes in food prices, typically

---

7   See Thaler (2016), Thaler and Sunstein (2008), and Sunstein and Thaler (2003).

8   Attempting to influence choices in this manor is sometimes referred to as "choice architecture" or "nudging" (Thaler and Sunstein 2008).

9   Examples of comparatively larger federal educational programs include the MyPyramid and MyPlate programs which work to educate low income households on healthy dietary habits.

10   See Philipson and Posner (1999) and Philipson (2001).

11   See Drewnowski and Specter (2004), Drewnowski and Darmon (2005), and Hruschka (2012).

12   The prices are artificial in the sense they would be higher or lower without government intervention.

lower-income consumers, are most affected by government induced price increases. As food prices rise, dietary quality decreases, increasing obesity and other health consequences.

For example, when the federal government subsidized corn production, the supply of corn and corn-based products increased. This resulted in the increased use of high fructose corn syrup since it was now a comparatively cheaper substitute for sugar. High fructose corn syrup is associated with increased risks of heart disease, obesity, and type 2 diabetes.[13] Although these health impacts were unintentional and unknown at the time, replacing sugar with high fructose corn syrup has deleteriously affected the health of countless US citizens.

Government interventions in the food market lead to harmful unintended consequences. A large percent of Mississippians face external conditions such as low incomes and low food budgets making them particularly vulnerable to governmental food policy and regulation that alter food prices.

Obesity and Poverty

In addition to holding one of the highest obesity rates in the US, Mississippi also has the lowest per-capita income, as described in Chapter 1. Mississippi also has the highest percent of population living below the poverty line at 22%. A common, somewhat paradoxical, finding is the association with low income and obesity.[14] Lower-income individuals have an incentive to purchase cheaper and lower quality food items, frequently resulting in less healthy food choices. This incentive structure places lower-income individuals at higher risk for obesity.

As depicted in Figure 15.1 below, this association is clearly prevalent in Mississippi. As the poverty rate has increased over time, so has the obesity rate. Although the percent of Mississippi's population below the poverty line increased at a slower rate than the obesity rate, poverty and income are related, with a correlation value of 0.87 after 2003.

Current county level data, as depicted Figure 15.2, also demonstrates a strong relationship between poverty and obesity. The correlation between the county population below the poverty line and obesity is 0.50. Furthermore, 77 out of 82 counties, or 94% of all counties, simultaneously hold poverty and obesity rates above the national average.[15] As income declines, so does

Figure 15.1: Mississippi Poverty and Obesity, 1990-2015

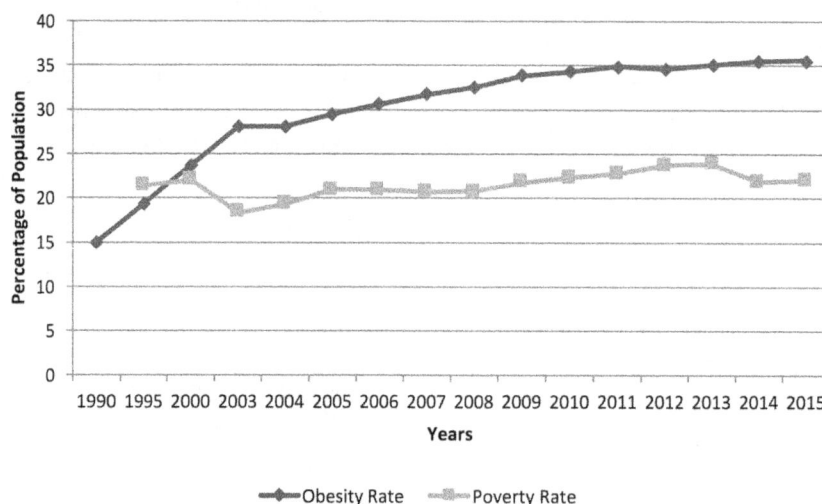

Source: Robert Wood Johnson Foundation's State of Obesity 2016 Report and US Census Bureau.

---

13 See Taubes (2006) and Goran, Ulijaszek, and Ventura (2013).

14 See Levine (2011).

consuming healthy, relatively pricier food choices, like fruits and vegetables. The Center for Disease Control's 2016 State Nutrition, Physical Activity, and Obesity Profile finds approximately 50% of low-income adults in Mississippi reported consuming no vegetables and 31% consumed no fruit on a daily basis. MSDH's Obesity Action plan 2016 finds similarly low consumption patterns for children where 10% of children in low income-households in Mississippi did not consume a serving of fruit or vegetables in the previous week.

Mississippi places additional burdens on low-income consumers by taxing groceries. Mississippi is only1 of 6 states which tax grocery purchases, and it is only 1 of 2 states which tax grocery purchases at the same rate as the state sales tax (7%), as discussed in Chapter 5. This raises the prices of all grocery goods. High grocery taxes place high financial burdens on low-income consumers. Furthermore, elevated price levels for food items provide a strong incentive to purchase unhealthy but calorie dense foods to economize on income allocated to consumption.

Obesity and Government Food Programs

Low-income households face the highest risk for not being able to afford a sufficiently nutritious diet. To reduce this risk, the Food Nutrition Service (FNS), an agency of the USDA, implemented the Supplemental Nutritional Assistance Program (SNAP) and the Women, Infants, and Children's Nutritional Program (WIC). Each program provides certain food items (either directly or through pre-paid electronic transfer cards) to program participants. By offering goods at no cost, participants are provided an incentive to consume food items provided by the programs rather

Figure 15.2: Mississippi Obesity and Poverty, 2014

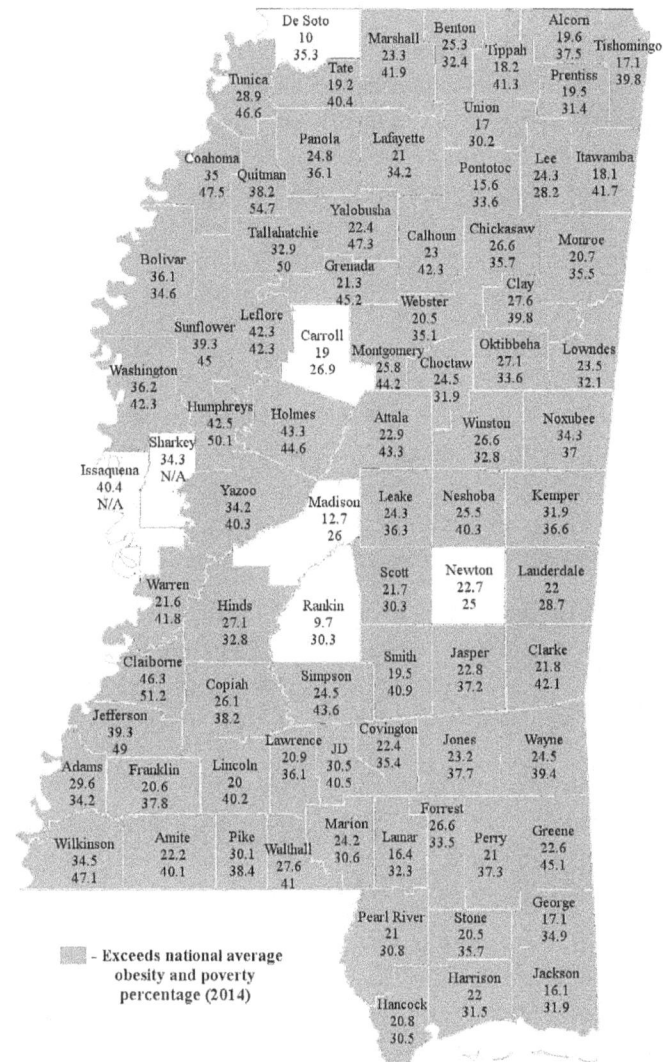

Note: Top numbers below the county names represents the percent of county population living below the poverty line as of 2014. Bottom numbers below the county names represent the percentage of county population considered obese. For clarity, Jefferson Davis County is shortened to "JD".

Source: County poverty line figures were obtained from the USDA's Economic Research Initiative. County obesity data was collected from 2011-2014 by the MSDH and were reported in the State of Obesity Action plan 2016. Sharkey and Issaquena county obesity data were considered "unreliable". Thus, the rates are excluded from the figure.

---

15 In 2014, the national percentage of adults considered obese was approximately 27.7% where the percentage of the population below the poverty line was approximately 13.5%.

than higher priced goods not provided by the program. Furthermore, because participants have lower-incomes, they are the least able to substitute toward healthy, higher priced foods. Although unintentional, both programs are associated with negative health consequences, primarily obesity.

SNAP is the largest federal program, in terms of cost and total participation designed to assist low-income individuals and households to afford a sufficient supply of food.[16] As of 2016, approximately 44 million participants nationwide received approximately $67 billion in benefits from the SNAP program. Mississippi has one of the highest SNAP participation rates with approximately 19.4% of the population receiving benefits as of 2013 (only trailing Oregon by 0.4%). Because SNAP provides food items to its participants, recipients have a strong incentive to consume the food provided by SNAP and only to acquire additional food items with personal income when necessary. Currently, SNAP benefits can be used to purchase unhealthy food items including soda, candy, cookies, ice cream, bakery cakes, and energy drinks.[17]

SNAP's contribution to the obesity problem is twofold. First, it provides additional incentives to consume food items which increase the risk of becoming obese. Second, because it provides food items to low-income consumers, its targeted consumers are strongly disadvantaged by not utilizing these benefits. Both factors make SNAP participation a reinforced incentive to consume less healthy food items. Empirical evidence illustrates that SNAP participation increases the risk for elevated BMI and obesity.[18] Furthermore, when compared to eligible but nonparticipating households, empirical evidence indicates participating households consume more sugary foods, fatty foods, and soda.[19]

SNAP eligibility in Mississippi is largely based on household size and income thresholds set by the state government. Mississippi has more lenient eligibility requirements than many other areas with income thresholds set well below the national average. Income eligibility requirements for households between 1-5 people are shown in Figure 15.3. Figure 15.3 demonstrates that Mississippi's current maximum income threshold for SNAP eligibility is consistently 23% higher than the national average. As a consequence, eligibility requirements are comparatively less restrictive.[20]

County level data finds that higher SNAP participation is associated with higher obesity rates. Figure 15.4 illustrates an unsurprising relation between SNAP participation rates and obesity rates at the county level. SNAP and obesity are highly correlated

Figure 15.3: SNAP Eligibility in Mississippi

Household Size	SNAP Maximum Eligible Monthly Income Threshold (US Average)	SNAP Maximum Eligible Monthly Income Threshold (Mississippi)	% Difference
1	$990	$1287	23%
2	$1335	$1736	23%
3	$1,680	$2,184	23%
4	$2025	$2633	23%
5	$2,370	$3081	23%

Note: All figures are for 2016-2017 eligibility.

Source: Figures on US average maximum SNAP eligibility income were obtained from the FNS. Maximum SNAP eligibility incomes for Mississippi were obtained from mybenefits.gov. Monthly income is used because SNAP eligibility is based on monthly rather than annual income.

---

16 This is sometimes referred to as "food insecurity".

17 Energy drinks are only covered by SNAP benefits if they have a nutritional facts label. SNAP benefits do not extend to vitamins, medicines, or health supplements because the Food and Drug Administration does not consider these food items.

18 See Leung and Villamar (2010), Baum (2011), DeBono, Ross, and Berrang-Ford (2012). It is important to note some literature does not find a consistent relationship between SNAP participation and obesity (Ver Ploeg, Mancino, Lin, and Wang 2006; Gunderson 2013). However, these studies are limited in considering socio-economic, local food market, and family composition factors.

19 See Wilde, McNamara, and Ranney (1999) and Whitmore (2002).

20 From 2009-2013, the median household size in Mississippi was 2.65 which is similar to the US average over the same period (2.63).

at 0.59. Additionally, 74 out of 82 counties exceed both the national average for SNAP participation and obesity rates.

In response to concerns regarding SNAP's association with obesity and other detrimental health outcomes, the federal Food and Nutrition Service agency introduced an educational sub-component of SNAP named SNAP-ed. SNAP-ed's role is to educate participants on healthy eating habits and effective budgeting strategies to make healthier food items more affordable. In 2017, Mississippi spent over $4 million dollars on SNAP-ed programs.[21] Unfortunately, obesity rates for low-income households have not diminished. Evidence for SNAP-ed's success remains mixed.[22]

WIC, also a federal program, is designed specifically to assist low-income women and children under 5 years old.[23] WIC is funded through matching programs where the federal government matches the funds allocated by state governments. WIC also provides educational programs to assist low-income women to understand their nutritional needs and of their children. Like SNAP, WIC eligibility requirements are determined by state governments.

The majority of WIC participants in Mississippi are infants and children (approximately 81% from October-September 2013) according to the National WIC Association. Mississippi WIC benefits supply participating infants and children with formula, infant cereal, and juices at no cost to the parents. Mississippi WIC policy also makes SNAP eligible households automatically eligible for WIC (assuming the household has a child below the age of 5).

Figure 15.4: SNAP Participation and Obesity in Mississippi, 2014

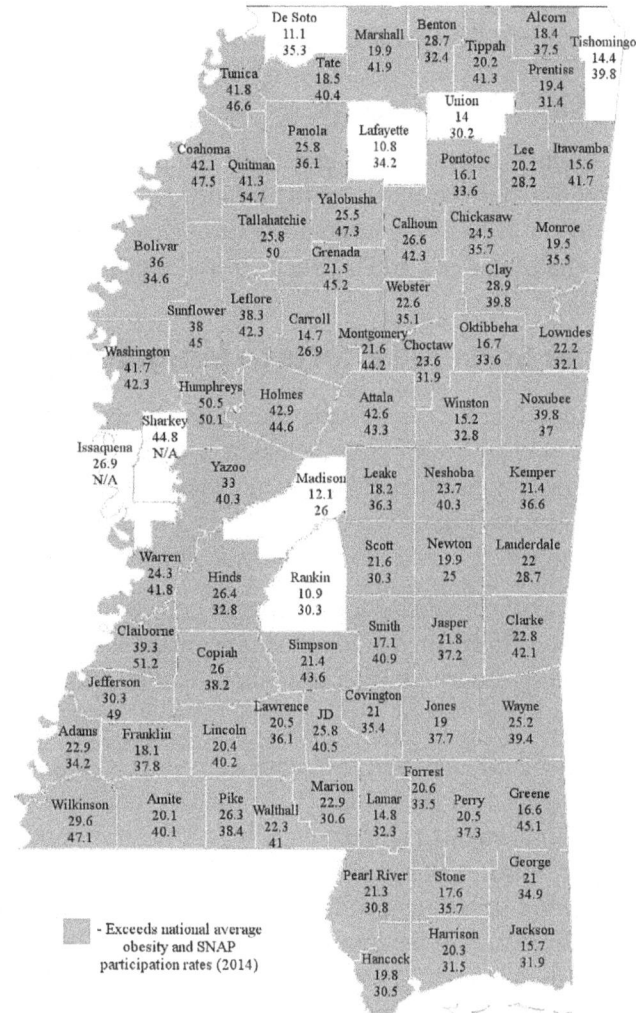

Note: Top numbers below the county names represents the percent of county population participating in the SNAP program as of 2011 (the most recent data available). Bottom numbers below the county names represent the percentage of county population considered obese. For clarity, Jefferson Davis County is shortened to "JD".

Source: County obesity data was collected from 2011-2014 by the MSDH and were reported in the State of Obesity Action plan 2016. Data for Sharkey and Issaquena counties are "unreliable" and are therefore excluded in the figure.

---

21 The federal government matches state level spending for SNAP-ed.

22 For a brief account of studies examining the effectiveness of SNAP-ed, see; Leung et al. (2013), Nguyen et al. (2015), and March et al. (2017).

23 Newborns, infants, and children can apply separately from their parents or legal guardians. However, frequently both are eligible to receive benefits.

WIC is also associated with higher levels of obesity. Unlike SNAP, WIC is specifically associated with higher rates of childhood obesity. According to the Center for Disease Control, from 2011-2014, toddlers participating in WIC held an obesity rate of approximately 15%. In contrast, the obesity rate for nonparticipating toddlers was approximately 9%.[24] As of 2015, Mississippi ranked slightly below the national average for toddlers participating in WIC at 14.5% which was still above the national nonparticipating average at 9%. Additionally, Mississippi is among only 15 states where WIC participants between the ages of 2-4 did not demonstrate a decrease in obesity rates from 2010-2014.

Childhood obesity is an important component of the obesity problem because, as most obesity research finds, obese children are significantly more likely to become obese adults, and obese infants are significantly more likely to remain obese through adulthood.[25] Unfortunately, this trend holds in Mississippi where children, teens, and high school students have the highest obesity rates in the nation.

Further State-led Efforts to Mitigate Obesity

Rather than explaining wide-spread obesity as the consequence of poor food choices made by a large number of cognitively limited consumers, wide-spread obesity is the result of federal and state policies incentivizing unhealthy consumption patterns. It follows that policy or intervention, rather than consumers, are key contributors to the obesity problem. A critical insight stemming from the findings above is further policy efforts are likely to provide little benefit in deterring obesity.

Instead of eliminating these perverse policies, state legislators are likely to double down and increase policy efforts in an attempt to influence consumer choices. This can come in the form of additional taxes on unhealthy foods or further restrictions to unhealthy food options. Both efforts affect all citizens within a state.

Taxing food items and restricting consumer access is problematic. Although taxes increase the price of food items, and should lower the amount consumed, research efforts find considerably high taxes must be implemented to meaningfully reduce consumption. For example, one estimate finds a 20% tax on sugary drinks would result in a total weight loss of approximately 2 pounds.[26] Additionally, changing the prices of unhealthy goods may not result in consuming healthier foods. Soda taxes are associated with increased consumption of more sugary fruit juices and alcoholic beverages (Lusk 2013). Taxing fast-food meals is associated with substitutions into more fatty foods consumed at home, which may lead to more weight gain than consuming fast-food meals (Schroeter, Lusk, and Tyner 2008). Conversely, efforts to promote healthy eating by providing financial incentives also have little evidence for success (Brambila-Macias et al. 2011).

The alternative method of restricting access may result in making vulnerable parties worse off. Reducing access to unhealthy foods, which are more likely to be consumed by low-income consumers, reduces access to food for those who have the least access to food. As a result, such interventions are disproportionately harmful to lower-income consumers. Furthermore, restricting the choices of specific demographics could result in stigmatizing low-income and minority segments of the population.[27]

---

24 The study also notes the national obesity rate for toddlers was previously higher. The overall obesity rate for toddlers was estimated at 15.5% in 2004 and 15.9% in 2010. As the rates of toddler obesity for WIC and non WIC participants have diverged since 2010, this indicates the WIC program likely contributes to toddler obesity.

25 See Serdula et al. (1993), and Charney et al. (1976).

26 The current highest tax on sugary drinks is 2 cents per ounce.

27 See Shenkin and Jacobson (2010) and Gunderson (2013).

Mississippi's state government's most recent efforts to curtail obesity are outlined in the MSHD's Obesity Action Plan 2016. An incomplete list of the plan's desired outcomes include: linking public health goals (including reducing obesity) in ways that give stores an incentive to enhance local food environments, educating consumers on how to read nutritional labels, increasing the number of healthy food choices available to employees in all appropriate work site venues, and increasing lactation (breastfeeding) consulting.[28] Each of these goals, although well intended, are costly to implement and have been tried previously with policies in other states where they demonstrated little success. Additionally, each goal faces the potential to lead to further unintended consequences.

Government efforts exhibit high costs with little benefit. The primary reason previous and potential future policy efforts to curb obesity fall short of their intended goals is a failure to address the underlying reasons for widespread obesity, persistent poverty and the resultant lack of choice in selecting healthier food options. The consequences of these policies are particularly damaging because the majority of those affected by their unintended consequences are the least well off members of society.

Private Efforts to Mitigate Obesity

For health and personal reasons, consumers have an incentive to avoid obesity or to lose weight if they are obese. Producers have an incentive to provide goods and services to help consumers avoid and reverse obesity because of the profit motive. Consumers looking to lose weight and improve their health can exchange portions of their income with entrepreneurs providing goods and services to help the consumers accomplish their weight-loss and health goals. Provided that regulatory efforts do not curtail the efforts of consumers and producers, these exchanges should result in more health products from suppliers and more healthy consumers. Empirical evidence overwhelmingly finds such transactions take place and do so frequently. Globally, some have predicted health and wellness industry sales to reach $1 trillion dollars.[29]

The US is one of the largest consumers of health goods and services. In 2016, specialty food sales reached $127 billion in the US.[30] US citizens spent nearly $20 billion on dietary books, drugs, and surgeries in 2012. Private interests to meet consumer demand for health products and services constitute a growing section of the US economy where, according to the Bureau of Labor Statistics, nutritionist and dietitian occupations are expected to grow 16% each year from 2014-2024. Regardless of whether these products and services are successful, the evidence demonstrates consumers appear health-conscious enough to take action and producers work to meet consumer desires.

It is not sufficient to review the goods and services provided on a macro scale to address Mississippi's obesity problem. To combat the obesity faced by a large percentage of Mississippians, private actors must find ways to provide these goods and services to lower-income consumers. Evidence of provision for this specific demographic would demonstrate the market can provide solutions to the obesity problem to those facing the highest risk for becoming obese and with the lowest access to health products.

Fortunately for those most vulnerable, the market has provided. Entrepreneurship has worked to lower prices to attract low-income food purchasers. In 2014, Los Angeles entrepreneurs Sam Polk and David Foster developed the restaurant Everytable.[31]Everytable was designed to offer healthy meal options for

---

28 The entire program contains 4 broad goals with 13 strategies and 57 bullet points outlining how to achieve the strategies. However, the main goals outlined in this section provide a broad representation of the program's intended outcomes.

29 The industry measures include dietary and physical activity goods and services. See Pilzer (2010) for details.

30 According to the Specialty Foods Association's Annual State of the Industry Report.

Southern Los Angeles inhabitants who hold an annual per-capita income of approximately $13,000. Polk and Foster cite noticing the only dining options in the area were fast-food restaurants as their motivation for starting a business.[32] The venture was successful and, as of 2017, there are three Everytable locations in Los Angeles.

In a similar story, noticing a shortage of grocery stores in low-income areas, entrepreneur Olympia Auset opened a low-priced, organic food supermarket named SÜPRMARKT in Los Angeles. SÜPRMARKT offers subscriptions to receive inexpensive food packages, free nutritional information, and recipes on its website, and engages in frequent outreach efforts to expand its consumer base. Auset notes her business serves as a substitute for government food policy: "The success of my entrepreneurship venture is enough to prove to anyone that they can tackle societal issues without relying on anyone".[33]

Private efforts at the communal level also work to provide support and information to breastfeeding mothers. The largest organization dedicated to this cause is La Leche League (LLL). LLL started in 1956 by 7 women concerned by decreases in breastfeeding rates in the US. Today, LLL is an international organization of volunteers offering free counseling through regular meetings, a "breast feeding helpline", and online podcasts. The organization does sell merchandise, but primarily finances itself through donation.

The examples above provide a sliver of entrepreneurial and local solutions providing means to prevent and reverse obesity. Local private solutions demonstrate more success in providing goods and services to combat the obesity problem because they work within and change the underlying conditions which incentivize obesity. Supermarkets and restaurants which specialize in providing healthy alternatives to food options available in low-income neighborhoods work within the external constraints faced by the consumer. Similarly, LLL provides local assistance to breastfeeding mothers. Rather than steering choices, these private options provide additional choices by offering new more accessible products or information.

Concluding Remarks and Recommendations

Mississippi's obesity problem affects a considerable component of the population medically and financially. Obesity is the result of widespread incentives to choose unhealthy foods; thus, economic analysis can provide insight into why a large number of consumers consistently make such choices.

State policy and government interventions have exacerbated Mississippi's obesity problem. State policies are inflexible, costly to implement, and do not account for external conditions faced by individual consumers. The result is unintended consequences.

Local and private efforts to reduce obesity can be more successful because private and local mechanisms address the specific circumstances of consumers. Freedom, in the form of allowing as much choice as possible, provides the most effective means to combat obesity. Private efforts to provide information and healthy alternatives allow for low-income consumers to improve their health and reduce the risk of obesity. Reducing taxes which stifle consumption choices such as grocery taxes would also provide more consumers the ability to consume healthier (but more expensive) food items. The efforts of private producers to supply healthy goods, services, and information on how to improve health do not require legislative actions nor regulation to serve the needs of consumers. Legislation and regulation, however, can

---

31 Details of the restaurants mission, location, story, and menu are available at https://www.everytable.com.

32 See https://www.everytable.com/about.

33 See http://yourblackworld.net/2017/06/08/26-year-old-black-woman-entrepreneur-launches-low-cost-organic-grocery-store/.

stifle and prevent such efforts from improving health and reducing obesity. The analysis and examples provided demonstrate this unfortunate, but predictable, trend.

Obesity is fundamentally the result of consistently consuming food items which lead to weight gain. Restricting food choices through regulatory efforts and policies fail to address why these foods are consumed, demonstrating an incomplete understanding of the obesity problem. Private actors' goods and services on the market increase the choices available to consumers. Economic freedom and markets remain the most effective means to increasing wealth, improving health, addressing social issues, and promoting prosperity. Reducing wide-spread obesity is no exception.

References

Baum, Charles L. 2011. The Effects of Food Stamps on Obesity. *Southern Economic Journal*. 77(3): 623-651.

Brambila-Macias, Jose, Bhavani Shankar, Sara Capacci, Mario Mazzocchi, Federico J. A. Perez-Cueto, Wim Verbeke, and W.B. Traill. 2011. Policy Interventions to Promote Healthy Eating: A Review of What Works, What Does Not, and What is Promising. Food and Nutrition Bulletin. 32(4): 365-375.

Charney, Evan, Helen Chamblee Goodman, Margaret McBride, Barbro Lyon, Rosalie Pratt, Burtis Breese, Frank Disney, and Kurt Marx. 1976. Childhood Antecedents of Adult Obesity – Do Chubby Infants Become Obese Adults? *New England Journal of Medicine*. 295: 6-9.

DeBono, Nathaniel L, Nancy A .Ross, and Lea Berrang-Ford. 2012. Does the Food Stamp Program Cause Obesity? A Realist Review and a Call for Place-Based Research. *Health and Place*. 18(2): 747- 756.

Drewnowski, Adam, and S.E. Specter. 2004. Poverty and Obesity: The Role of Energy Density and Energy Cost. *The American Journal of Clinical Nutrition*. 79(1): 6-16.

Drewnowski, Adam, and Nicole Darmon. 2005. The Economics of Obesity: Dietary Energy Density and Energy Cost. *The American Journal of Clinical Nutrition*. 82(1): 2655-2735.

Goran, Micheal, Stanley Ulijaszek, and Emily Ventura. 2013. High Fructose corn Syrup and Diabetes Prevalence: A Global Perspective. *Global Public Health*. 2012: 1-10.

Gunderson, Craig. 2013. SNAP and Obesity. University of Kentucky Center for Poverty Research Discussion Paper Series DP 2013-02. Online: http://uknowledge.uky.edu/cgi/viewcontent.cgi?article=1018&context=ukcpr_papers. (cited July 25th, 2017).

Hruschka. 2012. Do economic constraints on food choice make people fat? A critical review of two hypotheses for the poverty-obesity paradox. *American Journal on Human Biology* 24(3): 277-285

Kyureghian, Gayaneh, Rodolfo M. Nayga, Suparna Bhattacharya. 2013. The Effect of Food Store Access and Income on Household Purchases of Fruits and Vegetables: A Mixed Effects Analysis. *Applied Economic Perspectives and Policy*. 35(1): 69-88.

Leung, Cindy, and Eric L. Villamor. 2011. Is Participation in Food and Income Assistance Programmes Associated with Obesity in California Adults? Results from a State-wide Survey. *Public Health Nutrition*. 14(4): 642-652.

Levine, James. 2011. Poverty and Obesity in the US. Diabetes. 60(11), 2667-2669.

Lusk, Jayson. 2013. The Food Police: A Well Fed Manifesto About the Politics of Your Plate. Crown Forum: New York.

Pettus, Emily. 2013. Mississippi's New 'Anti-Bloomberg' Law Bans Restrictions on Food Portions. CNS News. 19 March. Online: http://www.cnsnews.com/news/article/mississippis-new-anti-bloomberg-law-bans- restrictions-food-portions-0.

Philipson, Thomas J, and Richard Posner. 1999. The Long-Run Growth in Obesity as a Function of Technological Change. NBER Working Paper No. 7423. Online: http://www.nber.org/papers/w7423.pdf. (cited July 25th, 2017).

Philipson, Thomas J. 2001. The World Wide Growth in Obesity: An Economics Research Agenda. *Health Economics*. 10(1): 1-7.

Pilzer, Paul Z. 2007. The New Wellness Revolution: How to Make a Fortune in the Next Trillion Dollar Industry. Wiley. Hoboken, New Jersey.

March, Raymond J, Conrad P. Lyford, Carlos E. Caprio, Tullaya Boonsaeng. 2017. Do SNAP Recipients Get the Best Prices? Working Paper. Available: https://ssrn.com/abstract=2824260. (cited August 2nd, 2017).

Mississippi Center for Obesity Research. Online: https://www.umc.edu/Research/Centers-and- Institutes/Mississippi-Center-for-Obesity- Research/Home-Page.html. (cite July 15th, 2017).

Mississippi State Department of Health. 2016. Obesity Action Plan 2016. Online: http://msdh.ms.gov/msdhsite/_static/resources/6164.pdf. (cited July 21st, 2017).

Mississippi State Department of Health. Fruits and Vegetables: More Matters. Online: http://msdh.ms.gov/msdhsite/index.cfm/43,0,213,242,html. (cited July 15th, 2017).

Nguyen, Bihn T, Kerem Shuval, Farryl Bertmann, and Amy L. Yaroch. 2015. The Supplemental Nutrition Assistance Program, Food Insecurity, Dietary Quality, and Obesity Among US Adults. *American Journal of Public Health*. 105(7): 1453-1459.

Neporent, Liz. 2013. Mississippi Governor Signs 'Anti-Bloomberg' Bill. ABC News. 19 March.Online: http://abcnews.go.com/Health/mississippi-governor-signs-anti-bloomberg- bill/story?id=18731896.

Schroeter, Christiane, Jayson Lusk, and Wallace Tyner. 2008. Determining the Impact of Food Price and Income Changes on Body Weight. *Journal of Health Economics*. 27(1): 45-68.

Serdula, Mary K, D. Ivery, R.J. Coates, D. Freedman, D. Williamson, and T. Byers. 1993. Do Obese Children Become Obese Adults? A Review of the Literature. *Preventative Medicine*. 22(2): 167-177.

Shenkin, Jonathan D and Michael F. Jacobson. 2010. Using the Food Stamp Program and Other Methods to Promote Healthy Diets for Low-Income Consumers. *American Journal of Public Health*. 100(9): 1562-1564.

Taubes, Gary. 2006. Good Calories, Bad Calories: Fats, Carbs, and the Controversial Science of Diet and Health. Alfred A. Knopf. New York.

Thaler, Richard. 2016. Misbehaving : The Making of Behavioral Economics. W. W. Norton & Company. New York.

Thaler, Richard. and Cass L. Sunstein. 2008. Nudge: Improving Decisions About Health, Wealth, and Happiness. Penguin Books. New York.

Thaler, Richard. and Cass L. Sunstein. Libertarian Paternalism. *American Economic Review*. 93(2): 175-179.

Ver Ploeg, Michele, Lisa Mancino, Lin Biing-Hwan, and Chia-Yih Wang. 2007. The Vanishing Weight Gap: Trends in Obesity Among Adult Food Stamp Participants (US) (1976- 2002). *Economics and Human Biology*. 5(1): 20-36.

Whitmore, Diane. 2002. What are Food Stamps Worth? Princeton University Working Paper #468. Online: https://msu.edu/~dick-ertc/301f06/whatarefoodstampsworth.pdf. (cited July 15th, 2017).

Wilde, Parke E, Paul E. McNamara, and Christine K. Ranney.1999. The Effect of Income and Food Programs on Dietary Quality: A Seemingly Unrelated Regression Analysis with Error Components. *American Journal of Agricultural Economics*. 81(4): 959-971.

Yan, Holly. 2013. No Soda Ban Here: Mississippi passes 'Anti-Bloomberg' bill CNN. 21 March. Online: http://www.cnn.com/2013/03/21/us/mississippi-anti-bloomberg-bill/index.html.

16

Criminal Justice
Reform in Mississippi

Trey Goff

16

Criminal Justice Reform in Mississippi

Trey Goff

Mississippi perpetually ranks firmly at the bottom of nearly every measure of success, prosperity, and wealth amongst the 50 states. However, Mississippi does hold the distinct honor of being in the top five of one list: incarceration rates. Yes, Mississippi has the 4th highest incarceration rate of any state in the United States, which has the highest incarceration rate of any country in the world by a large margin.[1] This puts Mississippi firmly atop the world rankings of incarceration rates at 609 prisoners per 100,000 population as of 2016.

However, this is not an achievement Mississippians should be proud of. Mississippi's tendency to imprison more people than almost anywhere else in the world has had a powerful negative impact on the state's economy, not to mention a violation of the most fundamental of human rights: freedom. Statistics detailing just how severe the impact of the criminal justice system has been on the people of Mississippi will be detailed below. Furthermore, the impact of incarceration on not just the incarcerated individual, but their extended social network is a powerful negative one with far-reaching economic consequences. Even worse, this systemic incarceration contains profound racial disparities that play a significant role in keeping average African-American incomes well below the poverty level in Mississippi, further intensifying the despondent economic conditions of Mississippi's largest minority group.

Although these facts may seem disheartening, all hope is not lost. There are a number of reforms Mississippi could enact to ameliorate these conditions. These reforms could significantly improve Mississippi's economic malaise while saving the state government millions of dollars in reduced criminal justice expenditure at the same time. These reforms will be detailed at the end of the chapter.

---

1   Criminal Justice Facts, The Sentencing Project, 2017

Mississippi: Land of the Criminals

The magnitude of mass incarceration in Mississippi is staggering. According to the Sentencing Project, Mississippi has 609 prisoners per 100,000 population. This number is meaningless, however, without being nested in the context of the incarceration rate of other states and other wealthy western nations. For example, nearby states such as Tennessee, Arkansas, North Carolina, and South Carolina all have rates below 500 per 100,000 population. Our direct neighbor, Louisiana, has the highest incarceration rate in the world imprisoning 873 per 100,000. Louisiana is also one of the most corrupt states in the union. All states exist under the same federal criminal justice system just as Mississippi does, raising questions as to why states like Mississippi and Louisiana imprison so many additional citizens compared to the national average. [2]

An additional comparison with wealthy industrialized countries further highlights the relative severity of Mississippi's mass incarceration. Canada, Germany, France, Italy, The United Kingdom, and all Scandinavian countries have incarcerations rates at or below 120 per 100,000 population, with most countries imprisoning under 100 per 100,000.[3] Thus, Mississippi's incarceration rate is six times that of almost all other western nations. In fact, Mississippi's incarceration rate is higher than both Communist Cuba (510 per 100,000) and Communist China (121 per 100,000) (although the numbers for these two regimes may not be accurate). Mississippi even imprisons more citizens than Russia (475 per 100,000), where freedom of the press is nearly nonexistent and political activism is a jailable offense.[4] Figure 16.1 presents these comparative incarceration rates graphically.

Mississippi's relatively high incarceration rate is not a result of increased crime either. According to the FBI's Uniform Crime Report, Mississippi's rates of both violent and property crime peaked in 1996 and have been steadily declining since, as Figure 16.2 indicates. This is commensurate with the national trend as well.[5] This decrease in crime rates cannot be explained by our heightened incarceration rates. As John Pfaff notes in *Locked in*, "rising crime over the 1970s and 1980s can explain, at most, half of the increase in prison population in those decades. That relationship weakened drastically during the

Figure 16.1: Incarceration Rates across Countries

Prison Population per 100,000

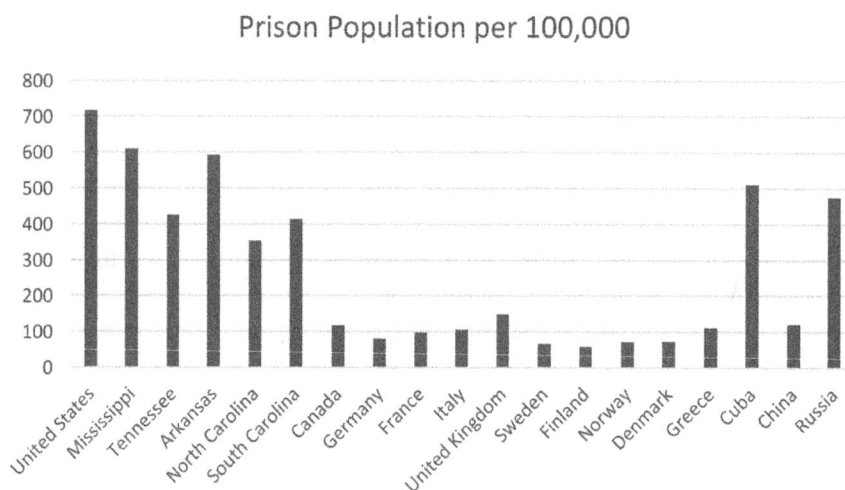

Source: World Prison Population List, Roy Walmsley, Institute for Criminal Policy Research, 2016 (http://www.prisonstudies.org/sites/default/files/resources/downloads/world_prison_population_list_11th_edition_0.pdf)

---

2   Maine, for example, has the lowest incarceration rate at 132 per 100,000 population. This suggests state policy has a far larger impact on incarceration rates than federal policy.

3   World Prison Population List, Roy Walmsley, Institute for Criminal Policy Research, 2016

4   Freedom in the World 2016, Freedom House, 2016

5   FBI Uniform Crime Report 2015

1990s, as prison populations continued to rise even as crime declined."[6] The disparity between rising incarceration rates and falling crime rates only continues to grow over time. This begs the obvious question: if more crimes aren't being committed, then why are more people imprisoned?

Figure 16.2: Mississippi's Violent Crime Rate, 1960-2012

Source: FBI, Uniform Crime Reports, prepared by the National Archive of Criminal Justice Data (https://www.ucrdatatool.gov/Search/Crime/State/RunCrimeStatebyState.cfm)

The answer lies with nonviolent criminals. In 2014, Pew Charitable Trusts created a policy brief that provided a detailed overview of Mississippi's criminal justice system (this research was part of a criminal justice reform effort in 2014 which will be discussed later.) In this brief, it is noted that 45% of Mississippi's incarcerated population are in prison for nonviolent crimes. Figure 16.3 depicts this graphically. According to Pew, nonviolent criminals "accounted for more than two-thirds of the increase in prison admissions between 2002 and 2012."

These facts indicate that it is not violent criminals in dire need of separation from the general population that are being imprisoned, but rather individuals who have not bodily harmed anyone, having instead broken a nonviolent crime law such as possession or trafficking of an illegal substance. Enforcement of these nonviolent crime laws has a myriad of other negative unintended consequences, from in-

---

6   *Locked In*, John Pfaff, Basic Books, 2017

centivizing an increase in drug potency, to a lack of adequate quality monitoring of the substances, to encouraging violent gangs to increase drug trafficking activity, to an increase in drug prices for highly addictive products with a relatively inelastic demand, to increased corruption in related government agencies.[7] [8]

Mississippi averages over 12,250 drug offense arrests per year.[9] Mississippi also has one of the highest per capita drug possession arrest rates in the nation.[10] More inmates are admitted for revocations of supervision than for actual new criminal convictions. Thus, it is plausible that a large majority of individuals being admitted into prison either committed a nonviolent crime or merely violated a technical supervision rule. If so, this requires a reexamining of the justice of their incarceration, an issue that will be discussed below.

Another factor exacerbating Mississippi's prison population is the ever-lengthening nature of sentencing in Mississippi. According to the aforementioned Pew report, "State data showed that the time inmates spend in prison grew significantly over the past decade...a dramatic length-

Figure 16.3: Mississippi's Type of Criminal Offenders, 2014

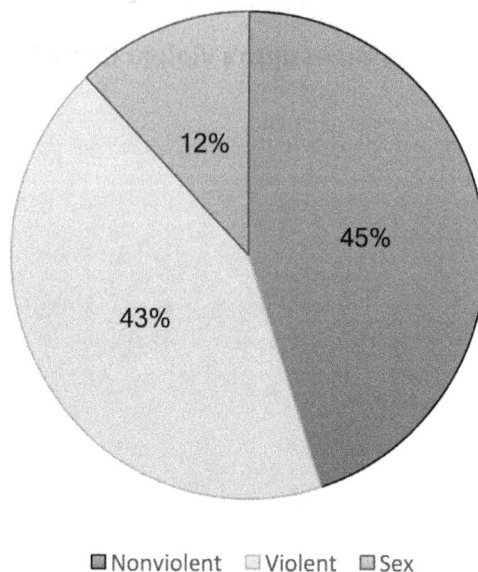

■ Nonviolent   □ Violent   ■ Sex

Source: "Mississippi's 2014 Corrections and Criminal Justice Reform," Pew Charitable Trusts, 2014 (http://www.pewtrusts.org/~/media/assets/2014/09/pspp_mississippi_2014_corrections_justice_reform.pdf)

ening of sentences (28 percent) between fiscal 2002 and 2012." This is at least in part a direct result of Mississippi's mandatory minimum sentencing provisions. For example, possession of at least 250 grams of marijuana carries a mandatory minimum of at least one year. These minimums only increase with an increase in the amount of marijuana in the arrested individual's possession. [11] Compare that to some of our surrounding states, such as Louisiana, where mandatory minimums don't kick in until 2.5lbs (1134 grams), or Arkansas, where mandatory minimums don't begin until 10lbs (4536 grams). Mississippi has disproportionate levels of punishment for marijuana possession, something that is legal elsewhere in the US. The sentences for possession of hash or marijuana concentrates is even higher, with a gram of concentrate carrying a prison sentence of up to three years.[12] Strict mandatory minimums mean Mississippians are going to prison more often and staying there longer once incarcerated.

The number of Mississippians who have a criminal record has also reached new heights. These criminal records follow Mississippians for the entirety of their lives, and can make life exceedingly difficult for them. From finding a job to renting an apartment, a criminal record can be a lifelong scarlet letter with intense economic ramifications. According to the Bureau of Justice statistics, at least 866,600 Mississippi-

7   The *Economics of Prohibition*, Mark Thorton, Mises Institute, 2014

8   "The price elasticity of demand for heroin: Matched longitudinal and experimental evidence," Olmstead et. Al., Journal of Health Economics, May 2015, pgs. 59-71

9   Mississippi, Drug Policy Alliance, 2017

10 "Every 25 Seconds," Human Rights Watch, 2016

11 Miss. Ann. Code § 41-29-139(c)(2)(B)

12 Miss. Ann. Code § 41-29-139(c)

ans have criminal records on file.[13] It should be noted that this figure can include anyone who has been arrested or taken into custody by police, regardless of whether the charges were ultimately dropped. This means many people who have never been convicted of a crime still have a lingering criminal history. Consequently, the Sentencing Project notes that nearly 7 percent of the adult voting-age population in Mississippi is disenfranchised because of a felony record.[14] These records are also either difficult or impossible to have sealed or expunged, a process which will be detailed later.

Our state's massive incarceration rates are not spread equally among the population. Large racial disparities exist within the Mississippi criminal justice system. According to the Sentencing Project, Mississippi's white incarceration rate is 346 per 100,000 population, while the black incarceration rate is 1052 per 100,000.[15] These figures indicate that the black incarceration rate is over three times that of their white counterparts in Mississippi. More than 65% of our prison population is black, too, despite the fact that African Americans are only 37% of our overall population. Even more distressing, 58% of all drug arrests in 2011 were for black Mississippians, despite the fact that whites use drugs at a slightly higher rate than blacks (53.4% to 47.7% lifetime use rates, respectively).[16] Such racial disparities in arrests and sentencing are deeply troubling, and have likely contributed to the continued economic despondence of African Americans in Mississippi.

However, the human impact of these policies can often be lost in translation. After all, it's one thing to discuss per capita personal income, government expenditures, and raw incarceration numbers; it's another thing entirely to attach a face, a name, a story to it in order to understand the gross injustice of the emotional and psychological impacts of these policies. Take the story of Atiba Parker.[17] Atiba, a resident of Columbus, Mississippi, was diagnosed with schizoaffective disorder. Schizoaffective disorder is described, according to the Mayo Clinic, as "a person experiences a combination of schizophrenia symptoms, such as hallucinations or delusions, and mood disorder symptoms, such as depression or mania." This would ordinarily be a debilitating disorder, but Atiba self-medicated with marijuana. He was arrested and charged with possession of marijuana in 2001, branding him with a criminal record. The combination of having a criminal record and having a mental illness made it difficult for him to earn money, so he could no longer afford his self-prescribed medication. He began selling small amounts of crack out of desperation to afford marijuana. He was soon set up by an informant, and was arrested on two charges of selling cocaine. He was eventually sentenced to 34 years in prison for selling 0.3 grams of crack-cocaine, with another 8 years tacked on for a 0.1 gram residue of cocaine found in his mother's car. A mentally ill man doing his best to make a life for himself found an effective medicine in marijuana, only to be jailed for 42 years for selling miniscule amounts of crack-cocaine in a desperate effort to afford it. He is currently serving his time without access to any psychiatric medication.

Consider the case of Mrs. Ruth Daniels, a 69 year old African-American widow.[18] In 2014, a bureau of narcotics helicopter spotted what appeared to be marijuana plants growing near her home in Macon. This led to a raid of her property, where the narcotics agents discovered 85 marijuana plants. After a lengthy legal battle, Mrs. Daniels entered a plea bargain, where she was sentenced to 10 years in prison.

---

13 "Survey of State Criminal Justice History Information Systems," Bureau of Justice Statistics, 2014

14 "State-Level Estimates of Felon Disenfranchisement in the United States, 2010", The Sentencing Project

15 "The Color of Justice: Racial and Ethnic Disparity in State Prisons," The Sentencing Project, Ashley Nellis, 2016

16 "Results from the 2015 National Survey on Drug Use and Health: Detailed Tables," Substance Abuse and Mental Health Services Administration

17 "Atiba Parker," Families Against Mandatory Minimums, 2016

18 "Macon woman, 70, serving decade prison term for pot," Isabelle Altman, The Dispatch, April 23, 2016

Mrs. Daniels had never received so much as a parking ticket before, and continues to assert that the plants were not hers. The 69-year-old grandmother was known as a paragon of the Macon community; she often handed out the food she grew in her garden to the neediest in the community. Now, she will most likely die sitting in a Rankin County prison cell, away from her beloved family or community.

Such is the brutal reality of the criminal justice system in Mississippi.

The Relation Between Incarceration and Impoverishment

Although there are many compelling ethical arguments against such mass incarceration, I will not be pursuing them here. We shall instead turn our minds towards the economic impact of incarceration on Mississippi. Not only does imprisoning and forever branding 7% of our population with a criminal record have a direct negative economic impact on the individual imprisoned, but also on their extended social networks. These negative impacts can be far reaching, echoing across generations of Mississippians. The effects have been most pronounced in keeping the black community of Mississippi perpetually ensnared in the jaws of poverty.

The negative economic impacts of mass incarceration act through a variety of mechanisms. The first, and most obvious, is simply pulling individuals out of the labor force. People in prison cannot work and cannot meaningfully contribute to society; they cannot produce anything, earn any wages, or start any businesses. As such, every day an individual spends in prison is another day of missed work, missed productivity, and missed prosperity for not only themselves, but the state as a whole. Consider the fact that Mississippi had approximately 22,000 people incarcerated in 2014 (most recent available data). [19] Now, assume that all 22,000 of those people were to have earned the average per capita personal income for the state of Mississippi in 2016-$36,266.[20] Also assume that those 22,000 incarcerated individuals would follow roughly the same labor force participation rate as the rest of the population of Mississippi-54.6%.[21] This leaves 12,012 of the original 22,000 working. If those 12,000 individuals were to earn the state average PCPI, they would have contributed $435.6 million to the state's economy.[22] Almost half a billion dollars were lost to mass incarceration in 2016 alone. This effect is only compounded for every year, meaning the actual total of wealth lost to the state of Mississippi over time could be a staggering amount.

However, the economic impact of these individual's removal from society is even worse. The time these individuals spend in prison keeps them from being able to accumulate any human capital while serving time. Thus, when they return to the labor market, their productivity levels are far lower than that of their counterparts who were never incarcerated. This lowered productivity level will persist throughout the remainder of their lifetimes, meaning that incarceration has erected a low ceiling of wealth through which it is nigh impossible for the once-incarcerated to pass.

But the economic misery of the incarcerated isn't done yet. No, the scarlet letter of a criminal record means they have vastly diminished job opportunities after release from prison. Whether fair or unfair, employers are far less likely to hire someone with a criminal record than someone with a clean one. In fact, a seminal 2003 paper in the American Journal of Sociology demonstrated just that: white job applicants with a criminal record were 17% less likely to receive a callback than ones with no criminal record, while

19 "Prisoners in 2014," Bureau of Justice Statistics, Ann Carson

20 Federal Reserve Bank of St. Louis Economic Research, 2017

21 Express Employment Professionals State-by-State Analysis of Labor Force Participation Rates, 2015

22 12,012*36,266=435,627,192

black job applicants with a criminal record were 9% less likely to receive a callback (it should be noted, however, that the absolute number of black applicants who received a callback was far lower; in fact, whites *with* criminal records received more callbacks than blacks *without* criminal records).[23]

Recall that black Mississippians comprise over 65% of the prison population and have six times the incarceration rate compared to their white counterparts.[24] These facts, combined with the findings above, paint a segregated picture of modern Mississippi: African Americans in our state are not only six times as likely to be incarcerated, but the negative effects of this incarceration after their release are nearly twice as powerful on them relative to their white counterparts. This could do much to explain why "blacks in Mississippi earn around 69% of what whites earn at the median, among fulltime, year-round workers."[25]

A criminal record is also difficult to shake. Expungement of a criminal record in Mississippi can only occur for select offenses, such as first-time drug offenders who utilize a rehabilitation program through drug court or minors in possession of alcohol. [26] Even these expunctions require a waiting period of anywhere from 1-5 years after conviction, after which time most of the debilitating damage of a criminal record may already done.

Unfortunately, the negative impacts of incarceration go far beyond economics. John Pfaff lays some of these out in vivid detail in *Locked In*:

> Even putting aside the various legal impediments former prisoners face, people who have been released from prison encounter a wide range of costs and risks. They are more likely to overdose on drugs (since drugs outside of prison are cheaper and more potent, and a person's tolerance declines while incarcerated); they leave prison less healthy than when they went in; their family ties are weakened, if not broken; they find it harder to get jobs; and the jobs they do find provide fewer hours, are less secure, and pay less per hour than the jobs they could have landed without a prison record.

Incarceration carries negative impacts beyond those on the directly incarcerated individual as well. Incarceration plays a large role in explaining why the African-American divorce rate is climbing, marriage rate is at an all-time low, and out-of-wedlock births are at an all-time high (the same is true for white Americans as well, but to a far lesser extent).[27] After all, a man or woman incarcerated cannot be there to interact with and strengthen the bonds amongst their family. This breakdown of the family can have far-reaching economic consequences, as seen in the case of unwed mothers. Unwed mothers enter into poverty more often, become welfare recipients more often, and earn less money than their wed counterparts.[28] These out-of-wedlock births also have an intergenerational effect: children born to single mothers have lower educational attainment and thus lower lifetime earnings and economic performance than their counterparts in two-parent homes. [29] Taken together, this evidence indicates the magnitude of the negative impact mass incarceration can have upon the economic performance of a state, as those who are incarcerated earn less, are employed less, are underemployed more, have poorer children with lower lifetime achievement, and are impoverished more often.

---

23 "The Mark of a Criminal Record", Devah Pager, American Journal of Sociology, 2003

24 "The Color of Justice: Racial and Ethnic Disparity in State Prisons," The Sentencing Project, Ashley Nellis, 2016

25 "The Economic Status of African Americans in Mississippi," Center for Policy Research and Planning, 2008

26 Mississippi Code § 99-19-71, 99-15-26(5), 99-19-71(4), 67-3-70(6)

27 "African American Marriage Patterns," Douglas J. Besharov and Andrew West, Hoover Press, 2001

28 "The Economic Consequences of Unwed Motherhood: Using Twin Births as a Natural Experiment," Stephen Bronars and Jeff Grogger, *American Economic Review*, 1994

29 Sheila F. Krein and Andrea H. Beller, "Educational Attainment of Children From Single-Parent Families: Differences by Exposure, Gender and Race," *Demography* 25, (May 1988): 221-234.

Mass incarceration also imposes steep costs on the state government. Of the $333 million budget of the Mississippi Department of Corrections, 93% of it is spent on prisons, even though only 36% of the correctional population is in prison.[30] It costs the corrections department, on average, $67.95 per day to house an inmate. This averages out to around $24,801 dollars per year per inmate kept in Mississippi correctional facilities.[31] If we combine the value of the labor lost to imprisonment calculated above and the cost to the state of keeping those people imprisoned, a rough estimate of the yearly opportunity cost of mass incarceration emerges. That total comes to over $991 million dollars.[32] That's nearly $1 billion a year of potential economic output lost for the already destitute state of Mississippi.

This means that a reduction in the prison population could go a long way toward reducing the overall cost of the Mississippi criminal justice system, potentially saving taxpayers millions of dollars in expenditures while simultaneously increasing tax revenue via increased economic growth. A reduction in mass incarceration is therefore beneficial not only to the state government, but to all citizens of Mississippi through the economic growth it may help create.

There is one final, grossly unjust way in which the Mississippi criminal justice system negatively impacts Mississippians: civil asset forfeiture. Civil asset forfeiture refers to the ability of policing and enforcement agencies to confiscate the property of an individual upon the mere suspicion of criminal activity-no convictions or charges required. It is a circumnavigation of the judicial system, as well a clear violation of the due process rights of Mississippians. In 2015 alone, nearly $4 million in property were seized by the Bureau of Narcotics in Mississippi.[33]

Civil asset forfeiture could have far-reaching economic consequences beyond just the value of the seized assets. Civil asset forfeiture is an abrogation of property rights institutions. This institution-that is, the right to own property unmolested by third parties-is the foundation of economic growth and prosperity. It is the protection and guarantee of the right to private ownership of property that creates the incentive to produce, innovate, and exchange goods. As such, a continued and systemic violation of property rights such as civil asset forfeiture could, if utilized on enough of a widespread scale, weaken public faith that the state will continue to protect the private property of its citizens and not plunder them instead. This, in turn, will create an incentive to move away for those already in the state, and will encourage entrepreneurs and producers to avoid the state at all costs. The economic impact of weakening property rights institutions is well established, and by nearly any measure of well-being, stronger property rights institutions are powerfully associated with higher levels of human well-being and prosperity.[34] As such, any weakening of property rights institutions-such as civil asset forfeiture- could become a dire threat to the economic well-being of an area.

A Path Forward

Although the situation may seem bleak, there is much cause for optimism: the Mississippi legislature has shown a willingness to enact reforms. There is much the legislature can do to ameliorate the harm caused by mass incarceration; these additional reforms will be laid out in detail below. However, it may be worth first evaluating the recent criminal justice reform bill the Mississippi legislature passed in 2014.

---

30 "Mississippi's 2014 Corrections and Criminal Justice Reform," Pew Charitable Trusts, 2014

31 "Mississippi Department of Corrections Fiscal Year 2014 Cost Per Inmate Per Day," Joint Legislative Committee on Performance Evaluation and Expenditure Review, Mississippi Department of Corrections, January 2015

32 (prison population*cost per inmate per year)+(value of lost economic activity of prisoners)=(22,400*$24,801.75)+($435,627,192)=$991,186,392

33 "Mississippi finally brings some transparency to asset forfeiture," C. J. Ciaramella, *Reason*, Mar. 14, 2017

34 "Private Property Rights, Economic Freedom, and Well Being," American Institute for Economic Research, Nov. 1, 2002

In 2014, Mississippi adopted a host of criminal just reform statutes under HB 585, adopted at the behest of a task force. The Corrections and Criminal Justice Task Force was a "bipartisan, interbranch group of state and local officials" which included "legislators, judges, prosecutors, law enforcement officials, defense attorneys, civil rights advocates, a county supervisor, and other criminal justice stakeholders" who were convened for the express purpose of developing a reform package.

HB 585 contained a number of meaningful, albeit small, reforms:

- Established time-served baselines to normalize early releases

- Improved parole release processes

- Allowed judges to utilize more alternative sentences such as probation and drug court

- Revised penalties for simple possession of drugs & reorganized drug tier statutes

- Raised felony theft threshold from $500 to $1000

- Implemented presumptive probation for crimes under $1000

- Expanded parole eligibility to many nonviolent offenders

- Developed risk assessment tools for probation concerns

- Reduced jail time for technical violations of probation (i.e. missed probation officer meeting, late to meeting, etc.)

- Required 10-year fiscal impact statements of future criminal justice legislation

Mississippi took a step in the right direction with this bill, especially insofar as it reduced penalties, increased alternative sentencing options, and expanded the availability and reliability of parole.

These reforms are small and incremental steps toward far greater goals. However, they do little to address some of the more overarching economic impacts of mass incarceration laid out above. Although they will marginally reduce prison populations over time, these reforms do nothing to address the deep-seated problems of nonviolent offense incarceration, relatively disproportionate sentence lengths for some violent crimes, racial disparity in the criminal justice system, and the sheer volume of Mississippians with criminal records. There are several more radical criminal justice reforms Mississippi could undertake to have a far more powerful impact on the Mississippi economy.

The first and most radical reform is a simple one: the decriminalization of all drugs at the state level. As radical as this may initially sound, it is the most logical reform to make to end the injustice of mass incarceration. In fact, both the Human Rights Watch and the American Civil Liberties Union endorsed this approach to reform in a massive 2016 report titled "Every 25 Seconds."[35] The reason a growing number of reputable organizations advocate this massive reform is simple: the war on drugs has been an abject failure. Federal, state, and local governments have spent more than $1.5 trillion on the war on drugs since its inception in 1970, yet the rate of drug addictions in the United States has remained unchanged.[36] Figure 16.4 shows both drug enforcement spending and drug addiction rates over time.

Furthermore, individuals addicted to drugs are not helped or "cured" by incarceration—they need medical rehabilitation, not jail time.

---

35 "Every 25 Seconds," Human Rights Watch, 2016
36 "A Chart That Says the War on Drugs Isn't Working," The Atlantic, October 12, 2012

Figure 16.4: US Spending on Drug Enforcement vs. Past-Month Drug Prevelance Rates

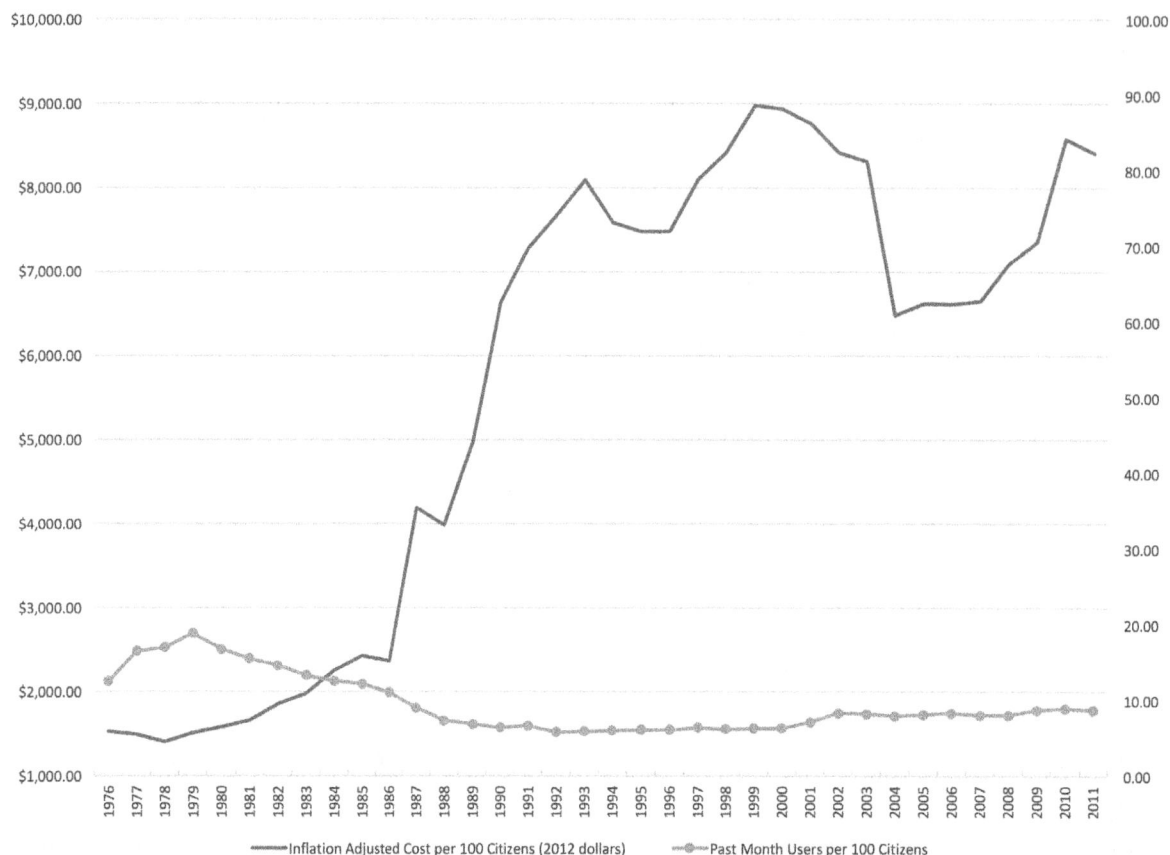

Inflation Adjusted Cost per 100 Citizens (2012 dollars) — Past Month Users per 100 Citizens

Source: "Updating the 1315 Chart," Matt Groff, The 1315 Project, October 23, 2012 (http://www.mattgroff.com/updating-the-1315-chart/)

Ending the war on drugs in Mississippi would put thousands of people back into the labor force, causing a boom in economic activity. It would have disproportionately positive effects on the poorest minority in Mississippi–African Americans. It would massively reduce the costs borne by the State government in both corrections and health spending, as drug addicts could finally obtain the help they need without fear of recrimination. Most importantly, it would allow addicts to be guided back to full health and rejoin the labor force.

Rectifying such powerful injustices as those faced by Abita Parker or Ruth Daniels will necessarily require the decriminalization of drugs. This isn't just a theoretical assumption, either: we have an empirical example of how well drug decriminalization works. In 2001, Portugal decriminalized all drugs and diverted the money required for drug enforcement to rehabilitation programs. The results were persuasive. Past-year drug use among adults has fallen, as have HIV rates.[37] Portugal now has the second-lowest drug overdose death rate in the entire European Union. Although studies regarding the pure economic impact of this are scant, one can deduce that the addition of healthy, productive laborers into the economy could only have a net positive impact on Portugal's economy. Just as importantly, Glenn Greenwald has pointed

---

37 "Why hardly anyone dies from a drug overdose in Portugal," Christopher Ingraham, *Washington Post*, June 5, 2015

out that "none of the nightmare scenarios touted by pre-enactment decriminalization opponents—from rampant increases in drug usage among the young to the transformation of Lisbon into a haven for "drug tourists"—has occurred."[38] Total drug decriminalization is an effective reform that Mississippi would do well to emulate.

Although this simple and radical reform would solve most of the negative economic outcomes associated with mass incarceration, it is highly unlikely to be enacted anytime soon. It is simply too politically costly within the current political climate. However, it should not be forgotten as the most effective potential reform.

A less radical and more politically feasible reform goal is marijuana legalization. It has already been legalized for recreational use in Colorado, Alaska, Washington, Washington, D.C., California, Maine, Massachusetts, Nevada, and Oregon. [39] Colorado was the first to legalize marijuana back in 2012, so a study of Colorado would be more informative than that of the other states who have joined more recently. According to a comprehensive Colorado Department of Public Safety report, marijuana use has marginally increased amongst adults; however, it has not increased amongst school-age children, nor have marijuana-related DUI's increased.[40] Importantly, both property crime and violent crime rates have also decreased in Colorado.

Although its beneficial impact on marijuana use and crime were small, the economic impact of marijuana legalization in Colorado was magnitudinous. According to a study by the Marijuana Policy Group, "legal marijuana activities generated $2.39 billion in state output, and created 18,005 new FullTime-Equivalent (FTE) positions in 2015...marijuana was the second largest excise revenue source, with $121 million in combined sales and excise tax revenues."[41]

This economic impact is a result of not only those who would have otherwise been incarcerated joining the labor force, but also the massive industry that has cropped up around the cultivation, production, and sale of marijuana in the state. This potent economic impact coupled with a few other criminal justice reforms could go a long way toward moving Mississippi out of last place economically while creating a more just society for all.

There are also a number of other policy reforms Mississippi could introduce to attenuate the problem of mass incarceration. Recall the discussion of mandatory minimums in Mississippi—potentially years in prison for a drug that is legal within other parts of the country.[42] Obviously, either drug decriminalization or marijuana legalization would abolish those laws. However, the other half of the prison population is, of course, violent criminals. Although there is no question that these people should certainly be separated from society and punished for violating someone else's safety or property, their incarceration does bear costs. It is at least worth considering that perhaps lengthy sentences for violent criminals may not be the most efficient, cost effective method of punishment, and that society may benefit more from differing punishment regimes. For instance, the criminology literature indicates that people age into and out of crime; that is, offending patterns move in a predictable way over the course of people's lives.[43] Generally speak-

38 "Drug Decriminalization in Portugal," Glenn Greenwald, Cato Institute, 2009

39 "here's where you can legally smoke weed now," Melia Robinson, *Business Insider*, Jan. 8, 2017

40 "Marijuana Legalization in Colorado: Early Findings," Colorado Department of Public Safety, March 2016

41 "The Economic Impact of Marijuana Legalization in Colorado," Marijuana Policy Group, October 2016

42 Miss. Ann. Code § 41-29-139

43 Sampson, Robert J, and John H Laub. 2005. "A Life-Course View of the Development of Crime." Annals of the American Academy of Political

ing, younger men are far more likely to commit a crime than older men; as such, it is worth considering that it may not be beneficial to keep offenders in jail beyond age 40 or 50. Further, the evidence to date suggests that increasing sentence length has zero deterrent effect on future crime—rather, the probability of apprehension in the first place is the true source of deterrence.[44]

Thus, if it is expensive for state governments to keep individuals in prison for excessively long sentences with no benefit to society in any meaningful sense, then why are violent offenders being imprisoned for so long? Of course, these arguments admittedly do not address philosophical justifications for longer punishment, such as retributivism. It is merely worth considering that some sort of scientifically-backed sentencing protocol may be a more rational and effective reform for violent offenders than simply locking them up and throwing away the key.

Another possible reform for Mississippi's criminal justice system would be to expand and streamline options for the expungement of a criminal record. As was detailed above, expungement is often not an option for many of the formerly incarcerated, and for those who are eligible, it involves a lengthy waiting period during which they still bear the marring of a record. Based upon the evidence presented above, it would be economically beneficial if Mississippi were to expand expungement options to all nonviolent misdemeanors with a reduced wait time—or ideally, with no wait time at all. Elimination of the waiting period for those convicted of misdemeanor, nonviolent crimes would allow them to re-enter the workforce immediately, rather than having an incubation period of several years before they may resume a normal life.

Along these lines, it would also be rational for the state to expand the scope of those eligible for expungement even to those who have committed low-level felony offenses like simple assault or drug trafficking. Expungement options should be vastly broadened and streamlined to allow more of the formerly incarcerated to return to the workforce more quickly. This could have the added benefit of reducing recidivism rates. If the formerly incarcerated were able to rapidly expunge their record and rejoin the labor force, they would be far less likely to fall into the trap of poverty as a result of the reduced job opportunities a criminal record causes, and as such would be less likely to return to criminal behavior out of economic desperation.

Luckily, some reform-minded Mississippi legislators are making attempts to chip away at the criminal justice leviathan. In the 2017 legislative session, HB 1033 was introduced to provide for a number of incremental reforms to the criminal justice system in Mississippi.[45] Most importantly, the bill ended the practice of jailing people for unpaid parking tickets in what has been referred to as modern-day debtor's prisons: "Incarceration shall not automatically follow the nonpayment of a fine, restitution, or court costs. Incarceration may be employed only after the court has conducted a hearing and examined the reasons for nonpayment and finds, on the record, that the defendant was indigent or could have made payment but refused to do so." The bill also contained a number of other provisions, including the removal of driver's license suspensions for controlled substance violations, expanded drug court usage in order to avoid incarcerating more nonviolent offenders, and an expansion of parole eligibility for those who have "not been convicted of committing a crime of violence, drug trafficking or as a habitual offender and he or she has served at least 25% of his or her sentence." These reforms could soften the heavy blow of drug policies in Mississippi but have not yet been enacted into law.

Before 2016, Mississippi did not track civil asset forfeitures. However, after the passage of HB 812, "the Mississippi Bureau of Narcotics will maintain a website showing descriptions and values of seized

---

and Social Science 602: 12-45.

44 Daniel S. Nagin, "Deterrence in the Twenty-First Century," Crime and Justice 42 (2013)

45 HB 1033, 2017 Legislative Session

property, which police department seized it, and any court petitions challenging the seizures."[46] This is an excellent step toward rectifying the injustice of asset forfeiture. More importantly, the bill requires law enforcement to obtain a seizure warrant within 72 hours of the seizure, effectively placing a procedural hurdle in front of the activity of law enforcement. This, combined with the detailed publication of seizures, should provide a powerful disincentive to deter law enforcement from attempting these kinds of seizures in the future.

Conclusion

Mass incarceration is a massive disadvantage for the Mississippi economy. The wholesale criminalization of the state effectively reduces employment, income, and productivity for a state already mired in economic malaise.

Recently, legislators have shown a willingness to work together toward reform. This momentum should be capitalized upon in order to enact some of the more radical reforms outlined above.

It is only through radical change that the gross injustice of mass incarceration, with all its concomitant negative economic consequences and racial disparities, can be permanently corrected. The prospects of progress in this area look bright, indeed.

References

Altman, I. 2016. *Macon Woman, 70, serving decade prison term for pot.* Retrieved from The Dispatch: http://www.cdispatch.com/news/article.asp?aid=49720

Besharov, Douglas. J., & West, Andrew. 2001. *African American Marriage Patterns.* Washington, D.C.: Hoover Press.

Bronars, Stephen., & Grogger, Jeff.1994. The Economic Consequences of Unwed Motherhood: Using Twin Births as a Natural Experiment. *American Economic Review*, 1141-1156.

Bureau of Justice Statistics. 2014. *Survey of State Criminal History Information Systems.* Washington, D.C.: U.S. Department of Justice.

Carson, Ann. 2015. *Prisoners in 2014.* Washington, D.C.: Bureau of Justice Statistics .

Center for Behavioral Health Statistics and Quality. 2016. *Results From The 2015 National Survey on Drug Use and Health: Detailed Tables.* Rockland: Substance Abuse and Mental Health Services Administration .

Ciaramella, C. J 2017. *Mississippi finally brings some transparency to asset forfeiture.* Retrieved from Reason: http://reason.com/blog/2017/03/14/mississippi-finally-brings-some-transpar

Colorado Department of Public Safety Division of Criminal Justice Office of Research and Statistics. 2016. *Marijuana Legalization in Colorado: Early Findings.* Denver: Colorado Department of Public Safety.

*Criminal Justice Facts.*2017. Retrieved from The Sentencing Project: http://www.sentencingproject.org/criminal-justice-facts/

Dai, Serena. 2012. *A Chart That Says the War on Drugs Isn't Working.* Retrieved from The Atlantic: https://www.theatlantic.com/national/archive/2012/10/chart-says-war-drugs-isnt-working/322592/

Drug Policy Alliance. 2017. *Mississippi.* Retrieved from Drug Policy Alliance: http://www.drugpolicy.org/mississippi

Express Employment Professionals. 2015, February 25. *Express Releases State-by-State Analysis of Labor Force Participation Rates.* Retrieved from Express Employment Professionals: https://www.expresspros.com/Newsroom/America-Employed/Express-Releases-State-by-State-Analysis-of-Labor-Force-Participation-Rates.aspx

Families Against Mandatory Minimums. 2016. *Families Against Mandatory Minimums.* Retrieved from Atiba Parker: http://famm.org/atiba-parker/

Federal Reserve Bank of St. Louis. 2017. *Per Capita Personal Income in Mississippi.* Retrieved from Economic Research Federal Reserve Bank of St. Louis: https://fred.stlouisfed.org/series/MSPCPI

Greenwald, Glenn. 2009. *Drug Decriminalization in Portugal: Lessons for Creating Fair and Successful Drug Policies.* Retrieved from Cato Institute: https://www.cato.org/publications/white-paper/drug-decriminalization-portugal-lessons-creating-fair-successful-drug-policies

---

46 "Mississippi Finally Brings Some Transparency to Asset Forfeiture," C. J. Ciaramella, *Reason*, Mar. 14, 2017

Hill, Marianne. 2008. *The Economic Status of African Americans in Mississippi*. Jackson, MS: Center for Policy Research and Planning.

Human Rights Watch. 2016. *Every 25 Seconds*. Washington, D.C.: Human Rights Watch.

Ingraham, Cristopher. 2015. *Why Hardly Anyone Dies From a Drug Overdose in Portugal*. Retrieved from Washington Post: https://www.washingtonpost.com/news/wonk/wp/2015/06/05/why-hardly-anyone-dies-from-a-drug-overdose-in-portugal/?utm_term=.fb1958620afb

Investigation, F. B.2015. *Uniform Crime Report*. Washington, D.C.: United States Department of Justice.

Joint Legislative Committee on Performance Evaluation and Expenditure Review. 2015. *Mississippi Department of Corrections' FY 2014 Cost Per Inmate Per Day*. Jackson, MS: Joint Legislative Committee on Performance Evaluation and Expenditure Review.

Krein, Sheila. F., & Beller, Andrea. H. 1988. Educational Attainment of Children Form Single-Parent Families: Differences by Exposure, Gender, and Race. *Demography*, 221-234.

Marijuana Policy Group. 2016. *The Economic Impact of Marijuana Legalization in Colorado*. Denver: Marijuana Policy Group.

Mayo Clinic Staff. 2016. *Mayo Clinic*. Retrieved from Schizoaffective Disorder: http://www.mayoclinic.org/diseases-conditions/schizoaffective-disorder/home/ovc-20258872

Nellis, Ashley. 2016. *The Color of Justice: Racial and Ethnic Disparity in State Prisons*. Washington, D.C.: The Sentencing Project.

Olmstead, Todd, et. al. 2015. The price elasticity of demand for heroin: Matched longitudinal and experimental evidence. *The Journal of Health Economics*, 59-71.

Pager, Devah. 2003. The Mark of a Criminal Record. *American Journal of Sociology*, 937-975.

Pfaff, John. 2017. *Locked In*. New York: Basic Books.

Powell, Benjamin. 2002. *Private Property Rights, Economic Freedom, and Well-Being*. Washington, D.C.: American Institute for Economic Research.

Puddington, Arch., & Roylance, Tyler. 2016. *Freedom in the World 2016*. Washington, D.C.: Freedom House.

Robinson, Melia. 2017, January 8. *it's 2017: here's where you can legally smoke weed now*. Retrieved from Business Insider: http://www.businessinsider.com/where-can-you-legally-smoke-weed-2017-1

Sampson, Robert. J., & Laub, John. H. 2005. A Life-Course View of the Development of Crime. *Annals of the American Academy of Political and Social Science*, 12-45.

Thorton, Mark. 1991. *Economics of Prohibition*. Salt Lake City: University of Utah Press.

Trusts, P. C. 2014. *Mississippi's 2014 Corrections and Criminal Justice Reform*. Washington, D.C.: Pew Charitable Trusts.

Uggen, Christopher., Shannon, Sarah., & Manza, Jeff. 2010. *State-Level Estimates of Felon Disenfranchisement in the United States, 2010*. Washington, D.C.: The Sentencing Project.

Walmsley, Roy. 2016. *World Prison Population List*. London: Institute for Criminal Policy Research.

17

Property Takings: Eminent Domain and Civil Asset Forfeiture

Carrie B. Kerekes

Property Takings: Eminent Domain and Civil Asset Forfeiture

Carrie B. Kerekes

On June 23, 2017, the United States Supreme Court delivered another blow to property rights in America in *Murr v. Wisconsin*.[1] The Murrs owned two pieces of property along the St. Croix River in Troy, Wisconsin. They wanted to develop one of the properties and sell the other; however, the properties had been merged under St. Croix County zoning regulations. The Murrs argued that the zoning regulation constituted a property taking by effectively denying them use of their second property. As such, they argued they should receive just compensation under the takings clause in the Fifth Amendment to the U.S. Constitution. The Supreme Court decided against the Murrs.[2] Court decisions like *Murr v. Wisconsin* weaken property rights, threaten individual liberty, and can have significant negative long-run consequences on the health of an economy.

This chapter discusses property rights in Mississippi and examines the effects of takings, specifically takings conducted through eminent domain and civil asset forfeiture. Secure private property rights make it easier for individuals to put their resources to productive uses. If other beneficial rules and policies are in place, secure property rights can ultimately translate to higher incomes and a better standard of living for residents across the state. Fortunately, Mississippi performs well relative to other states in protecting residents from eminent domain abuse. However, civil forfeiture laws in the state do not adequately protect property owners. Additional reforms to state laws are necessary for Mississippi residents to realize the full benefits of secure private property rights and the resultant gains in income and prosperity they produce.

---

1   *Murr v. Wisconsin*, 582 U.S. No. 15-214 (2017).

2   See Abbott (2017) and Somin (2017). Epstein (2017) provides a detailed discussion of the case and its relevance for takings law in the United States.

Institutions, Property Rights, and Economic Development

Institutions, or the rules of the game, provide the framework for any economy, as described in Chapter 2. When the rules of the game are uncertain or do not promote incentives for exchange, growth stagnates, and prosperity is elusive for most of the population.

Property rights are the cornerstone of a well-functioning economy. Property rights provide incentives to engage in socially productive activities through the incentive for exchange. Only when people own resources securely can exchange emerge. With property rights and exchange comes the emergence of prices. Prices provide incentives for the productive and efficient use of resources as relative prices provide information to owners regarding the value of their assets. Prices provide valuable information to property owners and make possible a system of profits and losses. This system of profit and loss provides incentive for innovation and is necessary for entrepreneurs to decide what goods and services to produce and how to produce them. Innovation and positive technological change lead to increases in productivity as scarce resources are combined in more efficient ways to produce more goods and services that people ultimately desire. It is this increase in productivity that ultimately causes economic growth.

Resources are more efficiently utilized when property owners can receive market signals through prices and act on them. Any intervention that interferes with prices or the profit/loss system distorts these valuable market signals. Interventions that reduce the security of property rights can potentially break the chain entirely. The result of these interventions is more waste, less efficient use of property and resources, and less innovation. Eventually, productivity will decline and the economy will stagnate or shrink.

When individuals are confident and their property rights are secure, they have incentives to put their property to its most efficient use and undertake investments because they know they will reap any increases in value (i.e. profits). The factors that make property rights important hold true for individual states as well as for entire nations. While the rules chosen at the federal level significantly affect the health of the economy for the United States, state rules and policies also play an important role in determining individual states' relative success or failure in terms of their economic productivity. Therefore, state level policies that weaken the security of property rights constitute a significant disadvantage for economic prosperity in Mississippi and are worthy of analysis.

Eminent Domain

One form of property taking that renders property rights more insecure is government's use of eminent domain. In the now infamous 2005 decision, the U.S. Supreme Court declared in *Kelo v. City of New London*[3] that private property could be taken by eminent domain and transferred to another private party for public benefit.[4] This decision created an uproar as it made property rights significantly less secure by expanding the scope for eminent domain.

The Fifth Amendment to the United States Constitution states, "nor shall private property be taken for public use, without just compensation."[5] The interpretation of 'public use' has undergone significant changes since the constitution was written. Traditionally, eminent domain was used for public projects

---

3 *Kelo et. al. v. City of New London*, 545 U.S. 469 (2005).

4 In *Kelo*, property was taken from residents near Fort Trumbull State Park for redevelopment. Specifically, the city's redevelopment plan included a hotel and shopping center, and research, office, and retail space to accompany a new facility for Pfizer, the pharmaceutical company. The reason for redevelopment was to increase the city's tax base.

5 U.S. Const. amend V.

and infrastructure, such as schools and roads. Over time, 'public use' came to mean 'public purpose'. The 'public purpose' interpretation allowed eminent domain to be used on the justification of eradicating blight[6] or reducing the concentration of land ownership[7]. In the aftermath of *Kelo*, eminent domain can now be used for 'public benefit'. For example, under this interpretation, eminent domain can be used to transfer property from one private owner to another if doing so will increase tax revenue or promote employment.

Eminent domain is a direct violation of private property rights. As such, its use is limited by the U.S. Constitution. Increases in the government's ability to use eminent domain reduce individuals' protection of their private property, distorting incentives for investment and negatively affecting economic growth. Economic development takings, like *Kelo*, are especially problematic and pose a grave threat to property rights.[8] Economic development takings are often initiated by special interest groups who have powerful political connections and can use the political process to their benefit at the expense of people with lower incomes or less political power. There is almost no limit to the reach of eminent domain if it can be used for development because supporters of the proposed project can claim the potential effects will have some public benefit that amounts to a public use. The only effective way to eliminate this potential expansion of eminent domain is for states to completely ban its use for economic development takings.

In addition to the U.S. Constitution, state constitutions also have provisions to protect private property rights. In the aftermath of *Kelo*, many states passed reforms to constitutions and laws in attempts to increase protections for private property rights. Several states drafted amendments to prevent property takings for private benefit, including economic development takings. Some states were more effective in their efforts to increase the security of property rights, while others made less significant changes that are little more than empty words on paper to appease voters. Many states that enacted reforms post *Kelo* still allow economic development takings to eradicate blight (usually defined as structures existing in states of abandonment or disrepair). However, loose definitions of 'blight' keep the door for eminent domain abuse open. While the overall effectiveness of the *Kelo* backlash in making property rights more secure is debatable, the response did ultimately cause many state legislatures to respond in some way to concerned voters.

Eminent Domain in Mississippi

Fortunately for Mississippi residents, eminent domain abuse does not currently appear to be a significant problem in the state. The Mississippi Constitution affords reasonable protection of private property. According to the Mississippi Constitution,

> "Private property shall not be taken or damaged for public use, except on due compensation being first made to the owner or owners thereof, in a manner to be prescribed by law; and whenever an attempt is made to take private property for a use alleged to be public, the question whether the contemplated use be public shall be a judicial question, and, as such, determined without regard to legislative assertion that the use is public."[9]

---

6   *Berman v. Parker*, 348 U.S. 26 (1954) and *Poletown Neighborhood Council v. Detroit*, 304 N.W. 2d 455 (1981).

7   *Hawaii Housing Authority v. Midkiff*, 467 U.S. 229 (1984).

8   Cohen (2006) discusses how problems of efficiency and group capture are particularly acute with economic development takings. Undercompensation for property owners is more likely in these cases than when the property is taken for a more traditional public use. Special interests are more likely to 'capture' the political process, making the government less likely to make efficient determinations when acquiring property. See also Somin (2004).

9   Miss. Const. Art. 3, § 17.

Mississippi state law allows for the use of eminent domain by persons or corporations to condemn private property for public use.[10] However, in 2011, residents voted for Initiative 31. This initiative amended the Mississippi Constitution to provide further protections against eminent domain use:

> "No property acquired by the exercise of the power of eminent domain under the laws of the State of Mississippi shall, for a period of ten years after its acquisition, be transferred or any interest therein transferred to any person, non-governmental entity, public-private partnership, corporation, or other business entity with the following exceptions:

> (1) The above provisions shall not apply to drainage and levee facilities and usage, roads and bridges for public conveyance, flood control projects with a levee component, seawalls, dams, toll roads, public airports, public ports, public harbors, public wayports, common carriers or facilities for public utilities and other entities used in the generation, transmission, storage or distribution of telephone, telecommunication, gas, carbon dioxide, electricity, water, sewer, natural gas, liquid hydrocarbons or other utility products.

> (2) The above provisions shall not apply where the use of eminent domain (a) removes a public nuisance; (b) removes a structure that is beyond repair or unfit for human habitation or use; (c) is used to acquire abandoned property; or (d) eliminates a direct threat to public health or safety caused by the property in its current condition."[11]

Initiative 31 amended the Mississippi Constitution to prohibit state and local governments from using eminent domain to confiscate private property for *Kelo*-style economic development takings. Exceptions include property taken for public projects, such as infrastructure and utilities, and situations involving property that is abandoned or severely dilapidated.

This amendment to the Constitution does provide more protection to property owners against eminent domain. However, the exceptions to this amendment leave the door open for potential eminent domain abuse. Property can still be confiscated if it is deemed to be a public nuisance or is dilapidated to the point where it poses a threat to public health or safety. These exceptions mean eminent domain can still be used for development takings to eradicate blight. As such, eminent domain still poses a threat in Mississippi, even though this reform is stronger than many enacted in other states.[12]

In 2007, the Castle Coalition released a report that graded states according to legislative reforms passed following the *Kelo* decision.[13] According to that report, Mississippi earned an F for its failure (at that time) to pass any legislative reforms to prevent *Kelo*-type property takings. More recently, the Castle Coalition gave Mississippi a B+.[14] This improvement is due to Initiative 31, which offers property owners significantly more protection from economic development takings than in the past.

One area related to eminent domain where Mississippi can improve is its determination of just compensation in property takings. For example, in 2005 Hurricane Katrina destroyed a restaurant and bar (Dan B's Restaurant and Bar) owned by Kenneth, Ray, and Audie Murphy in Bay St. Louis, Mississippi.[15] After the hurricane, the City of Bay St. Louis and the State of Mississippi proposed a redevelopment plan

---

10 Miss. Code § 11-27-1 (2016).

11 Miss. Const. Art. 3, § 17A.

12 Somin (2011) acknowledges the relative effectiveness of Initiative 31 in prohibiting eminent domain for economic development takings compared to other states' reforms. He does, however, caution that eminent domain could still be used for questionable condemnations by utility companies and common carriers.

13 Castle Coalition (2007).

14 http://castlecoalition.org/50-state-report-card

15 See Newman (2014).

for downtown Bay St. Louis. The plan included an access ramp and parking for a new harbor on property owned by the Murphy's. The State of Mississippi argued the property was public tideland, and confiscated the property without paying compensation to the Murphy's. The Murphy's took the state to court and a jury ultimately ruled against the state. The jury awarded the Murphy's $644,000 for their property.[16]

In *Bay Point Properties v. Mississippi Transportation Commission*[17] land was taken to build a public park, and the property owner was not awarded fair compensation for the taking. Prior to Hurricane Katrina in 2005, the State of Mississippi had an easement on the property and constructed a highway bridge. Hurricane Katrina destroyed the bridge, and the state decided to rebuild it elsewhere, not on the same piece of property. Rather than allow the property owner to use the land again, the state allowed the Mississippi Department of Transportation to use the land for a public park. Bay Point Properties sued the Mississippi Highway Commission for just compensation for the land. The case went to court on the argument that the State of Mississippi violated the just compensation clause in the Fifth Amendment. The jury did decide that the state had violated the Fifth Amendment. However, the judge instructed the jury to base compensation for the property as if it were encumbered because of the easement. As a result, the jury awarded $500 to the property owner.[18]

The case then went to the Mississippi Supreme court, but it sided with the lower court.[19] The Mississippi Supreme Court ruled that the jury had to value the land as if it were encumbered by the easement prior to the taking for the public park. The property owner, and parties filing amicus briefs on behalf of Bay Point Properties, argued that the land should have been considered unencumbered in determining just compensation because the State of Mississippi had abandoned the easement and now wanted to use the property for a different purpose for which the easement was originally obtained. The United States Supreme Court denied the petition for a writ of certiorari to hear the case.

While Mississippi courts can more carefully determine just compensation in future eminent domain cases, the Mississippi Constitution and state laws do offer reasonable protection for property owners from eminent domain. Unfortunately, property owners are not nearly as well protected from expropriation through civil asset forfeiture.

Civil Asset Forfeiture

Civil asset forfeiture is another form of property taking that reduces the security of property rights. Civil asset forfeiture is the process by which government can confiscate property that is alleged to have been used to commit a crime, regardless of whether the property owner was involved in or had any knowledge of its use in a crime. In these cases, the property is assigned a persona and held accountable for its actions. The forfeiture action is taken against the object, not the property owner. Civil asset forfeiture differs from criminal asset forfeiture. In criminal cases, the forfeiture accompanies a criminal prosecution.

Constitutional protections that apply to individuals do not apply to property in civil asset forfeiture cases, including the assumption of innocence until proven guilty, protection against "unreasonable searches and seizures", and requirements for due process.[20] For example, in criminal cases, the prosecution must prove the commission of a crime beyond a reasonable doubt; in civil forfeiture cases, they

---

16 *Murphy v. State of Mississippi*, Cause No. 12-0453 in the Circuit Court of Hancock County, Mississippi.

17 *Bay Point Properties v. Mississippi Transportation Commission*, Cause No. A2401-41-115 in the Circuit Court of Harrison County, Mississippi.

18 See Davis (2017) and Hearne et al. (2017).

19 *Bay Point Properties v. Mississippi Transportation Commission*, No. 2014-CA-01684-SCT.

20 U.S. Const. amend IV and U.S. Const. amend V.

must do so only by a preponderance of the evidence. This is a much lower burden of proof, with the result that individuals can lose their property even after being acquitted of the crime in question. Unlike in criminal proceedings, in most civil forfeiture cases the property owner does not have the right to a court-appointed attorney if he or she cannot afford one. The property owner must obtain legal counsel at his or her own expense. In many cases, the cost of hiring an attorney and the legal fees may be higher than the value of the property in question. As a result, assets valued below the cost of representation are often forfeited.

In the later 20th century, civil asset forfeiture was rationalized to fight the war on drugs. Its use has increased significantly over time as civil asset forfeiture can be attractive for law enforcement agencies. State and local law enforcement agencies rely on state budget allocations for funding. When state legislatures decrease funding for these agencies, the economic incentive for civil forfeiture increases, and it can be used as a revenue generating mechanism. In this manner, revenues from civil asset forfeitures may act as a substitute for state funding when state budgets shrink.[21]

The increasing use of civil asset forfeiture was compounded by the creation of the Equitable Sharing Program administered by the Department of Justice (DOJ). Most state civil forfeiture laws require seized funds to be deposited with the respective state and allocated by the state legislature to fund things like education. However, state and local law enforcement authorities can participate in equitable sharing to circumvent state laws. Through equitable sharing, federal authorities adopt state and local civil forfeiture cases. In return, the state and local law enforcement agencies share in the proceeds of the confiscated assets. These agencies can continue to supplement their budgets by retaining a portion of the seized assets. Thus, equitable sharing provides an economic incentive for law enforcement agencies to confiscate private property even when state laws are in place to try and prevent its use for this purpose. Between 2000 and 2008, equitable sharing payments to the states increased from approximately $200 million to $400 million.[22]

Many states do not require law enforcement agencies to track and report statistics on civil forfeiture, including the number of cases, values and descriptions of the seized assets, whether the property owner was convicted of a crime, or how the proceeds were used. This raises issues with government transparency and accountability. In addition, much of the burden in civil forfeiture cases falls on the property owner to prove their innocence, versus the government proving their guilt. These factors, combined with the aforementioned economic incentives, encourage law enforcement authorities to expropriate private property. Civil asset forfeiture is therefore one of the most serious threats to private property rights in the United States.

As individuals become more aware of this threat, and as forfeiture cases increasingly target innocent individuals, pressure from constituents has made civil forfeiture reform a priority. Many states have enacted reforms to forfeiture laws. Several states have enacted reforms that eliminate civil forfeiture without an accompanying criminal case. For example, Connecticut recently became the 14th state to require a criminal conviction for forfeitures.[23] Laws in Mississippi have also undergone change, but much more can be done to better protect residents and their property.

---

21 See Benson and Rasmussen (1996) and Blumenson and Nilsen (1998) for more detailed discussions of how law enforcement agencies use civil asset forfeiture as a revenue generating mechanism.

22 Kramer (2010).

23 Sibilla (2017a).

Civil Asset Forfeiture in Mississippi

Abuses of civil asset forfeiture are not uncommon in Mississippi. While recent legislation will help increase transparency, civil forfeiture will continue to pose a real threat to private property rights unless more substantial changes are made to state forfeiture laws.

The Institute for Justice (IJ) publishes *Policing for Profit*, a report that analyzes several factors to grade states according to their civil forfeiture laws.[24] IJ examines how lucrative and easy civil forfeiture is in each state. It examines the standard of proof, innocent owner burden, and the percentage of proceeds that go to law enforcement agencies. IJ also examines the extent to which each state utilizes equitable sharing. As this is often a means to circumvent state laws about how forfeiture proceeds will be allocated, more equitable sharing translates to a lower grade.

The first edition of the IJ report was published in 2010 and Mississippi earned a D+. At the time, laws in Mississippi were among the worst in the country for encouraging civil forfeiture and did little to protect property owners. At the time of the 2010 report, Mississippi had a very low standard of proof for property to be considered forfeitable. Police only had to show by a preponderance of the evidence that property was related to a crime. The burden was on the property owner to prove his or her innocence, and law enforcement agencies could collect 80% of the proceeds from forfeitures. Additionally, there was no requirement to collect or report any data on civil forfeitures.

By the publication of the second edition of the IJ report in 2015, Mississippi had improved its grade to a C-.[25] The only apparent area of improvement between the 2010 and 2015 reports is that state statutes have been interpreted as placing more of the burden of proof on the government versus the property owner.[26] There was still a low standard of proof for forfeitures, no conviction was required to seize assets, there were no reporting requirements, and law enforcement agencies continued to pocket 80% of the proceeds from forfeitures. If more than one agency is involved in the forfeiture, all of the proceeds go to law enforcement. This creates a strong economic incentive to seize assets, and it also creates a conflict of interests. The IJ report includes a striking example of this conflict. A $4.1 million training facility for law enforcement was built in Richland, Mississippi. The police boast that the facility was funded completely with proceeds from civil forfeitures conducted by the Richland police. Richland has a population of only 7,000 residents.[27]

The 2015 IJ report also ranks Mississippi 20th in the United States for federal forfeiture. Between 2000 and 2013, law enforcement agencies in the state worked in conjunction with the federal government and pocketed more than $47 million worth of assets through the Equitable Sharing Program. Using this figure, law enforcement agencies in Mississippi took in an average of $3.4 million from the Department of Justice (DOJ) each year.

In 2016, the Mississippi state legislature organized a Civil Asset Forfeiture Task Force to collect court records and data from 2015 to study civil forfeiture in the state.[28] According to the study, the Mississippi Bureau of Narcotics seized $4 million of assets in 2015. This figure includes 154 seizures with an average value of $66,773. Seized cash amounts ranged from $75 to $460,000. These numbers actually understate the extent of civil forfeiture because they do not include assets seized from police agencies that did not

---

24 Williams, Holcomb, and Kovandzic (2010). The full report is available online at http://ij.org/report/policing-for-profit-first-edition/.

25 Carpenter, Knepper, and McDonald (2015). The full report is available online at http://ij.org/report/policing-for-profit/.

26 Miss. Code § 41-29-179 (2013).

27 See Carpenter, Knepper, and McDonald (2015) and Wing (2015) for details.

28 See Ciarmella (2017) for more details from this report and examples of recent civil forfeiture cases in Mississippi.

work with the Bureau of Narcotics or assets taken in conjunction with federal authorities under the Equitable Sharing Program. Law enforcement officials seized everything from cash and cars to couches and comic books.

According to the Institute for Justice, Mississippi become the 18th state to pass legislation to reform forfeiture laws.[29] The findings of the Civil Asset Forfeiture Task Force prompted members of the legislature to draft House Bill 812. H.B. 812 was signed into law by Governor Phil Bryant on March 13, 2017.[30] The new law requires law enforcement agencies to report the location, description, and value of the seized assets and to indicate whether criminal charges were filed against the property owner. The Mississippi Bureau of Narcotics is required to build and maintain a searchable website reporting forfeiture information. The new law also requires a circuit or county judge to issue a civil seizure warrant within 72 hours. Failure to obtain a warrant from a judge would require the property to be returned.

Unfortunately, H.B. 812 does not mandate that law enforcement agencies report how they use forfeiture proceeds. While the new forfeiture reforms take some steps to improve transparency, stronger reforms are needed to provide property owners with any real protection against civil forfeiture abuse in Mississippi. If state residents and policy makers do not know how law enforcement agencies use forfeiture proceeds, then the new law has not achieved complete transparency. Furthermore, the new law does nothing to hold officials accountable for how they use the funds. Given the relative ease with which civil forfeiture can still be used in Mississippi, the incentives remain strong for law enforcement agencies to use civil forfeiture as a tool to increase revenues. As long as this tool is available to law enforcement, private property is at risk of expropriation.

Conclusion

Residents in Mississippi are fairly well protected from eminent domain abuses by the state and local governments. While the Mississippi Constitution still leaves room for potentially questionable economic development takings based on blight, it does prohibit state and local confiscations of property for private benefit in the style of *Kelo*. While property is relatively safe from eminent domain abuses in Mississippi, individuals should also be aware of regulations restricting land use or zoning laws. As demonstrated by *Murr v. Wisconsin*, zoning laws or land use regulations have the potential to effectively deprive individuals of the use of their property. Governments may rely more heavily on such regulations to utilize property if it becomes too difficult to seize property outright through eminent domain.

Mississippi residents are *not* well protected from civil forfeiture abuses. Mississippi should follow the example of several other states and require a criminal conviction to seize assets. Additionally, policy makers must recognize the current economic incentives in place that encourage law enforcement agencies to seize private property. Civil forfeiture is lucrative for law enforcement. Mississippi could make reforms along two fronts to significantly reduce the economic incentive. First, state laws should require forfeiture proceeds to be placed in a general fund that is allocated by the legislature. Secondly, laws should be reformed to prohibit participation in the Equitable Sharing Program so that law enforcement agencies do not try to circumvent state laws in efforts to keep forfeiture funds. These changes would eliminate much of the economic incentive for civil forfeiture and the number of seizures against innocent property owners would likely decline.

---

29 Sibilla (2017b).

30 See Wilson (2017).

As discussed in this chapter and Chapter 2, secure private property rights provide the incentives for individuals to undertake investments and make capital improvements to their property and businesses. To foster more innovation and entrepreneurship in the state and to promote prosperity, Mississippi policy makers should continue to improve laws and policies to restrict takings, including confiscations by eminent domain and civil asset forfeiture.

References

Abbott, Alden. 2017. How the Supreme Court Trampled on Private Property Rights in a Recent Decision. *The Daily Signal*, June 28. http://dailysignal.com/2017/06/28/supreme-court-trampled-private-property-rights-recent-decision/

Benson, Bruce L. and David W. Rasmussen. 1996. Predatory Public Finance and the Origins of the War on Drugs 1984-1989. *The Independent Review* 1(2): 163-189.

Blumenson, Eric and Eva Nilsen. 1998. Policing for Profit: The Drug War's Hidden Economic Agenda. *The University of Chicago Law Review* 65: 35-114.

Carpenter, Dick M., Lisa Knepper, and Jennifer McDonald. 2015. *Policing for Profit: The Abuse of Civil Asset Forfeiture*, 2nd Edition. Arlington, VA: Institute for Justice.

Castle Coalition. 2007. *50 State Report Card: Tracking Eminent Domain Reform Legislation Since Kelo*, http://ij.org/wp-content/uploads/2015/03/50_State_Report.pdf

Ciaramella, C. J. 2017. Inside Mississippi's Asset Forfeiture Extortion Racket. Reason.com, January 5. http://reason.com/blog/2017/01/05/inside-mississippis-asset-forfeiture-ext

Cohen, Charles E. 2006. Eminent Domain after *Kelo v. City of New London*: An Argument for Banning Economic Development Takings. *Harvard Journal of Law and Public Policy* 29: 491–568.

Davis, Stephen S. 2017. Bay Point Properties v. Mississippi Transportation Commission. Arent Fox, LLP, May 15. http://federaltakings.com/articles/bay-point-properties-v-mississippi-transportation-commission

Epstein, Richard A. 2017. Will the Supreme Court Clean up Takings Law in *Murr v. Wisconsin? NYU Journal of Law and Liberty* 11(1): 860-914.

Hearne, Thor, Stephen S. Davis, Meghan S. Largent, Ilya Shapiro and Trevor Burrus. 2017. Bay Point Properties v. Mississippi Transportation Commission. Cato Institute, April 6. https://www.cato.org/publications/legal-briefs/bay-point-properties-v-mississippi-transportation-commission

Kramer, John. 2010. Mississippi earns "D+" in "Policing for Profit" Report. Institute for Justice, March 29. http://ij.org/press-release/mississippi-earns-acanadacana-in-acanapolicing-for-profitacana-report/

Newman, Catherine. 2014. Mississippi Jury Awards Bayfront Restaurant Owners $644,000 in Inverse Condemnation Trial. PRWeb, August 20. http://www.prweb.com/releases/mississippi/inverse_verdict/prweb12110015.htm

Sibilla, Nick. 2017a. Connecticut Just Banned Civil Forfeiture Without a Criminal Conviction. Forbes.com, July 11. https://www.forbes.com/sites/instituteforjustice/2017/07/11/connecticut-just-banned-civil-forfeiture-without-a-criminal-conviction/#4a47bcfc52e7

Sibilla, Nick. 2017b. Mississippi Governor Signs Civil Forfeiture Reform. Institute for Justice, March 13. http://ij.org/press-release/mississippi-governor-signs-civil-forfeiture-reform/

Somin, Ilya. 2004. Overcoming *Poletown: County of Wayne v. Hathcock*, Economic Development Takings and the Future of Public Use. *Michigan State Law Review* 2004(4): 1005-1039.

Somin, Ilya. 2011. Vote Yes on Mississippi Measure 31. The Volokh Conspiracy, November 7. http://volokh.com/2011/11/07/vote-yes-on-mississippi-measure-31/

Somin, Ilya. 2017, A Loss for Property Rights in *Murr v. Wisconsin*. The Washington Post, June 23. https://www.washingtonpost.com/news/volokh-conspiracy/wp/2017/06/23/a-loss-for-property-rights-in-murr-v-wisconsin/?utm_term=.8fc26ace1d42

Williams, Marian R., Jefferson E. Holcomb, and Tomislav V. Kovandzic. 2010. *Policing for Profit: The Abuse of Civil Asset Forfeiture*. Arlington, VA: Institute for Justice.

Wilson, Steve. 2017. Mississippi Governor Signs Civil Asset Forfeiture Reform Bill Into Law. MississippiWatchdog.org, March 14. http://watchdog.org/290863/forfeiture-reform/

Wing, Nick. 2015. Police in Mississippi Town Buy New Station, Cruisers with Funds from Aggressive Civil Forfeiture Program. *The Huffington Post*, May 19. http://www.huffingtonpost.com/2015/05/19/richland-mississippi-civil-asset-forfeiture_n_7312988.html

18

The Small-Dollar Loan Landscape in Mississippi: Products, Regulations, Examples, and Research Findings on Interest Rate Caps

Thomas (Tom) William Miller, Jr.

18

The Small-Dollar Loan Landscape in Mississippi: Products, Regulations, Examples, and Research Findings on Interest Rate Caps

Thomas (Tom) William Miller, Jr.

Free markets promote prosperity by efficiently regulating prices—including the price of money, i.e., interest rates. Nevertheless, state legislatures often choke credit markets with interest rate caps. Despite the goal of improving consumer well-being, interest rate caps often harm the very people legislatures intend to help. Rate caps hit users of small-dollar loan products especially hard. Rate caps shift loans away from subprime borrowers and, because rate caps make the smaller dollar loans unprofitable, rate caps limit the supply of credit to these consumers. The Mississippi legislature can stimulate economic growth and prosperity in Mississippi by eliminating, or even greatly raising, interest rate caps in small-dollar loan markets.

What Consumer Credit Markets Do

Consumer credit serves a valuable economic purpose: Using credit, consumers can optimize their consumption of goods by shifting the timing of their cash inflows and outflows. Credit allows consumers to use a good, without having the cash on hand to purchase it. These markets also impose financial discipline on the borrower. To keep enjoying the good, the consumer must keep making payments, and figure out a budget that allows them to discharge the debt.

For well over 100 years, critics of consumer credit charge that credit allows people to "live beyond their means." Such a viewpoint ignores the fact that borrowers cannot increase debt levels indefinitely. Also, lenders will not extend more credit to borrowers with large debt levels because these borrowers are more likely to default. Calder's (1999) history of consumer credit in the United States discusses these points in great detail.

Many people are familiar with the notion of borrowing money to purchase a house, a vehicle, furniture, or household appliances. In these transactions, the consumer takes possession of the good in question, but the lender holds the title to the good. To pay off the debt, the consumer makes a known number of equal monthly payments, and there is no extra payment at the end of these payments. This loan structure is known as an installment loan. For houses and certain other property, we call this installment loan a mortgage. For vehicles, furniture, and household appliances, we call this installment loan sales financing.

Mortgages and sales financing, while important and familiar, are not the focus of this chapter. The focus of this chapter is another set of important, but not as familiar, non-bank supplied cash loans. A cash loan is not tied to the purchase of any good. Borrowers can use the proceeds from a cash loan in any manner they wish.

Prime borrowers, i.e., those with high credit scores, are likely unfamiliar with the variety of non-bank supplied cash loans. The reason is simple: Prime borrowers have access to bank-supplied credit, including credit cards. Consumers without access to bank credit, like sub-prime borrowers, are likely familiar with non-bank supplied cash loans.

Prime borrowers and sub-prime borrowers alike have a demand for consumer credit. Prime borrowers typically use credit products offered by banks—like installment loans and credit cards. Subprime borrowers, due to their limited or poor credit repayment histories, likely have less access to bank loans, but might have access to sub-prime credit cards. As a result, unfilled credit demand by these consumers must be met by other credit products.

The Non-Bank Supplied Small Dollar Credit Landscape

Despite wishes by many to the contrary, many Americans today live "paycheck to paycheck."[1] These households likely do not have a deep pool of cash reserves to meet unexpected bills. They might not have reserves to cover normal bills in the event of an unexpected income disruption, which many hourly workers often experience. So, these households are more likely to rely on some form of non-bank supplied credit. There is an ongoing policy debate around these credit products. Some observers, however, decry the competitive market-clearing interest rates for these loans as "astronomical," "abusive," or "predatory." Other observers explore whether these markets truly harm American consumers.

All along the small-dollar credit landscape, the Bureau of Consumer Financial Protection (i.e., the "CFPB"), keeps layering, or attempts to layer, federal regulations over state regulations. Although the Dodd-Frank Act explicitly prohibits the CFPB from regulating interest rates, the Bureau consults with and assists other entities, such as Congress, that can regulate interest rates.[2] The most notable example is the

---

1   Lusardi, Schneider, and Tufano (2011) examine the ability of American households to gather $2,000 within 30 days to help weather a financial shock. They document that approximately one-half of American households certainly could not, or probably could not, do so. The Federal Reserve (2015) places the hurdle even lower. In its report on the economic well-being of U.S. households, it finds that 47 percent of respondents "say they either could not cover an emergency expense costing $400, or would cover it by selling something or borrowing money."

2   President Barack Obama signed The Dodd–Frank Wall Street Reform and Consumer Protection Act (Pub.L. 111–203, H.R. 4173) into law on July 21, 2010. The Dodd-Frank Act contained legislation establishing the Bureau of Consumer Financial Protection (CFPB).

Talent-Nelson Military Lending Act of 2006, and its extension enacted in 2016.[3] In addition, State legislatures can, and do, regulate credit markets, often by setting allowable interest rates on loans.

To begin to understand this diverse set of consumer credit products, it is helpful to think of them as lying along a landscape, or forming a "financial ecosystem." Each product exists because it gives its user an assortment of benefits that cannot be exactly replicated by any other product.

Moreover, these products are not complex. The difference in these products lies in their simple terms. The examples given in this chapter clearly show the elementary nature of these loan products. Consumers can weigh the costs and benefits of each product before deciding which one to use. For example, a $40 fee to borrow $200 through a payday loan makes economic sense if the power bill is overdue and it costs $75 to restore the power if it is shut off.

Some consumers with prime credit might not appreciate the breadth and scope of the products that comprise the small-dollar loan landscape. One purpose of this chapter is to provide a brief description of some of the credit products that lie along this landscape in Mississippi.[4] In addition, the chapter contains examples of how each of these credit products work.

Another purpose of this chapter is to investigate the restrictions placed on these products in terms of the allowable interest rate.[5] The chapter also presents a brief overview of the findings from academic studies on the question of what happens to consumers when an interest rate cap exists. Research overwhelmingly shows that interest rate caps negatively affect consumers, which stymies economic growth and prosperity.[6]

Lump Sum Credit Products:
Pawn Loans, Vehicle Title Loans, and Payday Loans

The terms of a lump-sum loan are basic. These loans use the simple interest equation, which is:

$$\text{\$Interest} = \text{\$Principal} \times \text{Annual Rate} \times \text{Time} \tag{1}$$

Example 1. Sam borrows $300, at an annual rate of ten percent for six months. How much money must Sam repay at the end of six months? Using the simple interest formula:

$$\text{\$Interest} = \$300 \times .10 \times \frac{6}{12}$$

$$\text{\$Interest} = \$15.$$

In six months, Sam pays $15 of interest, and a total of $315 to repay the loan.

If a periodic rate and time measured in periods are given, the modified simple interest equation is used.

$$\text{\$Interest} = \text{\$Principal} \times \text{Periodic Rate} \times \text{Periods} \tag{2}$$

---

3   The Talent-Nelson Military Lending Act (MLA) of 2006, 10 U.S.C. § 987, imposes a 36% interest rate cap (and other restrictions) consumer loans made to service members and their dependents. New Department of Defense rules taking effect in October 2016 dramatically expands the MLA's coverage to nearly all forms of credit within the scope of the Truth in Lending Act of 1968.

4   Miller and Witt (2017) present a more detailed discussion of the non-bank supplied small dollar loan landscape, and current public policy issues surrounding these products.

5   Mississippi state law limits many other aspects of these credit markets. These other limitations are not discussed in this chapter, because the focus of this chapter is on interest rate caps.

6   Durkin, Elliehausen, Staten, and Zywicki (2014) contains detailed discussions of theories and research on a wide array of consumer credit topics.

Example 2. Dave borrows $300 for one month, at a monthly rate of twenty percent. How much money must Dave repay at the end of one month? Using the modified simple interest equation

$$\$Interest = \$300 \times .20 \times 1$$

$$\$Interest = \$60.$$

Dave pays $60 interest, and a total of $360 to repay the loan.

Pawnbroker Loans and Their Regulation in Mississippi

Pawnbroker loans have existed for thousands of years. In a negotiated pawn transaction, the consumer offers a tangible item to the pawnbroker, who gives cash to the consumer and takes possession of the item. The pawnbroker issues a detailed pawn ticket that contains the terms of the transaction and cost of redemption. Pawn transactions generally have a length of one month. A pawn transaction is not a loan in the traditional sense because the consumer has no obligation to repay the sum obtained in the pawn transaction.

After the pawn transaction, the consumer has three options: 1) Walk away with the cash and abandon the pawned item, 2) Repay the amount extended plus any fees charged for the month, or, 3) Extend the pawn transaction for another month by paying only the fees charged for the month. The pawnbroker has no recourse if the customer abandons the pawned item. The pawnbroker will notify the consumer when, as required by law, the title to the item will change hands.

While the pawn broker is in possession of the item, the consumer must pay charges for interest, storage, and other fees. State law sets the maximum allowable fees. In Mississippi, The Pawn Shop Act § 75-67-313 (2013) states: "A pawnbroker may contract for and receive a pawnshop charge in lieu of interest or other charges for all services, expenses, cost and losses of every nature not to exceed twenty-five percent (25%) of the principal amount, per month, advanced in the pawn transaction."

Example 3. Gene brings a Selmer tenor saxophone, complete with case, to a pawnshop. The pawn dealer assesses the pawn value of this personal treasure as $1,500. If the sax has considerable sentimental value to Gene, say $3,000, Gene is likely to redeem the pawn ticket. Assuming maximum allowable charges, at the end of the month Gene has three choices: 1) abandon the sax, 2) extend the pawn another month by paying $375 (=0.25 times $1,500) or, 3) pay $1,875 (=$1,500 plus $375) and reclaim possession of the sax.

Vehicle Title Loans and Their Regulation in Mississippi

A vehicle title loan is similar to a pawn loan, but with an important difference. In a pawn transaction, the consumer gives possession of the item to the pawnbroker. Under the terms of a vehicle title loan, the borrower retains possession of the pledged collateral. i.e., the vehicle. A basic vehicle title loan is a non-recourse one-month lump sum loan with the principal and interest due at the end of the month.

If, at the end of the month, the borrower cannot repay the principal, some states allow for an interest-only payment. In Mississippi, the title lender cannot allow an interest-only payment to extend the loan over for another month. Instead, the borrower must make the interest payment and a 10% reduction of the principal owed.

Like pawn loans, vehicle title loans are non-recourse: The consumer can walk away with the cash. As in a pawn loan, if the borrower defaults on a vehicle title loan, ownership of the vehicle transfers to the title lender. State laws specify how the lender can repossess the vehicle and begin the process to sell it. If the vehicle eventually sells for an amount that is less than the amount owed, the borrower does not have to make up the difference. In Mississippi, if the vehicle sells for more than the outstanding amount owed, the consumer receives 85% of the excess sale proceeds.

About seventeen states allow vehicle title lending. The variety in state laws makes for differences in the title loan transaction. In Mississippi, MS Code § 75-67-413 (2013) states "A title pledge lender may contract for and receive a title pledge service charge in lieu of interest or other charges for all services, expenses, cost and losses of every nature not to exceed twenty-five percent (25%) of the principal amount, per month, advanced in the title pledge transaction." States also regulate the loan amount of a title loan. In Mississippi, the maximum amount is $2,500.

The application process for a title loan is straightforward. To secure a title loan, the borrower must have a clear title to the vehicle, and the borrower must allow the title lender to place a lien on the vehicle. The consumer does not need to provide a credit history.

Example 4. Dewey brings a 2003 Chevrolet Tahoe Z71, and its clear title, to a title lender. The title lender can inspect the vehicle, if present, and/or look up values for similarly equipped vehicles. Suppose this Tahoe has a wholesale appraisal of about $4,900 and the lender makes an offer of $2,000. At the end of the month, Dewey has three choices: 1) walk away, and the process begins to transfer possession and ownership of the vehicle to the title lender, 2) extend the loan for another month by paying the title lender $500+$200 (=0.25 times $2,000, plus a required 10% reduction in the principal) or, 3) pay $2,500 (=$2,000 plus $500) to release the lien.

Payday Loans and Their Regulation in Mississippi

Payday loans are also known as cash advance loans, delayed deposit loans, and deferred presentment loans. In a traditional payday loan, a borrower writes a check to a lender in exchange for a short-term cash loan. The lender agrees not to cash the check until a date specified in the loan agreement.

To obtain a payday loan, lenders generally require borrowers to have an active checking account, provide proof of income, show valid identification, and be at least 18 years old. Payday lenders generally do not require a traditional credit report.

Under the *Mississippi Check Cashers Act*, a payday loan agreement must disclose the terms of the loan, including the loan amount and the annual percentage rate (APR). The lender will generally require the borrower to write a personal check for the loan principal plus a loan fee, i.e., interest on the loan. The loan agreement might allow the lender to withdraw (or attempt to withdraw) the sum owed from the borrower's bank account, i.e., cash the check, at the loan due date–regardless of whether the borrower has sufficient funds in the account. If the borrower does not have sufficient funds, the borrower will be subject to Non-Sufficient Funds (NSF) fees charged by their bank.

Under Mississippi law, the largest check a payday loan borrower can write is for $500. The amount of the check must include the loan principal and allowable fees. For a check written for $250 or less, Mississippi law allows a payday lender to charge a fee of up to $20 per $100 advanced to the borrower.

Example 5. Ruby writes a check for $240 to a payday lender who gives $200 to Ruby and keeps the check, which includes $40 in fees. In two weeks, the lender cashes the check, or receives money through an ACH (Automated Clearing House) agreement. If Ruby cannot repay the interest and principal, Ruby can extend the loan for another two weeks by paying, in this case, $40.

Installment Credit Products: Traditional Installment Loans From Finance Companies, Payday Installment Loans, and Vehicle Title Installment Loans

The terms of a fixed-rate installment loan are not complicated. Calculating the monthly payment of an installment loan might seem to be a daunting task to some people, but fortunately, there is a formula, taught in introductory finance classes, that makes this calculation straightforward. The formula used to calculate the monthly payment on a fixed-rate installment loan is:

$$\text{Principal} = \text{Monthly Payment} \times \left[\frac{1 - \frac{1}{(1+r)^n}}{r} \right] \qquad (3)$$

There are four unknown amounts in Equation (3): 1) Principal (i.e., the Amount Borrowed), 2) Monthly Payment, 3) Number of months, n, and 4) Monthly interest rate, r, which is the APR divided by 12. Given any three of these unknown amounts, a consumer can easily calculate the fourth amount using a financial calculator.

Here are two other handy equations to help the consumer calculate interest paid, i.e., the dollar cost of a loan. Because

$$\text{Total Interest and Principal} = \text{Monthly Payment} \times \text{Number of Payments} \qquad (4)$$

We can calculate

$$\text{Interest Paid} = \text{Total Interest and Principal} - \text{Amount Borrowed.} \qquad (5)$$

Traditional Installment Loans and Their Regulation in Mississippi

In the early 1900s, a battle raged against illegal "loan sharks." An alternate new loan source developed through the collaboration of lenders and consumer advocates, notably Arthur H. Ham of the Russell Sage Foundation. What emerged was the Uniform Small Loan Law (USLL) written in 1916. By 1940, all but nine states had adopted some version of this proposed law for cash installment loans.[7]

The striking feature of this law was that it allowed for interest rates higher than allowed under existing usury laws. Of course, illegal "loan sharks," and those who favored low interest rate caps, lobbied long and hard against this legislation. When collaborating on the Uniform Small Loan Law, the parties agreed: 1) Legal installment lenders must be able to earn a reasonable profit. Therefore, the interest rate was initially set at 3 to 3.5 percent per month; 2) Small loans were defined as "up to $300" (in today's dollars, more than $7,000), and; 3) the maximum interest rate would be re-examined periodically to sustain the industry.

For 100 years, i.e., until 2016, Mississippi Law set rates lower than the ones recommended by the USLL. As of 2016, Mississippi Law allows finance companies a choice concerning the interest rate on installment loans, either through the *Small Loan Regulatory Law* or *The Mississippi Consumer Alternative Installment Loan Act.*

---

7   For an excellent set of papers on the Uniform Small Loan Law and its implementation, see the conference proceedings on "Combating the Loan Shark," 1941.

Mississippi Code § 75-17-21 (2013) sets the maximum allowable finance charges by licensees operating under the *Small Loan Regulatory Law*. Mississippi law, like that of many states that impose an interest rate cap, imposes a set of allowable interest rates that change with the amount borrowed. The higher the amount borrowed, the lower the allowable interest rate.

The *Small Loan Regulatory Law* reads: "For an unpaid balance up to $1,000, the maximum annual rate is 36 percent (3 percent per month). For amounts over $1,000 up to $2,500 the maximum rate is 33 percent; for amounts over $2,500 to $5,000 the maximum rate is 24 percent, and; for amounts over $5,000 the maximum allowable annual rate is 14 percent." The resulting interest rate on a $4,000 loan is about 30 percent.

Example 6. Molly borrows $1,000 from a finance company. The lender makes the loan at 36 percent, and Molly will repay the loan in twelve equal installments. Molly does not buy any ancillary products (i.e., credit insurance). Ignoring the allowable closing fee, using Equation (3), with r = .36/12 and n = 12, Molly's monthly payment is $100.46. The total interest and principal she pays is $100.46 × 12 = $1,205.52. The interest is $205.52.

The Mississippi Consumer Alternative Installment Loan Act took effect July 1, 2016. Section 3 of this Act reads: "For any consumer installment loan that a licensee makes, the licensee has the option to either lend at the rates and fees indicated under the *Small Loan Regulatory Law* (§ 75-17-21), or at the rates and charges under Section 4 of this act."

Section 4 states: "In lieu of the interest and charges in §75-17-21, on loans of Four Thousand Dollars ($4,000.00) or less, a licensee may contract and charge a monthly finance charge not to exceed an annual percentage rate, calculated according to the actuarial method, of fifty-nine percent (59%) per annum on the unpaid balance of the amount financed."

Example 7. Violet borrows $2,000 from a finance company. The lender makes the loan at 59 percent, and Violet will repay the loan in twelve equal installments. Violet does not buy any ancillary products (i.e., credit insurance). Ignoring the allowable closing fee, using Equation (3), with r = .59/12 and n = 12, Violet's monthly payment is $224.59. The total interest and principal she pays is $224.59 × 12 = $2,695.08. The interest is $695.08.

Payday Installment Loans and Their Regulation in Mississippi

Under the *Mississippi Credit Availability Act*, payday lenders have a way to make "payday installment loans." Under Section 4(a) of this Act, borrowers can pay back loans up to $500 in four to six fully amortizing installments. For loans up over $500, but no more than $2,500, Section 4(b) states that borrowers can pay back these loans in six to twelve fully amortizing installments. For all loans up to $2,500 under the *Mississippi Credit Availability Act*: "A licensee may charge and collect a monthly handling fee for services, expenses, and costs not to exceed twenty-five percent (25%) of the outstanding principal balance of any credit availability account per month." In addition, Section 2(a) and Section 2(b) state: "The handling fee shall not be deemed interest for any purpose of law." In addition, Section 2(c) also states "...a licensee may also charge and collect an origination fee in the amount of one percent (1%) of the amount disbursed to the account holder or Five Dollars ($5.00), whichever is greater..."

Example 8. Salley borrows $500 from a payday installment lender. The monthly fee is 25 percent per month (equivalent to a 300 percent APR), there is a one percent per $100 origination fee, and Salley will repay the loan in four equal installments. Using Equation (3), with Principal = $505 ($500 plus $5 origination fee), r = 3.00/12 and n = 4, Salley's monthly payment is $213.84. The total interest and principal she pays is $213.84 × 4 = $855.36. The interest is $350.36.

Vehicle Title Installment Loans and Their Regulation in Mississippi

Many consumers are familiar with making a monthly payment to finance the purchase of a vehicle. It is important, however, to distinguish sales financing of a vehicle from a Vehicle Title Installment loan. Sales financing occurs at much lower interest rates, covers a bigger percentage of the vehicle's value, and is longer-term compared to a Vehicle Title Installment loan. In addition, dealers underwrite sales financing contracts by gathering income and expense data from the applicant and reviewing the applicant's credit report. Failure to perform on a sales finance contract lowers the credit score, and timely repayment improves the credit score.

The attributes above do not describe a Vehicle Title Installment loan. The *Mississippi Credit Availability Act* governs these loans. The maximum amount borrowed is $2,500, the allowable monthly fee is 25%, and a loan amount of the maximum amount is paid back over six to twelve months. Generally, these loans are not strenuously underwritten (the vehicle title alone secures the loan). Moreover, performance on these loans does not influence credit scores.

Example 9. Betty borrows $2,500 from a vehicle title installment lender. The monthly fee is 25 percent per month (equivalent to a 300 percent APR), there is a one percent per $100 origination fee, and Betty will repay the loan in six equal installments. Using Equation (3), with Principal = $2,525 ($2,500 plus $25 origination fee), with r = 3.00/12 and n = 6, Betty's monthly payment is $855.52. The total interest and principal she pays is $855.52 × 6 = $5,133.12. The interest is $2,608.12.

The Economics of Interest Rate Caps

Economic theory predicts that an interest rate cap set above the market-clearing interest rate does not restrain borrowing and lending. A binding interest rate cap is one that lies below the market-clearing interest rate. Economic theory also predicts that a binding interest rate cap will interfere with a credit market in three ways: 1) create shortages; 2) destroy gains from trade; 3) give rise to additional search costs.

A binding rate cap creates shortages because, at the rate cap, the amount of money sought by borrowers exceeds the amount of money lenders are willing to provide. Because a binding rate cap does not allow for a free market outcome, borrowers and lenders alike are worse off. There are some borrowers who would be better off getting a loan at a higher rate, as opposed to being shut out of the loan market at the cap rate. Lenders are also better off without a cap because they can profitably lend more money. A binding rate cap forces borrowers to seek out ways to obtain credit in other loan markets, or in other ways. When borrowers search out other ways to obtain credit, they expend time, effort, and money.

Interest Rate Caps Remain, Despite Their Predictably Detrimental Effects

Long before the creation of the model legislation known as the Uniform Small Loan Law of 1916, state legislatures were heavily involved in regulating the small loan market. State legislatures are still heavily involved in passing laws governing small dollar installment loan markets. As of 2016, seventeen states (and the District of Columbia) had *lower* rate caps than they did in 1935, and five states had the same rate cap as they did in 1935.[8]

Advocates of interest rate caps offer many arguments for the "need" for interest rate caps in small-dollar loan markets. One can collectively view these arguments simply as "being in the best interest of con-

---

8   See Foster (1941); Black and Miller (2016).

sumers." Black and Miller (2016) review the rate cap literature and find four themes that interest rate cap proponents use to support interest rate caps. These themes are: 1) Borrowers are naïve, and simply do not understand the loan terms; 2) Groups thought, by advocates, to be most vulnerable to exploitation by lenders—namely minorities, women, and the poor—need protection from "predatory" lenders; 3) Even if consumers are willing to borrow at high interest rates, society should protect these consumers from themselves because they are making themselves worse off, and; 4) Lenders, especially small dollar lenders, make abnormally high profits from lending at high interest rates because they have considerable market power. Black and Miller (2016) show that rigorous academic research rejects these four themes.

What happens to consumers when legislatures impose binding interest rate caps? Academic research provides strong evidence that imposing interest rate caps harms the very people that the cap is designed to protect. The strongest evidence is that rate caps weigh heaviest on consumers for whom credit is least available, i.e., poor people and/or those consumers who are sub-prime borrowers. Researchers find that imposing interest rate caps hurts financially challenged households by reducing the amount of credit given to high risk borrowers, i.e., the poor.[9]

The Effects on Consumer Welfare from Tightening Restrictions on Payday Lenders

Almost surely, some state legislatures will tighten payday lending laws with future laws. The Bureau of Consumer Financial Protection (CFPB) has drafted a proposed rule that, if enacted, will change the payday lending market drastically, perhaps resulting in a de facto ban on current practices of payday lenders. Some academic studies, however, find that banning payday lending likely reduces consumer welfare.

For example, Morgan and Strain (2008) examine the impact on consumers when legislation in Georgia (2004) and North Carolina (2005) closed payday lending operations in these two states. In general, Morgan and Strain (2008) find that after the ban, Georgia households bounced more checks, had more complaints about debt collectors, and were more likely to file for bankruptcy under Chapter 7. Rather than finding that Georgia and North Carolina households had fewer financial difficulties after banning payday lending, Morgan and Strain (2008) find that residents of these states had more financial difficulties.

What happens to consumer access to credit when a state lowers an interest rate cap on payday lenders? Oregon instituted an APR cap of 150 percent in 2007. Zinman (2010) estimates loan production costs result in a break-even APR rate of 390 percent for payday lenders. Not surprisingly, after Oregon imposed the interest rate cap, the number of payday lenders in Oregon dropped from 346 to 82 by September 2008. Zinman (2010) also finds that this reduction in the supply of credit for payday borrowers worsened their financial condition. In addition, borrowers who would have been payday customers shifted into what Zinman (2010) refers to as "plausibly inferior substitutes," such as pawnbrokers and internet lenders.[10]

Despite the intention to enhance consumer welfare, these studies show that banning payday lending or lowering interest rate caps on payday loans can harm consumers. In addition, Morse (2011) documents a causal relation between welfare and access to payday loan credit and concludes that payday lending is welfare enhancing and that "a move to ban payday lending is ill advised." Unfortunately, as of 2015, Black and Miller (2016) document that 13 states and the District of Columbia ban the payday lending product, and four more impose interest rate caps that result in a de facto ban on payday lending.

---

9   See the research studies by Bowsher (1974), Benmelech and Moskowitz (2010), and Rigbi (2013).

10 For borrowers who prefer pawn loans and internet loans, payday loans are the inferior substitute.

The Effects on Consumer Welfare from Interest Rate Caps on Traditional Installment Loans

Although traditional installment loans from finance companies have existed for a century, there is little academic research on this market. Recently, however, two studies show that differences in interest rate cap levels create differences in installment loan markets.

Durkin, Elliehausen, Hwang (2017) compare the small-dollar loan markets in Texas and Pennsylvania–with a lower allowable rate than Texas. They find a lower number of loans in Pennsylvania. In addition, they find that the size of the loans in Pennsylvania are larger than those made in Texas. Higher allowable rates in Texas mean that smaller loan sizes are profitable in Texas, but not in Pennsylvania. Durkin, Elliehausen, and Hwang (2017) also find empirical evidence consistent with Juster and Shay's (1964) theory of credit rationing. This theory predicts that borrowers who use small-dollar installment loans, are "rationed borrowers," that is, these borrowers are unable to borrow all they need at low rates from banks.

Arkansas has a 17 percent constitutionally imposed interest rate cap. There are no installment lenders who operate within the state of Arkansas, but there are installment lenders who operate in all six states that border Arkansas. Lukongo and Miller (2017) find that Arkansas residents obtain installment loans from lenders in these six other states. They also find that Arkansas residents living in perimeter counties hold 96.8 percent of these loans–an indication of a small-dollar installment loan "credit desert" in the interior counties of Arkansas.

The Effects of Interest Rate Caps on Subprime Borrowers

In a free market, the interest rate attached to a loan reflects the risk of the borrower. The greater the chance that the borrower will default, the higher the interest rate charged to the borrower. In a free market, lower risk borrowers pay lower interest rates, and higher risk borrowers pay higher interest rates. In a free market, all borrowers get credit. Prime borrowers will borrow from lenders who specialize in lending to prime borrowers. Sub-prime borrowers will borrow from lenders who specialize in lending to sub-prime borrowers.

When an interest rate cap is imposed, borrowers who are judged by a free market to have to pay a rate higher than the cap will not receive credit. Lenders will not extend credit because they are not compensated for the risk that these borrowers represent. The rate cap does not affect prime borrowers–their risk level lies below the interest rate cap.

What is the result? A greater share of the available loan funds flows to lower risk applicants–thereby increasing the volume of credit flowing to relatively wealthier borrowers. Relatively poorer borrowers and sub-prime borrowers, therefore, have a reduced access to credit.

Because rate caps make some small dollar installment loan sizes unprofitable, rate caps limit the supply of credit to small dollar borrowers. When the Uniform Small Loan Law of 1916 was written, lenders could profitably make installment loans under $100 at the interest rates suggested by this model law, i.e., an APR of 36 to 42 percent. The Uniform Small Loan Law of 1916 states that a rate established by legislators "should be reconsidered after a reasonable period of experience with it." Clearly, 100-plus years exceeds "a reasonable period." Nevertheless, Black and Miller (2016) show that 38 states had interest rate caps less than or equal to 36 percent APR, as of 2015.[11]

---

11 Source: Black and Miller (2016).

How to Create a Loan Desert With An Interest Rate Cap

These outdated interest rate caps create legal loan deserts in the small-dollar loan landscape. There is demand, but no supply. For example, in Table 1, the first column contains the revenue and cost numbers when an installment lender could profitably make a $100 loan, i.e., earn ten percent on equity ($2.00 of Net Income divided by $20 of Equity). So, the first column shows the market conditions in 1916. Since 1916, loan production costs increase because wages, benefits, rent, taxes, and other costs increase.

The second column in Table 1 represents a case where costs have doubled. In this case, to have $2.00 of Net Income which yields 10 percent on Equity, the loan size must increase to $190.25. The third column represents a case where loan production costs are ten times the base cost case. In this case, to earn ten percent on Equity, the loan size must be $912.19.

To provide some sense of a timeline, the Consumer Price Index (CPI) was 10.9 in 1916. The CPI was approximately twice as high, 22.3, in 1947 and about ten times higher, 103.9, in 1986. The CPI in 2016 was 240.0, more than twenty times the level in 1916.[12] In Figure 18.1, as loan production costs increase, so does the size of the loan needed to be profitable—defined as a ten percent ROE.

Over time, what happens to consumers who want to borrow $300? In the first two column of Figure 18.1 (i.e., representative of 1916 and 1947), these consumers can borrow $300, because lenders can make these loans profitably. If production costs in 1986 are approximated by the third column in Figure 18.1, then consumers cannot borrow only $300. At the 36% interest rate cap, the break-even loan size is over $900. Borrowers who want to borrow only $300 cannot obtain a traditional installment loan. If their financial situation does not allow them to repay a $900 loan, these consumers must find another source of credit. The persistence of the 36% rate cap in the face of ever-increasing loan production costs, creates a loan desert below the breakeven loan amount.

Focus on column three of Figure 18.1. A monthly payment of $91.64 means that the total interest received on a loan of $912.19 is $187.50. To make a $300 loan profitable, it must also generate interest of $187.50. At an interest rate cap of 36%, however, it generates only $61.68 of interest from monthly payments of $30.14. To generate $187.50 of interest, the monthly payment must increase by $10.49 to $40.63. In this case, the APR must increase from 36% to about 100%. Given the price levels of 2016, the APR would have to be even higher.

Figure 18.1: At a 36% APR, Loan Size Increases as Costs Increase

Item	Base Costs	Double Base Costs	Ten Times Base Costs
Amount Lent	$100.00	$190.25	$912.19
Monthly Payment	$10.05	$19.11	$91.64
Total of Payments	$120.55	$229.35	$1,099.69
Interest Received	$20.55	$39.10	$187.50
All Costs	$18.55	$37.10	$185.50
Net Income	$2.00	$2.00	$2.00
Equity	$20.00	$20.00	$20.00
Return on Equity	10.0%	10.0%	10.0%

---

12 Source: Minneapolis Federal Reserve. www.minneapolisfed.org/community/teaching-aids/cpi-calculator-information/consumer-price-index-and-inflation-rates-1913.

The National Commission on Consumer Finance (1972) contains a detailed study of breakeven interest rates when the loan amount does not change. Durkin, Elliehausen, and Hwang (2017) provide supporting evidence on the National Commission's (1972) findings that the production cost of making small-dollar installment loans, as well as their risk, means that suppliers of smaller dollar loans need a relatively higher interest rate to supply these loans. If there is no rate cap, then the market will determine which interest rates are profitable for a given loan size.

Conclusion

Unfettered access to credit is an economic freedom that fuels prosperity. The best way to foster economic growth and prosperity in Mississippi is to create laws where honest businesses thrive, and dishonest business perish. Setting good rules governing how legitimate businesses provide access to consumer credit is important for everyone living in Mississippi. Consumers know their cash inflow and cash outflows. If Mississippians have unfettered access to consumer credit, they can choose when and how to fix an imbalance between income and expenses.

The Overview of the Report of the National Commission on Consumer Finance (1972) contains a statement that is still relevant 45 years later: "Underlying the Commission's belief that competition is the best regulator of the consumer credit marketplace is its belief that a competitive system cannot be 'half-free.' If there is to be competition, then it follows that such competition should also be the governor of *rates* as well as other aspects of credit granting (amount, type, and so forth). It would be inconsistent to turn to the industry and attempt to regulate and eliminate practices which affect operating costs but at the same time limit the rate by fiat so that it cannot seek its own level. And yet this is precisely what legislators have done."

Mississippi consumers have access to as many small-dollar loan products as residents in any other state. Unlike some other states, Mississippi imposes rate caps (and other restrictions) on all small-dollar loan products available to Mississippi consumers. For lump sum loans, these caps are found under: *The Pawn Shop Act § 75-67-313* (Pawn Loans), MS Code § 75-67-413 (Vehicle Title Loans), and the *Mississippi Check Cashers Act* (Payday Loans). For installment loans, these caps are found under: *Mississippi Code § 75-17-21, The Small Loan Regulatory Law* or, recently, *The Mississippi Consumer Alternative Installment Loan Act* (Traditional installment loans from finance companies) and *The Mississippi Credit Availability Act* (for installment loans from payday and vehicle title lenders).

Economic theory predicts that free markets are the best regulator of prices—including interest rates. Nevertheless, the Mississippi state legislature fetters small-dollar credit markets with interest rate caps. They are not alone. Many state legislatures impose laws that impede prices in credit markets from seeking their market-clearing levels.

The recently enacted *Mississippi Consumer Alternative Installment Loan Act* nearly doubles the allowable interest rate on loans up to $4,000. This law is a move toward letting the free market determine the interest rate on any possible loan size. There is no economic reason to limit the loan size to $4,000. Given the predictions of economic theory and the findings by researchers, the Mississippi state legislature can greatly help Mississippi consumers by eliminating, or greatly raising, interest rate caps on all small-dollar loan markets.

References

Benmelech, Efraim and Tobias J. Moskowitz. 2010. The political economy of financial regulation: Evidence from U.S. usury laws in the 19th century. Journal of Finance, 65, pp. 1029-1073.

Black, Harold and Thomas W. Miller, Jr. 2016. "Examining Some Arguments Made by Interest Rate Cap Advocates," in "Rethinking Financial Regulation: Enhancing Stability and Protecting Consumers," Mercatus Center at George Mason University (Ben Klutsey and Hester Peirce, editors).

Board of Governors of the Federal Reserve System, "Report on the Economic Well-Being of U.S. Households in 2014," May 2015. See: https://www.federalreserve.gov/econresdata/2014-report-economic-well-being-us-households-201505.pdf

Bowsher, Norman N. 1974. Usury laws: Harmful when effective. Federal Reserve Bank of St. Louis Review, August.

Calder, Lendol. 1999. "Financing the American dream: A cultural history of consumer credit," Princeton University Press, Princeton, NJ.

"Combating the Loan Shark." 1941. Law and Contemporary Problems, Duke University Law School, Volume 8, Number 1.

Durkin, Thomas A., Gregory Elliehausen, and Min Hwang. 2017. "Rate ceilings and the distribution of small dollar installment loans from consumer finance companies: Results of a new survey of small dollar cash lenders," working paper, Washington, DC: George Washington University.

Durkin, Thomas A., Elliehausen, Gregory, Staten, Michael E, and Todd J. Zywicki. 2014. "Consumer Credit and the American Economy." Oxford University Press, New York, New York.

Juster, F. Thomas and Robert P. Shay. 1964. "Consumer Sensitivity to Finance Rates: An Empirical and Analytical Investigation." New York: National Bureau of Economic Research, Occasional Paper 88.

Lukongo, Ben, and Thomas W. Miller, Jr. 2017. "Some Consequences of the Binding Constitutional Interest Rate Cap in the State of Arkansas," *working paper,* Mercatus Center at George Mason University.

Miller, Thomas W., Jr., and Michael Wilt. 2017. "A Primer on Non-Bank Supplied Small Dollar Loans," *Mimeo,* Mercatus Center at George Mason University.

Morgan, D. P. and M. R. Strain. 2008. "Payday holiday: How households fare after payday credit bans," Staff Reports, Federal Reserve Bank of New York.

Morse, Adair. 2011. "Payday lenders: Heroes or villains?" *Journal of Financial Economics,* 102, pp. 28-44.

National Commission on Consumer Finance. 1972. Consumer Credit in the United States: The Report of the National Commission on Consumer Finance. Washington, D.C.: Government Printing Office.

Rigbi, Oren. 2013. The Effects of Usury Laws: Evidence from the Online Loan Market. *Review of Economics and Statistics,* 95(4): 1238-1248.

Zinman, Jonathan. 2010. "Restricting consumer credit access: Household survey evidence on effects around the Oregon rate cap," *Journal of Banking and Finance* 34, pp. 546-556.

19

Natural Disasters and Prosperity in Mississippi

Daniel Sutter

19

Natural Disasters and Prosperity in Mississippi

Daniel Sutter

Introduction

Extreme weather poses a risk for economic activity. History offers cases where hurricanes disrupted the exploration and settlement of the New World by Europeans, impacted military campaigns, or submerged an entire city. The potential loss to life and property from hurricanes, tornadoes, floods, winter storms, droughts, and heat waves threatens the economic health of communities and states. Economists like to use extreme weather as a textbook example of a negative supply shock, subjecting students to test questions which begin, "A freeze devastates the Florida orange crop...." Mississippi is vulnerable to a wide range of extreme weather and suffered from two of the worst weather disasters in U.S. history, the Great Flood of 1927, and Hurricane Katrina in 2005. Hurricanes and floods pose a further complication for high risk geographic areas: coastal zones for hurricanes and the flood plains of rivers. The high risk zones, however, also provide immense economic value; transportation and manufacturing frequently use water, while people value living and vacationing along coastlines.

Public policy affects where households and businesses locate and how they build. Government also provides or regulates much of the infrastructure necessary for economic use, like roads, bridges, highways, canals, and utilities. Households' and businesses' decisions, as influenced by policy, determine whether the economic benefits of hazard-prone areas will be realized and if the costs of extreme weather will be efficiently managed. Government policies affect the vulnerability of our communities when extreme weather occurs, the response to assist victims immediately afterwards, and the prospects for long term recovery by victims and communities.

A prosperous economy must overcome the challenges of extreme weather. The burden of extreme weather is typically managed through sharing of the costs, which can be done in three ways: through markets, primarily meaning insurance; through charitable assistance to the victims; and through government aid. The sharing of risks can also encourage excessive risk exposure; the Samaritan's Dilemma (Buchanan 1975, Coate 1995) looms large in any discussion of weather risk. The tale of the Good Samaritan teaches us to assist strangers who have suffered misfortune. The dilemma arises because knowledge that a Good Samaritan will be there to assist makes us more likely to put ourselves into positions where we get into trouble. Thus, while we want to care for those who have suffered from natural disasters, doing so may increase the number who suffer from such disasters in the first place. The societal impact of hurricanes, floods, and tornadoes is never exclusively due to nature, but rather a complex interaction of weather and peoples' choices to put themselves, and their property, in locations likely to be exposed to these extreme weather events.

The Affordability of Insurance, Development, and Fairness

Collectively, our wants and desires for goods and services exceed our production capacity, so we will never be able to afford everything we want. We experience our choice to do without a good we would like to have as a problem of affordability: if the price were a little lower, or if we had a little more money, we could buy the item. Concerns about people being unable to afford some goods are inevitable. Affordability of any good is not a market failure; indeed, affordability is essentially the rationing function of prices in the market. Unfortunately, a lack of understanding of this concept has led to the affordability of insurance being used to justify policy interventions. Advocates of the use of government aid to subsidize the high cost of wind or flood insurance often cite two specific negative impacts, disruptions to economic development and the well-being of families with modest incomes. Both concerns are worth exploring, and provide a background perspective on the problems posed by extreme weather.

Economic development is about persons, not places. People must live and work somewhere, but prosperity in a state never requires development of a specific locale, even if some locales have natural economic advantages. Hurricanes and floods increase the real opportunity or economic cost of building on the Gulf Coast or along a river relative to a safer location. Repair costs will be greater in a vulnerable location, or more costly construction will be needed to avoid destruction. These higher costs will be worth incurring if the hazard-prone location provides enough additional economic value to justify the cost. Higher insurance rates tell people that they should have a good reason to question building in a hazard-prone area. On the margin, higher insurance rates will reduce development in a high-risk locale, but the deterred or relocated development will be that for which the hazardous location does not provide corresponding extra value.

Wind and flood insurance is sometimes criticized as taxpayer subsidies for the wealthy. There is some truth to this; Census tracts immediately along the Gulf Coast do have higher incomes than the remainder of Mississippi (Sutter 2007). But not all coastal residents are rich by any stretch of the imagination. Mississippi's twelve Gulf Coast casinos employ around 10,000 people in total, and many of these families' budgets would be significantly impacted by a steep increase in insurance rates (Mississippi Gaming & Hospitality Association 2017). To keep wind insurance premiums low, the state appropriated almost $180 million to the Mississippi Windstorm Underwriting Association after Hurricane Katrina, while the Mississippi Insurance Commissioner sued the Federal government over proposed increases in National Flood Insurance premiums under the 2012 Biggert-Waters Act (Mississippi Insurance Department 2015). These policy actions raise an important question. Should affordability concerns for Mississippi families being able to live in disaster prone areas be an important policy goal?

A comprehensive answer to this question would depend on ethics, not just economics. But it is important to consider unintended consequences of such a policy. Research clearly demonstrates that low income households are less likely to evacuate in advance of an approaching hurricane (Dash and Gladwin 2007), for many reasons. For instance, low income households are less likely to have a car, may not have the savings to cover evacuation expenses, and are more likely to be hourly employees and lose earnings if they evacuate. I do not wish to judge or second guess these decisions, but they raise the question of whether public policy should be justified based on encouraging specifically those people who may lack the means to evacuate to live in dangerous areas and put their lives at risk.

If affordability is an important policy goal, assistance for low income individuals to pay market insurance premiums would be a better means to achieve this goal. Addressing affordability concerns only requires assisting the relatively small number of persons needing assistance, not distorting the price of insurance for everyone. Higher rates based on risk are an important signal that should affect location decisions.

Price Gouging and the Response to Disaster

Price gouging refers to charging a higher price than "normal" for items, or a price well in excess of cost. The term is often used to refer to high prices that might be charged for standard items in the aftermath of a disaster. Thirty-four states, including Mississippi, have passed laws criminalizing price gouging, and these laws affect the immediate response to a disaster. Mississippi's law does not allow the prices of goods to rise above the level charged prior to the declared emergency zone, except to cover additional costs of selling.[1]

Many economists have written on price gouging, which illustrates the effects of price ceilings and highlights the importance of time and space in economics.[2] Disasters can affect both the demand and supply sides of the market. On the demand side, disasters cause significant increases in demand for selected goods and services such as plywood, tarps, generators, building supplies, gasoline, and ice. Disasters typically reduce supply as well, through damage to retailers, disruption of the utilities businesses need to operate, and interference with transportation to the disaster area. Increases in demand and decreases in supply both increase the equilibrium price, meaning the price at which the available quantity of a good equals the quantity that consumers wish to buy *at that price*. Economic theory can easily rationalize huge increases in the equilibrium prices during the period of the distortion of demand and supply.

The post-disaster period highlights how valuable knowledge in economics depends on time and place, as Hayek (1945) first explained. While knowledge in the natural sciences is general (meaning it applies across different places) and timeless (the law of gravity holds each day), valuable knowledge in economics varies. Normally one cannot plan to sell ice for more than about $2 a bag, which is very close to the cost of making, storing, and shipping it to grocery and convenience stores. But on August 30, 2005, the day after Katrina's landfall, economic conditions in Mississippi were no longer normal. Mississippians had a great need for, and were willing to pay a lot for, ice, generators, and gasoline on that day and very near their homes. The fact that ice could be purchased for $2 a bag in Atlanta or Houston was irrelevant. Ice when and where it was needed was worth more than $2 a bag.

Although economists can understand why the post-disaster equilibrium price of ice might be $8 or $12 a bag, such a price shocks and appalls many people. The term price gouging suggests the equivalent

---

1   A list of state laws against price gouging (as of 2012) is available at: https://knowledgeproblem.com/2012/11/03/list-of-price-gouging-laws/

2   For economists' analyses of price gouging see Sowell (2004), Gibberson (2011), and Lee (2015).

at least of gouging a person's eyes out; President George W. Bush compared price gougers with looters after Katrina.[3] Philosopher Michael Sandel (2009, p.7) states the objection quite succinctly:

> In times of trouble, a good society pulls together. Rather than press for maximum advantage, people look out for one another. A society in which people exploit their neighbors for financial gain in times of crisis is not a good society.

Laws prohibiting this behavior signal society's disapproval of this behavior.

The cost of supplying ice to communities across Mississippi was certainly more than $2 a bag after Katrina. Let's say it was $8 a bag. I would agree with Professor Sandel that selling ice for $12 a bag instead of $8 a bag (the current cost) is ethically questionable. An economic case for this can be made (Sowell 2004), but the persistence of laws against price gouging might show that perhaps morality is trumping economics on this issue. However, the more significant point is that prohibiting price gouging does *nothing* to provide victims with ice and other badly needed supplies. The harm and suffering of victims is due to the hurricane, tornado, or ice storm. Nature produces conditions under which victims willingly pay $12 a bag for ice. Competition in markets if often the best way for dealing with many anti-social behaviors. We can keep someone from selling ice to victims for $12 instead of $8 a bag by letting other sellers undercut their price. The ultimate goal after a disaster is to get the needed supplies to people at the lowest price possible. Higher prices for needed goods would incentive more individuals to supply these goods to the affected area, simultaneously providing needed goods more quickly and through competition putting downward pressure on prices for these same products. The information generated by the market response is critical in providing the supplies actually needed. The important role of economic knowledge in successfully assisting victims is illustrated by FEMA's poor performance after Katrina (Sobel and Leeson 2006, Leeson and Sobel 2007). Instead of simply prohibiting price increases after weather disasters, Mississippi could offer tax credits to retailers for losses incurred selling below cost after emergencies.

Post Disaster Reconstruction and Occupational Licensing

Natural disasters can place an enormous strain on the capacity of the construction industry. The stock of housing stock is large, but houses are long-lived investments, so the amount of new housing constructed in any given year is much smaller. Mississippi has 1.3 million housing units, and yet over the past five years, an average of less than 6,700 housing units and 5,500 single family homes have been built. Construction requires both specialized equipment and skilled workers in a variety of trades; expanding this capacity takes time. The building capacity in any one community is even more limited naturally. For example, an average of 197 total housing units and 87 single family homes have been built annually in the Hattiesburg metro, a community hit hard by Katrina and several recent tornadoes. The capacity of experienced contractors to repair damaged homes and buildings is similarly limited.

Hurricane Katrina resulted in 483,000 insurance claims state wide, with 236,000 just in the three coastal counties (Hancock, Harrison, and Jackson; Mississippi Insurance Department, 2015). Significant extreme weather events can definitely produce a demand for construction and contractors exceeding the capacity of the state's builders. A shortage of builders and contractors can lead to long delays in reconstruction forcing residents to seek alternative living arrangements or live in an unrepaired home longer. This increases the cost and hardship of a disaster.

---

3   Julie Mason, "Bush: 'Zero tolerance' for looters, price gougers," September 1, 2005, available at: http://www.chron.com/news/hurricanes/article/Bush-Zero-tolerance-for-looters-price-gouging-1923045.php

Markets can help meet such demand surges. Building supplies can be reallocated from other states, and contractors can also temporarily relocate as well. Occupational licensing can limit the mobility of contractors (and other professionals). As was discussed in Chapter 9, Mississippi licenses too many professions; indeed, the state licenses all 28 residential and commercial contractor trades reported by the Institute for Justice (Carpenter et al. 2012). Licensing can restrict the ability of contractors licensed in other states from moving to Mississippi. While rolling back occupational licensing requirements in the state would be the best way to deal with any artificial restriction in the supply of builders, a temporary relaxation of licensing after a disaster should be a priority. Florida allowed contractors licensed in other states to work in the state after four major hurricanes struck in 2004. A study found that customer complaints were not higher for the out-of-state contractors than for Florida licensed contractors (Skarbek 2008).

Property Insurance

Coastal properties exposed to hurricane risk pose a particular challenge for property insurers, for two reasons. First, hurricane risk is correlated. Insurance normally works through the pooling of independent risks. For example, property insurance covers house fires, and even though every house in Mississippi faces a risk of fire, something which causes a fire in one home, say faulty electric wiring, does not make fires more likely in other homes. House fires will happen every year, but the chance of say 100,000 house fires in a given year is extremely remote. Insurers promise to have the funds needed to pay off all covered losses incurred by their customers. Consequently, they face a risk of bankruptcy typically only if a large proportion of covered homes have fire losses in the same year. Since this is unlikely, house fires and similar risks like auto accidents or lightning strikes can be insured relatively easily.

A hurricane is dramatically different. In most years, Mississippi will not be hit by a hurricane and insurers will have no losses for this hazard, but when a major hurricane hits, such as Camille in 1969 or Katrina in 2005, a large proportion of policy holders will suffer a loss, especially those in the coastal counties. The insurance company must pay all of these losses at the same time - they must have access to tens or hundreds of millions of dollars to pay the claims. Insurance companies use reinsurance contracts and other financial instruments to ensure that they can pay catastrophe claims, but reinsurance is costly. Insuring correlated risks like hurricanes is more financially challenging than insuring against house fires or auto accidents.

Furthermore, extreme weather events, as the name suggests, occur relatively infrequently. For example, a major hurricane (Categories 3, 4 and 5 on the Saffir-Simpson Scale) has not made landfall in the United States since October 2005. Insurers learn from losses, which allows them to better estimate future losses. Weather records extend back at most only to the latter half of the 1800s, which is a short sample to estimate the exact likelihood of events occurring once every ten, twenty, or hundred years. Insurers can use risk models to try to refine estimates of occurrence probabilities, but there will be ambiguity concerning the underlying risk, which insurers do not like to have to price (Kunreuther et. al 1995). There will be more potential for learning after an event, which might reveal that a company was underestimating losses, leading them to want to write less of a type of insurance in a state.

Consequently, hurricane wind insurance can be subject to periodic shortfalls of capacity, meaning insurers will not want to write as many policies as the number of coastal zone structures needing insurance (Born and Viscusi 2006). Furthermore, modest increases in premiums may not induce insurers to write additional policies in the near term, yet mortgagees and businesses legally must maintain insurance, creating a problem. States maintain "residual" markets to deal with such shortfalls for auto and property insurance. Insurance is a highly regulated industry, and regulated primarily by the states. When a state faces a significant residual risk, like hurricane winds, a dedicated residual market mechanism is often established. Mississippi and six other Southeastern states have hurricane pools, or Fair Access to Insurance Requirements (FAIR) plans. FAIR plans are established under the authority of a 1968 act of Congress addressing a shortage of insurance produced by the urban riots of the 1960s. Mississippi's wind pool is the Mississippi Windstorm Underwriting Association (MWUA 2011), created in 1987 and authorized to write wind policies in six coastal counties (Hancock, Harrison, Jackson, Pearl River, Stone, and George). MWUA and other wind pools are mixed public-private sector entities ultimately under state insurance regulators.

MWUA addresses the occasional, short term problems of availability, but creates a mechanism for subsidizing insurance for coastal properties. The subsidy is not explicit, so we must trace through the exact mechanism to recognize that it is equivalent to a government subsidy. State insurance commissions have regulatory authority over the setting of prices (premiums), in addition to other elements of an insurance contract. Mississippi regulates based on prior approval, meaning that companies must get rates approved by the Mississippi Insurance Department before they can charge them to customers. A large residual market persisting for any length of time almost always indicates premiums set too low by regulators: "But where residual markets grow large, it generally represents evidence that regulatory restrictions have prevented insurers from meeting consumers' needs by disallowing what would otherwise be market-clearing prices" (Lehmann 2016, p. 16). In other words, a large residual market reflects the shortage created by a price ceiling in the primary market.

The residual market becomes the means by which to get high risk coastal properties insured at these artificially low premiums, and this amounts to the subsidy. Charging higher premiums to customers will allow a company to purchase additional reinsurance at a market price, which is how insurance ends up paying for rebuilding after a disaster.[4] The MWUA, however, can remain in an exposed position because they possess the legal authority to impose assessments on insurance policies from across the state after a hurricane if needed. The assessments are imposed on insurance companies based on policies written in the state and are equivalent to a tax. Insurance buyers and companies across the state end up paying wind pool losses. Hurricane Katrina illustrates the operation of this mechanism. MWUA had $1.8 billion in exposure for the 2005 season and only $175 million in reinsurance and ended up with losses in Katrina exceeding $700 million (Mississippi Insurance Department 2015). A regular insurance company in such a circumstance would have, in all likelihood, had to declare bankruptcy. But before this, they likely would have purchased additional reinsurance or accumulated investments to pay the losses. The assessment mechanism allows purchase of less reinsurance to cover a given exposure, and shifts the losses after the next major hurricane to other policy holders.[5]

Ensuring the availability of insurance for the Mississippi Gulf Coast, even during capacity crises, is important to enable economic activity, but this does not require a permanent wind pool. The long term goal should be to phase out the MWUA and rely on a deregulated private market charging risk-based premiums. As mentioned, low income families could be given a subsidy to help afford coverage at market rates. If MWUA is retained, it should rely on reinsurance to cover events up to at least the 100 year (0.01 probability of annual occurrence) storm, and perhaps the 250 or 500 year storm.[6] Government assistance

---

4 Voluntary market insurance is not a subsidy, even though customers who experience a loss may receive a larger payment for a loss than they have (or ever will pay) in premiums. The nature of insurance involves such payments. If an insurance company voluntarily sells coverage, the company is not giving anything away - they are being adequately compensated for taking on the risk, even when they pass some of the risk on to others through reinsurance.

5 Or potentially state tax payers, because no state residual market has ever gone bankrupt (Lehmann 2016).

to the wind pool, if provided, should be through state appropriations to purchase reinsurance annually as opposed to hidden assessment taxes. The assessment mechanism obscures the commitment to effectively tax Mississippians to pay for hurricane losses. Such disguised forms of transfers exploit rational ignorance on the part of citizens (Boudreaux 1996). Requiring the legislature to appropriate funds to for reinsurance for MWUA is more explicit and consequently easier to potentially control. Indeed, $178 million in government funding was provided to MWUA for this purpose in the years after Katrina. Policy details should remain transparent so that citizens can readily become informed about an issue should they want to do so. Politicians who believe that all Mississippians should pay to keep wind insurance inexpensive should have to make the case annually for appropriations, not planting a time bomb that explodes after the next Katrina.

Flood Insurance

Flood insurance also affects vulnerability to extreme weather. Although the Federal government runs the National Flood Insurance Program (NFIP), states and local governments play a role in the overall system. Establishment of the NFIP in 1968 is best viewed as establishing government management of the nation's flood-prone areas. Policies sold under the NFIP are effectively subsidized by the Federal government, a factor which by itself promotes excessive building in flood plains.[7] The NFIP involves state and local governments in managing development in flood plains and controlling access to the subsidy. Communities must join the NFIP to allow residents to purchase policies, and this involves adopting government flood plain management. This injects politics into the decision about building in flood plains or rebuilding after a flood.

The separation of flood insurance from standard homeowners' insurance causes confusion and delay after hurricanes with significant storm surge like Katrina. Insurance companies and FEMA can go back and forth about what portion of losses will be covered by which policy, what Emily Chamlee-Wright (2010) labeled the flood - no flood tango. However, this dance is costly. Debate and litigation delays the payment of claims, increasing how long residents must fund alternative living arrangements. Homes rebuilt after a flood must be elevated to the base flood elevation (the level of the 100 year flood plain), adding to the cost of rebuilding which may not be covered by insurance. FEMA may seek to redraw flood plain maps, delaying establishment of the level for elevating structures. Political control over rebuilding would be unnecessary if flood insurance were provided in private markets, or if structures which were not flood proofed could purchase coverage at higher premiums. NFIP provides a reminder that government subsidies may not even benefit the recipients that much once the controls frequently accompanying the subsidies are factored in.

Building Codes and Mitigation

The quality of the built environment (homes, apartments, businesses, and infrastructure) affects the damage caused by natural disasters (Ryland 2006). Shoddy construction imposes both direct costs (repairing or replacing structures and damage to contents) and indirect costs like temporary housing, lost production, and longer driving times due to damaged roads. The story of The Three Little Pigs teaches children how higher quality construction will reduce losses when disasters occur. Indeed, engineers

---

6   Other options exist consistent with self-funding, including self-insurance by accumulating a large surplus, the use of post-event assessments but only applied to customers, and risk sharing pools with other states facing hurricane risk.

7   Unlike state wind pools, NFIP borrows from the U.S. Treasury if it has losses it cannot pay, without ever having to repay the loan.

know how to build structures to withstand even the strongest tornadoes and earthquakes, but mitigation (the term referring to designs and techniques for buildings better able to survive hazards) is costly and disasters incur frequently, so mitigation may never be "used" against a hazard.

Natural hazard mitigation is an important dimension on which individuals can reduce the impact of extreme weather on our lives. Consequently, efficient investment in mitigation is tremendously important in managing weather risk. Mitigation involves two quality assurance questions: first, whether a given design or product will reduce damage as promised; and second whether mitigation is installed correctly in a given structure. Communities across America rely on building codes enacted and enforced by local governments to assure the quality of both residential and commercial buildings, meaning public sector certification of the quality of the built environment. Building codes date to the early 20th Century, and were first adopted to deal with fire risk. In the 19th Century, wooden construction, narrow streets, and structures built closely together created the potential for city-wide fires like the Chicago Fire of 1871. This made early fire codes a public policy issue. Public certification of quality remains the norm today, even though contemporary building codes include many elements not connected to an externality.

Public sector assurance of the quality of the built environment through building codes has numerous problems. Perhaps the best recognized is the enforcement problem. Quality is always costly; ensuring the quality of construction requires multiple inspections by trained inspectors to ensure use of the specified materials and proper workmanship. This process does not occur automatically, and home buyers and insurers have difficulty observing if a finished home was built to code. Hurricane Andrew struck Miami in 1992. South Florida was regarded at the time by as having one of the best wind codes in the country. Research after the hurricane, however, found that 25% of the damage was due to poor enforcement of the existing building code (Mileti 1999). A number of factors contributed to this, including the hiring of too few inspectors and approval of inferior materials and techniques as meeting the code. Andrew was hardly unique; poor enforcement of California's seismic code increased damage in 1994's Northridge Earthquake.

Economics and public choice suggest that the problems with public sector quality assurance will be systemic and irremediable (Holcombe 1995). Adopting the International Building Code is relatively inexpensive for a government, requiring merely the passing of a law or an ordinance. The costs arise in supplying high quality enforcement of these laws, just as assuring the quality of cars or furniture is costly for the private sector. Adopting a building code allows elected officials to appear to act on behalf of the public. The details of enforcement are far less visible and are costly: hiring properly trained inspectors, using higher quality materials, halting work while waiting for an inspection, redoing work of poor quality. The incentive always exists to relax on quality assurance. Without a profit incentive, government officials will not incur the costs of quality.

Building codes continue to be poorly enforced. The Insurance Services Office developed a Building Code Effectiveness Grading Scale (BCEGS) after the problems revealed by Hurricane Andrew. The scale assigns grades on a scale from 1 (best) to 10 (worst) based on administration, review of building plans, and field inspections for participating communities.[8] The enforcement of residential and commercial codes is graded separately. Nationally only 6 out of 19,000 rated communities currently have a score of 1 for their residential code, and only 16% receive a score of 3 or better, and this is just among rated communities; ISO does not report the number of communities which do not participate, and thus have no effective enforcement program. The Mississippi State Rating Bureau performs its own BCEGS ratings for communities in the state, based on the same type of criteria as the ISO grades. Figure 19.1 reports the distribution of current ratings, and com-

---

8   For details on the BCEGS ratings see: https://www.isomitigation.com/bcegs/what-why-when-and-what-do-i-do.html

munities across Mississippi also have a building code enforcement problem. For personal lines, no community currently has a rating better than 4, and half of all the rated communities have a rating of 99, described as "does not meet minimum criteria for BCEGS program.[9] Mississippians buying homes across the state probably presume that they have been built to code, but the public sector is actually providing no assurance of this.

Mississippi passed its first state-wide building code in 2014. Instead of trying to improve public sector performance, a better approach would be greater reliance on private sector quality certification for buildings and homes. This could occur either through builder reputation or third party quality certification on the model of the highly successful Underwriter's Laboratory (Holcombe 1995). Some efforts toward market-based quality assurance for homes are underway. The Institute for Business and Home Safety's Fortified for Safer Living program includes a number of building features which go beyond the current code and protect against a range of natural hazards.[10] Home builders can participate in this voluntary program. Homes certified as built to the Fortified for Safer Living standards are eligible for a premium discount of up to 25% on MWUA policies.[11] The Mississippi Insurance Board also allows homeowners in a community without an effective building code enforcement program to hire an engineer or architect to certify construction of a new home to the standards of the current International Residential Code. This certification allows the home to receive the same premium discount available for a home built in a community with a BCEGS score of 1 (25% on MWUA policies).[12]

A second approach to encouraging mitigation has been to offer tax-funded subsidies or mandate insurance premium discounts for mitigation. Subsidies have frequently been funded out of the hazard mitigation component of Federal disaster assistance. The rationale for this set-aside has been that spending dollars on mitigation after today's disaster will reduce future government disaster assistance. Some states have also invested in mitigation; Florida and South Carolina have funded state subsidies for wind storm mitigation. Although many mitigation measures are efficient, politics distorts disaster assistance (Garrett and Sobel 2003) and could easily lead to inefficient mitigation selection.

Figure 19.1: Building Code Effectiveness Grades for Mississippi

Category	Personal Lines		Commercial Lines	
	Number	Percent	Number	Percent
1	0	0	0	0
2	0	0	0	0
3	0	0	1	1.2
4	11	13.6	11	13.6
5	7	8.6	8	9.9
6	12	14.8	13	16.0
7	4	4.9	6	7.4
8	4	4.9	4	4.9
9	1	1.2	1	1.2
10	1	1.2	1	1.2
99	41	50.6	36	44.4

Scores range from 1 (best) to 10 (worst), and 99 represents "does not meet minimum criteria for BCEGS program."
Source: Authors' counts using Mississippi State Rating Bureau BCEGS scores available at:
https://www.msratingbureau.com/bcegs-manual

---

9   The Mississippi BCEGS ratings are available at: https://www.msratingbureau.com/bcegs-manual.

10   For more information on the Fortified for Safer Living program see: https://disastersafety.org/fortified/

11   See https://www.msplans.com/mwua/wind-mitigation-programs

12   Ibid.

Insurance premium discounts are the key to efficient mitigation investments by property owners. But will the politicized process of insurance regulation select the proper discounts? The danger exists that excessive, mandated discounts for mitigation can become a form of hidden subsidy. Regulators could set risk-based rates for coverage, and then mandate excessive discounts, resulting in below market rates. Mississippi currently mandates premium discounts of up to 25% for properties with a BCEGS score of 1. Whether this is appropriate or not is a challenging question.

Market competition provides the best way to determine the proper discount for specific mitigation measures. Insurance companies need freedom to both charge premiums and discounts for mitigation as they see fit. Insurers rely on their own proprietary formulas for assessing risk and charging premiums, when not restricted via regulation. Competition will push insurers to offer discounts reflecting their estimate of the expected savings from mitigation instead of simply pocketing the savings from homeowners' and businesses' investments. Furthermore, insurers have no incentive to offer discounts for ineffective mitigation measures or discounts in excess of losses avoided. The selection of which mitigation and design features to incentivize, and by how much, will be far more efficient if left to profit-and-loss incentives than the political process.

Recovery

As a community gets past the immediate aftermath of a hurricane, tornado, or flood, as retailers reopen, the basic necessities of life are available again, utilities restored and debris removed, emphasis turns to the long-term task of rebuilding lives, businesses, and communities. Long term recovery involves two specific policy-relevant questions: whether residents and businesses will have adequate resources to rebuild, and whether individuals' efforts will be coordinated enough to enable community recovery.

Insurance should provide the bulk of the resources for rebuilding. Encouraging homeowners and businesses to be adequately insured, including coverage for alternate living expenses or business interruption loss, assumes primary significance. To encourage individual savings, in 2015 Mississippi established Catastrophe Savings Accounts allowing residents to make (state) tax-exempt deposits to cover an insurance deductible or self-insure their primary residence. Beyond markets, many people have a natural desire to assist disaster victims, both through charitable organizations and through our governments. Charitable organizations like Habitat for Humanity and Samaritan's Purse will build new homes for victims of natural disasters to assist with recovery. Most government long term assistance comes in the form of subsidized loans from the Small Business Administration or supplemental Congressional appropriations and will not be considered here. However, research after Katrina found that Mississippians rated federal government and state and local governments as two of the least effective categories of assistance (Chappell et al. 2007). Government can provide large dollar amounts of assistance but appears to provide less bang for the buck than voluntary sector.

Long term recovery planning is a task increasingly viewed as requiring coordination and planning undertaken by governments. FEMA provides guidance for such a process through the National Disaster Recovery Framework (Department of Homeland Security 2016), which "defines how the whole community, including emergency managers, community development professionals, recovery practitioners, government agencies, private sector, nongovernmental organization (NGO) leaders, and the public will collaborate and coordinate..." (DHS 2016, p.1) Presidential disaster declarations under the Stafford Act require such a planning process (DHS 2016, p.3), usually undertaken by local governments.[13] Whether

---

13 This of course presumes that government-led planning and coordination is necessary to effectively accomplish these recovery tasks, meaning that they cannot be coordinated through a decentralized, market based process. For an assessment of market failure claims for long term recovery planning, see Smith and Sutter (2017).

the planning contributes to timely recovery is unclear. Chamlee-Wright (2010) discusses long term planning in New Orleans after Katrina. The plan initially designated certain neighborhoods to not be redeveloped, interfering with these residents' efforts to begin rebuilding. The plan was subject to change, and by joining the planning process, residents could attempt to protect what presumably should be part of their property rights. At a minimum, the long-term planning introduced extra uncertainty and diverted residents' scarce time, energy, and resources from rebuilding. While required for Federally-declared disasters, substantial variation exists across communities in the extent of such planning, and whether the planning process restricts the exercise of property rights (Smith and Sutter 2013). Governments should focus on restoring their services after a disaster and allow residents, businesses, churches, and others to proceed with returning their lives to normalcy.

Policy Uncertainty and Natural Disasters

Economic decisions inevitably involve considerable, irreducible uncertainty. Market forces are beyond anyone's control and nearly impossible to predict, and they can cause wages or home prices to rise or fall or render business investments uneconomic. Government policy can itself be a source of uncertainty (Higgs 1997), making economic decisions even more risky. More significantly, the uncertainty due to government policy is frequently avoidable. Unfortunately, government policy often contributes to uncertainty after natural disasters in Mississippi, impairing response and recovery. This section considers two cases of disaster-related policy uncertainty.

The first is Mississippi's law against price gouging. Mississippi's law declares unjustified price increases after disasters illegal. The Attorney General's office periodically reminds (one might say threatens) businesses about price gouging after disasters.[14] Consequently, businesses trying to respond to demand and supply shocks must also guess whether a price increase might attract the ire of the Attorney General or local prosecutors. The consequences of guessing wrong provides an incentive for businesses not to incur the extra costs of trying to open immediately after a disaster. Research on business closures has found that variables like the severity of a disaster and a business' pre-disaster preparations do not explain why businesses remain closed (Webb, Tierney and Dalhamer 2000). One explanation for these findings could be uncertainty due state laws against price gouging.

Insurance regulation also generates uncertainty. After Katrina, Mississippi Attorney General Jim Hood filed lawsuits to force insurance companies to pay for storm surge losses. At a philosophical level, the Attorney General might have had a case: the winds of Hurricane Katrina blew water from the Gulf toward the coast, and this produced the devastating storm surge. But legally the argument went directly against the common understanding of the flood exclusion on homeowners' policies. Courts rejected the argument (Hartwig and Wilkinson 2010). If successful, the suit would have saddled insurers with billions of dollars in losses they had not been collecting premiums to cover. The effort demonstrated a willingness of state politicians to rewrite contracts to benefit their constituents. Trying to estimate losses on infrequent extreme weather events is challenging enough, but it becomes almost impossible if elected officials might then try to change the rules based on politics. The total coverage of the MWUA increased to $12 billion after Katrina (Mississippi Insurance Department 2015), reflecting the poor environment for insurance. Furthermore, the policy uncertainty in this case has also plausibly contributed to popular confusion. Five years after Katrina, 35 % of residents of Mississippi and Louisiana still thought that homeowners' insurance covered storm surge flooding (Hartwig and Wilkinson 2010).

---

14 See http://www.ago.state.ms.us/releases/attorney-general-issues-price-gouging-reminder/

Conclusion

Rising losses from extreme weather have been offered as evidence that human-caused climate change is already starting to occur. Such a conclusion is unwarranted because a number of studies have shown no time trend in normalized losses various from extreme weather, including hurricanes (Pielke et al. 2008), floods (Downton, Miller and Pielke 2005), and tornadoes (Simmons, Sutter and Pielke 2013). Damage normalizations control for changes in population and wealth in addition to inflation. With a larger population and greater wealth per capita than fifty or one hundred years ago and every corner of the nation vulnerable to some type of extreme weather, America will inevitably see more large dollar losses today. The evidence is clear: increases in the number of persons and value of property in harm's way explains rising damages from extreme weather (Pielke 2014). Each and every weather event causes more damages than in the past, and affects more individuals.

Increasing societal vulnerability explains why extreme weather causes more costly disasters. It does not follow, however, that prosperity requires minimizing our exposure to extreme weather. Such a goal would not increase prosperity. To see the fallacy in this line of thinking, the United States could reduce traffic fatalities to zero by banning cars and trucks, but this would make us poorer. Prosperity requires a balancing: accepting and possibly mitigating the risk when this makes sense, while not encouraging excessive exposure to risk.

The key to this balancing is ensuring that the persons who chose to live in disaster prone areas *also bear the extra costs of their choices.* Only when their taking risks is subsidized and paid for by others does the problem become excessive. Market processes and economic freedom accomplish this extremely well in most instances. Insurance can share the costs of losses in a mutually agreeable manner and provide an incentive to relocate economic activity unless the high risk areas provide a commensurate benefit. Insurance also provides an incentive to invest in mitigation when the benefits (losses avoided) exceed the cost. Home prices will also reflect higher quality construction able to withstand disasters.[15]

Prices and profits provide businesses an incentive to supply goods and services needed by victims of a disaster, while competition will keep prices as low as possible. The generosity of Americans as channeled by the charitable sector can fill in many of the remaining gaps (Skarbek 2014). Large scale shifting of the costs of extreme weather, and thus incentives to take on excessive exposure, typically results from government policies, like the suppression of risk-based insurance premiums.

Economic freedom not only leads to prosperity, it also reduces conflict between persons in society. People differ in their tolerance of risk. Economic freedom allows people to assume the risk from extreme weather consistent with their personal preferences. A person who is scared of tornadoes can build a safe room in their home capable of withstanding even an EF-5 tornado. The cost of a safe room is considerable, but when people pay for their own decisions, one person's fear (or fearlessness) does not spill over to others. By contrast, government subsidies allow some peoples' choices to a financial burden on others, creating conflict. Subsidies almost always come with restrictions on personal choice to try to constrain such costs. We cannot stop extreme weather or eliminate its cost, but market-based policies can help to promote prosperity in Mississippi, making it more prosperous, resilient, and harmonious.

---

15 For documentation of price differentials and for safer construction, see Simmons, Kruse, and Smith (2002), Simmons and Sutter (2007), Sutter and Simmons (2007), and Dumm, Sirmans, and Smersh (2011, 2012).

References

Born, Patricia H., and W. Kip Viscusi. 2006. The Catastrophic Effects of Natural Disasters on Insurance Markets. *Journal of Risk and Uncertainty*, 33: 55-72.

Boudreaux, Donald J. 1996. Was Your High School Civics Teacher Right After All? Donald Wittman's The Myth of Democratic Failure. *Independent Review*, 1(1): 111-128.

Buchanan, James M. 1975. The Samaritan's Dilemma. In *Altruism, Morality, and Economic Theory*, edited by E.S. Phelps. New York: Russell Sage Foundation.

Carpenter, Dick M., Lisa Knepper, Angela C. Erickson, and John K. Ross. 2012. *License to Work: A National Survey of Burdens from Occupational Licensing*. Washington DC: Institute for Justice.

Chamlee-Wright. 2010. *The Cultural and Political Economy of Recovery: Social Learning in a Post-Disaster Environment*. New York: Routledge.

Chappell, William F., Richard G. Forgette, David A. Swanson, and Mark V. Van Boening. 2007. "Determinants of Government Aid to Katrina Survivors: Evidence from Survey Data." *Southern Economic Journal*, 74(2): 344-362.

Coate, Stephen. 1995. Altruism, the Samaritan's Dilemma, and Government Transfer Policy. *American Economic Review*, 85(1): 46-57.

Dash, Nicole, and Hugh Gladwin. 2007. Evacuation Decision Making and Behavioral Responses: Individual and Household. *Natural Hazards Review*, 8: 69-77.

Department of Homeland Security. 2016. *National Disaster Recovery Framework*, Second Edition. Available at: https://www.fema.gov/media-library-data/1466014998123-4bec8550930f774269e0c5968b120ba2/National_Disaster_Recovery_Framework2nd.pdf

Downton, M. W., J. Z. B. Miller, and R. A. Pielke, Jr. 2005. Reanalysis of the U. S. National Flood Loss Database. *Natural Hazards Review*, 6: 13-22.

Dumm, Randy E., G. Stacy Sirmans, and Greg Smersh. 2011. The Capitalization of Building Codes in House Prices. *Journal of Real Estate Finance and Economics*, 42: 30-50.

Dumm, Randy E., G. Stacy Sirmans, and Greg T. Smersh. 2012. Building Codes, Wind Contours, and House Prices. *Journal of Real Estate Research*, 34(1): 73-98.

Garrett, Thomas A., and Russell S. Sobel. 2003. The Political Economy of FEMA Disaster Payments. *Economic Inquiry*, 41(3): 496-509.

Gibberson, Michael. 2011. The Problem with Price Gouging Laws: Is Optimal Pricing During an Emergency Unethical?" *Regulation*, Spring, pp. 48-53. Available at: https://object.cato.org/sites/cato.org/files/serials/files/regulation/2011/4/regv34n1-1.pdf

Hartwig, Robert P., and Claire Wilkinson. 2010. *Hurricane Katrina: The Five Year Anniversary*. New York: Insurance Information Institute. Available at: http://www.iii.org/sites/default/files/1007Katrina5Anniversary.pdf

Hayek, Friedrich A. 1945. The Use of Knowledge in Society. *American Economic Review*

Higgs, Robert. 1997. Regime Uncertainty: Why the Great Depression Lasted So Long and Why Prosperity Returned After the War. *Independent Review*, 1(4): 561-590.

Holcombe, Randall G. 1995. *Public Policy and the Quality of Life: Market Incentives versus Government Planning*. Westport CT: Greenwood Press.

Kunreuther, Howard, Jacqueline Meszaros, Robin M. Hogarth, and Mark Spranca. 1995. Ambiguity and Underwriter Decision Processes. *Journal of Economic Behavior and Organization*, 26: 337-352.

Lee, Dwight R. 2015. Making the Case Against 'Price Gouging' Laws: A Challenge and an Opportunity. *Independent Review*, 19(4): 583-598.

Leeson, Peter T., and Russell S. Sobel. 2007. The Use of Knowledge in Disaster Relief Management. *Independent Review*, 11(4): 519-532.

Lehmann, R. J. 2016. *2016 Insurance Regulation Report Card*. Washington DC: R Street. http://www.rstreet.org/policy-study/2016-insurance-regulation-report-card/

Mileti, Dennis J. 1999. *Disasters by Design*. Washington DC: Joseph Henry Press.

Mississippi Gaming & Hospitality Association. 2017. *Annual Report 2017*. Available at: http://msgaming.org/wp-content/uploads/2017/01/MGHA17_annual_report-5.pdf

Mississippi Insurance Department. 2015. *Insurance in Mississippi 10 Years After Katrina*. Available at: http://www.mid.ms.gov/newsroom/pdf/Insurance-10Years-After-Katrina.pdf

Mississippi Windstorm Underwriting Association. 2011. *Mississippi Windstorm Underwriting Association Plan of Operation*. Available at: https://www.msplans.com/sites/default/files/MWUA/MWUA%20Plan%20of%20Operation.pdf

Pielke, Jr., Roger A. 2014. *The Rightful Place of Science: Disasters and Climate Change*. Tempe AZ: Consortium for Science, Policy & Outcomes.

Pielke, Jr., R. A., J. Gratz, C. Landsea, D. Collins, M. Saunders, and R. Musulin. 2008. Normalized Hurricane Damage in the United States: 1900-2005. *Natural Hazards Review*, 9:29-42.

Ryland, Harvey G. 2006. Providing Economic Incentives to Build Disaster-Resistant Structures. In *On Risk and Disaster: Lessons from Hurricane Katrina*, edited R.J. Daniels, D.F. Kettl, and H. Kunreuther, pp. 223-228. Philadelphia: University of Pennsylvania Press.

Sandel, Michael J. 2009. *Justice: What's the Right Thing to Do?* New York: Farrar, Straus and Giroux.

Simmons, Kevin M., and Daniel Sutter. 2007. Tornado Shelters and the Housing Market. *Construction Management and Economics*, 25(11): 1119-1126,

Simmons, Kevin M., Jamie Brown Kruse, and Douglas A. Smith. 2002. Valuing Mitigation: Real Estate Market Response to Hurricane Loss Reduction Measures. *Southern Economic Journal*, 68(3):660-671.

Simmons, Kevin M., Daniel Sutter, and Roger A. Pielke, Jr. 2013. Normalized Tornado Damage in the United States, 1950-2011. *Environmental Hazards*, 12(2): 132-147.

Skarbek, David. 2008. Occupational Licensing and Asymmetric Information: Post-Hurricane Evidence from Florida. *Cato Journal*, 28(1): 73-82.

Skarbek, Emily. 2014. The Chicago Fire of 1871: A Bottom Up Approach to Disaster Relief. *Public Choice*, 160(1): 155-180.

Smith, Daniel J., and Daniel Sutter. 2013. Response and Recovery from the Joplin Tornado: Lessons Learned and Lessons Applied. *Independent Review*, 18(2): 165-188.

Smith, Daniel J., and Daniel Sutter. 2017. Recovery Fast or Slow? The Costs of Post-Disaster Planning to Reduce Hazard Vulnerability. Working paper, Manuel H. Johnson Center for Political Economy, Troy University.

Sobel, Russell S., and Peter T. Leeson. 2006. Government's Response to Katrina: A Public Choice Analysis. *Public Choice*, 127(1/2): 55-73.

Sowell, Thomas. 2004. Price Gouging in Florida. *Jewish World Review*, September 14. Available at: http://www.jewishworldreview.com/cols/sowell091404.asp

Sutter, Daniel. 2007. *Ensuring Disaster: State Insurance Regulation, Coastal Development, and Hurricanes*. Mercatus Center Policy Comment #14.

Sutter, Daniel, and Daniel J. Smith. 2016. Coordination in Disaster: Nonprice Learning and the Allocation of Resources After Natural Disasters. *Review of Austrian Economics*, forthcoming, DOI: 10.1007/s11138-016-0369-5.

Webb, Gary R., Kathleen J. Tierney, and James M. Dalhamer. 2000. Businesses and Disasters: Empirical Patterns and Unanswered Questions. *Natural Hazards Review*, 1(2):83-90.

20

Learning from Disasters in Mississippi

Stefanie Haeffele and Virgil Henry Storr

20

Learning from Disasters in Mississippi

Stefanie Haeffele and Virgil Henry Storr

This chapter examines disaster recovery in Mississippi and how policies that foster entrepreneurship might help spur disaster recovery and promote prosperity going forward. Based on our broader research on community recovery after Hurricane Katrina across the Gulf Coast and, specifically, in Mississippi, and after Hurricane Sandy in New York, we argue that entrepreneurs are key to disaster recovery. Entrepreneurs can spur community revival by increasing the benefits and reducing the costs associated with returning and rebuilding.

Natural disasters are no strangers to Mississippi. Indeed, Mississippi has experienced hurricanes, severe storms, floods, and tornadoes throughout its history (also see Chapter 19 for details on Mississippi's disaster history). In 1906, for instance, the Mississippi hurricane caused millions of dollars in damage to infrastructure, buildings, and cotton crops in Macon, Jackson, Brookhaven, Vicksburg, and McComb. In 1969, Hurricane Camille, a category 5 hurricane, destroyed homes along the Mississippi coastline and caused almost a billion dollars in damage throughout the state. Likewise, in 1971, a tornado outbreak along the Lower Mississippi River Valley destroyed multiple communities in Mississippi. Recently, on April 30, 2017, tornadoes and flooding caused $5.5 million in damages to homes in Holmes and Montgomery counties.[1]

In the past few decades, several disasters have severely impacted the citizens and environment of Mississippi. Hurricane Katrina made landfall on August 29, 2005, wreaked havoc on the Mississippi coastline, and then passed over the length of the state, producing heavy rainfall, high winds, and debilitating tornadoes. The storm resulted in 238 deaths in the state alone; in total, there were over 1,800 deaths

---

1   Rigsby (2017)

and over $100 billion in damage across the Gulf Coast associated with Hurricane Katrina.[2] The tornado outbreak on April 24, 2010, also impacted the state, resulting in ten deaths.[3] Furthermore, severe flooding plagued the state in both 2011 and 2016. The storms in April and May 2011, coupled with high levels of snowmelt, caused the Mississippi River watershed to overflow, flooding communities all along the western border of Mississippi.[4] Record levels of rainfall in March and August 2016 caused the Mississippi River delta to overflow, flooding parts of Louisiana and Mississippi.[5]

Mississippi also seems particularly vulnerable to future disasters. Based on the disasters that occurred between 2006 and 2015, leaving out the impact of Hurricane Katrina, Kiplinger and the National Weather Service identified Mississippi as the seventh most likely state in the United States to be impacted by disaster. From 2006 to 2015, 113 deaths in the state were weather-related, and there was over $4.4 billion in disaster-related property damage.[6] Since Hurricane Katrina in 2005, Mississippi has received 19 disaster declarations from the Federal Emergency Management Agency (FEMA).[7]

These disasters caused hundreds of deaths and billions of dollars in property damage as well as emotional and physical distress. Citizens, and their communities, faced the challenge of dealing with the disasters and finding ways to return their lives to normalcy. This is, of course, no easy task. Not only does recovery depend on access to resources—such as personal savings, insurance, federal assistance, donations, etc.—to rebuild damaged and destroyed homes and businesses, but recovery can also depend on disaster victims being able to rely on their social ties for material and emotional support. These potentially disrupted social networks can also prove to be significant for recovery efforts, as families displaced by the disaster decide whether to move elsewhere or to return and rebuild.

In this post-disaster scenario, characterized with immense uncertainty, local commercial, social, and political entrepreneurs—including business owners, community organizers, and religious leaders—are essential to community rebound.[8] In our research on disaster response and recovery after Hurricanes Katrina and Sandy, we saw that time after time, entrepreneurs played a crucial role in (1) providing the necessary goods and services after the storm, (2) restoring disconnected social networks, and (3) signaling that recovery is already taking place. These actions encourage others to return and recover from disasters by ensuring that affected residents have the material and emotional support they need as well as showing that fellow citizens are committed to rebuilding their communities. These individuals also often find novel and innovative ways to (a) encourage others to return, (b) acquire resources for the community, and (c) foster new opportunities within the community. We argue that these findings are important for understanding how policies impact disaster recovery. Policies can either hinder recovery or foster an environment where local entrepreneurs have the space and incentive to act. In order to foster entrepreneurship and promote prosperity, Mississippi should learn these lessons and implement policies that reduce uncertainty and promote community rebound.

This chapter proceeds as follows. The next section, "Entrepreneurs Drive Disaster Recovery," examines the uncertainty of the post-disaster context and the key role that local, commercial, and social entrepreneurs, including business owners and community leaders, play in disaster recovery. Then the

---

2   Beven et al. (2008)

3   Potter (2010)

4   See U.S. Army Corps of Engineers (2012).

5   See Martinez, Payne and Alsup (2016) and Di Liberto (2016).

6   For more information on the Kiplinger and National Weather Service rankings, see http://www.kiplinger.com/slideshow/insurance/T028-S001-10-states-most-at-risk-of-disaster/index.html.

7   For a list of federal disaster declaration in Mississippi, see https://www.fema.gov/states/mississippi.

8   Storr, Haeffele-Balch and Grube (2015)

"Looking at Mississippi Disasters" section explores several examples from Mississippi to highlight this research. The final section concludes with some policy recommendations.

Entrepreneurs Drive Disaster Recovery

The post-disaster context is characterized by extreme uncertainty for affected citizens. In some cases, citizens have evacuated and can remain displaced even after the disaster has passed as government officials assess damage, public utilities remain offline, and their neighborhoods remain uninhabitable. These displaced residents need to figure out when they are able to return home, discover what damage their house or business has sustained, and decide whether to rebuild or use the opportunity to start anew elsewhere. In other cases, citizens are not able to evacuate and, instead, must ride out the storm or shelter in place as the storm passes through. After the storm, affected citizens must deal with damage to their homes, power outages, and limited supplies. After the initial days following the disaster, they then must assess the state of their community and determine whether to rebuild or not. These decisions do not happen in a vacuum, but are dependent upon the decisions of other community members.

This sort of challenge is known as a collective action problem in economics. It is a scenario where all group members would benefit if they could cooperate, but where no individual member will contribute to the group effort until they are confident that others will contribute as well. The costs associated with repairing and rebuilding damaged buildings can be significant. Additionally, the costs of replacing damaged and destroyed automobiles, equipment, appliances, and personal items can be quite high. There are, of course, real benefits associated with reopening your damaged business and remaining a member of your community. However, those benefits are reduced if others do not rebuild and are increased if they do. If only a small portion of your neighbors return, your community will not be the same as before. If many neighbors do return, you will not only be able to stay in a community you call home, but you will also have access to economic opportunities, public assistance, and other goods and services. Garbage collection or electricity, for instance, may not return unless a certain number of neighbors are present to take advantage of the services. Community members' inability to get answers to a myriad of questions relevant to decisions regarding the rebuilding process, including questions about the decisions of other citizens and the prospects for the community after the recovery process, only exacerbate the difficulty and uncertainty inherent in the recovery process.

It is important to note that this challenge of rebuilding does not just affect residents, but also the decisions of government officials that live in the disaster area. Government officials must decide where to deploy scarce government resources. That is, they must decide where to restore public utilities, which public schools to focus on first, which roads to repair, and which neighborhoods to protect at a time when there is a great deal of pressure for public services. Moreover, government officials, police officers, and firefighters not only have to respond to the community, but they also must deal with their own personal situations.

The worse the disaster, the more difficult to it is to overcome this challenge of gaining sufficient traction to rebuild a community. Losses are more extreme, including death, property damage, lost family objects, job loss, etc. Not only are more resources required to spur recovery, but the benefits and costs of returning are even more uncertain. After a disaster, like a major hurricane that destroys whole neighborhoods, displaces residents, and damages infrastructure, it can be hard to locate and coordinate with other community members whose cooperation your successful recovery depends on.

In such a scenario, it is rational for community members to wait to see how others will respond to the disaster. It is also rational for officials to wait to see which communities are recovering before deploying scarce resources. Of course, if everyone behaves "rationally" then disaster recovery will not occur. While everyone waits for others to act first no actions occur, and no actual recovery may take place.

However, we see recovery occurring after every disaster. We argue, based on our research on Hurricanes Katrina and Sandy, that local entrepreneurs rise to this challenge and are some of the first movers to drive recovery. By doing so, they reduce the costs and increase the benefits of returning to affected communities, and increase the likelihood that other people return as well.

Our research builds off a larger project that began after Hurricane Katrina ravaged the Gulf Coast in 2005.[9] A group of scholars, affiliated with the Mercatus Center at George Mason University, sought to understand the impact of the costliest natural disaster in U.S. history by examining the response and recovery efforts by the government (local, state, and federal), the business community, and the communities themselves. Groups of researchers analyzed macro level empirical data, conducted case studies, and went into the field and conducted in-depth structured interviews with residents, business owners, and individuals who work for faith-based groups and nonprofit organizations. In all, over 300 interviews were conducted in the Gulf Coast region (including the greater New Orleans area in Louisiana as well as in Mississippi) and 53 interviews in Houston, Texas between 2006 and 2009. Interviews focused on the state of the community before and after the storm, individuals' experiences during the storm and its immediate aftermath, the process of rebuilding (or relocating), and what people, organizations, and resources were important to or hindered recovery. This approach enabled scholars to examine the storm from multiple perspectives and attempt to understand the complex reality of disaster recovery.[10]

Studies on the federal government response detail both failures and successes. For instance, Sobel and Leeson examine how FEMA struggled to obtain and analyze the knowledge necessary to deliver effective disaster management, and argue that this knowledge problem is crucial to understanding the limits of centralized disaster management.[11] Alternatively, Horwitz analyzes the U.S. Coast Guard's response to Hurricane Katrina and determines that their approach of delegating authority to local managers led to successful response efforts.[12] Horwitz also found that Walmart engaged in a similar management approach and, as a result, proved to be helpful to the response and recovery efforts.[13] Furthermore, local business owners played important roles in recovery either by reopening their business or by opening new businesses to fulfill unmet needs.

Similarly, Storr, Haeffele-Balch, and Grube highlighted the efforts of local gas stations in providing necessary provisions in the early stages of recovery, furniture stores providing equipment and furniture during rebuilding, and new coffee shops providing food, internet services, and social spaces for citizens to complain to one another and share their experiences.[14] Indeed, studies that examined community recovery found several common themes that spurred recovery in seemingly different neighborhoods. For instance, Chamlee-Wright and Storr explore the role of collective narratives in encouraging or discouraging recovery and the importance of social capital in overcoming the collective action problem.[15] Storr and Haeffele-Balch also highlight how communities with relatively loose social ties can still come together to spur return.[16] Grube and Storr identify that communities that engage in organized self-governance in mundane times are more likely to rebound more quickly after disaster.[17]

---

9 For a summary on the broader project, see https://medium.com/mercatus-scholar-commentary/10-years-later-katrina-and-the-political-economy-of-everyday-life-6722ab3c3258.

10 See a list of research that came from this project here: https://ppe.mercatus.org/expert_commentary/mercatus-disaster-recovery-research.

11 Sobel and Leeson (2007)

12 Horwitz (2009a)

13 Horwitz (2009a), (2009b)

14 Storr, Haeffele-Balch and Grube (2015)

15 Chamlee-Wright and Storr (2011)

16 Storr and Haeffele-Balch (2012)

This research was later expanded to include the response and recovery of Hurricane Sandy, the second-costliest disaster in U.S. history. Specifically, we interviewed members of the Orthodox Jewish community in Rockaway, New York over the summers of 2013 and 2014. 16 in-depth, structured interviews were conducted, following the same interview structure and methods as those conducted after Hurricane Katrina. Similar patterns and themes emerged from examining this community, including the importance of social capital and local leaders in driving community rebound.

After years of conducting fieldwork and research on natural disasters, including studying the costliest and most-complex disasters in U.S. history, we have found that community leaders and local entrepreneurs are vital to response and recovery in state after state and neighborhood after neighborhood.[18] While the details of each community are different, entrepreneurs in each community find unique ways to fulfill three major roles: 1) providing necessary goods and services after the storm, 2) restoring disconnected social networks, and 3) signaling that recovery is already taking place. These actions encourage others to return and recover from disasters by showing that fellow citizens are committed to rebuilding their communities.

Three examples from our research highlight the key role that entrepreneurs, in particular commercial and social entrepreneurs, play in spurring recovery. After Hurricane Sandy, in the Orthodox Jewish community of Rockaway, New York, for instance, Rabbi Bender, the founder and president of the Achiezer Community Resource Center,[19] and his network of rabbis were able to provide one of the most important goods and services needed after a disaster: monetary assistance.

Achiezer is a social organization aimed at helping members of the community navigate health issues and other personal crises. While not an official disaster relief center, Achiezer is also the place people call when they are in need, including in the lead up to and aftermath of Hurricane Sandy. They sent out email updates to around 10,000 individuals, and their hotline received around 1,500 phone calls a day, with people asking for updates on the storm, evacuation options, and available resources. They also received phone calls about sending supplies and money to the community, and soon became a hub for donations.

In order to process and distribute the influx of monetary donations, Rabbi Bender worked with the Davis Memorial Fund to reinstitute the Community Assistance Fund (CAF). CAF was originally used to provide small amounts of funds to community members in need during the recession, and became the mechanism for distributing aid after Sandy. A board of trustees was created, and rabbis in the Orthodox Jewish community on the Rockaway Peninsula helped spread the word, take applications, and assess needs.

CAF was distributed in three phases, with graduated applications and assessments to ensure the funds were going to credible needs: 1) $2,000-3,000 for emergency needs; 2) $10,000 for quick repairs, like pumping out water, clearing mold, and repairing walls; and 3) major financial assistance for substantial home repairs. As Storr, Haeffele-Balch and Grube summarize,

> Overall, over $11 million was raised, and CAF helped more than 1,000 families in the Orthodox Jewish community on the Rockaway Peninsula. Less than a year after the storm, Rabbi Bender expressed pride in his team's ability to raise and distribute the funds quickly and efficiently, "The staggering fact from this, which I am extremely proud of, and I want you to watch the media and the Attorney General speaking about the fact that a lot of places who raised money for Sandy, but it still didn't [get] out. We raised it, $11 million, and we gave out $11 million and there was no overhead costs." (2015, 84)

---

17 Grube and Storr (2014)

18 Storr, Haeffele-Balch and Grube (2015)

19 For more information on Achiezer, see http://www.achiezer.org.

The resources available through the CAF were critical in helping the community recover.

After a disaster, citizens are dispersed, and communication networks are overwhelmed, making it difficult to connect with loved ones, employers, neighbors, etc. This may seem even more daunting in a diverse neighborhood, with loose social ties. However, in the diverse neighborhood of Broadmoor in New Orleans, residents were able to communicate with one another and band together to ensure rebuilding after Hurricane Katrina by using the information and structure of their neighborhood association, the Broadmoor Improvement Agency (BIA).[20]

Broadmoor suffered severe flooding after Katrina, with an average of eight feet of water. Every home in the neighborhood sustained damage. In early 2006, when few residents had returned to the area, the first New Orleans redevelopment plan was released, part of the Bring New Orleans Back (BNOB) Commission. The BNOB plan called for Broadmoor to become green space. Residents were shocked. In order to keep their homes, communities would have to prove that at least 50 percent of their populations would return. The president of the BIA, LaToya Cantrell, knew she had to do something to rally the neighborhood and called for a meeting, reaching out to residents through the BIA's preexisting records. The meeting was widely attended and resulted in the creation of website, a marketing campaign for the neighborhood, and a strategy for contacting and tracking residents. These efforts were successful because of the vast skills within the community. As Storr, Haeffele-Balch and Grube note,

> ... the BIA used the skills and tools available in the diverse community to prove viability, highlighting the ability of private citizens to effectively tap into dispersed knowledge and use it to their advantage during recovery. Maggie Carroll articulated this nicely, "We've realized that we have such capacity here, and it already exists. People have so much expertise, and we're just able to really hone in and use those skills for the betterment of the entire neighborhood." (2015, 92)

Their efforts paid off. Broadmoor was not only intact in subsequent versions of the redevelopment plan, but subsequent versions also included Broadmoor's own community driven post-disaster development plan. Cantrell and the BIA were able to utilize their preexisting social networks to contact and band together residents; furthermore, they used their diverse skillsets to not only prove community vitality but to also spur recovery.

Lastly, after Hurricane Katrina, Father Vien of the Mary Queen of Vietnam (MQVN) Catholic Church in New Orleans East went above and beyond his role as religious leader in order to signal that recovery was underway.

The MQVN community was badly damaged after Katrina, with flood waters of five to twelve feet deep. After the storm, Father Vien travelled the country visiting displaced parishioners, encouraging them to return. He also started holding church services only six weeks after the storm. As such, when he petitioned the utilities company to turn electricity back on, he was able to share his knowledge of the commitment of his parishioners to return as well as show pictures of residents who promised to return.

The displaced members of the MQVN community did, indeed, return. Father Vien, then, worked to get FEMA trailers for elderly members of the community and led petitions when city officials planned to build a landfill nearby. Father Vien not only worked hard to ensure his community rebounded but encouraged others to actively participate in recovery, including creating their own development corporation that focused on bringing a charter school, retirement center, and health clinic to the area. Father Vien also

---

20 For more information on the BIA, see http://www.broadmoorimprovement.com.

rallied youth in the community to be politically active, and they created the Vietnamese-American Youth Leadership Association (VAYLA). As Storr, Haeffele-Balch and Grube observe,

> It is clear that Father Vien acted as a focal point for community rebound and spokesperson for the MQVN community after Hurricane Katrina… Had Father Vien not acted, the dynamic in the MQVN community would likely have been very different. Fortunately, Father Vien did act and spurred a rapid recovery for the MQVN community. Less than two years after Katrina, the overwhelming majority of his parishioners had returned, most of the businesses they owned had reopened, and the community was well on its way to being rebuilt. In fact, by the summer of 2007, about 90 percent of the residents had returned to the MQVN community while the repopulation rate in New Orleans overall was only 47 percent. By expanding his role from spiritual leader to community spokesperson and political activist, Father Vien ensured the MQVN community returned and was taken seriously by the political actors in charge of the overall recovery of New Orleans. (2015, 110)

As multiple members of the MQVN community suggested, the neighborhood would not have bounced back so quickly without Father Vien's efforts.

After a disaster, entrepreneurs often find novel and innovative ways to a) encourage others to return, b) acquire resources for the community, and c) foster new opportunities within the community. For instance, Rabbi Bender was able to repurpose a community fund, CAF, that ensured that monetary donations were processed and distributed appropriately and quickly. LaToya Cantrell and the BIA were able to tap into local talent and find unique solutions to prove vitality and spur recovery. Finally, Father Vien ignited his parishioners, both young and old, to become politically active and take control of the fate of their community. These local entrepreneurs were essential to community rebound.

Looking at Mississippi Disasters

Like we found in multiple neighborhoods after Hurricanes Katrina and Sandy, the people of Mississippi are proud of their community, their skills, their hardworking attitude, and their resilience. As one person we interviewed in Waveland, Mississippi noted after Katrina,

> We just get up and do it again. You know, you just do it. I mean you just do it. And maybe it's because our hearts are big. I don't know. We just do it. We got up, pulled up our bootstraps and just went to work. You do that, because you see your friends and neighbors and they're in need … and in some ways, they might not be able to provide for themselves. So, you gotta help them and provide.

Likewise, Carpenter analyzed four communities along the Mississippi coast and found that the two that rebounded quickest, Waveland and Ocean Springs, were composed of citizens with strong social ties and networks. Carpenter concludes that, "strong local networks of support and a varied built environment tend to be associated with higher community resilience" (2013, 1). Smith also argues that the people of Mississippi were their own source of resilience and recovery, and also highlights issues with public assistance.[21]

Mississippi's experience provides similar evidence toward the importance of community leaders and local entrepreneurs for disaster rebound. Faith-based groups and religious leaders have played important

---

21 Smith (2012)

roles in spurring recovery after disasters in Mississippi. Like Father Vien, pastors throughout the Gulf Coast sought to signal recovery after Katrina. For instance, Reverend Edward Murphy of Bay St. Louis, Mississippi worked hard to get his church open for services, noting that "Virtually everybody who comes into Bay St. Louis comes by this church ... I want it to be a shining light."[22] Rev. Murphy recognized that in order to restore his community meant a need to restore the spiritual and social center as well. Likewise, the editor of the *Baptist Record* stated that "We need to get these houses of worship in order as soon as possible before more people drift away."

Nonprofits and businesses also worked together to get employees back to work or in new jobs after Hurricane Katrina. For instance, Oreck Corp. reopened its vacuum cleaner plant quickly after the storm, using generators and providing shelter for workers.[23] United Way helped set up job fairs for evacuees who settled in northern Mississippi after the storm.[24]

Furthermore, nonprofits in Mississippi have weathered hurricanes, tornadoes, floods, and oil spills, and are finding ways to learn from these experiences, collaborate with one another, and better serve citizens in need.[25] Consider, for instance, the efforts of The Carpenter's Helper, a United Way agency that works to correct poor housing conditions, especially for the elderly, or those with disabilities or low incomes.[26] The Carpenter's Helper helped to repair homes in Hattiesburg after several recent tornadoes and floods.[27]

Nonprofits are also finding ways to utilize the contacts they created in the wake of past disasters, allowing them to better serve their clients. For example, as Wallace reported in *The Chronicle of Philanthropy,* "When Vietnamese-speaking shrimpers lost their main source of income after the BP spill, a local nonprofit group-the Mississippi Center for Justice-knew just where to turn: to a Vietnamese-American group of lawyers in California who had volunteered their services to help homeowners resolve rebuilding disputes after Katrina and Rita."[28]

If religious leaders, business owners, and nonprofits find unique ways to deal with disasters and learn from past experiences, Mississippi policymakers can and should as well.

Policy Recommendations and Conclusion

Based on our research, we argue that local entrepreneurs matter for disaster recovery. This understanding of the role of entrepreneurs in disaster recovery has implications for the types of disaster-related policies that Mississippi should implement. If we are correct that entrepreneurs are key drivers of post-disaster recovery, officials should develop policies that ensure that entrepreneurs have the space to act in the wake of disaster. Moreover, officials should avoid policies that can hinder recovery by (1) stalling recovery efforts through introducing excessive bureaucratic processes and red tape in applying for assistance or petitioning for resources and (2) introducing uncertainty that exacerbates the collective action problem and discourages activities of disaster recovery.

---

22 Byrd (2006)

23 Horsley (2005). While the vacuum cleaner plant has since left the area, its efforts after Katrina provided employment and a commitment to return.

24 Seid (2005)

25 Wallace (2010)

26 For more information, see https://www.unitedwaysems.org/carpenters-helper.

27 See WDAM (2016).

28 Wallace (2010)

First, some policies that might be appropriate during regular times can unintentionally hinder entrepreneurial activity and stall recovery after a disaster. Such policies include zoning laws, building codes, occupational licensing, and changing procedures and eligibility of assistance.[29] Zoning laws aimed at separating residential and commercial property can limit the availability of goods and services in the post-disaster environment. After a disaster, for instance, communities may need access to health care, food services, and community spaces. However, zoning laws often restrict these entities from forming. For example, when a nurse from the Ninth Ward in New Orleans attempted to open a clinic in order to provide low-cost medical care to residents, zoning restrictions delayed its opening for months since the donated building was a residence before the storm. Building codes may also prevent businesses from operating and providing necessary goods to the community. While building codes might ensure safety in mundane times, allowing a hardware store to open up while repairs are being made would allow for people to buy the supplies needed to rebuild their homes and businesses. Likewise, occupational licensing rules can hamper recovery by restricting the ability of outsiders to provide construction, plumbing, and electrical services. Skarbek examines how Florida relaxes licensing requirements after hurricanes, and argues that such activities quicken recovery without increased safety or fraud.[30] Sutter, in chapter 19, also examines the negative effects of building codes, zoning laws, and occupational licensing, as well as other regulations that impact disaster recovery.

Second, policies can introduce uncertainty into the post-disaster environment, even when designed and implemented with the best intentions. Chamlee-Wright calls this type of hindrance "signal noise."[31] Signal noise occurs when the policy space is changing rapidly and when policies and government programs have vague eligibility requirements or unclear benefits. For instance, after a disaster, flood maps are often found out of date and require updating before flood insurance benefits are allotted. Residents waiting to find out if their home or business are covered in the new flood maps are unsure whether to go about rebuilding or to wait. Likewise, after a disaster, federal and state governments often implement tax breaks for individuals and businesses impacted by the storm. Such tax breaks can give citizens access to needed resources for rebuilding. However, the programs are often not announced or implemented until months after the storm and after rebuilding is already underway. These programs give resources back to citizens, but often not when they are needed most (in the immediate aftermath of the storm).

Major redevelopment planning efforts can also introduce signal noise into the recovery process. Often the intent is to engage in a robust planning effort that ensures that cities rebound, that building practices help mitigate future disasters, or that new and better urban planning principles are implemented. However, redevelopment planning efforts can take months or years to complete, and go through several iterations before being finalized. Planners must negotiate between differing goals and interests, and settle on a set of plans for the entire community. In the case of post-Katrina New Orleans, the city went through multiple planning commissions and a handful of drafts over the years after the storm.[32] With each iteration, local residents felt undermined or neglected. Both Broadmoor and New Orleans East, mentioned above, had been identified as potential green space in the initial redevelopment plans and had to prove that the residents would return and that demolishing their neighborhood was not a vital option. Evans-Cowley and Gough examined the redevelopment planning process in Mississippi and noted that resources were not directly provided for county-level planning. They argued that large-scale planning should build community trust and can benefit from an experienced team of outsiders to facilitate the

---

29 For an in-depth look at policies and regulations for insurance, price-gouging laws, and occupational licensing, see Chapter 19.

30 Skarbek (2008)

31 Chamlee-Wright (2010)

32 Storr, Haeffele-Balch and Grube (2015)

conversation and community buy-in. In Harrison County, for instance, citizens decided on their future with the help of a planning team from Ohio State University.[33]

In all these examples, signal noise adds uncertainty to recovery. Individuals and communities must try to estimate what policies will impact them and be ready to adapt when policies change, instead of being able to primarily focus on actual recovery.[34]

In order to foster entrepreneurship and promote prosperity, Mississippi should learn from these lessons and implement policies that reduce uncertainty and promote community rebound. In order to do this, we provide three major policy recommendations: 1) temporarily suspend policies that hinder recovery, 2) articulate simple and predictable policies that reduce signal noise, and 3) devise a disaster policy framework before a disaster starts. This broad framework, in many ways, complements the specific policy recommendations in Chapter 19, including suspending or altering zoning laws, price gouging laws, and occupational licensing.

First, we recommend that Mississippi, and the counties and cities within the state, temporarily suspend policies that hinder entrepreneurial action, including zoning laws, building codes, and occupational licensing. By allowing citizens to quickly reopen their businesses, even if they are in bare-bones structures or minimally staffed, can provide goods and services that enable others to return and rebuild. For instance, allowing the hardware store to open even while it is still under repair means that residents are able to start their recovery process much sooner. Additionally, relaxing the teacher-student ratio required for day-care services would mean that children are not spending their day on a construction site but at a day-care facility. In a study of the tornado outbreak in 2011, Smith and Sutter compared the policy environment for businesses in Joplin, Missouri and Tuscaloosa, Alabama and found that Joplin, which relaxed requirements and expedited processing, recovered more quickly.[35]

Second, we recommend that Mississippi develop simple and predictable policies for disaster recovery in a timely manner. Such policies reduce signal noise because they are easier for citizens to understand and comply with. For example, if tax breaks will be offered for individuals and business owners, they should be announced quickly after a disaster with clear eligibility requirements and details. Likewise, assistance programs, programs that buy-out destroyed homes, and flood insurance metrics should be written in plain language, have clear eligibility requirements, and a simple process for applying and receiving assistance. Not only will such policies reduce signal noise, but they will also ensure that vulnerable populations—that often lack resources and the social and political capital needed to navigate the bureaucratic red tape—can take advantage of the aid.[36]

Third, we recommend that Mississippi takes the time to develop a policy framework that consists of suspending policies that hamper recovery and establish simple and predictable programs before the next disaster strikes, rather than devise a new framework after each time a disaster strikes. By having the

---

33 Evans-Cowley and Gough (2008)

34 Smith (2012) also highlights stalled recovery efforts in Mississippi, specifically detailing issues with housing programs and the hindrance of bureaucratic red tape.

35 Smith and Sutter (2013)

36 Several critiques of federal and state programs have identified that the most vulnerable are often the least likely to get assistance. While clear language and simple processes may help, policymakers should also aim to design programs that help those who need it most. For a discussion on how housing programs in Mississippi after Katrina neglected renters and low-income residents, see Jopling (2008) and Lowe (2012). For an in-depth study on several differences and vulnerabilities in Mississippi disaster recovery post-Katrina, see Cutter et al. (2014). For an analysis of how post-Katrina planning allowed for politically-advantaged groups to reform policy in ways that neglected minorities and the poor, see Derickson (2014). Further, Weber and Hilfinger Messias (2012) argue that front-line aid workers in Mississippi, who are well-suited to match vulnerable populations and with needed assistance, felt hindered in their efforts and had disaster-fatigue after Katrina. Empowering those aid workers to be entrepreneurial could provide aid to those in need.

plan written out ahead of time, policymakers can quickly pull it off the shelf and implement policies that encourage recovery. This quick, visible action will show that policymakers care about their citizens and are taking steps to empower entrepreneurs to spur rebound.

In summary, community leaders and local entrepreneurs help solve the challenges inherent in the post-disaster context and spur recovery. To promote prosperity, Mississippi should recognize the lessons from our research and implement policies that empower entrepreneurial activity in the wake of disasters leading to the fastest possible recovery for disaster stricken communities

References

Beven II, John L., Lixion A. Avila, Eric S. Blake, Daniel P. Brown, James L. Franklin, Richard D. Knabb, Richard J. Pasch, Jamie R. Rhome, and Stacy R. Stewart. 2008. Annual Summary: Atlantic Hurricane Season of 2005, *Monthly Weather Review,* 136: 1109-1173.

Byrd, Sheila. 2006. Churches reaching out to community while rebuilding worship houses, *Tulsa World,* May 6 [electronic file]. Online: http://www.tulsaworld.com/news/churches-reaching-out-to-community-while-rebuilding-worship-houses/article_b04b3183-9e7e-5b41-a9a7-281bd8d7971b.html?mode=image&photo=0 (cited: July 15, 2017).

Carpenter, Ann. 2013. Building Community Resilience: Four Case Studies from Post-Katrina Mississippi, *Paper for the Federal Reserve Community Affairs Internal Research Symposium* [electronic file]. Washington, DC. Online: https://www.frbatlanta.org/-/media/Documents/news/conferences/2013/resilience-rebuilding/13resiliencerebuildingpaperCarpenter.pdf (cited: July 15, 2017).

Chamlee-Wright, Emily. 2010. *The Cultural and Political Economy of Recovery: Social Learning in a Post-Disaster Environment.* London: Routledge.

Chamlee-Wright, Emily, and Virgil Henry Storr. 2011. Social capital as collective narratives and post-disaster community recovery, *The Sociological Review,* 59(2), 266-282.

Cutter, Susan L., Christopher T. Emrich, Jerry T. Mitchell, Walter W. Piegorsch, Mark M. Smith, and Lynn Weber. 2014. *Hurricane Katrina and the Forgotten Coast of Mississippi.* New York: Cambridge University Press.

Derickson, Kate Driscoll. 2014. The Racial Politics of Neoliberal Regulation in Post-Katrina Mississippi, *Annals of the Association of American Geographers,* 104(4): 889-902.

Di Liberto, Tom. 2016. August 2016 extreme rain and floods along the Gulf Coast, *ClimateWatch Magazine,* August 19 [electronic file]. Online: https://www.climate.gov/news-features/event-tracker/august-2016-extreme-rain-and-floods-along-gulf-coast (cited: July 15, 2017).

Evans-Cowley, Jennifer S., and Megan Zimmerman Gough. 2008. Citizen Engagement in Post-Katrina Planning in Harrison County, Mississippi, *Cityscape: A Journal of Policy Development and Research,* 10(3): 21-37.

Grube, Laura E., and Virgil Henry Storr. 2014. The capacity for self-governance and post-disaster recovery, *Review of Austrian Economics,* 27(3), 301-324.

Haeffele-Balch, Stefanie, and Virgil Henry Storr. 2015. Austrian contributions to the literature on natural and unnatural disasters in Christopher J. Coyne and Virgil Henry Storr (eds.), *New Thinking in Austrian Political Economy (Advances in Austrian Economics,* Vol. 19). Bingley, UK: Emerald.

Horsley, Scott. 2005. Vacuum Maker Oreck to Stay after Katrina, *NPR,* September 14 [electronic file]. Online: http://www.npr.org/templates/story/story.php?storyId=4846583 (cited: July 15, 2017).

Horwitz, Steven G. 2009a. Best responders: Post-Katrina innovation and improvisation by Wal-Mart and the U.S. Coast Guard, *Innovations,* 4(2), 93-99.

Horwitz, Steven G. 2009b. Wal-Mart to the rescue: Private enterprise's response to Hurricane Katrina, *The Independent Review,* 13(4), 511-528.

Jopling, John. 2008. Two Years after the Storm: The State of Katrina Housing Recovery on the Mississippi Gulf Coast, *Mississippi Law Journal,* 77: 873-894.

Lowe, Jeffrey S. 2012. Policy versus politics: post-Hurricane Katrina lower-income housing restoration in Mississippi, *Housing Policy Debate,* 22(1): 57-73.

Martinez, Michael, Ed Payne, and Dave Alsup, D. 2016. Flooding spreads across southern Louisiana and Mississippi, *CNN,* March 12 [electronic file]. Online: http://www.cnn.com/2016/03/12/us/southeast-weather/index.html (cited: July 15, 2017).

Potter, Ned. 2010. Mississippi Tornadoes: Unusual Outbreak, or Warning for Spring? *ABCNews,* April 26 [electronic file]. Online: http://abcnews.go.com/WN/Eco/mississippi-tornadoes-worst-natural-disaster-hurricane-katrina-forecast/story?id=10478481 (cited: July 15, 2017).

Rigsby, Mark. 2017. Mississippi Requests Federal Money to Help After Tornadoes Damaged Rural Areas, *Mississippi Public Broadcasting,* May 15 [electronic file]. Online: http://www.mpbonline.org/blogs/news/2017/05/15/mississippi-requests-federal-money-to-help-after-tornadoes-damaged-rural-areas/ (cited: July 15, 2017).

Seid, Dennis. 2005. Evacuees look for answers and a return to normalcy, *Northeast Mississippi Daily Journal,* October 13.

Skarbek, David. 2008. Occupational Licensing and Asymmetric Information: Post-hurricane Evidence from Florida, *Cato Journal,* 28(1), 73–82.

Smith, J. P. 2012. *Hurricane Katrina: The Mississippi Story.* Jackson, MS: University Press of Mississippi.

Smith, Daniel J., and Daniel Sutter. 2013. Response and Recovery after the Joplin Tornado, *The Independent Review* 18(2): 165-188.

Sobel, Russell S, and Peter T Leeson. 2007. The use of knowledge in natural-disaster relief management, *The Independent Review,* 11(4), 519-532.

Storr, Virgil Henry, and Stefanie Haeffele-Balch. 2012. Post-disaster community recovery in heterogeneous, loosely connected communities, *Review of Social Economy,* 70(3), 295-314.

Storr, Virgil Henry, Stefanie Haeffele-Balch, and Laura E. Grube. 2015. *Community Revival in the Wake of Disaster: Lessons in Local Entrepreneurship.* New York, NY: Palgrave Macmillan.

U.S. Army Corps of Engineers. 2012. *Mississippi River and Tributaries 2011 Post Flood Evaluation* [electronic file]. Vicksburg, MS: U.S. Army Corps of Engineers. Online: http://www.mvd.usace.army.mil/Missions/Flood-Risk-Management/Regional-Flood-Risk-Management-Program/MR-T-Post-Flood-Report/ (cited: July 15, 2017).

Wallace, Nicole. 2010. The Legacy of Katrina for Gulf Coast Charities: 5 Years After the Hurricanes, Gulf Coast Grapples with Recovery, *The Chronicle of Philanthropy,* August 6 [electronic file]. Online: https://www.philanthropy.com/article/The-Legacy-of-Katrina-for-Gulf/160189 (cited: July 15, 2017).

WDAM. 2016. The Carpenter's Helper repairs homes of flood victims, *WDAM,* April 20 [electronic file]. Online: http://www.wdam.com/story/31775630/the-carpenters-helper-repairs-homes-of-flood-victims (cited: July 15, 2017).

Weber, Lynn, and DeAnne K. Hilfinger Messias. 2012. Mississippi front-line recovery work after Hurricane Katrina: An analysis of the intersections of gender, race, and class in advocacy, power relations, and health, *Social Science & Medicine,* 74: 1833-1841.

Summary of
Chapter Conclusions

PART 1. Introduction: The Role of Government and Economic Growth

Chapter 1: The Case for Growth—Russell S. Sobel, The Citadel, and J. Brandon Bolen, Mississippi State University

- Mississippi is the poorest state in the United States in terms of per capita income. Mississippi underperforms economically relative to all of its bordering states.

- Focusing on policies that generate economic growth is the most viable pathway to alleviating Mississippi's weak economic condition.

- Very small changes in economic growth rates may yield vast positive changes in the quality of life for Mississippi residents within as little time as one to two generations.

- Focusing on economic growth does not mean that other important policy goals such as improving health and education and reducing crime are neglected.

Chapter 2: The Sources of Economic Growth—Russell S. Sobel, The Citadel, and J. Brandon Bolen, Mississippi State University

- The economic activity of a state necessarily occurs within that area's institutional context, including the legal, regulatory, and tax environments, as well as the degree of private property rights. The quality of these institutions affects the output of economic activity.

- Capitalism is an economic system based on the private ownership of productive assets within an economy.

- Abundant evidence demonstrates that areas with institutions that allow capitalism to thrive experience much higher levels of prosperity relative to areas that do not rely upon capitalism.

Chapter 6: "Selective Incentives," Crony Capitalism and Economic Development— Thomas A. Garrett, University of Mississippi, and William F. Shughart II, Utah State University

- This chapter evaluates the costs and benefits of targeted tax incentives designed to lure new private business enterprises to Mississippi.

- Our analysis demonstrates that Mississippi is poorer, not richer, by funding incentive programs.

- Reasons that incentive packages fail include no new employment since many individuals hired were previously employed, the additional tax cost to accommodate the new population growth, and resources allocated to funding the subsidies could have been spent on better schools, roads, or used to finance a reduction in tax rates for all.

- The funds now being spent to benefit a handful of private business owners could be used to finance broad-based reductions in tax rates and lightening the regulatory burden on all Mississippians.

Chapter 7: Incentive-Based Compensation and Economic Growth— Brandon N. Cline and Claudia R. Williamson, Mississippi State University

- Incentive based compensation is a payment method where an individual's pay is in some way tied to their performance. Economic literatures studying incentive based pay for executives show that use of incentive based pay improves company performance and by extension state economies.

- Empirical data shows that firms in Mississippi use incentive-based compensation less than similar firms in other states.

- Mississippi can help improve its economic position by restructuring parts of its tax code to allow for greater use of incentive based executive compensation.

Chapter 8: Mississippi Shadow Economies: A Symptom of Over-Regulated Markets and Measure of Missed Opportunities—Travis Wiseman, Mississippi State University

- This chapter discusses Mississippi's regulatory environment and the state's cumbersome habit of maintaining outdated and burdensome regulation, far longer than other states.

- Several sensible and low-cost reforms are introduced that can help curtail unwanted shadow economic activity, and promote prosperity in Mississippi.

- A case study of one industry that Mississippi over-regulates – the brewing industry – is discussed.

Chapter 9: Occupational Licensing in Mississippi—Daniel J. Smith, Troy University

- Occupational licensing, the regulation of individual entry to a profession, enables industry practitioners to restrict entry to their profession and raise prices on consumers.

- The effects of occupational licensing fall heaviest on low-income residents who must pay higher prices or resort to lower-quality home-production or black market provision.

- Mississippi has at least 118 different occupational categories with licensing, representing nearly 20 percent of Mississippi's labor force.

- The total estimated initial licensing costs in Mississippi exceed $48 million and the estimated annual renewal costs add up to over $13.5 million.

- Mississippi policymakers can promote prosperity in Mississippi by removing unnecessary and overtly burdensome licensing laws.

Chapter 10: Prosperity Districts: A Ladder Out of Last Place—Trey Goff, Out of Last Place Alliance

- Prosperity districts are geographically self-contained areas that reduce or eliminate unnecessary government restrictions on business activity, including regulation, taxation, and private subsidization

- Prosperity districts can be a unique and promising solution to the state's economic woes by allowing specific areas to be exempt from unproductive policies.

- Prosperity districts allow experimentation to determine which policies work best.

- Real world examples of the potential success of prosperity districts can be seen in the closely related concept of special economic zones, which have seen tremendous economic growth and development in places such as Singapore.

Chapter 11: Promoting Prosperity in Mississippi through Investing in Communities—Ken B. Cyree, University of Mississippi, and Jon Maynard, Oxford Economic Development Foundation

- We investigate the impact of investing in community livability and the relation to the change in total employment to promote prosperity in Mississippi.

- We document the decline in Mississippi employment, on average, from 2007-2016, and especially the decline in manufacturing employment.

- Our analysis shows that increased employment is significantly related to better school rankings, higher changes in wages, and higher changes in per capita retail sales. New business creation is not statistically related to employment.

- Our results suggest that in order to promote prosperity in Mississippi, we should invest in quality of life for the community.

Chapter 12: Local Governments Run Amok? A Guide for State Officials Considering Local Preemption—Michael D. Farren, George Mason University, and Adam A. Millsap, Florida State University

- Local governments sometimes implement regulations and ordinances that stifle economic growth.

- Preemption is a legal doctrine asserting that state law takes precedence over local law. In some cases it should be used by state governments to overrule local governments.

- State officials should consider preemption when local rules violate the principles of generality or free exchange. Such policies often involve barriers to entry, price controls, or business practice mandates.

- Violations of generality and free exchange harm economic growth because they inhibit economic activity and the efficient allocation of resources. Conversely, preempting such policies promotes economic growth.

Chapter 13: School Choice: How To Unleash the Market in Education—Brett Kittredge, Empower Mississippi

- The United States has fallen behind other countries in K-12 education. One study found that American students ranked 38th out of 71 countries when tested in math, reading, and science.

- A government monopoly has existed in our delivery of education in the United States. Students are assigned to a school based on their zip code and the year they were born.

- Because students are assigned to a school based on a district line, real estate prices naturally rise in neighborhoods within a desirable school district. This has the effect of pricing out many families and forcing them to live in areas with less desirable schools.

- To improve quality, our education system should be student centered and market based. Parents should have options available to craft a custom education for their child based on their specific learning needs.

- The legislature can adopt a market based education through a universal school choice program that has broad eligibility, autonomy for all schools, and level funding across the various educational sectors.

Chapter 14: Medicaid: A Government Monopoly That Hurts the Poor—Jameson Taylor, MS Center for Public Policy

- State health care policy revolves around Medicaid, which is a government-subsidized insurance program consuming one-third of Mississippi's budget.

- Health outcomes for Medicaid insurance patients are very poor; patients with no insurance at all fare better.

- Medicaid's number one problem, like that of many American insurance plans, is that it incentivizes the over utilization of health care while insulating recipients from the financial consequences of poor lifestyle choices.

- Medicaid is crowding out the development of innovative products and policy ideas.

- Reforms aimed at unleashing the power of health care pricing including large HSAs, direct surgical care, and comparative shopping incentives can begin to disrupt Medicaid's monopoly.

Chapter 15: Tipping the Scales: Curbing Mississippi's Obesity Problem— Raymond J. March, San Jose State University

- Widespread obesity has serious health and financial consequences in Mississippi.

- Government policy, although well intended, is associated with increased levels of obesity especially for lower-income households.

- State-led efforts to reduce obesity are costly and unlikely to succeed because they fail to address the underlying causes of why less healthy food options are consumed.

- Private and local solutions are more effective in promoting health and reducing obesity.

- The most effective way to combat widespread obesity is the market, not the government.

Chapter 16: Criminal Justice Reform in Mississippi—Trey Goff, Out of Last Place Alliance

- Despite decreasing rates of both violent and property crime since 1996, Mississippi incarceration rates have steadily increased.

- Mississippi has an incarceration rate that is among the highest in the world, most due to incarcerating non-violent crimes.

- The economic drain from this level of mass incarceration is extremely detrimental for the state economy in terms of both the cost of maintaining incarceration and the negative effects of incarceration upon individuals in the labor market.

- Reevaluating and restructuring the criminal justice system in Mississippi to reduce incarceration rates would be an extremely effective tool to increase the economic strength and wellbeing of the state.

Chapter 17: Property Takings: Eminent Domain and Civil Asset Forfeiture— Carrie B. Kerekes, Florida Gulf Coast University

- Secure private property rights provide incentives for individuals to undertake investments and make capital improvements to their property and businesses. To promote prosperity, Mississippi policy makers should continue to improve laws and policies to restrict property takings.

- Following reforms passed in 2011 to protect against development takings, property owners in Mississippi are reasonably protected from eminent domain takings.

- Citizens are significantly less protected in the case of civil asset forfeiture. Civil asset forfeiture laws in Mississippi provide incentives for law enforcement agencies to seize private property.

Chapter 18: The Small-Dollar Loan Landscape in Mississippi: Products, Regulations, Examples, and Research Findings on Interest Rate Caps—Thomas (Tom) William Miller, Jr., Mississippi State University

- The best fuel for economic growth and prosperity is free market prices, including interest rates.

- Despite the goal of improving consumer welfare, interest rate caps often harm the very people legislatures intend to help—especially users of small-dollar loan products.

- Despite their well-known harmful effects on consumers, laws continue to fetter consumer credit markets with interest rate caps.

- Setting good rules governing how legitimate businesses provide access to consumer credit is important for everyone living in Mississippi.

- The Mississippi legislature can greatly help consumers by eliminating, or greatly raising, interest rate caps in all small-dollar loan markets.

Chapter 19: Natural Disasters and Prosperity in Mississippi—Daniel Sutter, Troy University

- Extreme weather poses a severe financial risk for a state economy. Mississippi is particularly exposed to the threat of damage from natural disasters.

- Free market practices often perform better at meeting the challenges posed by natural disasters rather than government policies. Removal of harmful policies such as occupational licensing and building codes during disaster may better allow the market to speed disaster recovery.

- Some government policies such as flood and wind insurance may exacerbate exposure to natural disasters. Other policies slow recovery time by creating uncertainty after the occurrence of a natural disaster.

Chapter 20: Learning from Disasters in Mississippi—Stefanie Haeffele and Virgil Henry Storr, George Mason University

- This chapter examines disaster recovery in Mississippi and how policies that foster entrepreneurship might help spur disaster recovery going forward.

- Entrepreneurs can spur disaster recovery by providing needed goods and services, restoring disrupted social networks, and acting as focal points around which other residents can coordinate their recovery efforts.

- To promote prosperity in Mississippi, officials should develop policies that ensure that entrepreneurs have the space to act in the wake of disaster.

About the
Institute for Market Studies
at Mississippi State University

The Institute for Market Studies (IMS) at Mississippi State University, created in 2015, is a nonprofit research and educational organization conducting scholarly research and providing educational opportunities to advance the study of free enterprise.

The IMS's mission is to support the study of markets and provide a deeper understanding regarding the role of markets in creating widely shared prosperity. This includes advancing sound policies based on the principles of free enterprise, individual liberty, and limited government. The IMS pursues its mission by bringing together leading scholars to conduct timely research on current economic and financial issues.

About the Authors

Editors:

Brandon N. Cline, Ph.D., is the John "Nutie" and Edie Dowdle Associate Professor of Finance. His research focuses on insider trading, executive compensation, equity offerings, and corporate governance. His work has been published in numerous finance journals, including: *Journal of Financial Economics, Financial Management, Journal of Corporate Finance, Journal of Banking and Finance, Journal of Empirical Finance, The Journal of Financial Research,* and *The Financial Review.* Dr. Cline has received invitations to present his work at prestigious conferences such as the American Finance Association. He has also received various research awards including the 2014 Wharton School-WRDS Outstanding Paper in Empirical Research, the 2012 Journal of Financial Research Outstanding Article Award, the 2010 Eastern Finance Association Outstanding Paper Award, the 2009 Eastern Finance Association Outstanding Paper Award, the 2008 Southern Finance Association's Outstanding Paper Award in Corporate Finance, and the 2017 Mississippi State College of Business Faculty Research Award. His research has also been the subject of feature stories in *Fortune, The Wall Street Journal, Harvard Business Review, Bloomberg Radio, FoxBusiness, CNNMoney, RealClearMarkets,* and the *Harvard Law School Forum on Corporate Governance and Financial Regulation.* Prior to joining Mississippi State, Dr. Cline taught both graduate and undergraduate courses in corporate finance and financial derivatives at Clemson University. In 2006, Dr. Cline received the Outstanding Finance Faculty Award at The University of Alabama. Dr. Cline has served on the faculty of the Graduate School of Banking at LSU since 2016 and is currently the Vice President – Program for the Southern Finance Association.

Russell S. Sobel, Ph.D., is a native of Charleston, South Carolina. He earned his Bachelor's degree in business economics from Francis Marion College in 1990, and his Ph.D. in economics from Florida State University in 1994. Dr. Sobel has authored or co-authored over 200 books and articles, including a nationally-best-selling college Principles of Economics textbook. His research has been featured in the *New York Times, Wall Street Journal, Washington Post, US News and World Report, Investor's Business Daily, and The Economist Magazine,* and he has appeared on CNBC, Fox News, CSPAN, NPR, and the CBS Evening News. He serves on the editorial board for three academic journals, and on the advisory board for four university centers. He has won numerous awards for both his teaching and his research, including the 2008 Sir Anthony Fisher Award for best state policy publication of the year. His recent research focuses on economic policy and entrepreneurship. Dr. Sobel is a Professor of Economics & Entrepreneurship in the Baker School of Business at The Citadel, and a Visiting Fellow at the South Carolina Policy Council.

Claudia R. Williamson, Ph.D., is an Associate Professor of Economics and the Drew Allen Endowed Fellow at Mississippi State University. She is also Co-Director of the Institute for Market Studies at Mississippi State University. Her research focuses on applied microeconomics, the role of culture in development, and the political economy of development policies, such as foreign aid. She has authored over 30 articles in refereed journals including the *Journal of Law and Economics, World Development, Journal of Comparative Economics, Public Choice, Journal of Corporate Finance, Journal of Institutional Economics, European Journal of Political Economy, Defense and Peace Economics,* and *the Southern Economic Journal.* She has also contributed multiple chapters to edited books, written book reviews, and policy briefs. Her research has appeared in popular press outlets, such as *The Economist* and the BBC. She currently serves on the editorial board for *Public Choice* and the Executive Board for the Association of Private Enterprise Education. Claudia is a native of West Virginia. She earned her B.B.A. in economics from Marshall University in 2000, and she completed her Ph.D. in economics at West Virginia University in 2008. She spent the 2007-2008 year at George Mason University as the F.A. Hayek Visiting Scholar in Philosophy, Politics, and Economics. She was a post-doctoral fellow at the Development Research Institute of New York University from 2009-2012, and she spent the 2008-2009 year as an assistant professor of economics at Appalachian State University. During the summer of 2007, she performed fieldwork on land titling in rural Peru. Additional information can be found at www.claudiawilliamson.com.

Contributing Authors

J. Brandon Bolen is a Ph.D. candidate in Applied Economics at Mississippi State University. His main research interests lie at the intersection of applied economic development and political economy. He has also published in the Journal of Sports Economics highlighting the importance of evaluating college athletic programs on the basis of both athletic and academic achievement. Brandon is originally from Madison, MS and has been teaching economics to Mississippi students for six years.

Ken B. Cyree, Ph.D, is Dean, the Frank R. Day/Mississippi Bankers Association Chair of Banking, and Professor of Finance at the University of Mississippi School of Business Administration. Dr. Cyree received his doctorate and MBA from the University of Tennessee. His research interests are in banking and financial markets. His published works have appeared in the *Journal of Business, Journal of Banking and Finance, Financial Management, Journal of Financial Research, the Journal of Financial Services Research, the Journal of Financial Markets, and Financial Review* among many others. He is currently an associate editor at the *Journal of Financial Research*. Cyree has conducted numerous media interviews including National Public Radio, Mississippi Public Broadcasting, View Point television, the Marshall Ramsey Radio Show and the Dave Foster Radio Show. He has been quoted in the *Clarion Ledger, the Hattiesburg American, the Mississippi Business Journal, the Tupelo Daily Journal,* along with online news sites such as Bloomberg and Fox Business. He has spoken to the Conference of Bank State Supervisors, the St. Louis Federal Reserve, the Mississippi Bankers Association, and testified before the Mississippi State Legislature Banking Committee. He is a board member of the Mississippi Young Bankers Association.

Michael D. Farren, Ph.D., is a Research Fellow at the Mercatus Center at George Mason University. His research focuses on the effects of government favoritism, specializing in labor markets, economic development, and transportation policy. His research and commentary have been featured in numerous media outlets, including the *Washington Post, Los Angeles Times, the Miami Herald, The Dallas Morning News,* and *NPR*. He blogs about economic policy at Concentrated Benefits.

Thomas A. Garrett, Ph.D., is Associate Professor of Economics at the University of Mississippi, where he has been employed since 2012. Prior to joining the University of Mississippi, he was an economist in the Research Division at the Federal Reserve Bank of St. Louis for 10 years and an assistant professor at Kansas State University for 3 years. He graduated from West Virginia University with a Ph.D. in Economics in 1998. His primary areas of interest are state and local public finance, state lotteries, public choice, and applied microeconomics. He has published over 30 articles in scholarly economics journals, and has written numerous policy briefs on various subjects including casino gaming, state lotteries, income inequality, personal bankruptcy, social security reform, and state budgeting.

Trey Goff is a recent graduate of Mississippi State University, where he obtained a bachelor's degree in Economics and Political Science. He is an Alumni of the Charles Koch Institute's Summer Fellows program, and has been published at the Foundation for Economic Education. Trey was heavily involved in the student liberty movement throughout college, and is now a leading voice in the free societies movement. Trey is currently actively involved in a variety of ongoing free society projects, as well as the Mississippi-focused Out of Last Place Institute

Stefanie Haeffele, Ph.D., is the Deputy Director of Academic and Student Programs, and a Senior Fellow for the F. A. Hayek Program for Advanced Study in Philosophy, Politics and Economics at the Mercatus Center at George Mason University. She earned her Ph.D. in economics at George Mason University. After receiving an MA in economics at George Mason University in 2010, she completed a Presidential Management Fellowship where she worked in emergency and disaster management at both the Federal Emergency Management Agency and then the U.S. Forest Service. She is the coauthor of *Community Revival in the Wake of Disaster: Lessons in Local Entrepreneurship* (Palgrave, 2015), along with Virgil Henry Storr and Laura E. Grube.

Carrie B. Kerekes, Ph.D, is an Associate Professor of Economics at Florida Gulf Coast University. She received her Ph.D. in Economics from West Virginia University in 2008. Her research interests are in the areas of applied microeconomics; public economics; and economic development, with an emphasis on institutions and private property rights. Dr. Kerekes has published several articles in refereed journals including the *Journal of Law and Economics, the American Law and Economics Review, The American Journal of Economics and Sociology, the Cato Journal, and the Review of Law and Economics*. Dr. Kerekes conducted field research on land titling in rural Peru in 2007. Dr. Kerekes regularly attends the meetings of the Association of Private Enterprise Education (APEE) and the Southern Economic Association (SEA), and she has served on the APEE Executive Board. Dr. Kerekes serves on the Board of Directors and is the Treasurer of the Freedom and Virtue Institute (FVI), a nonprofit organization that promotes individual liberty, self-reliance, and human dignity.

Brett Kittredge is Director of External Relations for Empower Mississippi, a Mississippi-based public policy organization that promotes school choice in the state. In his position, Kittredge oversees all communications and outreach for Empower. Kittredge has authored two reports for Empower, *The Special Needs ESA: What Families Enrolled In The Program Are Saying After One Year* and *Exploring Mississippi's Private Education Sector: The Mississippi Private School Survey*. Previously, Kittredge served as Communications Director for the Office of the State Auditor under State Auditor Stacey Pickering. Prior to that, he was the Communications Director for the Mississippi Republican Party. Kittredge received his Bachelor's Degree from the University of Mississippi in 2007 and his Master's Degree from Abilene Christian University in 2010.

Raymond J. March, Ph.D., is Assistant Professor of Economics at San Jose State University. He earned his Ph.D. From Texas Tech University in 2017. His research examines the public and private provision and governance of healthcare in the United States, particularly in pharmaceutical markets. Dr. March's research has appeared in the *Journal of Institutional Economics, the Journal of Entrepreneurship and Public Policy,* and *the International Review of Economics*.

Jon Maynard is President and CEO of the Oxford-Lafayette County Economic Development Foundation and Chamber of Commerce. Mr. Maynard holds a Bachelor of Science degree in Business Administration from Northwestern State University of Louisiana. He is a graduate of the University of Oklahoma Economic Development Institute. Has been in professional economic development for 11 years. He began his economic development career as a volunteer board member in 1991 in Natchitoches, LA. In 2006, he was hired for his first professional position in Minden, LA working for the Northwest Louisiana Economic Development Foundation (now NLEP). He was recruited to work in Starkville, MS in 2008 and then in Oxford, MS in 2012. He has a varied employment background that includes running a small movie theatre business and an officer at a bank in Louisiana where he ran two branches.

Thomas (Tom) William Miller, Jr., Ph.D., is Professor of Finance and inaugural holder of the Jack R. Lee Chair in Financial and Consumer Finance at Mississippi State University. Professor Miller is also a Senior Affiliated Scholar at the Mercatus Center at George Mason University. His current research concerns various aspects of consumer credit and, specifically, small dollar installment loans. Professor Miller is a frequent speaker on consumer credit issues at national conferences. Professor Miller has been honored with many research and teaching awards. Professor Miller is co-author (with Bradford D. Jordan and Steve Dolvin) of *Fundamentals of Investments: Valuation and Management*, 8th ed. (McGraw-Hill/Irwin. Professor Miller enjoys playing blues and jazz on his tenor saxophone.

Adam A. Millsap, Ph.D., is the Assistant Director of the Hilton Center at Florida State University and a Senior Affiliated Scholar at the Mercatus Center at George Mason University. His research focuses on urban development, population trends, labor markets, and federal and local urban public policy. His commentary has appeared in national outlets such as *US News and World Report, USA Today,* and *The Hill,* as well as regional outlets such as the *Detroit Free Press, Cincinnati Enquirer, and Orange County Register*, among others. He is also a *Forbes* contributor. In addition to his research and writing he has taught economics at Clemson University and George Mason University.

William F. Shughart II, Ph.D., research director of the Independent Institute (Oakland, Calif.), is J. Fish Smith Professor in Public Choice at Utah State University's Jon M. Huntsman School of Business. He is a past president of the Southern Economic Association, has been editor in chief of *Public Choice*, a peer-reviewed academic journal, since 2005, and was on the economics faculty at Ole Miss from 1988 to 2011.

Daniel J. Smith, Ph.D., is an Associate Professor of Economics at Troy University and the Associate Director of the Manuel H. Johnson Center for Political Economy. He also serves as the Book Review Editor for *The Review of Austrian Economics*. Daniel received his Ph.D. in economics from George Mason University. Dr. Smith's academic research uses both Austrian and public choice economics to analyze market and governmental institutions, including social and economic cooperation, monetary policy and institutions, and public pensions. His public policy work primarily uses Austrian and public choice economics to address barriers to economic mobility and prosperity. He has published op-eds in newspapers across the nation, including the *Wall Street Journal, CNBC,* and *Investor's Business Daily*.

Virgil Henry Storr, Ph.D., is the Senior Director of Academic and Student Programs at the Mercatus Center, and the Don C. Lavoie Senior Fellow in the F.A. Hayek Program in Philosophy, Politics and Economics, Mercatus Center, George Mason University. He is also a Research Associate Professor of Economics in the Department of Economics, George Mason University. He holds a Ph.D. in Economics from George Mason University. He is the author of *Enterprising Slaves and Master Pirates* (Peter Lang, 2004), *Understanding the Culture of Markets* (Routledge, 2012), and the coauthor of *Community Revival in the Wake of Disaster: Lessons in Local Entrepreneurship* (Palgrave, 2015), along with Stefanie Haeffele and Laura E. Grube.

Daniel Sutter, Ph.D., is the Charles G. Koch Professor of Economics and Interim Director of the Manuel H. Johnson Center for Political Economy at Troy University and is a Ph.D. graduate of George Mason University. His research interests include the societal impacts of extreme weather and disasters, the economics of the news media, the markets for economists and economic research, environmental regulation, and constitutional economics. He hosts Econversations on Troy University's Trojan Vision channel, which discusses economics, markets, and policy, and writes a weekly column in the *Troy Messenger*. Dr. Sutter is a Senior Affiliated Scholar with the Mercatus Center at George Mason University and a Policy Advisor with the Heartland Institute.

Jameson Taylor, Ph.D., is vice president for policy at the Mississippi Center for Public Policy. He has spent most of his public policy career working at the state level, with a focus on health care, constitutional rights, life and family issues, and regulatory issues. He is a three-time Earhart Fellow, a Publius Fellow with the Claremont Institute, and an E.A. Morris Fellow. In 2017, he was appointed to the Mississippi Governor's Faith-Based Council. Dr. Taylor holds an A.B. in government from Bowdoin College and a Ph.D. in politics from the University of Dallas. He has written numerous policy guides, briefs and op-eds, and his work has appeared in *Citizen, Clements' International Report, Commentary, Logos, This Rock, and The Review of Metaphysics*.

Travis Wiseman, Ph.D., is Director and Clinical Assistant Professor of International Business at Mississippi State University. He earned his Ph.D. from West Virginia University in 2013. His applied research focuses on relationships between institutions – both formal and cultural – entrepreneurship, and shadow economies, and has been published in the *Southern Economic Journal, the Journal of Institutional Economics, Constitutional Political Economy, the Journal of Entrepreneurship and Public Policy, Contemporary Economic Policy, Public Finance Review, the Review of Law & Economics, the Journal of Regional Analysis & Policy, and the American Journal of Entrepreneurship*. His work has also been featured in several popular news outlets, including *New York Magazine, Inc. Magazine, Reason Magazine and Pacific Standard*.

www.ingramcontent.com/pod-product-compliance
Lightning Source LLC
Chambersburg PA
CBHW080513220326
41599CB00032B/6072